BY JAMES HENRY BREASTED

CHARLES SCRIBNER'S SONS

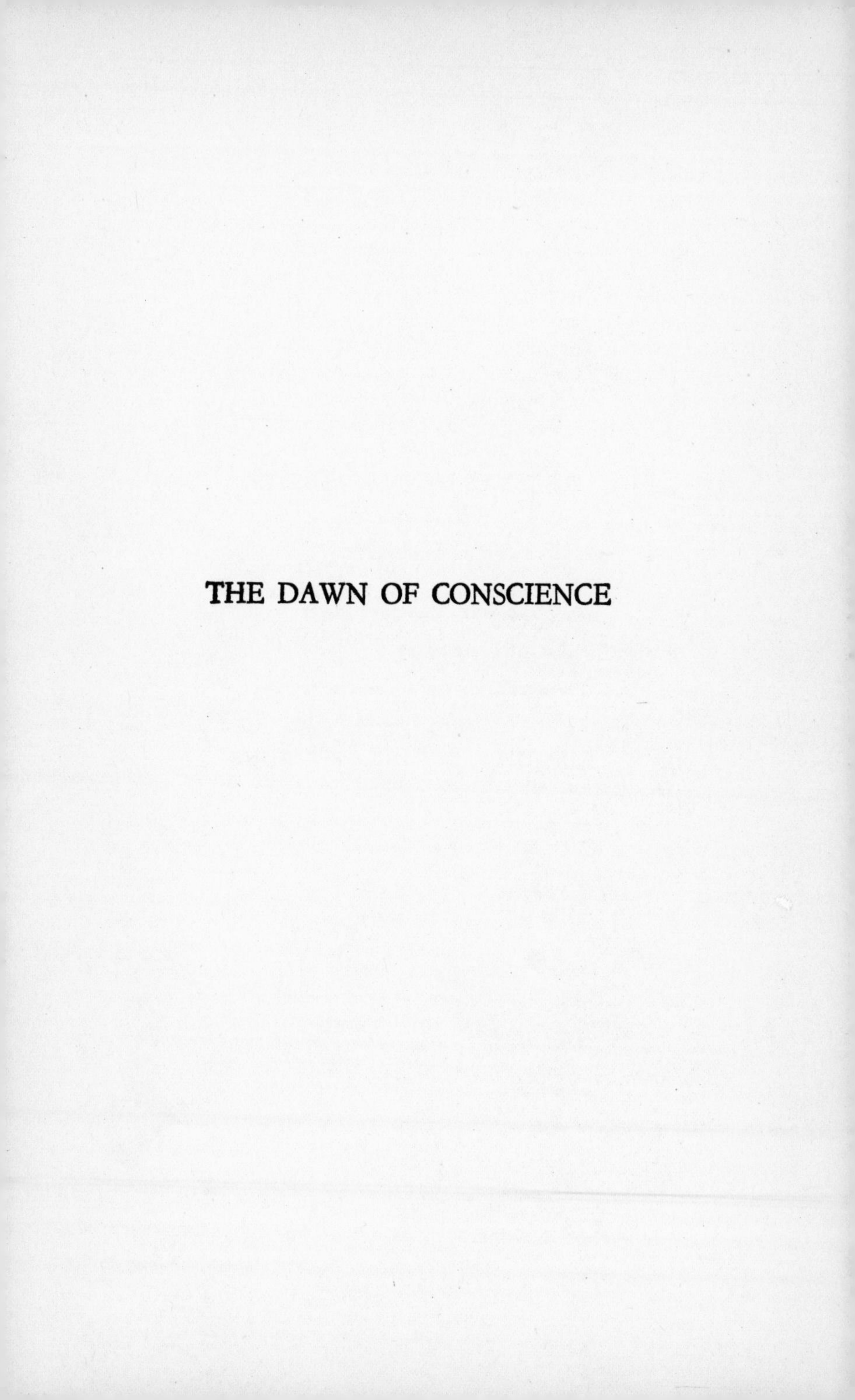

THE DAWN OF CONSCIENCE

THE DAWN OF CONSCIENCE

By

James Henry Breasted

"We think our civilization near its meridian, but we are yet only at the cock-crowing and the morning star. In our barbarous society the influence of character is in its infancy."

EMERSON, Essay on Politics.

CHARLES SCRIBNER'S SONS
NEW YORK · LONDON
1950

Printed in the United States of America

"Established is the man whose standard is righteousness, who walketh according to its way."

The Grand Vizier Ptahhotep of Memphis, Twenty-seventh Century B.C.

"More acceptable is the virtue of the upright man than the ox of him that doeth iniquity."

Instruction Addressed to Prince Merikere by his Father, an Unknown Pharaoh of Heracleopolis, Twenty-third Century B.C.

"Righteousness is for eternity. It descendeth with him that doeth it into the grave, . . . his name is not effaced on earth, but he is remembered because of right."

The Eloquent Peasant of Heracleopolis, Twenty-third Century B.C.

"A man's virtue is his monument, but forgotten is the man of evil repute."

From an Egyptian Tombstone, about the Twenty-second Century B.C.

"The people of his time shall rejoice, the son of man shall make his name forever and ever, . . . Righteousness shall return to its place, unrighteousness shall be cast out."

Neferrohu, Prophet of Egypt, about 2000 B.C.

"O Amon, thou sweet Well for him that thirsteth in the desert; it is closed to him who speaketh, but it is open to him who is silent. When he who is silent cometh, lo he findeth the Well."

An Ancient Egyptian Wise Man of about 1000 B.C.

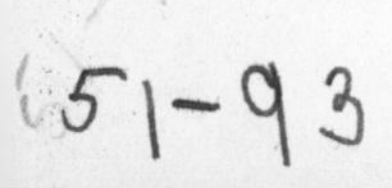

FOREWORD

It has now become a sinister commonplace in the life of the post-war generation that man has never had any hesitation in applying his increasing mechanical power to the destruction of his own kind. The World War has now demonstrated the appalling possibilities of man's mechanical power of destruction. The only force that can successfully oppose it is the human conscience—something which the younger generation is accustomed to regard as a fixed group of outworn scruples. Every one knows that man's amazing mechanical power is the product of a long evolution, but it is not commonly realized that this is also true of the social force which we call conscience—although with this important difference: as the oldest known implement-making creature man has been fashioning destructive weapons for possibly a million years, whereas conscience emerged as a social force less than five thousand years ago. One development has far outrun the other; because one is old, while the other has hardly begun and still has infinite possibilities before it. May we not consciously set our hands to the task of further developing this new-born conscience until it becomes a manifestation of good will, strong enough to throttle the surviving savage in us? That task should surely be far less difficult than the one our savage ancestors actually achieved: the creation of a conscience in a world where, in the beginning, none existed.

The most fundamentally important thing in the developing life of man has been the rise of ideals of conduct and the emergence of character, a transformation of human life which can be historically demonstrated to have begun but yesterday. At a time when the younger generation is throwing inherited morals into the discard, it would seem to be worthwhile to re-appraise these ancient values which are being so light-heartedly abandoned. To gain any adequate conception of the value of ideals of conduct to the life of man we must endeavour to disclose the process by which men first gained discernment of character and appreciation of its value. As we look back into human beginnings we discover at once that man began as an *un*moral savage. How did it come about that he ever gained any moral dictates or eventually submitted to the moral mandate when once it had arisen? How did a world totally without any vision of character rise to social idealism and learn to listen with reverence to voices within? Over against the visible and tangible advantages of material conquests how did it eventually happen that there arose the first generation of men with comprehension of unseen inner values? Why should not the young man or woman of today reject as outworn the inherited moral standards of the past, of whose origin neither of them has any knowledge?

The ancient documents which furnish an answer to these questions, and which reveal the origins of our inherited ideals, are presented in this book in translations accompanied by enough discussion to make them fairly intelligible. They disclose the dawn of conscience, the rise of the earliest ideals of conduct, and the resulting Age of Character—a development not only wonderfully fascinating to follow step by step, but also a new vision of hope in times like these. Some of these ancient sources are delightfully picturesque oriental tales, and such the reader will traverse with ease and even pleasure. Others are not so easily assimilated and if the young reader—for this book is intended especially for the new generation—finds himself mired in rather heavy going and inclined to give it up, I suggest that he read at least the epilogue, which serves to put the amazing human development from barbarism to the Age of Character as disclosed in this book into its proper setting and against its appropriate background.

Like most lads among my boyhood associates I learned the Ten Commandments. I was taught to reverence them because I was assured that they came down from the skies into the hands of Moses, and that obedience to them was therefore sacredly incumbent upon me. I remember that whenever I fibbed I found consolation in the fact that there was no commandment, "Thou shalt not lie," and that the Decalogue forbade lying only as a "false witness" giving testimony before the courts where it might damage one's neighbor. In later years when I was much older, I began to be troubled by the fact that a code of morals which did not forbid lying seemed imperfect; but it was a long time before I raised the interesting question: How has my own realisation of this imperfection arisen? Where did I myself get the moral yardstick by which I discovered this shortcoming in the Decalogue? When that experience began, it was a dark day for my inherited respect for the theological dogma of "revelation." I had more disquieting experiences before me, when as a young orientalist I found that the Egyptians had possessed a standard of morals far superior to that of the Decalogue over a thousand years before the Decalogue was written.

Such personal experiences have now become fading memories as I look back upon them across more than forty years of researches carried on in the endeavour to determine what evidences on this fundamental question of the origin of morals have been preserved among the ancient monuments in oriental lands. As these researches have progressed, I have been more and more convinced that the results should be made intelligible to any average reader, and that the present generation of young people, who may be troubled with such fundamental questions as I was, should be able to ascertain the facts. From time to time I have formulated historical sketches of the development of early man's higher life before the rise of civilised Europe, especially summaries of the facts drawn from the monuments of Egypt. In 1912 some of these results went into a simply written historical textbook for American schools. A more mature discussion of the moral and religious development of ancient man was presented in the same year to the students of Union Theological Seminary in the Morse Lectures, and later to the students of Cornell University in the introductory course of the Messenger Lectures under a new foundation devoted to "Evolution," established by Doctor Messenger. Of these two courses the Morse Lectures were duly published.[2]

Finally at Bryn Mawr College, in the introductory course under the new foundation of the Mary Flexner Lectures, the author undertook a more developed survey

[2] James Henry Breasted, *The Development of Religion and Thought in Ancient Egypt*. (New York, 1912).

of the whole subject, which, however, like the Messenger Lectures at Cornell, has never been published. Fundamental conclusions drawn from those lectures and some of the actual text of the Morse Lectures are included here without quotation marks. For assistance in the arrangement of these earlier materials, in the compilation of the illustrative scheme, and in the preparation of the index, proof-reading, etc., I am greatly indebted to Doctor Edith Williams Ware.

As far back as 1912 in the Morse Lectures then published, the author stated his conviction that a group of Egyptian papyri written in the Feudal Age around 2000 B.C. were more than merely showy literary products, as the prevailing opinion of Egyptologists had at that time long considered them. In the author's opinion these compositions contained clear evidence of being social tractates, the earliest known discussions of society, written by their ancient authors as campaign propaganda in the earliest crusade for social justice. Their authors were thus the first social prophets. Over twenty years of subsequent contemplation of these documents has only confirmed the author's opinion. To accept a social interpretation of these sources is to do for the evolution of Egyptian civilisation what socially enlightened historical critics, the so-called "higher critics," had long ago done for the development of Hebrew civilisation. In the case of Hebrew civilised development, however, historical criticism was very slow to apprehend and accept this social reconstruction and interpretation. The same has been true of the author's interpretation of the social evolution of Egyptian religion and morals, especially on the basis of the above papyri of the Feudal Age. His interpretation has, however, been hospitably received in France. It was accepted and used by his lamented colleague, Georges Bénédite of the Louvre and the Institut de France; and has likewise been taken up and elaborated by Alexandre Moret, Maspero's successor in the Collège de France, and Bénédite's successor in the Institut. It can hardly be doubted that this social interpretation of the Egyptian sources and a social reconstruction of Egyptian religion as the earliest adequately known chapter in the evolution of morals and social idealism will find general acceptance, just as the analogous interpretation of Hebrew history has done.

Since the lectures mentioned above were delivered the discovery of new documents, especially in Egypt, has not only substantially increased our knowledge, but has also made quite certain the social significance of the Feudal Age papyri. The most extraordinary revelation has been the fact that the Wisdom of Amenemope, preserved in an Egyptian papyrus in the British Museum, was translated into Hebrew in ancient times and, circulating in Palestine, was the source for a whole section of the Old Testament Book of Proverbs.

How many modern clergymen, requested to preach before some convention of business men, have taken as text the quotation from the Book of Proverbs "Seest thou a man diligent in business, he shall stand before kings"? It is not likely that any such clergyman ever prefaced his sermon with the observation that this text was taken by the Hebrew editor of Proverbs from a much older Egyptian book of moral wisdom. This discovery has added profound significance to the fact that civilised development in the countries surrounding Palestine was several thousand years earlier than that of the Hebrews. It is now quite evident that the ripe social and moral development of mankind in the Nile Valley, which is three thousand years older than that of the Hebrews, contributed essentially to the formation of the Hebrew literature which we call the Old Testament. Our moral heritage therefore derives from a wider *human* past enormously older than the Hebrews, and it has come to us rather *through* the Hebrews than *from* them. The rise of man to social idealism took place long before the traditional theologians' "age of revelation" began. It was a result of the social experience of *man himself* and was not projected into the world from the outside.

The fact that the moral ideas of early men were the product of their own social experience is one of profoundest meaning for thinking people of today. Out of prehistoric savagery, on the basis of his own experience, man arose to visions of character. That achievement which transformed advancing life, human or animal, on our globe was one from a characterless universe, as far as it is known to us, to a world of inner values transcending matter—a world for the first time aware of such values, for the first time conscious of character and striving to attain it. With that achievement man had discovered a new country, but he had not yet explored it. The *discovery itself* was an incomparably more difficult achievement than the subsequent explorations. The discovery is a *recent* event and the explorations have consequently but just begun. They are an unfinished process which must be continued by us—by *every* generation.

What we of this generation need more than anything else, therefore, is *confidence in man.* I believe that the story of his rise is an incomparable basis for full confidence. Among all the conquests which made that rise possible the supreme achievement is the discovery of character. Not projected from the outside into a world of unworthy men by some mystic process called inspiration or revelation, but springing out of man's own life two thousand years before the theologians' "age of revelation" began, illumining the darkness of social disillusionment and inner conflict, a glorious vindication of the worth of man, the dawn of the age of conscience and character broke upon the world. No conception of a spot-light of Divine Providence shining exclusively on Palestine shall despoil man of this crowning glory of his life on earth, the discovery of character. It is the greatest discovery in the whole sweep of the evolutionary process as far as it is known to us.

In the course of that evolution the position of the Hebrews is now historically established, and this volume endeavours to make that position clear. In this connection there are reasons why the author would like to call attention to the fact of his life-long interest in Hebrew studies. For years he taught Hebrew in university classes, and had among his students many future rabbis. Among modern Jews he has many valued friends. The opinions regarding the historical place of Hebrew civilisation set forth in this book are based solely on judicially minded study of the ancient documents; but in a world in which anti-Semitic prejudice is still regrettably evident it seems appropriate to state that the book was not written with the slightest anti-Semitic bias. On the contrary the author's admiration of Hebrew literature, which began in his boyhood, has always been such that his judgment of it was much more likely to be affected by a favourable bias than otherwise. The ancient civilisation of the Hebrews was a great demonstration of developing human life—of the advance of man toward new visions of character and of social idealism. It is for us now to recognise the larger human process transcending racial boundaries—a process in which the Hebrews occupied an intermediate stage—and to catch the full significance of the fact that man arose to high moral vision two thousand years before the Hebrew nation was born.

JAMES HENRY BREASTED.

BURRO MOUNTAIN HOMESTEAD, NEW MEXICO,
June 28, 1933.

CONTENTS

CONTENTS

ILLUSTRATIONS

INTRODUCTION

I BELIEVE it was Diderot who attempted to instruct his daughter in the philosophical bases of moral conduct, as she was passing from childhood into womanhood, and failing to discover any such bases, found himself in an embarrassing dilemma.[1] As a matter of experience in actual living, however, Diderot never relinquished his dauntless belief in the value of virtuous conduct. In an age like ours, in which there are many, who, while not wholly repudiating Diderot's conviction, nevertheless insist on their own personal standards of virtue, one feels the necessity of being able to look back into the remoter reaches of the human career and to discern something of the historical origins of our ideas of moral conduct.

There was a time when man was completely unaware of conduct—when all that he did was a matter of instinct. It was an enormous advance when he first became *aware* of his conduct, and a still greater advance when he reached a point where he discerned conduct as something to be approved or disapproved. The appearance of this discernment was a step towards the emergence of conscience. As conscience developed it finally became a powerful social force, reacting to influence the same society which had earlier produced it.

In the life of the prehistoric hunter, struggling to survive among the fierce and terrible mammals about him, it was a profound change, a fundamental advance, when

[1] The place of this dilemma in Diderot's life has been interestingly discussed by Carl Becker, "The Dilemma of Diderot," *Philosophical Review*, Vol. XXIV, No. 1 (January, 1915).

he first began to hear whispers from a new world which was dawning within him. Here was a new trumpet call which, unlike the tug of hunger or the panic call of self-preservation, did not stir one impulse alone while leaving all the others cold, but for the first time marshalled all the battalions of the human soul. What was the source of these new inner voices, how did they gain such mandatory power in the life of the individual man, and how did they rise to become such deep-seated and commanding forces in human society? We repeat that this whole development was a social process, the later stages of which are well within the range of our observation, for they took place within the historic age, that is, within the age of written documents. The decipherment of the lost languages of the Ancient Near East has enabled us to read the written records which disclose the dawn of conscience, the stages by which it became a social force and produced the Age of Character, at the beginning of which we still stand. It required probably not less than a million years of human development for man to build up an enlightened life out of which began to issue the Age of Character. The slow transition to it was an achievement of yesterday, although the man of today is not yet aware that he has so recently entered a new country which he has not yet learned to possess.

His failure to discern that he is wandering in unfamiliar country only very recently entered is in some measure due to his historians. They tell him that human history falls into great periods such as the Age of Monarchy, the Age of the Empires, the Age of Democracy, etc.—useful and instructive distinctions, which however do not penetrate far into the nature of advancing human life. Another type of historian recognises the importance of the Mechanised Age and the accompanying Industrial Revolution, while the engineers who tout "technocracy" summarise the advance of man exclusively in terms of power. The archæologists find it convenient to divide the earlier course of human life into several periods: the Stone Age, the Copper Age, the Bronze Age, and the Iron Age; while the palæontologists, after enumerating an impressive series, the successive stages of rising animal life, tell us that we are now reaching the close of the Age of Mammals. Convenient or necessary as these terms all may be, they inevitably remain in some respects superficial. Even the Age of Democracy and the Mechanised Age, as terms, suggest little of the intellectual emancipation which brought them about. Much more instructive and significant designations of the stages of human progress would be the Age of Conscience and Character which began some five thousand years ago, and the Age of Science ushered in by Galileo over three hundred years ago. To these fundamental human developments history-writing has hitherto usually devoted but scanty attention.

Man became the first implement-making creature not later than the beginning of the Ice Age, probably a million years ago, and possibly earlier. At the same time he also became *the first weapon-making creature.* For perhaps a million years therefore he has been improving those weapons; but it is less than five thousand years since men began to feel the power of conscience to such a degree that it became a potent *social force.* Physical force, reinforced by triumphant science during the last three centuries, wielding ever more cunningly devised weapons, has been operating for something like a million years;

higher and more elusive inner capacities arising from social experience have been socially at work for only about five thousand years. The Age of Weapons is thus doubtless a million years old; while the Age of Character made its slow and gradual beginning between four and five thousand years ago. It is time that the modern world should catch something of the profound significance of this fundamental fact; it is time that it should become a part of modern education. It is therefore the purpose of this book to set forth the historical facts and to present the leading ancient records from which they are drawn, showing that we are still standing in the gray dawn of the Age of Character—facts that are a fair basis for dreams of a noonday, still very far away to be sure, but nevertheless yet to follow upon that dawn.

After this book had been written I noticed the prophetic observation which I have placed on the title page, and which my memory of youthful reading of many years ago had failed to retain. By sheer force of intuitive vision as a philosophic seer, the High Priest of New England transcendentalism discerned what is perhaps the most significant truth in the entire range of modern life. In Emerson's day it could not have been demonstrated to be more than a belief or an impression; but since the sage of Concord has passed on, investigation of the ancient history of the Orient has disclosed it as a historical fact. It is the purpose of this volume to make accessible to the average reader the historical evidence upon which our new knowledge of this great fact is based.

THE DAWN OF CONSCIENCE

EXPLANATORY NOTE

ON THE TRANSLATIONS HEREIN

It has been the author's endeavour to include in this volume English renderings of all the important sources employed, or such portions of them as are essential to document the historical development. For the most part the reader has not been burdened with the references. As far as the venerable Pyramid Texts are concerned, practically all the references which students may wish to verify will be found in the author's published Morse Lectures, which have been copiously employed in this book without quotation marks. In the English versions the reader should note the following:

Words enclosed in half-brackets, ⌜thus⌝, are of uncertain meaning in the original.

Words enclosed in brackets are restorations, supposed to have been either originally in the source and now lost, or justifiably to be understood as the meaning of the original.

Words enclosed in parentheses are explanations by the author and are not in the original.

therefore included both Northern Africa and Western Asia.[2] There was thus an extensive Near Eastern World of Early Stone Age man embracing Northern Africa and Western Asia, forming a vast stage, whose footlights in front stretched from the Black Sea on the north through Syria and Palestine to the distant cataracts of the upper Nile on the south, and whose back-stage perspective is deepened by the drop-curtain of the Persian mountains in the background.

The picture is likewise very deep in time as well as in space. At least several hundred thousand, and perhaps a million, years ago, when the polar ice cap was beginning to creep down over Europe, men were already leading a hunting life on this great Near Eastern stage. If we may judge from the type of prehistoric man who was already living in Eastern Asia near modern Pekin, the brain of our Western hunter was one-third smaller than that of his historical successors in the same region. He has left his stone weapons lying plentifully strewn on the surface of Northeastern Africa, and also far over the hills of neighbouring Asia and beyond the Persian mountains.

The lapse of time involved is measured rather in terms of geological processes than in years. The *first* of these geological time scales was the creation of the great river valleys of the region. These prehistoric men of the East were of course unaware that they were watching the formation of the Nile Valley and the valley of the Tigris and the Euphrates, in an age when what is now the Nile Delta was still a gulf of the Mediterranean, and the Persian Gulf extended far northward over what is now the Babylonian plain to the latitude of the northeast corner of the Medi-

[2] There is now no doubt that the range of Early Stone Age (Palæolithic) man extended far eastward likewise, into farther Asia.

terranean. The *second* time scale now discernible alongside the advancing life of man was the widespread gradual desiccation. The deserts with which we are so familiar in this region had not yet appeared. All North Africa was a region of plentiful rains and rich vegetation, forming an ideal hunting ground. I have found the Nile boats of the plateau hunters carved on the rocks in the wastes of the Nubian Sahara behind Abu Simbel, and Doctor Sandford, Field Director of the Prehistoric Survey of our Oriental Institute, has recently discovered the flint weapons of these prehistoric hunters far out in the southern Sahara a thousand miles or more from the Nile. Still lying where their owners lost them some hundreds of thousands of years ago, these flint implements and weapons are mute witnesses of the wide range, both of the hunters and of the game they pursued, when all North Africa was still green and fertile. It is important to understand that the places where these silent tokens of vanished human life are found at the present day are remote and desolate regions, where no modern hunter would dare to penetrate into the desert and hope to return alive across the waterless waste.

It was in the middle of the Old Stone Age that the rainfall began to decline and thereupon followed the far-reaching desiccation which transformed the fertile plateau of North Africa into the vast desert which we now call the Sahara.[3]

At that time, however, geological forces had already long been at work preparing a new and much more fa-

[3] The researches of the Prehistoric Survey conducted by the Oriental Institute of the University of Chicago, under Doctor Kenneth S. Sandford as field director, have shown that the desiccation of North Africa began with the Mousterian stage of the Palæolithic period, that is, the middle of the Old Stone Age, and continued into the Neolithic. See K. S. Sandford and W. J. Arkell, *Paleolithic Man and the Nile-Faiyum Divide* (University of Chicago Press, 1929).

vourably situated home for the Stone Age hunters in the northeast corner of Africa. Here tropical Africa stretched forth across the Sahara to the southeastern corner of the midland sea, a fertile and sheltered corridor teeming with luxuriant vegetable and animal life from inner Africa, and offering to the Stone Age hunters a home of inexhaustible resources in a situation of unexampled safety and protection from hostile intruders.

Driven from the plateau by the growing scarcity of food as the vegetation became too scanty to support life, the animals of Northeastern Africa must have early taken refuge along the shores of the great river at the bottom of the deep Nile gorge, where there thus grew up a game preserve of unexampled plenty. Into this Eden of the lower Nile Valley, which we now call Egypt, the Stone Age hunters of the North African plateau from the beginning had been sometimes lured by the chase, and having eventually been forced by the desiccation to follow the game thither, they began to make their permanent home in the Nile gorge. Around this hunter's Paradise the desiccation finally laid down a protective barrier of impenetrable desert on three sides of Egypt, east, west, and south, and transformed the lower Nile Valley into an isolated social laboratory without its like anywhere else. *For the Nile is the only river on our globe which rises in the tropics and flows northward to penetrate for nearly 700 miles into the climatic belt where the first great national organisations of men arose,* the temperate "sub-tropical belt of old empires" lying between north latitude 25 and 45 degrees, within which all the ancient empires grew up.[4] Furthermore, in prehistoric times the Nile Valley en-

[4] See the useful essay by Sten De Geer in *Geografiska Annaler,* Vol. X, pp. 205–244 (Stockholm, 1928).

joyed an additional unique advantage in that it was not exposed to the rigours of the Ice Age in Europe, from which it was separated and protected by the broad and tempering waters of the Mediterranean Sea, while the life of the European Stone Age hunters on its north was retarded in its development by arctic winds and the irresistible march of the glaciers.

In strong contrast with Egypt, Western Asia, with a mountainous highland belting its northern zone from the Bosphorus to Persia, was seriously exposed to the destructive glacial drainage and the cold of the Ice Age winter. It is not unlikely that it was a vague tradition of one of the outgoing glacial inundations which gave rise to the early Babylonian and later Biblical story of a universal deluge. Such disturbing *natural* forces, intruding from the northern highlands of Western Asia, were curiously anticipatory of the successive *racial* inundations which, likewise coming from the highlands, periodically overwhelmed the region, repeatedly overturning the existent social and governmental organisations, so that when the human development in the region had passed through the elementary stages of social evolution, it was continually broken down and thrown back, to go toilsomely through the same processes over and over again. Thus in succession the shifting forces both of Nature and of Man broke up the continuity of social evolution in Babylonia. Although we must recognise the stimulus of foreign invasion as a creative force, it has nevertheless been much overemphasised by some historians. A giant tree stands and defies the winds by the strength of those tough rings of annual growth which may have been developing for centuries, and remain deep in the inner structure of its great trunk. The accumulated strength of such a tree may serve to

Fig. 1. THE WESTERN SHORE OF THE NILE AT THEBES

With an uninhabitable desert plateau behind the cliffs, the Nile gorge furnished an isolated and protected situation, a unique social laboratory. It was on the black soil, which the river deposited along its shores for over seven hundred miles, that the earliest agricultural nation of several million souls arose. (*Oriental Institute photograph.*)

illustrate that of a developing national organisation which has gained lasting increments of power; but the tree which has been repeatedly blown down and uprooted always remains dwarfed and stunted. It is no accident that, after the culmination of Babylonian civilisation under Hammurapi's dynasty, its fall in the Eighteenth Century B.C., together with the invasion of the Kassites resulted in a cultural stagnation which persisted for a thousand years or more.

On the other hand we have just observed that the desiccation of North Africa isolated the lower Nile Valley and created there the only such sheltered corridor on our globe, extending north and south, with one end in the tropics and the other opening upon a great inland sea in the temperate zone. Enjoying unparalleled physical advantages, it was so isolated and protected that it made possible a human evolution which, notwithstanding some foreign intrusions, continued for several thousand years without serious interruption. Today we excavate along the margin of the Egyptian alluvium on the edge of the desert the graves of the oldest known cemeteries in the world, and we find lying in these graves the descendants of the Nile hunters of the Stone Age, just beginning the transition to metal well back of 4000 B.C., and not improbably much earlier. They had already acquired all the leading domestic animals, and had made the transition to the settled agricultural life. The evidence is in favour of the conclusion that these prehistoric Egyptians of the early cemeteries, or their ancestors, were the earliest large society on earth able to insure themselves an uninterrupted food supply by the domestication of the wild sources, vegetable and animal, while their subsequent conquest of metal and their development of the earliest known system of phonetic writing, gave them the leadership in the long advance towards civilisation.

This jungle valley of Egypt lying athwart the eastern Sahara not only gathered between its contracted rocky walls the prehistoric hunters scattered along the North African coast, but it also held them together in the possession of all the resources necessary for the unhampered development of human life under conditions so favourable that the once local communities were slowly consolidated into the first great society of several million souls, swayed by one sovereign hand and in possession of the leading fundamentals of civilisation. Thus in the centuries between 5000 and 3500 B.C. arose the first great civilised state at a time when Europe and most of Western Asia were still inhabited by scattered communities of Stone Age hunters.

The first coalescence forming a united nation took place probably not later than 4000 B.C. The result was some centuries of union which I have begun to call the First Union, and which resulted in the foundation of a centralised government, the earliest known human organisation embracing several million souls.[5] Subsequently, with the formation of the Second Union, there began a national evolution, an impressive development, governmental and economic, social and religious, architectural, artistic, and literary, which went steadily on for a thousand years, from the Thirty-fifth to the Twenty-fifth Century B.C. This period of a thousand years is a unique stage in the life of man on earth, for it represents the first chapter of developing human life as a social process, disclosing to us the first rise of social forces and their effect on human society. It is im-

[5] The First Union is a matter of recent discovery, and was not known when the numbering of the historic dynasties was introduced. The numbered dynasties therefore begin with the Second Union.

portant to emphasise the word "unique" as used in the preceding sentence, for there was in this early age no such consecutive and uninterrupted development anywhere else in the ancient world. It was this thousand years of social experience which placed Egypt morally and culturally far in advance of Babylonia where the struggle of contending city kingdoms, representing insignificant local interests, continued throughout this same thousand years, and long afterwards was still going on. *Preceding* this fundamentally important initial millennium of social development the main drift in the great human drama was that of man's advancing conquest of the *material* world. The Nile Valley is for us therefore the earliest social arena, where we may observe man victoriously emerging from an age-long *struggle with nature,* and entering this new arena of social forces, to begin the baffling *struggle of mankind with himself*—a struggle which has hardly passed beyond its beginnings at the present day.

We of America are especially fitted to visualise and to understand the wonderful transformation of a wilderness into a land of splendid cities. But our fathers, whose efforts have planted great and prosperous cities along the once lonely trails of our own broad land, received art and architecture, industry and commerce, social and governmental traditions, as an inheritance from our European ancestry. There was an age, however, when the transition from barbarism to civilisation, with all its impressive outward manifestations in art and architecture, had to be made *for the first time*. The significance of the appearance of civilisation along the Nile does not lie in the splendour of its buildings alone, but in the fact that as a continuous and uninterrupted social evolution steadily moving on for over a thousand years it was rising *for the first time on our globe,* and furnishing the first demonstration that the highest vertebrate creature which had appeared on earth could thus rise from savagery to social idealism, and to express in human life something which, as far as we know, was appearing for the first time in the Universe.

Today the traveller on the Nile enters a wonderland at whose gates rise the colossal pyramids of which he has had visions from earliest childhood. As he ascends the river he sees expanding behind palm-fringed shores vast temple precincts, to which avenues of sphinxes lead up from the shore, dominated by the mighty shafts of tall obelisks and stately colonnades. But rarely does it occur to the traveller that, just as in America, so there on the Nile *the wilderness preceded all this.* Where those vast monuments of stone now rise once stretched the tangled jungle of the Nile canyon, pathless for thousands of years save where the hunter's narrow trail wound through the whispering reeds to the water's edge. There was no civilised ancestry from whom the prehistoric Nile-dweller might receive an inheritance of culture. In their own deepening experience and broadening vision we must find the magic which transformed these primitive hunters and their little settlements of wattle huts into a great society dominated by masterful men of grandly spacious imagination, of imposing monumental vision, whose prodigal hands, untrammelled by tradition, stretched out over the one-time jungle, and not only scattered these gigantic monuments far up and down the river, but also caught a noble vision of social values and unselfish character which had never before dawned on the world. He who knows the story of the transition from the prehistoric hunters of the Nile jungle to the sovereigns and statesmen, the architects, engineers, and craftsmen, the sages and social prophets of a great organised society, which wrought these monumental wonders along the Nile at a time when all Europe was still living in Stone Age barbarism and there was none to teach a civilisation of the past—he who knows all this knows the story of the *first rise of a civilisation of profound moral vision anywhere on the globe.*

Civilisation in the highest sense was thus born at the southeast corner of the Mediterranean. From the first, however, there were important advances towards civilisation in neighbouring Western Asia, especially in Babylonia, where there eventually arose a culture, characterised by persistent progress in practical, legal, and commercial matters, and at the same time so devoted to the belief that human destiny might be read in the stars that its extraordinary skill in the study of the celestial bodies ultimately furnished the data which became in the hands of the Greeks the foundations of the science of astronomy. Babylonian civilisation, however, was dominated throughout by a spirit of calculating commercialism, of hard and mechanical requirements, which deprived the social evolution of the Babylonians of the very foundations of altruistic development. The basic moral requirement of equal justice to all was totally lacking, and the famous code of Hammurapi's laws dispenses justice according to the social station of the litigant or the offender. The complete obliteration of social distinctions before the law, which is one of the finest achievements of Egyptian civilisation, was unknown in Babylonia, and as a result of this fact, Babylonian morals have contributed little if anything to the moral heritage of the Western world.

The interfusion of the early civilisations in the Near Orient led to the creation of what we may call an Egypto-Babylonian or Near-Oriental culture nucleus. Until our own generation the peoples of the West have left almost unnoticed the profoundly important fact that both in Egypt and Babylonia civilisation had culminated and was on the decline before Hebrew civilisation had arisen. We are all aware that Egypto-Babylonian culture set European civilisation going; but few modern people have observed the fact, so important in the history of morals and religion, that *Egypto-Babylonian culture also set Hebrew civilisation going*. Later a current of early oriental influences, of which Christianity is the most noticeable, continuing to set towards Europe, eventually transformed the Roman State at Constantinople into an oriental despotism and continued to be felt until long after the Crusades.

Considerations like these disclose at once an impressive degree of unity in the career of man. The recognition of the Near Orient as lying behind the history of Europe, just as the history of Europe lies behind that of America, and the further possibility of pushing back behind the Ancient Near East of historic times into the ages of man's *prehistoric* development thus giving us the ever remoter stages, America, Europe, the Near Orient, prehistoric man, the geological ages—these latest reconstructions of the new historian disclose to us the career of man for the first time *as one whole,* to be regarded as a consecutive development from the stone fist-hatchet to the shell fragments of 1914, buried side by side on the battlefields of the Somme. A comprehensive study of the Ancient Near East, carried on with open eyes and with larger objects in view than the statistics of the dative case, long so dear to the hearts of our classical colleagues, reveals to us the well-known historic epochs of the career of European man for the first time set in a background of several hundred thousand years. In this vast synthesis, which only a study of oriental history makes possible, there is thus disclosed to us an imposing panorama of the human career in a vista of successive ages such as no earlier generation has ever been able to survey.

This is the New Past.

However it may be with science and philosophy, history, morals, and theology have thus far made little account of this tremendous synthesis. In the history of morals the New Past suddenly discloses to us the long unsuspected fact that Hebrew civilisation, with its important and profoundly influential records of religious and moral experience, is one of the latest, outgoing stages of early human development, which was preceded by ages of productive and creative social and moral experience along the Nile and the Euphrates. We must therefore adjust our minds to the fact that the moral heritage of modern civilised society originated in a time far earlier than the Hebrew settlement in Palestine, and has descended to us from a period when the Hebrew literature now preserved in the Old Testament did not yet exist.

In a sermon delivered recently by one of the ablest American preachers I find the following glance forward to a time when historians of the future, reviewing our epoch, may hail it as a "momentous period when the Sun of righteousness rose with healing in his wings."[6] This familiar figure was of course drawn from Hebrew literature; but, as we shall see, the Hebrews borrowed it from Egypt, where the "Sun of righteousness" rose over two thousand years earlier than he did in Palestine. If he is to rise again on our own generation, it will be as the culmination of a process of human development which had

[6] From a sermon by Doctor Henry Sloane Coffin, October 2, 1932, as quoted in *The New York Times,* Monday, October 3, 1932, p. 13. The above is not intended to classify Doctor Coffin as one of the "traditional theologians."

been unfolding in the life of man for thousands of years before the "age of revelation" so long accepted by traditional theologians.

We are now to see what the New Past, as disclosed to us by the most recent researches, reveals to us regarding the early human experience which brought to man his first realisation of the highest values, so that his adventure culminated in the dawn of conscience and introduced the Age of Character.

CHAPTER II

THE NATURE GODS AND HUMAN SOCIETY: THE SUN-GOD

IT is a matter of not a little interest to observe what humankind becomes in the course of five thousand years in such an Island of the Blest as Egypt; to follow him, as we are now able to do, from his obsolescent stone tools and weapons in a few generations to the copper chisel and the amazing extent and accuracy of the Great Pyramid masonry; from the wattle-hut to the sumptuous palace, gorgeous with glazed tile, rich tapestries, and incrusted with gold; to disengage all the golden threads of his many-sided life, as it was interwoven at last into a rich and noble fabric of civilisation. We are now endeavouring to follow but one of these many threads, as its complicated involutions wind hither and thither throughout the whole fabric.

There is no force in the life of ancient man the influence of which so pervades all his activities as does that of his religion. In the most primitive stage it is but an endeavour in vague and childish fancies to explain and to control the world about him and the gods he sees there; its fears become his hourly master, its hopes are his constant mentor, its feasts are his calendar, and its outward usages are to a large extent the education and the motive towards the evolution of art, literature, and science. Life is not only touched by religion at every point, but life, thought, and religion are inextricably interfused in an intricate complex of impressions from without and forces from within. Responding to such stimuli, religion cannot remain static, but becomes a *process,* passing from stage to stage. It has always been so, as far back as we can observe it, and there is every reason to conclude that it will always continue to be a development, an evolution. We are now to see something of this development, in which the world *about* man and the world *within* him successively wrought and fashioned the religion and gradually created the morals of the earliest great society for over three thousand years.

We shall be able to follow the process more clearly if we first undertake a rapid bird's-eye survey, furnishing a historical summary of ethical development among the Egyptians. At this point it is important to bear in mind the now commonly accepted fact that in its primitive stages, religion had nothing to do with morals as understood by us of today. Furthermore, the earliest morals were only folk custom which might have nothing to do with the gods or with religion. As among all other early peoples, it was in his natural surroundings that the Egyptian first saw his gods. The trees and springs, the stones and hill-tops, the birds and beasts, were creatures like himself, or possessed of strange and uncanny powers of which he was not master. *Nature* thus made the earliest impression upon his mind, the visible world was first explained in terms of religious powers and the earliest gods were the controlling forces of the *material* world. A *social* or *political* realm, or a domain of the *spirit* where the gods should reign supreme, was not at first perceived. Least of all did the worshippers of such a god conceive of him as having any ideas of right or wrong, or any desire to lay such requirements upon his worshippers, who considered themselves as expected only to present certain propitiatory offerings just as they might present them to a local chieftain. Such divinities as these were for the most part local, each known only to the dwellers in a given locality but migration or diffusion might carry the belief in a god far across the ancient world.

After 4000 B.C. the state, the political organisation by which the two successive unions were governed, began to assume a place in the minds of men, alongside the natural world. These two unions, the earliest great national organisations of men in history, brought before the minds of men an imposing fabric of the *state* which at length made a profound impression upon religion. The forms of the state began to pass over into the world of the gods, and an important god would be called a "king."

At the same time the relations of *social* life had likewise long been influencing religion. The realm of family life reached a high development as a world of tender emotions, inevitably inclining to become those of approval and disapproval, and leading to notions of praiseworthy or reprehensible conduct. Voices within began to make themselves heard, and moral values as we know them were discerned for the first time. Thus both the organised power of man *without* and the power of the moral imperative *within,* came to be early forces in shaping Egyptian religion. The surviving sources would indicate that the moral mandate was felt earlier in Egypt than anywhere else. The earliest known discussion of right and wrong in the history of man is embedded in a Memphite drama celebrating the supremacy of Memphis and dating from the middle of the Fourth Millennium B.C. It is obviously a semi-theological, semi-philosophical discussion of origins, produced by a priestly body of temple thinkers. It does not reflect the life of the Egyptian people as a whole. At a later period they also were to feel the moral conviction impelling their own lives. Moral discernment thus descended gradually from the aristocrats of the royal court and the temple priesthoods to the provincial nobles first and then to the masses.

Under the dominion of a stable government in the Second Union ruling by standards of justice, there arose the earliest conception of a moral order, designated by a significant word "righteousness," "justice," or "truth" (Egyptian *Maat*), which endured for a thousand years from the Thirty-fifth to the Twenty-fifth Century B.C. and made a profound impression on the human mind.

When it fell at the end of that thousand years, the catastrophe was like the fall of the Eternal City in Europe and essentially altered the human outlook. In an ensuing interval of political feebleness, the imperishable inner values began to be discerned more clearly and in the Twenty-third Century B.C. an otherwise unknown king of Heracleopolis set forth to his son and successor the supreme value of character.

Left prostrate by the fall of the ancient order, the collapse of Maat itself, and assessed by more sensitive moral discernment, the corrupt and disorganised society which followed the Pyramid Age appeared hopeless to the horrified eyes of some of the social sages who contemplated the wreck of the old order. The earliest known age of pessimism and disillusionment ensued. The social prophets painted a terrible picture of corruption and disorganisation which they denounced in unsparing terms—in one case even addressing these denunciations to the king himself. Nevertheless there were some among these Egyptian sages who had not lost hope, and they carried on the earliest crusade for social justice. It is very surprising that their social idealism took the form of Messianism, the belief in a righteous ruler yet to come, one who should usher in a golden age of justice for all mankind, a belief later inherited by the Hebrews.

With the restoration of ordered government and development of provincial society in the Feudal Age, beginning some centuries before 2000 B.C., the effect of the social crusade is discernible in the demand for social justice which found expression in the conception of a gracious and paternal kingship, maintaining high ideals of social equity. The world of the gods, continuing in sensitive touch with the political conditions of the nation, at once felt this influence, and through the idealised kingship social justice passed over into the character of the state god, enriching the ethical qualities which in some degree for more than a thousand years had been imputed to him. In the minds of his worshippers the god had long been a king; he now became a *righteous* king in a social sense, exacting right conduct also in the lives of his worshippers.

The belief that the god would decree life for the good and death for the wicked had already been expressed in the Memphite drama in the middle of the Fourth Millennium B.C. The idea of a judgment beyond the grave had then become more and more definite after 3000 B.C. In its earliest form it had not implied a judgment before which all men must necessarily appear; but a court of justice like those on earth, to which any one might appeal for righting a wrong. It was at first therefore only an *accused* person who must appear to justify himself before the court in the hereafter. Before 2000 B.C., however, in the early part of the Feudal Age, the conception of a general judgment arose. Subsequently in the early Empire (Sixteenth Century B.C.), the judgment not only included a detailed scrutiny of all transgressions, but became an ethical ordeal, a test of the entire moral quality of every man's life. The consciousness of such an impending judgment was becoming a powerful moral influence as the sages who were its authors intended it to be; but its influence was early blighted by magical agencies of the Book of the Dead, devised for gain by the temple priests to enable the dead to delude and deceive the dreaded judge.

Beginning in the Sixteenth Century B.C. a period of international expansion, both political and religious, enlarged the arena of religious thinking and after 1400 B.C. culminated in the earliest known monotheism. The supremacy of a world-god, however, did not enrich the moral development of the Egyptians. Imperial wealth debased the priesthoods, and the last great development in Egyptian religion which ensued took place seemingly outside of the temples and the state religion (1300–1000 B.C.). It was a development towards a realisation of sinfulness, a recognition of the believer's own unworthiness, combined with deep personal confidence in the goodness and paternal solicitude of God, resulting in a relation of spiritual communion with him. It was especially in this age that the teachings of the Egyptian sages exerted a profound influence on Hebrew religious thinking and, having thus effected lodgment in Palestine, they had advanced through the first stage in their long transition from Egypt to us of the modern world. In Egypt itself, however, this oldest known age of personal piety in a deep spiritual sense degenerated under the influence of sacerdotalism into the exaggerated religiosity of Græco-Roman days in Egypt.

Thus unfolding during some three thousand years, beginning about 4000 B.C., there passes before us an imposing chapter of human experience, disclosing the first great human society, as it moved from stage to stage of the longest ethical evolution which we can follow in the career of any human society. It was a development the more impressive because, in so far as we know, it was taking place *for the first time,* and was thus demonstrating a fact before unknown: that the highest mammal which had emerged on this planet was not only able to rise to a civilised level as we have before noted, but that this rise also included a discernment of new and supreme values which shifted human development into an incomparably loftier world. In revealing this new world to man it thus for the first time introduced such ethical possibilities into the great movement of early human life, both in Egypt and abroad. The life and literature of a great nation developing an experience like this for three thousand years necessarily exerted a profound and growing influence, especially on the life of its nearest neighbor, Palestine, but also throughout the Near East. The movement which it stimulated among the Hebrews created a religious and moral tradition, which passed to Western civilisation, and its later stages have thus continued as a powerful moral force in modern life.

With this rapid summary in mind we are now in a position to follow a fuller consideration of the long development in the Nile Valley by which its people rose to social ideals of character. The evidences for studying the earlier ethical development of such an ancient people are very scanty until we reach the introduction of writing and the production of written sources. The earliest of these do not begin to serve us in Egypt until after 3000 B.C., although sources of later date do throw important light backward upon remoter stages of ancestral development. But the written sources can never carry us back to the beginning of the development.

For our knowledge of the earliest human life in the Nile Valley we are dependent upon purely material documents, almost exclusively stone weapons and implements. Later the prehistoric cemeteries, with thousands of archaic burials strewn along the margin of the alluvium, disclose to us something of the religious beliefs of the Nile dwellers in remote days of the Late Stone Age. From the earliest to the latest of such prehistoric evidences the period of time involved is several hundred thousand years at the very least. It is safe to conclude that, like modern natives still surviving in a primitive stage of life, the earliest Egyptians had only unmoral local gods, and a body of customs which had not yet become morals. Some further light is thrown on ideas current in the age before writing if we examine Egyptian religion in its earliest surviving written documents and endeavour to disengage the greatest impressions which we find reflected there, and which the Egyptians had received from the natural world.

It is evident that two great phenomena of nature had made the most profound impression upon the Nile-dwellers, and that the gods discerned in these two phenomena dominated religious and intellectual development from the earliest times. These are the sun and the Nile or the vegetation which its waters supported. These two, the Sun-god, Re, and the Verdure-god, Osiris, were the great gods of Egyptian life. Very early they entered upon a rivalry for the highest place in the religion of Egypt—a rivalry which ceased only with the annihilation of Egyptian religion at the close of the Fifth Century of the Christian Era. He who knows the essentials of the story of this long rivalry will know the main course of the history of Egyptian religion, not to say one of the most important chapters in the history of man.

The all-enveloping power and glory of the Egyptian sun is the most insistent fact in the Nile Valley even at the present day as the modern tourist views him for the first time. The Egyptian saw him in different, doubtless originally local forms.

Probably the oldest notion of him goes back to the days when the prehistoric Egyptians were still leading a hunting life in the Nile marshes, when they pictured the Sun-god as a hunter poling or paddling himself across the reed-grown marshes in a boat made by lashing together two bundles of reeds like a catamaran (*cf.* note on p. 77). Glimpses of this archaic notion are still preserved in the oldest passages of the Pyramid Texts, which often picture the Sun-god ferrying across the celestial marshes in the "double reed-boat." This was Re, the physical sun, whom the earliest Nile-dwellers already envisaged in human form, and localised at Heliopolis, where he displaced an ancient Sun-god called Atum and became the greatest god of Egypt.

At Edfu, in Upper Egypt, the Sun-god appeared as a falcon, for the lofty flight of this bird, which seemed a very comrade of the sun, had led the early fancy of the Nile peasant to believe that the sun must be such a falcon, taking his daily flight across the heavens, and the sun-disk with the outspread wings of the falcon became the commonest symbol of Egyptian religion. It has come down to us through Hebrew literature in such pictures as "the wings of the morning" and "the sun of righteousness . . . with healing in his wings." As falcon the Sun-god bore the name Hor (Horus or Horos), or Harakhte, which means "Horus of the horizon." Survivals of the distinctions between the archaic local Sun-gods are still to be found in the Pyramid Texts, but a process of coalescence early began, which merged them all so that the Sun-god might be called "Re-Harakhte" or "Re-Atum." This process was hastened by local pride as each sanctuary sought to gain honour by associating itself with the birth of the Sun-god.

For ages of prehistoric time the Sun-god remained a nature god. In the remotest past therefore it was only with material functions that the Sun-god had to do. In the earliest sun-temples at Abusir, he appears as the source of life and increase. Men said of him: "Thou hast driven away the storm, and hast expelled the rain, and hast broken up the clouds." These were his enemies, and of course they were likewise personified in the folk-myth, appearing in a tale in which the Sun-god loses his eye at the hands of his enemy.

But as the Nile Valley, where the Sun-god had so long appeared as a power of Nature, was slowly being transformed into a great nation, his field of action was inevitably to become one of human life and national affairs. Of the historical processes which brought about the First Union, we know nothing but it is certain that a prince of On, the city later called by the Greeks Heliopolis, had subdued the other prehistoric principalities of Egypt and united the country for the first time under one sovereign, probably not later than 4000 B.C. Not an echo of his name has ever reached us across the interval of some six thousand years which has elapsed since then; but his work left a permanent mark on Egyptian life and civilisation, for he founded and set going the first great national organisation of men, controlling the life of a population of sev-

FIG. 2. FIGURE OF TUTENKHAMON IN THE FORM OF OSIRIS, PROTECTED BY HIS *BA* (ON LEFT) AND *KA* (ON RIGHT)

This remarkable wood carving is only about twelve inches long and is an example of the beauty of craftsmanship which characterises even the smallest objects from the tomb of Tutenkhamon. The inscription explains that the figure was a funerary gift to the king from the director of the royal cemetery. (*Cairo Museum. By courtesy of Mr. Howard Carter.*)

FIG. 3. THE WINGED SUN-DISK ADORNING THE SARCOPHAGUS OF KING EYE

This magnificent sarcophagus, carved from a single block of red granite, has four goddesses standing at the corners with wings spread protectingly over the sides, which are further adorned by exquisitely sculptured winged sun-disks: "the sun of righteousness . . . with healing in his wings." (*Fourteenth Century* B.C.)

eral millions of souls. We recall that this First Union lasted for some centuries, and that after it broke up again an interval of disunion was followed, about 3400 B.C., by another conquest of the political fragments which coalesced into what we have called the Second Union. The leadership of Heliopolis under the First Union gave the city a place of influence and prestige which it never lost. On Egyptian civilisation it made a profound impression, in which the Sun-god occupied an exalted place, and it was from the Egyptian state under the First Union that the forms and characters of earthly government passed over into the whole régime of the Sun-god as national god at Heliopolis. He became the sovereign of all gods; men said to him, "Thou art he who overlooks all gods; there is no god who overlooks thee." He likewise at the same time became the supreme ruler over the destinies of men.

From the world of nature, the Sun-god thus shifted to the world of men, where he became an ancient king who, like a Pharaoh, had once ruled Egypt. His outward manifestations were correspondingly changed. The "double reed-boat" of remote prehistoric days was succeeded by a gorgeous royal barge like that of the earthly Pharaoh. In this luminous sun-barque, one for the morning and the other for the evening, it was believed that the Sun-god majestically crossed the celestial ocean as the Pharaoh sailed the Nile. Many folk-myths telling of his earthly rule arose, but of these only fragments have survived, like that which narrates the ingratitude of his human subjects, whom he was obliged to punish and almost exterminate before he retired to the sky. While the Egyptians continued to refer with pleasure to the incidents which made up these primitive tales, and their religious literature to the end was filled with allusions to these myths, nevertheless as the unified nation emerged they were already discerning the Sun-god in the exercise of functions which lifted him far above such childish fancies and made him the great arbiter and ruler of the Egyptian nation.

This fundamental transition, the earliest of its kind known to us, thus shifted the activities of the Sun-god from the realm of exclusively *material* forces to the domain of *human affairs*. A sun-hymn which probably arose in this period of the First Union is preserved to us in the Pyramid Texts of later days. In this, the earliest sun-hymn which we possess, it is the Sun-god's supremacy in the *affairs of Egypt* which is celebrated. It sets forth not only the god's beneficent maintenance and control of the land of Egypt, but also rolls on in line after line extolling the great god's protection of Egypt against her enemies.

Similarly the Sun-god is the ally and protector of the Pharaoh. The Pyramid Texts say of him: "He settles for him Upper Egypt, he settles for him Lower Egypt; he hacks up for him the strongholds of Asia, he quells for him all the people,[1] who were fashioned under his fingers." Having thus entered the realm of human affairs, the Sun-god, like any earthly subject of human government, or member of earthly society, began, in the thinking of men, to feel the influences of human society, which were thus eventually to shape and fashion him into the earliest moral and righteous god in human history.

[1] The word used applies only to the people of Egypt.

CHAPTER III

THE SUN-GOD AND THE DAWN OF MORAL IDEAS

Not a single royal monument surviving from the period of the First Union is now accessible. If any have survived they still lie deeply buried under the water-logged alluvium of the Nile Delta, where it has been accumulating over the remains of prehistoric Heliopolis for many thousands of years. Nevertheless, as we have already noticed, later ages have transmitted to us echoes and reminiscences of these far-off times, or even of the remoter age before Egypt was united under one king. Indeed the actual text of a document written at the beginning of the Second Union has come down to us in a later copy inscribed on a black stone now in the British Museum. It last served as a nether millstone, on which modern Egyptian villagers ground their flour. For years they turned the upper millstone round and round on the inscribed surface, little realising what they were obliterating.

Priceless are the mutilated passages which still remain legible on this venerable block. We learn something of its origin at once from a line of stately hieroglyphs at the top, where we find the name of the Ethiopian Pharaoh Shabaka, who ruled Egypt in the Eighth Century B.C. Following his name his inscription states: "His majesty (meaning himself) wrote out this writing anew in the house of his father Ptah-South-Of-His-Wall. His majesty had found it as a work of the ancestors, it having been eaten of worms and not legible from beginning to end.

Then his majesty wrote it out anew, so that it was more beautiful than it was before." In the Eighth Century B.C. then, this pious Ethiopian king of Egypt was interested in preserving an ancient writing "of the ancestors"—a writing which must have been on papyrus, otherwise it could not have been "eaten of worms." In order to save it permanently, Shabaka, very fortunately for us, transferred his new copy to *stone,* where even so, a few more years of grain-grinding would have destroyed the oldest drama in the world and the earliest known philosophical discussion.

It is now a generation ago that I spent many stifling summer days, sitting on a low stool under a window in the British Museum endeavouring to reflect some light from the window above, by means of a hand mirror, to the stone below, installed as it was *under* the window sill so that no light from the window fell upon it. It was before the days of the modern powerful electric hand lanterns, and copying such a worn and sometimes totally illegible inscription on a dead black stone was slow and difficult. The inscription was in columns, or vertical lines, and the order of the columns in reading such an inscription may be from right to left, or left to right according as the hieroglyphs face towards the reader's right or towards his left; that is, in such columns the signs usually face the beginning of the inscription.

In this inscription the hieroglyphs all faced towards the right, indicating that the beginning was on the right, and so I had begun copying with the first right-hand column, and was proceeding column by column towards the left. All at once, however, I noticed that a phrase at the bottom of one column was continued, *not* by the next column on the left but by the next column on the *right.* It was thus suddenly evident that the inscription was one of a few which we know were written with reversed signs, that is, signs not facing in the customary direction, and that it had therefore hitherto been read in inverted order, as a series of disjointed sections following each other *from the end to the beginning!* Read in the proper order these columns of text began to tell a remarkable story; but it was a fragmentary story and in parts so illegible that it was exceedingly difficult to understand. The upper millstone had revolved in the middle of the inscribed surface and there also the miller had cut a hole with channels radiating from it like spokes from a hub. The merciless millstone had almost completely obliterated the middle third of the ancient text, leaving only a scanty third on the left at the beginning, and a similar amount on the right at the end. It was impossible to discern any connection between the group of columns on the left and those on the right.

Since I published the text of the inscription with a preliminary attempt to interpret it, it has required the further efforts of a generation of scholars, among whom Erman and Sethe have contributed the most, to gain an adequate understanding of its character and content, and not least to establish its date. The Ethiopian Shabaka in the Eighth Century B.C. called it a "work of the ancestors," a vague term suggesting that his learned scribes had no idea that the writing they were copying was at that time over two thousand five hundred years old. But the language and the content of the ancient writing leave us in no doubt about its remote origin. The language contains archaisms which show that the document is enormously old, and the text discloses an historical situation which is obviously only to be found at the beginning of the Second Union, that is, at the founding of the First Dynasty by Menes about 3400 B.C. It is therefore a product of Egyptian civilisation in the middle of the Fourth Millennium B.C. As such we have mirrored in it *the oldest thoughts of men that have anywhere come down to us in written form.*

The distressing gap in the middle, as I have already indicated, has left us a beginning, at the left, and, at the right, a conclusion. The text of the beginning is cut up by frequent divisions into short sections, most of which are utterances by various gods to each other. At the beginning of such an utterance we often find the hieroglyphs for the names of two gods, so arranged that the signs face each other, as if one god were speaking to the other, as the content of the speeches would indicate that they were in fact doing. A similarly arranged group of speeches has since been found by Sethe on a papyrus dating nearly 2000 B.C., accompanied by notes and pictures which can only be understood as stage directions.[1] That is to say, the papyrus investigated by Sethe is an ancient drama. The arrangement of its text in columns is identical with that of our British Museum stone, and this fact demonstrates that on this stone also we have an archaic drama, as indeed Erman had suspected.[2] The conclusion of this oldest known drama is lost in the gap in the middle caused by the millstone. As we pass on beyond the gap towards the right end, we find a philosophical discussion, which it seems difficult to connect with the drama. Sethe has suggested we should understand that some important ecclesiastic or priestly lector delivered much of the presentation in the form of a long narrative address

[1] K. Sethe, *Dramatische Texte zu altægyptischen Mysterienspielen* (Leipzig, 1928).

[2] A. Erman, "Ein Denkmal memphitischer Theologie," in *Sitzungsberichte der Königlich Preussischen Akademie der Wissenschaften,* Vol. XLIII (1911).

in the course of which, whenever an incident in the myth was narrated, the divinities concerned appeared and introduced the incident in the form of a dialogue. There were thus interspersed the dialogues carried on by the various gods participating in the presentation, which at such points is therefore dramatic in form and strikingly like the sacred narratives presented in the Christian mystery plays of mediæval times, of which the Memphite drama is the earliest ancestor.

In both the drama and the discussion we find the god Ptah of Memphis playing the rôle of the Sun-god as the supreme god of Egypt. It is an illustration of the practice, to which we have already referred above (p. 26), by which a local god sought to gain the prestige and splendour of the Sun-god by assuming his position and appropriating his rôle in the mythical history of Egypt and its origins. The supremacy of Ptah in this drama clearly denotes the political leadership of his native city of Memphis—a supremacy in this case due to the triumph of Menes, the founder of the First Dynasty, who, although he was a native of Thinis in Upper Egypt, established Memphis as the capital and royal residence. Notwithstanding its Memphite origin, the ultimate source of the content of this extraordinary Memphite drama, as we may now call the composition, was without question Heliopolis. We thus have in it the philosophising theology of the priests of Heliopolis as it had developed during the First Union, when it had reached a stage which we find the Memphite priests appropriating for their own god Ptah.

It discloses to us the old nature god, the Sun-god Re, completely transformed into an arbiter of human affairs, already viewed from a moral angle. He rules in a world in which he must guide human life in accordance with distinctions between right and wrong. It is very surprising to find that such ideas as these had already arisen by the middle of the Fourth Millennium B.C.

The content of this venerable drama may be summarised as an effort to account for the origin of all things, including the moral order of the world, and to show that they had their origin in Ptah of Memphis. All subsidiary agencies or beings who had any part in the creation of the world were merely forms or aspects of Ptah, who was the local Memphite god of the artisans and craftsmen and became the patron deity of all craftsmanship.

When Menes conquered Egypt and made Memphis, lying in the midst between Upper and Lower Egypt, the capital and royal residence, it was but a step to see in Ptah the master craftsman who had created the world. The effort to assume this rôle was of course substantially aided by assigning to Ptah also the prestige and unique supremacy of Re, who had for centuries led the gods of Egypt from the vantage point of his splendid seat at Heliopolis. The Memphite drama discloses to us the supreme place claimed for Ptah in the concluding passages, which we must now examine. We learn first that "Ptah the Great is the heart and the tongue of the gods." This extraordinary statement becomes more intelligible when we learn that "heart" means "mind" or "intelligence," while "tongue" is the designation of the spoken word, the authoritative utterance, by which the thoughts of the mind become objective, that is, are projected into a world of objective reality. We are now in a position to follow the meaning of the ancient narrative, as it proceeds to recount the origin of things.

FIG. 4. "PTAH THE GREAT IS THE HEART AND THE TONGUE OF THE GODS"

Head of black granite statue of the god Ptah of Memphis.

(*From the Oriental Institute collections.*)

1. Thought and Its Expression as the Origin and Sustaining Power of Both the Divine and Earthly Order

"It came to pass that heart and tongue gained the power over every member, teaching that he (Ptah) was (in the form of the heart) in every breast and (in the form of the tongue) in every mouth, of all gods, all men, all cattle, all reptiles, [all] living, while he (Ptah) thinks and while he commands everything that he desires." After we are told how the Memphite group of gods are still in the mouth of Ptah, "which pronounced the names of all things," we learn that these gods, who have earlier been enumerated as forms of Ptah, "created the sight of the eyes, the hearing of the ears, the breathing of the nose, that they may transmit to the heart. It is he (the heart) who causes that every conclusion should come forth, it is the tongue which announces the thought of the heart. Thus all gods were fashioned, Atum and his Divine Ennead (group of nine gods); while every divine word came into being through that which the heart thought and the tongue commanded; and thus the stations (official positions) were made and the functions (of government) were assigned, which furnished all nutrition and all food, by this (preceding) speech," meaning the argument that precedes.

2. The Earthly Order

"(As for) him who does what is loved and him who does what is hated, life is given to the peaceful and death is given to the criminal."

"Thus are carried on every work and every craft, the action of the arms, the going of the legs, the movement of every member, according to this command which the heart thinks, which has come forth from the tongue, and which makes the worth of everything."

3. The Divine Order

"It came to pass that it was said regarding Ptah, 'He who made Atum (an old Solar divinity at Heliopolis), and caused the gods to be.' He is Tatenen (an old name of Ptah), who fashioned the gods. Everything has come forth from him, whether food, or nutrition, or food of the gods, or any good thing. Thus was it found and perceived that his (Ptah's) strength was greater than all gods, and thus was Ptah satisfied after he had made all things and every divine word."

"He fashioned the gods, he made the cities, he founded the nomes (baronies), he set the gods on their holy places, he established their sacred revenues, he equipped their shrines, he made likenesses of their bodies as their heart desired. Thus the gods entered into their bodies of every kind of wood, of every kind of mineral, of every kind of clay, and everything that grows upon him (Ptah as earth-god), in which they had taken form."

"Thus the gods and their functions gathered to him, the Peaceful, the Reconciler, as Lord of the Two Lands (Egypt; a title of Pharaoh). The Divine Granary was the Great Throne (Memphis) rejoicing the heart of the gods who are in the House of Ptah, mistress of all life, from which the life of the Two Lands (Egypt) is furnished."

In order to explain why Memphis had become the granary of Egypt the narrative passes at this point to the story of Osiris. We shall have to defer the consideration of Osiris in the Memphite drama until we have completed the discussion of the Sun-god's functions which we have just seen appropriated by Ptah. As we scan the content of the above discussion of Ptah it is obvious that there is much repetition of the same ideas, so that the three subjects which I have attempted to disengage and to indicate by sub-titles are by no means mutually exclusive. They overlap noticeably. The archaic priestly thinker is especially unable to refrain from dwelling on the production of food, whenever he touches the divine order, because even though it belongs primarily to the earthly order, it is a process dependent on the power of the gods.

The extraordinary basis of this early system is the fundamental assumption that mind or thought is the source of everything; for all things "came into being through that which the heart (mind) thought and the tongue (speech) commanded." Not being given to abstractions and believing that the heart was the seat of intelligence the ancient Egyptian employed the word "heart" for "mind" or "understanding." The agency by which mind became creative force was the spoken word which enunciated the idea and gave it reality. The idea thus took on being in the world of objective existence. The god himself is identified with the heart which thinks, and the tongue which speaks. Are we to recognise here the prehistoric background of the Logos doctrine of New Testament days? "In the beginning was the Word, and the Word was with God, and the Word was God"—is there here an echo of remote human experience on the Nile?

It is obvious that this tremendous idea, appearing so early in human history, or, perhaps we would better say, prehistory, is in itself evidence of surprisingly advanced maturity at such a remote date. We are abruptly, and without any gradual transition stages, shifted out of the world of nature gods into a ripe and developed civilisation, in which the organisers of religion and government are producing mature abstract thinking. They see the world about them functioning intelligibly and therefore conclude that it was brought forth and is now maintained by a great all-pervading intelligence, which, by a touch of pantheism, they believe is still active in every breast and every mouth of all living creatures. It is an idea which long survived and we find the Egyptian of nearly two thousand years later believing in "the oracle of the god which is in every body"; or referring to "the god that is in thee."

It is quite clear that ordered society and organised government had made a great impression on these early thinkers. "Stations" of rank and official position and "functions" of government, by which human society maintains itself, were thought to have been ordained by the supreme intelligence and called into being by his word. The practical operations of every-day living, in work and craftsmanship, were in accord with the mandate "which the heart thinks and which has come forth from the tongue."

Already at this remote stage of human development there is recognition of the fact that some conduct is approved and some disapproved. Each is treated accordingly. "Life is given to the peaceful (literally "to the one bearing peace"), and death is given to the guilty" (literally "the one bearing guilt"). It is very noticeable that these early thinkers do not use here the terms "good and evil." The peaceful is "he who does what is loved" and the guilty is "he who does what is hated." These are *social* judgments, designating what is approved ("loved"), and what is disapproved ("hated"). These two terms, "what is loved" and "what is hated," occurring here for the first time in human history, form the earliest known evidence of man's ability to draw the distinction between good and bad conduct. They had a long subsequent history and continued in use for many centuries. It was long before they were displaced by right and wrong.

The suspended construction of the introductory phrases of this brief paragraph on the moral order is not wholly clear. On the stone itself the words are arranged thus:

"He who does { what is loved,"
what is hated,"

and seem to be disconnected from the following by a separative particle. It is a question whether the rendering above has brought out the whole meaning. In the first place the word rendered "does" means also "make," and being here in a participial form, "he who does" might possibly mean "he who makes," that is, "maker," and thus designate the god as "the maker of what is loved and what is hated." If so, we have the god here called the creator of both good and evil. Erman, thinking this unacceptable, interpreted the two opposing terms as "good fortune" and "misfortune"; but this interpretation, as Sethe has noted, is shown to be impossible by the following opposed terms, "peaceful" and "guilty," which are obviously ethical. Moreover these terms, as we have already mentioned, have a subsequent history, in which they are unmistakably ethical in use. In order to give the suspended terms some connection, Sethe concludes that there has been an omission in copying by the ancient scribe and suggests that the omitted words should be restored from a passage in the Book of the Dead, which would give us the following:

"[Thus Right is given to] "[and Wrong is given to]	him who does	what is loved" what is hated."

The chief objection to this restoration is the introduction of the terms "right" and "wrong," derived from a source so much later. The lack of these latter terms in our drama is a very important fact, suggesting their later development. Otherwise the restoration, though exceedingly daring, is attractive, and supplies perfect parallelism with the following two opposed clauses.

Among the qualities or characteristics of the Sun-god which we can clearly discern after 3000 B.C. are two called "Command" and "Understanding." The two were often personified as deities, just as the Hebrews personified "Wisdom." As successor of the Sun-god, the Pharaoh was often hailed by his courtiers, thus: "It is Command who is in thy mouth, it is Understanding who is in thy heart," and Gardiner has made the attractive suggestion that when this idea was appropriated for Ptah, the Memphite authors of the drama modified the terms they found in the solar theology, substituting "heart" for the solar "Understanding" and "tongue" for the solar "Command." We would thus have the two parallel pairs:

1. Original Qualities
   of the Sun-god: Understanding: Command.
2. Substituted Qualities
   of Ptah : Heart : Tongue.

It is evident that the idea of a supreme personality was for the first time dawning upon the human mind. These early thinkers were struggling with the whole imposing conception and were endeavouring to recognise and disengage the constituent characteristics which distinguish such personality. As an idea it was to have a profound influence upon human life. It is quite clear that it came out of the kingship, or better out of the actual reign and administration of the king, in whom the whole idea was personalised. For the first time in human history men beheld, in the Pharaoh, a glorious vision of outstanding personality and of personified power, and the idea thus began to become a force reacting first on the tiny nucleus of thinking men, and eventually on human society.

The Memphite drama discloses to us the earliest known recognition of conduct as approved or disapproved, and these two reactions, as we have already observed, were social, and the product of social evolution. The total lack of contemporary documents prevents us from discerning the source and the character of this evolution. Surviving from later stages of the development, we shall find plentiful evidences disclosing to us the nature of the sources which led early men to recognise some conduct as "loved" and some as "hated"—a stage of morals as primarily custom. Even at this very early stage, the development had already gone far enough so that conduct had become a subject of reflection in the minds of the earliest thinkers known to us in the remote centuries of the First Union of Egypt. In other words we have in this Memphite drama a brief hint of the earliest reflective morality. The virtuous man is called the "peaceful," literally the "bearer of peace," evidently a social term, designating a virtuous man's relations with those about him. Opposed to him is the "bearer of crime," the "criminal," who is an offender against those about him. There must already have been law which recognised these two kinds of conduct, and meted out death to the offender and granted life to the inoffensive.

All this implies a social and ethical development that lies far below our earliest historical horizon. It is important to determine just how far this development had proceeded when it first emerges in the dawn of history. Later conditions make it quite evident that the source of law, the source of life and death, was the Pharaoh. The effect of conduct was a purely external matter concerning exclusively this life on earth. The Pharaoh might look forward to a glorious hereafter sailing the celestial ocean with his father the Sun-god; but for every one else an acceptable or a reprehensible course of conduct was a matter of purely external, earthly consequences, and had no effect on any life hereafter. Right and wrong were things decreed by the Pharaoh, and, as the Memphite drama shows, were discussed by his priestly thinkers. It was to be long before such ideas had been humanised and socialised to become a great social force introducing the age of conscience and of character, many centuries later.

CHAPTER IV

THE SOLAR FAITH AND THE STRUGGLE WITH DEATH

In following the emergence of Egypt's oldest gods, we have been watching ages of prehistoric human development in the Nile Valley, and we have seen how the world of nature gradually impressed itself upon the minds of the earliest Nile dwellers. Sunshine and verdure were insistent, natural manifestations which continuously wrought upon the thought and imagination of the earliest Egyptian, and we have seen how he personified these mysterious powers of nature as great gods. We recall that these two gods were at first, and long continued to be, merely natural forces, operating chiefly if not solely in the realm of nature. We have seen the Sun-god gradually shifting into a world of organised human affairs, and we shall later watch the Verdure-god going through the same process. After they had thus entered this common arena of action they were both inevitably brought into relations with each other.

It was an imposing new world in which they were becoming involved. The prehistoric hunter, whose self-expression had been quite content to ply the flint graving tool in carving symmetrical lines of game beasts along the ivory haft of a stone dagger, had been transformed by fifty generations of social evolution into a royal architect launching great bodies of organised craftsmen upon the quarries of the Nile cliffs and summoning thence stately and rhythmic colonnades, imposing temples of the gods, and a vast rampart of pyramids, the greatest tombs ever erected by the hand of man. What was to become of the old nature gods in a world like this?

Nor was it a world transformed only by the grandeur of its outward and merely material expressions of advancing social and governmental organisations; for man's unfolding *inner* life had obviously kept even pace with these visible but unwritten evidences. The appearance of the earliest known architecture in stone and the first colonnaded buildings were not only evidences of the advancing efficiency of organised community life, but likewise revelations of new and expanding human vision. The builders of this time were the first poet-architects to thrust out their hands among the palm groves and the marshes of the Nile and plucking thence the lotus, the papyrus, and the tufted palm, to range them as colonnades along the temple porticoes—the first artists to bring into the temple courts something of the sunny and verdant beauty of the outside world. Thus even in the temple, sunshine and verdure commingled to beautify the outward forms of the sanctuary as they did likewise inwardly the religious beliefs of the age.

As the greatness of the state began to find expression in architectural forms of dignity and splendour, these forms were chiefly religious. The impressive outward magnificence of organised religion is a measure of the profound influence of the new state and government on religion. Thus formally organised by the state, religion responds but slowly to social influences, but these state forms are favourable to the reception of reciprocal influences from one priestly or temple community to another.

Under these circumstances we find that the local beliefs begin to interpenetrate. This has already been evident in the case of the Sun-god at Heliopolis and the craftsman-god Ptah at Memphis. It was still more true of the sunshine and the verdure, the Sun-god and Osiris.

The fact of death made a tremendous impression on Egyptian religion and it profoundly affected both the Solar and the Osirian theology. It is especially in examining the mortuary beliefs of the Egyptians that we shall be able to discern the interfusion of Solar and Osirian faith. We shall not be able to understand the commingling of these two faiths until we have given some attention to Egyptian notions of life after death and the extraordinary practices which these ideas brought forth.

Among no people, ancient or modern, has the idea of a life beyond the grave held so prominent a place as among the ancient Egyptians. This insistent belief in a hereafter may perhaps have been, and experience in the land of Egypt has led me to believe that it was, greatly favoured and influenced by the fact that the conditions of soil and climate resulted in such remarkable preservation of the human body as may be found under natural conditions perhaps nowhere else in the world. While working on the inscriptions of Nubia, many years ago, I was not infrequently obliged to pass through the corner of a cemetery, where the feet of a dead man, buried in a shallow grave, had been uncovered and extended directly across my path. They were very much like the rough and calloused feet of the workmen in our excavations. How old the grave was I do not know, but any one familiar with the cemeteries of Egypt, ancient and modern, has found bodies or portions of bodies indefinitely old which sometimes seemed almost as well preserved as those of the living. This must have been a frequent experience of the ancient Egyptian likewise, and like Hamlet with the skull of Yorick in his hands, he must often have pondered deeply as he contemplated these silent witnesses. The surprisingly perfect state of preservation in which he found his ancestors when the digging of a new grave may have disclosed them, must have greatly stimulated his belief in their continued existence, and aroused his imagination to more detailed pictures of the realm and the life of the mysterious departed.

The earliest and simplest of these beliefs began at an age so remote that they have left no trace in surviving remains. The cemeteries of the prehistoric communities along the Nile, discovered and excavated since 1894, disclose a belief in the future life which was already in an advanced stage. Thousands of graves, the oldest of which undoubtedly reach back far into the Fifth Millennium B.C., were dug by these primitive people in the desert gravels along the margin of the alluvium. In the bottom of the pit, which is but a few feet in depth, lies the body with the knees drawn up towards the chin and surrounded by a meagre equipment of pottery, flint implements, stone weapons, and utensils, beside rude personal ornaments—all of which were of course intended to furnish the departed for his future life.

From the archaic beliefs represented in the earliest of such burials as these it is presumably a matter of not less than fifteen hundred years to the appearance of the earliest written documents surviving to us—documents on which we have above been drawing, and which disclose the more developed faith of a people rapidly rising towards a high material civilisation. We are thus able, on the basis of written sources, to take up the course of the development under the Second Union, about 3000 B.C.

We then have before us the complicated results of a commingling of originally distinct beliefs which have long since interpenetrated each other and have for many centuries circulated thus, a tangled mass of threads which it is now very difficult or impossible to disentangle.

These difficulties are complicated by the early Egyptian's notion of the nature of a person. The actual personality of the individual in life consisted, according to the Egyptian notion, in the visible body, and the invisible intelligence, the seat of the last being considered the "heart" or the "belly," which indeed furnished the chief designations for the intelligence. Then the vital principle which, as so frequently among other peoples, was identified with the breath which animated the body, and was not clearly distinguished from the intelligence. The two together were pictured in one symbol, a human-headed bird with human arms, which we find in the tomb and coffin scenes depicted hovering over the mummy and extending to its nostrils in one hand the figure of a swelling sail, the hieroglyph for wind or breath, and in the other the so-called *crux ansata,* or symbol of life.[1] This curious little bird-man was called by the Egyptians the *ba.* The remarkable fact has been strangely overlooked that originally the ba came into existence really for the first time at the death of the individual. All sorts of devices and ceremonies were resorted to that the deceased might at death become a ba. It is evident that the Egyptian, like ourselves, could not dissociate a person from the body as an instrument or vehicle of sensation, and they resorted to elaborate devices to restore to the body its various channels of sensibility, after the soul (ba), which compre-

[1] As first noticed by Battiscombe Gunn, this sign is really a sandal-latchet, the Egyptian word for which has the same consonants as the word for "life." Gunn's suggestion seems to me correct, although it is not accepted by all.

hended these very things, had detached itself from the body. The Egyptian thought of his departed friend as existing in the body, or at least as being in outward appearance still possessed of a body, as we do, if we attempt to picture the departed at all. Hence, when depicted in mortuary paintings, the deceased friend of course appears as he did in life.

In harmony with these conceptions was the desire of the surviving relatives to insure physical restoration to the dead. Gathered with the relatives and friends of the deceased at the tomb, the mortuary priest stood over the silent body and addressed the departed: "Thy bones perish not, thy flesh sickens not, thy members are not distant from thee." However effective these injunctions may have been, they were not considered sufficient. The motionless body must be resuscitated and restored to the use of its members and senses. This resurrection might be the act of a favouring god or goddess, as when accomplished by Isis or Horus; or the priest addressed the dead and assured him that the Sky-goddess would raise him up: "She sets on again for thee thy head, she gathers for thee thy bones, she unites for thee thy members, she brings for thee thy heart into thy body." But even when so raised the dead was not in possession of his senses and faculties, nor had he the power to control and use his body and limbs. Several devices were necessary to make of this unresponsive mummy a living person, capable of carrying on the life hereafter. He had not become a ba, or a soul, merely by dying, and it was necessary to aid him to become one. Osiris when lying dead had become a soul by receiving from his son Horus the latter's eye, wrenched from the socket in his conflict with Set. Horus, recovering his eye, gave it to his father, and on receiving it

Osiris at once became a soul. From that time any offering to the dead was commonly called the "eye of Horus," and might thus produce the same effect as on Osiris. "Raise thee up," says the priest, "for this thy bread, which cannot dry up, and thy beer which cannot become stale, *by which thou shalt become a soul.*" The food which the priest offered therefore possessed the mysterious power of effecting the transformation of the dead man into a soul, as the "eye of Horus" had once transformed Osiris.

From these facts it is evident that the Egyptians had developed a rude psychology of the dead, in accordance with which they endeavoured to reconstitute the individual by processes *external to him,* and under the control of the survivors, especially the mortuary priest who possessed the indispensable ceremonies for accomplishing this end. We may summarise it all in the statement that after the resuscitation of the body, there was a mental restoration or a reconstitution of the faculties one by one, attained especially by the process of making the deceased a "soul" (ba), in which capacity he again existed as a *person,* possessing all the powers that would enable him to subsist and survive in the life hereafter. It is therefore not correct to attribute to the Egyptians a belief in the *immortality* of the soul strictly interpreted as imperishability or to speak of his "ideas of immortality."

In beginning the new and untried life after death, the deceased was greatly aided by a protecting guardian spirit called the *ka,* which came into being with each person, followed him throughout life, and passed *before* him into the life hereafter. On the walls of the temple of Luxor, where the birth of Amenhotep III was depicted in sculptured scenes late in the Fifteenth Century before Christ, we find the little prince brought in on the arm of the Nile-god, accompanied apparently by another child. This second figure, identical in external appearance with that of the prince, is the being called by the Egyptians the *ka.* He was a kind of superior genius intended especially to guide the fortunes of the individual *in the hereafter,* where every Egyptian who died found his ka awaiting him. It is of importance to note that in all probability the ka was originally the exclusive possession of kings, each of whom thus lived under the protection of his individual guardian genius, and that by a process of slow development the privilege of possessing a ka became universal among all the people.

We cannot doubt that the weapons of the primitive hunter, together with jars of food and drink, besides his personal ornaments, had been laid beside him in his grave for thousands of years before there was any king or kingdom in the Nile Valley. Gradually the monarchy and the advancing civilisation which went with it evolved an elaborate material equipment, a monumental tomb with its mortuary furniture. The earliest massive masonry tomb, called by the modern Egyptians a *mastaba* (or "bench"), was like a truncated pyramid with very steep sides. It was but the rectangular descendant of the prehistoric burial mound with a retaining wall around it, once of rough stones, now of carefully laid hewn-stone masonry, which had taken on some of the incline of its ancient ancestor—the sand heap or the tumulus—still encased within it. In the east side of the superstructure, which was often of imposing size, was a rectangular room, perhaps best called a chapel, where the offerings for the dead might be presented and these ceremonies on his behalf might be performed. For, notwithstanding the elaborate reconstitution of the dead as a person, he was not unquestionably able to maintain himself in the hereafter without assistance from his surviving relatives. All such mortuary arrangements were chiefly Osirian, for in the Solar faith the Sun-god did not die among men, nor did he leave a family to mourn for him and maintain mortuary ceremonies on his behalf. It was altogether natural to consign the dead to the protection of Osiris, as a son of Geb the Earth-god.

From the Thirty-fourth Century on, as the tombs of the First Dynasty at Abydos show, it had become customary for favourite officials and partisans of the Pharaoh to be buried in the royal cemetery, forming a kind of mortuary court around the monarch whom they had served in life. Gradually the king became more and more involved in obligations to assist his nobles in the erection of their tombs and to contribute from the royal treasury to the splendour and completeness of their funerals. The favourite physician of the king receives a requisition on the treasury and the royal quarries for the labour and the transportation necessary to procure him a great and sumptuous false door of massive limestone for his tomb, and he tells us the fact with great satisfaction and much circumstance in his tomb inscriptions. We see the Pharaoh in the royal palanquin on the road which mounts from the valley to the desert plateau, whither he has ascended to inspect his pyramid, now slowly rising on the margin of the desert overlooking the valley. Here he discovers the unfinished tomb of Debhen, one of his favourites, who may have presumed upon a moment of royal complaisance to call attention to its unfinished condition. The king at once details fifty men to work upon the tomb of his *protégé,* and afterwards orders the royal engineers and quarrymen who are at work upon a temple in the vicinity to bring for the fortunate Debhen two false doors of stone, the blocks for the façade of the tomb, and likewise a portrait statue of Debhen to be erected therein. One of the leading nobles who was flourishing at the close of the Twenty-seventh Century B.C. tells us in his autobiography how he was similarly favoured: "Then I besought . . . the majesty of the king that there be brought for me a limestone sarcophagus from Troja (royal quarries near Cairo, from which much stone for the pyramids of Gizeh was taken). The king had the treasurer of the god (= Pharaoh's treasurer) ferry over, together with a troop of sailors under his hand, in order to bring for me this sarcophagus from Troja; and he arrived with it in a large ship belonging to the court (that is, one of the royal galleys), together with its lid, the false door . . . (several other blocks the words for which are not quite certain in meaning), and one offering-tablet."

In such cases as these, and indeed quite frequently, the king was expected to contribute to the embalmment and burial of a favourite noble. The Pharaoh sent out his body of mortuary officials, priests, and embalmers to meet the nobleman Sebni, returning from the Sudan with his father's body (p. 118). Similarly he despatched one of his commanders to rescue the body of an unfortunate noble who with his entire military escort had been massacred by the Bedouin on the shores of the Red Sea while building a ship for the voyage to Punt, the Somali coast, in all likelihood the land of Ophir of the Old Testament. Although the rescuer does not say so in his brief inscription, it is evident that the Pharaoh desired to secure the body of this noble also in order to prepare it properly for the hereafter. Such solicitude can only have been due to the sovereign's personal attachment to a favourite official.

This is quite evident in the case of Weshptah, one of the viziers of the Fifth Dynasty about 2700 B.C. The king, his family, and the court were one day inspecting a new building in course of construction under Weshptah's superintendence, for, besides being grand vizier, he was also chief architect. All admire the work and the king turns to praise his faithful minister when he notices that Weshptah does not hear the words of royal favour. The king's exclamation alarms the courtiers, the stricken minister is quickly carried to the court, and the priests and chief physicians are hurriedly summoned. The king has a case of medical rolls brought in, but all is in vain. The physicians declare his case hopeless. The king is smitten with sorrow and retires to his chamber, where he prays to Re. He then makes all arrangements for Weshptah's burial, ordering an ebony coffin made and having the body anointed in his own presence. The dead noble's eldest son was then empowered to build the tomb, which the king furnished and endowed. A noble whose pious son wished to rest in the same tomb with him (p. 118) enjoyed similar favour at the king's hands. The son says: "I requested as an honour from the majesty of my lord, the king of Egypt, Pepi II, who lives forever, that there be levied a coffin, clothing, and festival perfume for this Zau (his dead father). His majesty caused that the custodian of the royal domain should bring a coffin of wood, festival perfume, oil, clothing, 200 pieces of first-grade linen and of fine southern linen . . . taken from the White House (the royal treasury) of the court for this Zau."

Interred thus in royal splendour and equipped with sumptuous furniture, the maintenance of the departed, in theory at least *through all time,* was a responsibility which he dared not intrust exclusively to his surviving family or eventually to a posterity whose solicitude on his behalf must continue to wane and finally disappear altogether. The noble therefore executed carefully drawn wills and testamentary endowments, the income from which was to be devoted exclusively to the maintenance of his tomb and the presentation of oblations of incense, ointment, food, drink, and clothing in liberal quantities and at frequent intervals. The source of this income might be the revenues from the noble's own lands or from his offices and the perquisites belonging to his rank, from all of which a portion might be permanently diverted for the support of his tomb and its ritual every day.

In a number of cases the legal instrument establishing these foundations has been engraved as a measure of safety on the wall inside the tomb-chapel itself and has thus been preserved to us. At Siut, Hepzefi (the count and baron of the province) has left us ten elaborate contracts on the inner wall of his tomb-chapel, intended to perpetuate the service which he desired to have regularly celebrated at his tomb or on his behalf.

The amount of the endowment was sometimes surprisingly large. In the Twenty-ninth Century B.C., the tomb of Prince Nekure, son of King Khafre of the Fourth Dynasty, was endowed from the prince's private fortune with no less than twelve towns, the income of which went exclusively to the support of his tomb. A palace steward in Userkaf's time, in the middle of the Twenty-eighth Century B.C., appointed eight mortuary priests for the service of his tomb; and a baron of Upper Egypt two centuries and a half later endowed his tomb with the revenues from eleven villages and settlements. The income of a mortuary priest in such a tomb was, in one instance, sufficient to enable him to endow the tomb of his daughter in the same way. In addition to such private resources, the death of a noble not infrequently resulted in further generosity on the part of the king, who might either increase the endowment which the noble had already made during his life, or even furnish it entirely from the royal revenues.

The privileges accruing to the dead from these endowments, while they were intended to secure him against all apprehension of hunger, thirst, or cold in the future life, seem to have consisted chiefly in enabling him to share in the most important feasts and celebrations of the year. Like all Orientals the Egyptian took great delight in religious celebrations, and the good cheer which abounded on such occasions he was quite unwilling to relinquish when he departed this world. The calendar of feasts, therefore, was a matter of the greatest importance to him, and he was willing to divert plentiful revenues to enable him to celebrate all its important days in the hereafter as he had once so bountifully done among his friends on earth. He really expected, moreover, to celebrate these joyous occasions among his friends in the temple just as he had once been wont to do, and to accomplish this he had a statue of himself erected in the temple court. Sometimes the king, as a particular distinction granted to a powerful courtier, commissioned the royal sculptors to make such a statue and to erect it inside the temple door. In his tomb likewise the grandee of the Pyramid Age set up an extraordinary lifelike stone or wooden portrait statue of himself painted in the hues of life. It was concealed in a secret chamber hidden in the mass of the tomb masonry. Such statues, too, the king not infrequently furnished to the leading nobles of his government and court. It was evidently supposed that this portrait statue, the earliest of which we know anything in art, might serve as a body for the disembodied dead, who might thus return to enjoy a semblance at least of bodily presence in the temple, or again in the same way return to the tomb-chapel, where he might find other representations of his body in the secret chamber close by the chapel.

We discern in such usages the rise of a more highly developed and more desirable hereafter, which gradually supplanted the older and simpler views. These new views involved the first discernible tendency towards a recognition of individuality as shown in these earliest-known portrait statues. They depict for us only the proud patricians, the men and women of the noble class. The common people doubtless still thought of their dead either as dwelling in the tomb, or at best as inhabiting the gloomy realm of the West, the subterranean kingdom ruled by the old mortuary gods eventually led by Osiris. But for the great of the earth, the king and his nobles at least, a happier destiny had now dawned. They might dwell at will with the Sun-god in his glorious celestial kingdom. In the royal tomb we can henceforth discern the emergence of this Solar hereafter (*cf.* pp. 74 *ff.*).

The Pharaoh himself might reasonably expect that his imposing tomb would long survive the destruction of the less enduring structures in which his nobles were laid, and that his endowments, too, might be made to outlast those of his less powerful contemporaries. The pyramid as a stable form in architecture has impressed itself upon all time. Beneath this vast mountain of stone, as a result of its mere mass and indestructibility alone, the Pharaoh looked forward to the permanent survival of his body and of the personality with which it was so indissolubly

FIG. 5. THE PYRAMIDS OF GIZEH FROM THE AIR

The largest were built to serve as permanent and indestructible resting places for the bodies of three kings of the Fourth Dynasty of Egypt (after 2900 B.C.). The small pyramids belonged to members of the royal family and the other tombs to court officials.
(*Oriental Institute photograph by Reed N. Haythorne.*)

linked. It would carry us too far afield to discuss the origin of the pyramid as a form of architecture;[2] it is important to notice, however, that the pyramidal tomb was a solar symbol of the highest sacredness, rising above the mortal remains of the king, to greet the Sun, whose offspring the Pharaoh was.

The king was buried under the same symbol of the Sun-god which stood in the holy of holies in the Sun-temple at Heliopolis, a symbol upon which, from the day when he created the gods, the Sun-god was accustomed to manifest himself in the form of the Phœnix; and when in mountainous proportions the royal pyramid rose above the king's sepulchre, dominating the royal city below and the valley beyond for many miles, it was the loftiest object which greeted the Sun-god in all the land, and his morning rays glittered on its shining summit long before he scattered the shadows in the dwellings of humbler mortals below. On the apex of a pyramid, a magnificent pyramidal block of polished granite, found lying at the base of Amenemhet III's pyramid at Dahshur, on the side which undoubtedly faced the east, we find a winged sun-disk, surmounting a pair of eyes, beneath which are the words "beauty of the sun," the eyes of course indicating the idea of beholding, which is to be understood with the words "beauty of the sun." Below is an inscription of two lines beginning: "The face of King Amenemhet III is opened, that he may behold the Lord of the Horizon when he sails across the sky" (see Fig. 6).

In the adoption of the pyramid, the greatest of the Solar symbols, as the form of the king's tomb, we must

[2] See the author's *Development of Religion and Thought in Ancient Egypt*, pp. 70 *ff*.

therefore recognise another evidence of the supremacy of the Solar faith at the court of the Pharaohs. It is notable in this connection that it was chiefly against Osiris and the divinities of his cycle that protection was sought at the dedication of a royal pyramid tomb.

The pyramid did not stand alone. It was a part, and the most conspicuous part, of an imposing architectural complex occupying a prominent position on the margin of the desert plateau overlooking the Nile Valley. On its east side, and abutting on the masonry of the pyramid, rose a low temple, with a beautiful colonnaded portico in front, leading to a charming colonnaded court, with surrounding storage chambers on either side, and in the rear a holy place. The back wall of this "holy of holies" was the east face of the pyramid itself, in which was a false door. Through this the dead king might step forth to receive and enjoy the offerings presented to him here. A covered causeway of impressive length, built of massive masonry, led up from the Nile Valley below to the level of the plateau where pyramid and temple stood, and extended to the very door in front of the temple, with whose masonry it engaged. At the lower end of the causeway and forming a sumptuous colonnaded entrance to it, like a monumental portal, was another temple appropriately called by Reisner the "valley temple," which was probably within the walls of the royal residence city below. These temples were of course the home of the elaborate mortuary ritual maintained on behalf of the king, and were analogous in origin to the chapel of the noble's tomb already discussed. The whole group or complex, consisting of pyramid, temple, causeway, and valley temple below, formed the most imposing architectural conception of this early age, and its surviving remains have

FIG. 6. THE CAPSTONE FROM THE PYRAMID OF AMENEMHET III AT DAHSHUR

The eyes, which are those of the dead king, faced the rising sun and thus each morning could "behold the beauty of the Sun." The inscription below begins: See p. 57. (*Cairo Museum.*)

FIG. 7. (*Right*) THE SUN-GOD RISING AS A FALCON: PAINTED VIGNETTE IN A BOOK OF THE DEAD

Below in two curves is the sandy desert on which the deceased lady Inhai appears twice as a human-headed bird (*Ba;* see p. 47) standing on the roof of her tomb. She and all the figures above her are lifting their arms in worship of the Sun-god, rising from the desert as a splendid falcon with a sun-disk on his head. (*British Museum.*)

contributed in the last few years an entirely new chapter in the history of architecture.

Each Pharaoh of the Third and Fourth Dynasties (about 3000 to 2750 B.C.) spent a large share of his available resources in erecting this vast tomb, which was to receive his body and insure its preservation after death. Thus to insure the sovereign's survival in the hereafter became the chief object of the state and its organisation. More than once the king failed to complete the enormous complex before death, and was thus thrown upon the piety of his successors, who had all they could do to complete their own tombs. When completed the temple and the pyramid were dedicated by the royal priests with elaborate formulæ for their protection.

Resting beneath the pyramid, the king's wants were elaborately met by a sumptuous and magnificent ritual performed on his behalf in the temple before his tomb. Of this ritual we know nothing except such portions of it as have been preserved in the Pyramid Texts. These show that the usual calendar of feasts of the living was celebrated for the sovereign, though naturally on a more splendid scale. Evidently the observances consisted chiefly in the presentation of plentiful food, clothing, and the like. One hundred and seventy-eight formulæ or utterances, forming about one-twentieth of the bulk of the Pyramid Texts, contain the words spoken by the royal mortuary priests in offering food, drink, clothing, ointment, perfume, and incense, revealing the endless variety and splendid luxury of the king's table, toilet, and wardrobe in the hereafter. The magnificent vases discovered by Borchardt at Abusir in the pyramid-temple of Neferirkere (Twenty-eighth Century B.C.) are a further hint of the royal splendour with which this ritual of offerings was maintained, while the beauty and grandeur of the pyramid-temples themselves furnished an incomparable setting within which all this mortuary magnificence was maintained. Pronouncing some six or eight score formulæ of the offering ritual besides some others scattered through the Pyramid Texts, the priest laid before the dead king those creature comforts which he had enjoyed in the flesh. In doing so the priest entered the mysterious chamber behind the temple court, where he stepped into the presence of the pyramid itself. There before him rose the great false door through which the spirit of the king might re-enter the temple from the royal sepulchre far beneath the mountain of masonry now towering above it. Standing before this false door, the priest addressed the king as if present and presented a vast array of the richest gifts, accompanying each with the prescribed formula of presentation which we have already discussed. But the insistent fact of death cannot be ignored even in these utterances which existed solely because the dead king was believed to live and to feel all the needs of the living. In the silent chamber the priest keenly felt the unresponsiveness of the royal dead lying entombed beneath the mountainous pyramid, and hence from time to time called upon him to rise from his sleep and behold the food and the gifts spread out for him. In order that none of these might be omitted, the priest summarised them all in the promise to the king: "Given to thee are all offerings, all oblations, even thy desire, and that by which it is well for thee with the god forever." Added to all this elaborate ritual of gifts there were also charms potent to banish hunger from the vitals of the king, and these, too, the priest from time to time recited for the Pharaoh's benefit. Maintained in this way, the kings of the early Pyramid

Age in the Thirtieth Century B.C. evidently believed that they might confidently look forward to indefinite survival in the life hereafter. But would the posterity of an oriental sovereign never weary in giving him mortuary offerings every day? We shall see.

Such maintenance required a considerable body of priests in constant service at the pyramid-temple, though no list of a royal pyramid priesthood has survived to us. They were supported by liberal endowments, for which the power of the royal house might secure respect for a long time. The priesthood and the endowment of the pyramid of King Snefru at Dahshur (Thirtieth Century B.C.) were respected and declared exempt from all state dues and levies by a royal decree issued by Pepi II of the Sixth Dynasty, three hundred years after Snefru's death. Moreover, there had been two changes of dynasty since the decease of Snefru. But such endowments, accumulating as they did from generation to generation, must inevitably break down at last. In the Thirtieth Century B.C., Snefru himself had given to one of his nobles "one hundred loaves every day from the mortuary temple of the mother of the king's children, Nemaathap." This queen had died at the close of the Second Dynasty, some two generations earlier. Snefru, while he may not have violated her mortuary income, at least disposed of it, after it had served its purpose at her tomb, in rewarding his partisans. In the same way the Pharaoh Sahure, desiring to reward Persen, one of his favourite nobles, found no other resources available and diverted to Persen's tomb an income of loaves and oil formerly paid to the Queen Neferhotepes every day. These arrangements make it evident that the mortuary offerings were not consumed, but were still available after having been presented in a tomb.

There is in these acts of Snefru and Sahure, therefore, a hint of one possible means of meeting the dilemma as the number of tomb endowments increased, viz., by supplying one tomb with food-offerings which had already served in another.

Even so the increasing number of royal tombs made it more and more difficult as a mere matter of management and administration to maintain them. Hence even the priests of Sahure's pyramid in the latter part of the Twenty-eighth Century B.C., unable properly to protect the king's pyramid-temple, found it much cheaper and more convenient to wall up all the side entrances and leave only the causeway as the entrance to the temple. They seem to have regarded this as a pious work, for they left the name of the particular phyle of priests who did it, on the masonry of the doorways which they thus closed up. After this the accidentally acquired sanctity of a figure of the goddess Sekhmet in the temple, a figure which enjoyed the local reverence and worship of the surrounding villages, and continued in their favour for centuries, resulted in the preservation of a large portion of the temple which otherwise would long before have fallen into ruin. Sahure's successor, Neferirkere, fared much worse. A few years after his death a successor of the same dynasty (Nuserre) broke away the causeway leading up to the pyramid-temple that he might divert it to his own temple near by. The result was that the mortuary priests of Neferirkere, unable longer to live in the valley below, moved up to the plateau, where they grouped their sun-dried brick dwellings around and against the façade of the temple where they ministered. As their income dwindled these dwellings became more and more like hovels, they finally invaded the temple court and chambers, and the priests, by this time in a state of want, fairly took possession of the temple as a priestly quarter. Left at last without support, their own tumble-down hovels were forsaken and the ruins mingled with those of the temple itself. When the Middle Kingdom opened, six hundred years after Neferirkere's death, the temple was several metres deep under the accumulation of rubbish, and the mounds over it were used as a burial ground, where the excavations disclosed burials a metre or two above the pavement of the temple.

The great Fourth Dynasty cemetery at Gizeh experienced the same fate. The mortuary priests, whose ancestors had once administered the sumptuous endowments of the greatest of all pyramids, pushed their intrusive burials into the streets and areas between the old royal tombs of the extinct line, where they too ceased about 2500 B.C., four hundred years after Khufu laid out the Gizeh cemetery. Not long after 2500 B.C. indeed, the whole sixty-mile line of Old Kingdom pyramids from Medûm on the south to Gizeh on the north had become a desert solitude. This melancholy condition is discernible also in the reflections of the thoughtful in the Feudal Age five hundred years later as they contemplated the wreck of these massive tombs (see pp. 161 *ff.*).

What was so obvious centuries after the great Pharaohs of the Pyramid Age had passed away, was already discernible long before the Old Kingdom fell. The pyramids of Egypt represent the culmination of the belief in *material equipment* as completely efficacious in securing felicity for the dead. They are the imposing final manifestation of the age-long struggle for the conquest of purely physical forces—a struggle which had been going on for perhaps a million years. Carried on for ages by the individual prehistoric hunter single-handed, that struggle was now being maintained by the disciplined forces of a whole nation. The great pyramids of Gizeh represent the effort of titanic energies absorbing all the resources of a great organised state as they converged upon one supreme endeavour to sheath eternally the body of a single man, the head of the state, in a husk of masonry so colossal that by these purely material means the royal body might defy all time and by sheer force of mechanical supremacy make conquest of immortality. The decline of such vast pyramids as those of the Fourth Dynasty at Gizeh and the final insertion of the Pyramid Texts in the pyramids, beginning with the last king of the Fifth Dynasty about 2625 B.C., puts the emphasis on wellbeing elsewhere, a belief in felicity in some distant place not so entirely dependent upon material means, and recognises in some degree the fact that piles of masonry cannot confer that immortality which a man must win in his own soul. The earliest "technocrats" were learning their first lesson and the Age of Character was about to lay a paralysing hand upon the work of the pyramid builder.

CHAPTER V

THE PYRAMID TEXTS AND THE PHARAOH'S ASCENT TO THE SKY

TOGETHER with the Memphite Drama the Pyramid Texts furnish us the oldest chapter in human thinking which has survived to mankind. We have in these sources the remotest reach in the intellectual history of man which we are now able to discern. It had always been supposed that the pyramids were all without inscriptions, until the native workmen employed by Mariette at Sakkara in 1880, the year before his death, penetrated the pyramid of Pepi I and later that of Mernere. There they found the walls of the galleries, passages, and chambers of these pyramids covered with thousands of lines of hieroglyphic writing. It is these writings which we call the Pyramid Texts. They are found in five of the pyramids of Sakkara, the ancient cemetery of Memphis, and they were placed there by a group of Pharaohs including the last king of the Fifth Dynasty and his four successors, the first four kings of the Sixth Dynasty. They thus cover a period of about a century and a half, beginning about 2625 and extending to possibly 2475 B.C., that is the whole of the Twenty-sixth Century and possibly a quarter of a century before and after it. It is evident, however, that they contain material much older than the age of the copies which have come down to us. The five copies themselves refer to material then in existence which has not survived. We read in them of the "Chapter of Those Who Ascend" and the "Chapter of Those Who Raise Themselves Up," which purport to have been used on the occasion of various incidents in the myths. These chapters were thus regarded as older than our Pyramid Texts. There are also references to the hostilities between the kings of the North (Lower Egypt) and those of the South (Upper Egypt), showing that such passages must have been written before the Second Union, that is, before the Thirty-fourth Century B.C.; and also others which belong to the early days of the Second Union when the hostilities had not yet ceased, when the kings of the South were nevertheless maintaining control of the North and preserving the united kingdom. All these are written from the southern point of view. On the other hand some of the Pyramid Texts were composed as late as the Old Kingdom itself, like the formulæ intended to protect the pyramid, which of course are not earlier than the rise of the pyramid-form in the Thirtieth Century B.C. Within the period of a century and a half covered by our five copies also differences are noticeable. Evidences of editing in the later copies, which, however, are not found in the earlier copies, are clearly discernible. The processes of thought and the development of custom and belief which brought them forth were going on until the last copy was produced in the early Twenty-fifth Century B.C. They therefore represent a period of at least a thousand years, and a thousand years, it should not be forgotten, which was ended some four thousand five hundred years ago. Such a great mass of documents from the early world exists nowhere else and forms a storehouse of experience from the life of ancient man which largely remains to be explored.

While their especial function may be broadly stated to

be *to insure the king felicity in the hereafter,* they constantly reflect, as all literature does, the ebb and flow of the life around them, and they speak in terms of the experience of the men who produced them, terms current in the daily life of palace, street, and bazaar, or again terms which were born in the sacred solitude of the inner temple. To one of quick imagination they abound in pictures from that long-vanished world of which they are the reflection. While they are concerned chiefly with the fortunes of the king, these do not shut out the world around. Of the happiness of the king beyond the grave it is said: "This that thou hast heard in the houses and learned in the streets on this day when King Pepi was summoned to life." Of this life in the houses and on the streets of five thousand years ago we catch fleeting glimpses: the swallows twittering on the wall; the herdman wading the canal immersed to his middle and bearing across the helpless young of his flock; the crooning of the mother to her nursing child at twilight; "the hawk seen in the evening traversing the sky"; the wild goose withdrawing her foot and escaping the hand of the baffled fowler in the marsh; the passenger at the ferry with nothing to offer the boatman for a seat in the crowded ferry-boat, but who is allowed to embark and work his passage wearily bailing the leaky craft; the noble sitting by the pool in his garden beneath the shade of the reed booth; these pictures and many others are alive with the life of the Nile-dweller's world. The life of the palace is more fully and picturesquely reflected than that of the world outside and around it. We see the king in hours heavy with cares of state, his secretary at his side with writing kit and two pens, one for black and the other for the red of the rubrics; again we discern him in moments of relaxation leaning familiarly on the shoulder of a trusted friend and counsellor, or the two bathe together in the palace pool and royal chamberlains approach and dry their limbs. Often we meet him heading a brilliant pageant as he passes through the streets of the residence with outrunners and heralds and messengers clearing the way before him; when he ferries over to the other shore and steps out of the glittering royal barge, we see the populace throwing off their sandals, and then even their garments, as they dance in transports of joy at his coming; again we find him surrounded by the pomp and splendour of his court at the palace gate, or seated on his gorgeous throne adorned with lions' heads and bulls' feet. In the palace-hall "he sits upon his marvellous throne, his marvellous sceptre in his hand; he lifts his hand towards the children of their father and they rise before this king; he drops his hand towards them and they sit down (again)." To be sure these are depicted as incidents of the life beyond the grave, but the subject-matter and the colours with which that life is portrayed are drawn from the life here and the experience here. It is the gods who cast off their sandals and their raiment to dance for joy at the arrival of the king, as he crosses the celestial Nile; but they are of course depicted as doing that which the Pharaoh's subjects were always accustomed to do along the earthly Nile. It is the gods who dry the Pharaoh's limbs as he bathes with the Sun-god in the "lake of rushes," but here too the gods do for the Pharaoh what his earthly chamberlains had been wont to do for him.

But notwithstanding the fact that these archaic texts are saturated with the life out of which they have come, they form together almost a *terra incognita*. As one endeavours to penetrate it, his feeling is like that of entering a vast primæval forest, a twilight jungle filled with strange forms and elusive shadows peopling a wilderness through which there is no path. An archaic orthography veils and obscures words with which the reader may be quite familiar in their later and habitual garb. They serve too in situations and with meanings as strange to the reader as their spelling. Besides these disguised friends, there is a host of utter strangers, a great company of archaic words which have lived a long and active life in a world now completely lost and forgotten. Hoary with age like exhausted runners, they totter into sight above our earliest horizon for a brief period, barely surviving in these ancient texts, then to disappear forever, and hence are never met with again. They vaguely disclose to us a vanished world of thought and speech, the last of the unnumbered æons through which prehistoric man has passed till he finally comes within hailing distance of us as he enters the historic age. But these hoary strangers, survivors of a forgotten age, still serving on for a generation or two in the Pyramid Texts, often remain strangers until they disappear; we have no means of making their acquaintance or forcing them to reveal to us their names or the message which they bear, and no art of lexicography can force them all to yield up their secrets. Combined with these words, too, there is a deal of difficult construction, much enhanced by the obscure and elusive nature of the content of these archaic documents; abounding in allusions to incidents in lost myths, to customs and usages long since ended, they are built up out of a fabric of life, thought, and experience largely unfamiliar or entirely unknown to us.

We have said that their function is essentially to insure the king's felicity in the hereafter. The chief and dominant note throughout is insistent, even passionate, protest against death. They may be said to be a reflection of humanity's earliest supreme revolt against the great darkness and silence from which none returns. The word death never occurs in the Pyramid Texts except in the negative or applied to a foe. Over and over again we hear the indomitable assurance that the dead lives. "King Teti has not died the death, he has become a glorious one in the horizon"; "Ho! King Unis! Thou didst not depart dead, thou didst depart living"; "Thou hast departed that thou mightest live, thou hast not departed that thou mightest die"; "Thou diest not"; "This king Pepi dies not"; "King Pepi dies not by reason of any king . . . (nor) by reason of any dead"; "Have ye said that he would die? He dies not; this king Pepi lives forever"; "Live! Thou shalt not die"; "If thou landest (euphemism for "diest"), thou livest (again)"; "This king Pepi has escaped his day of death"—such is the constant refrain of these texts. Not infrequently the Utterance concludes with the assurance: "Thou livest, thou livest, raise thee up"; or "Thou diest not, stand up, raise thee up"; or "Raise thee up, O this king Pepi, thou diest not"; or an appendix is added as a new utterance by itself: "O lofty one among the Imperishable Stars, thou perishest not eternally." When the inexorable fact must be referred to, death is called the "landing" or the "mooring," as we have seen it above, or its opposite is preferred, and it is better to mention "not living" than to utter the fatal word; or with wistful reminiscence of lost felicity once enjoyed by men, these ancient texts recall the blessed age "before death came forth."

While the supreme subject of the Pyramid Texts is life, eternal life for the king, they are a compilation from the most varied sources. Every possible agency and influence was brought to bear to attain the end in view, and all classes of ancient lore deemed efficacious or found available for this purpose were employed by the priests who put together this earliest surviving body of literature.

The content of the Pyramid Texts may be said to be in the main sixfold: a funerary ritual and a ritual of mortuary offerings at the tomb, magical charms, very ancient ritual of worship, ancient religious hymns, fragments of old myths, prayers and petitions on behalf of the dead king. In their modern published form, including the variants, they fill two quarto volumes containing together over a thousand pages of text. The ancient editor has divided them into 714 "Utterances."

While the *content* of the Pyramid Texts may thus be indicated in a general way, a precise and full analysis is a far more difficult matter. The *form* of the literature contained is happily more easily disposed of. Among the oldest literary fragments in the collection are the religious hymns, and these exhibit an early poetic form, that of couplets displaying parallelism in arrangement of words and thought—a form taken over by the Hebrews two thousand years later, and now familiar to us all in the Hebrew psalms as "parallelism of members." It is carried back by its employment in the Pyramid Texts into the Fourth Millennium B.C., by far earlier than its appearance anywhere else. It is indeed the oldest of all literary forms known to us. Its use is not confined to the hymns mentioned, but appears also in other portions of the Pyramid Texts, where it is, however, not usually so highly developed.

Besides this form, which strengthens the claim of these fragments to be regarded as literature in our sense of the term, there is here and there, though not frequently, some display of literary quality in thought and language. There is, for example, a fine touch of imagination in one of the many descriptions of the resurrection of Osiris: "Loose thy bandages! They are not bandages, they are the locks of Nephthys," the weeping goddess hanging over the body of her dead brother. The ancient priest who wrote the line sees in the bandages that swathe the silent form the heavy locks of the goddess which fall and mingle with them. There is an elemental power too in the daring imagination which discerns the sympathetic emotion of the whole universe as the dread catastrophe of the king's death and the uncanny power of his coming among the gods of the sky are realised by the elements. "The sky weeps for thee, the earth trembles for thee" say the ancient mourners for the king, or when they see him in imagination ascending the vault of the sky they say:

"Clouds darken the sky,
The stars rain down,
The Bows (a constellation) stagger,
The bones of the hell-hounds tremble,
The [porters] are silent,
When they see King Unis
Dawning as a soul."

When we recall that these mortuary texts were written only in the royal tombs, there can be no doubt that they were all intended exclusively for the benefit of the king, and as a whole contain beliefs which apply only to him. It is a significant fact that the nobles of the age made practically no use of the Pyramid Texts in their own tombs.

While the Pyramid Texts have not been able to shake off the old view of the sojourn at the tomb, they give it little thought, and deal almost entirely with a blessed life in a distant realm. It is of not a little interest that this distant realm is the sky, and that the Pyramid Texts know practically nothing of the gloomy hereafter in the Nether World. The realm of the dead, therefore, is a celestial one, using the term with none of its frequent theological significance in English. That the conception of a celestial paradise, later universal in the Christian world, had its origin in the same enormously old Egyptian belief can hardly be doubted.

Two ancient doctrines of this celestial hereafter have been commingled in the Pyramid Texts: one represents the dead as a star, and the other depicts him as associated with the Sun-god, or even becoming the Sun-god himself. It is evident that these two beliefs, which we may call the stellar and the Solar hereafter, were once in a measure independent, and that both have then entered into the form of the celestial hereafter which is found in the Pyramid Texts. In the cloudless sky of Egypt it was a not unnatural fancy which led the ancient Nile-dweller to see in the splendour of the nightly heavens the host of those who had preceded him; thither they had flown as birds, rising above all foes of the air, and there with the coming shadows every night they swept across the sky as eternal stars. It is especially those stars which are called "the Imperishable Ones" in which the Egyptian saw the host of the dead. These are said to be in the north of the sky, and the suggestion that the circumpolar stars, which never set or disappear, are the ones which are meant is hardly to be doubted. Much discussion has been caused by the fact that the sloping entrance passage of the Great Pyramid points directly towards the Pole Star. The hitherto unnoticed reason is obviously disclosed in the Pyramid

Texts. When the king's soul emerged from this passage its direction carried it straight towards the circumpolar stars.

While the stellar and the Solar elements are found side by side, the Solar beliefs predominate so strongly that the Pyramid Texts as a whole and in the form in which they have reached us may be said to be of Solar origin. The Solar destiny was perhaps suggested by the unfailing daily reappearance of the sun. Death was on earth; life was to be had only in the sky, where the king is lifted high above the universal doom of mortal men,

> "Men fall,
> Their name is not.
> Seize thou King Teti by his arm,
> Take thou King Teti to the sky,
> That he die not on earth
> Among men."

This idea that life was in the sky is the dominant notion, far older than the Osirian faith in the Pyramid Texts. So powerful was it that Osiris himself is necessarily accorded a celestial and a Solar hereafter in the secondary stage, in which his myth has entered the Pyramid Texts.

The prospect of a glorious hereafter in the splendour of the Sun-god's presence is the great theme of the Pyramid Texts. Even the royal tomb, as we have seen, assumed the form of the Sun-god's most sacred symbol. The state theology, which saw in the king the bodily son and the earthly representative of Re, very naturally conceived him as journeying at death to sojourn forever with his father, or even to supplant his father and be his successor in the sky as he had been on earth. The Solar hereafter is properly a royal destiny, possible solely to a Pharaoh; it is only later that ordinary mortals gradually assert the right to share it, though, as we shall see, this could be done only by assuming also the royal character of every such aspirant.

Passing as the Pharaoh did to a new kingdom in the sky, even though the various notions of his status there were not consistent, he was called upon to undergo a purification, which is prescribed and affirmed in the texts with wearisome reiteration. It was usually a purification by water and might be accomplished by libations or by bathing in the sacred lake in the blessed fields, with the gods even officiating at the royal bath with towels and raiment. This purification might also have moral aspects. We have here again an enormously old oriental ceremony of purification which has continued into modern times in the rite of baptism.

In the Solar faith the region towards which the king fared was the east of the sky. Not only was the Sun-god born there every day, but also the other gods. In this sacred place are the doors of the sky, before which stands "that tall sycamore east of the sky whereon the gods sit." Again we hear of "the two sycamores which are on yonder side of the sky," which the king seizes when "they ferry him over and set him on the east side of the sky." Here in this sacred place too the dead king finds the Sun-god, or is found by him, here he ascends to the sky, and here lands the ferry which brings him over.

When the deceased Pharaoh turned his face eastward towards this sacred region he was confronted by a lake lying along the east which it was necessary for him to cross in order to reach the realm of the Sun-god. It was on the farther, that is eastern, shore of this lake that the eye of Horus had fallen in his combat with Set. It was called the "Lily-lake," and it was long enough to possess "windings," and must have stretched far to the north and south along the eastern horizon. Beyond it lay a strange wonder-land, alive with uncanny forces on every hand. *All* was alive, whether it was the seat into which the king dropped, or the steering-oar to which he reached out his hand, or the barque into which he stepped, or the gates through which he passed. To all these, or to anything which he found, he might speak; and these uncanny things might speak to him, like the swan-boat of Lohengrin. Indeed it was a wonder-world like that in the swan-stories or the Nibelungen tales of the Germanic traditions, a world like that of the Morte d'Arthur, where prodigies meet the wayfarer at every turn.

To the dweller along the Nile the most obvious way to cross the Lily-lake was to embark in a ferry-boat. He found it among the rushes of the lake-shore with the ferryman standing in the stern poling it rapidly along. To do so he faces backward, and is therefore called "Face-behind," or "Look-behind." He rarely speaks, but stands in silence awaiting his passenger. Numerous are the pleas and the specious petitions by which the waiting Pharaoh seeks to cajole this mysterious boatman with averted face. We hear him assured with deceptive cunning that "this king Pepi is the herdman of thy cattle who is over thy breeding-place," and who must therefore be ferried over at once in the ferryman's own interests. Or the king brings with him a magic jar the power of which the boatman cannot resist, or the ferryman is assured that the Pharaoh is "righteous in the sight of the sky and of the earth," and of the isle to which they go. Again the king is the dwarf or pigmy of the royal dances "who gladdens the (king's) heart before the great throne," and he must therefore be hastened across to the palace and the court of Re to gladden the Sun-god. Indeed this is matter of common knowledge, as the ferryman is now told: "This is what thou hast heard in the houses and learned in the streets on this day when this king Pepi was summoned to life. . . ." We hear the boatman's challenge of the newcomer: "Whence hast thou come?" and the dead king must prove his royal lineage. If in spite of all the king's efforts the shadowy boatman proves obdurate and refuses to bring his boat to the shore, then the king addresses the oar in the ferryman's hand: "Ho! Thou who art in the fist of the ferryman," and if his words are powerful enough, the oar brings in the boat for the king.

From the earliest days the prehistoric peasant might cross the Nile on two reed floats bound firmly together side by side like two huge cigars.[1] One of the earliest folk-tales on the Sun-god's voyage depicted him as crossing the celestial waters on such a pair of floats, and however primitive they might be, their use by the Sun-god had become common and involuntary belief. It required but the proper "sympathetic" transference of their use by Re to the dead Pharaoh, to insure him certain passage like that of the Sun-god. Thus just as "the two floats of the sky are placed for Re that he may ferry over therewith to the horizon," so "the two floats of the sky are placed for King Unis that he may ferry over therewith to the horizon to Re."

1 The writer was once, like the Pharaoh, without a boat in Nubia, and a native from a neighbouring village at once hurried away and returned with a pair of such floats made of dried reeds from the Nile shores. On this somewhat precarious craft he ferried the writer over a wide channel to an island in the river. It was the first time that the author had ever seen this contrivance, and it was not a little interesting to find a craft which he knew only in the Pyramid Texts of five thousand years ago, still surviving and in daily use on the ancient river in far-off Nubia. There can be no doubt that this is the craft so often called the "two floats" in the Pyramid Texts.

But even these many devices for crossing the eastern sea might fail and then the king must commit himself to the air and make the ascent to the sky. "Thy two wings are spread out like a falcon with thick plumage, like the hawk seen in the evening traversing the sky," says a mysterious speaker to the king. "He flies who flies; this king Pepi flies away from you, ye mortals. He is not of the earth, he is of the sky. . . . This king Pepi flies as a cloud to the sky, like a masthead bird; this king Pepi kisses the sky like a falcon, this king Pepi reaches the sky like the Horizon-god (Harakhte)." The speaker also sees him escaping from the hands of men as the wild goose escapes the hand of the fowler clutching his feet and flies away to the sky; "the tips of his wings are those of the great goose." Thus he "flies as a goose and flutters as a beetle." "His face is (that of) falcons and his wings are (those of) geese"; "King Unis flaps his wings like a *zeret*-bird," and the wind bears him on high. "King Unis goes to the sky, King Unis goes to the sky! On the wind! On the wind!" "The clouds of the sky have taken him away, they exalt King Unis to Re." He "has ascended upon the raincloud." Or the priest sees strange forms in the cloud of incense that soars above him and he cries: "He ascends upon the smoke of the great incense-burning."

In the oblique rays of the sun also, shooting earthward through some opening in the clouds, they beheld a radiant stairway let down from the sky that the king might ascend. "King Pepi has put down this radiance as a stairway under his feet, whereon King Pepi ascended to this his mother, the living Uræus that is on the head of Re." Again the broad sunbeams slanting earthward seem like a ladder to the imagination of this remote people and they say, "King Unis ascends upon the ladder which his father Re (the Sun-god) made for him." The spectacle of the ascending king calls forth the admiration of the gods: "'How beautiful to see, how satisfying to behold,' say the gods, 'when this god (meaning the king) ascends to the sky. His fearfulness is on his head, his terror is at his side, his magical charms are before him.'" Men and gods together are called upon in mighty charms to lift the king. "O men and gods! Your arms under King Pepi! Raise ye him, lift ye him to the sky, as the arms of Shu (the Atmosphere) are under the sky and he raises it. To the sky! To the sky! To the great seat among the gods!"

But the possibility remained that the gates of the celestial country might not be opened to the new-comer. Over and over again we find the assurance that the double doors of the sky are opened before the Pharaoh: "Opened are the double doors of the horizon; unlocked are its bolts" is a constant refrain in the Pyramid Texts. That art which opened the door for Ali Baba and the Forty Thieves had opened many a gate in the Ancient East, thousands of years before the Arabian Nights made it familiar to us of the Western world.

It will be seen that in spite of the conviction of life, abounding life, with which the Pyramid Texts are filled, they likewise reveal the atmosphere of apprehension which enveloped these men of the early East as they contemplated the unknown and untried dangers of the shadow world. Whichever way the royal pilgrim faced as he looked out across the eastern sea he was beset with apprehensions of the possible hostility of the gods, and there crowded in upon him a thousand fancies of danger and opposition which clouded the fair picture of blessedness beyond. There is an epic touch in the dauntless courage with which the solitary king, raising himself like some elemental colossus, and claiming sway over the gods themselves, confronts the celestial realm and addresses the Sun-god: "I know thy name. I am not ignorant of thy name. 'Limitless' is thy name. The name of thy father is 'Possessor-of-Greatness.' Thy mother is 'Satisfaction,' who bears thee every morning. The birth of 'Limitless' in the horizon shall be prevented, if thou preventest this king Pepi from coming to the place where thou art." The king wielding his magical power thus makes himself sovereign of the universe and will stop the very rising ("birth") of the sun if he is halted at the gate of the Sun-god's realm.

And so at last the departed king draws near the eastern shore of the Lily-lake, and "this king Pepi finds the glorious by reason of their equipped mouths,[2] sitting on the two shores of the lake, . . . the drinking-place of every glorious one by reason of his equipped mouth." Then they challenge the new arrival and the king replies: "I am a glorious one by reason of his equipped mouth." " 'How has this happened to thee,' say they to King Pepi, . . . 'that thou hast come to this place more august than any place?' 'Pepi has come to this place more august than any place, because the two floats of the sky were placed,' says the morning-barque, 'for Re' "; and at the story of his successful crossing as Re had crossed, the celestials break out into jubilee. Thereupon the Pharaoh lands, takes up their manner of life, and sits before the palace ruling them. Again we hear a solitary voice issuing from the world of the dead and challenging the king as he ascends and passes through the gates of the sky, led by Geb: "Ho! Whence comest thou, son of my father?" And another voice answers: "He has come from the Divine

[2] This curious term means mouths equipped with magical charms which have enabled their possessors to become "glorious ones."

Ennead that is in the sky, that he may satisfy them with their bread." Again comes the challenge: "Ho! Whence comest thou, son of my father?" and we hear the reply: "He has come from the Divine Ennead that is on earth, that he may satisfy them with their bread." The questioner is still unsatisfied: "Ho! Whence comest thou, son of my father?" "He has come from the *Zenedzender*-barque." And then we hear the question for the last time: "Ho! Whence comest thou, son of my father?" "He has come from these his two mothers, the two vultures with long hair and hanging breasts, who are on the mountain of *Sehseh*. They draw their breasts over the mouth of King Pepi, but they do not wean him forever." Thereafter the challenging voice is silent and the Pharaoh enters the eternal kingdom of the sky.

CHAPTER VI

THE SOLAR FAITH AND THE CELESTIAL HEREAFTER

We have followed the royal pilgrim as he passed through the celestial gates, where he awaited announcement of his arrival to the Sun-god, in whose realm he must now abide. We behold his heralds hastening to announce his advent. "Thy messengers go, thy swift messengers run, thy heralds make haste. They announce to Re that thou hast come, (even) this king Pepi." We hear their message as they shout, " 'Behold, he comes! Behold, he comes!' says Sehpu. 'Behold the son of Re comes, the beloved of Re comes,' says Sehpu." The gods crowd down to the shore. "This king Pepi found the gods standing, wrapped in their garments, their white sandals on their feet. They cast off their white sandals to the earth, they throw off their garments. 'Our heart was not glad until thy coming,' say they." Again they are overcome with awe as they hear the proclamation of the heralds and behold the king approaching. Re stands before the gates of the horizon leaning upon his sceptre, while the gods are grouped about him. "The gods are silent before thee, the Nine Gods have laid their hands upon their mouths," says the herald voice.

We of the older generation in this modern world, who grew up as children to believe in a realm beyond the skies peopled with celestial beings living in eternal bliss, may find it not a little interesting to read the earliest known musings of the human mind regarding such a life beyond the grave. For in the Pyramid Texts we find the oldest surviving pictures of a celestial hereafter—ideas which grew up over five thousand years ago, and in which we must without doubt recognise the original background out of which came those beliefs regarding a blessed realm in the skies which we were taught in childhood. The sky has always wrought profoundly upon the minds of men, and that impression of mystery in the skyey deeps of cloud-land has left its record in literature from the often awesome pictures in the Pyramid Texts to the enraptured wonder of Shelley contemplating the loveliness of summer clouds.

The men in whose hands the Pyramid Texts grew up took the greatest delight in elaborating and reiterating in ever new and different pictures the blessedness enjoyed by the king, protected, maintained, and honoured in the Sun-god's celestial realm. Their imagination flits from figure to figure, and picture to picture, and, allowed to run like some wild tropical plant without control or guidance, weaves a complex fabric of a thousand hues which refuse to merge into one harmonious or coherent whole. At one moment the king is enthroned in oriental splendour as he was on earth, at another he wanders in the Field of Rushes in search of food; here he appears in the bow of the Solar barque, yonder he is one of the Imperishable Stars acting as the servant of the Sun-god. There is no endeavour to harmonise these inconsistent representations, although in the mass we gain a broad impression of the eternal felicity of a godlike ruler, "who puts his annals (the record of his deeds) among his people, and his love among the gods." "The king ascends to the sky among the gods dwelling in the sky. He stands on the great ⌜dais⌝, he hears (in judicial session) the (legal) affairs of men. . . . He (Re) gives thee his arm on the stairway to the sky. 'He who knows his place comes,' say the gods. O Pure One, assume thy throne in the barque of Re and sail thou the sky. . . . Sail thou with the Imperishable Stars, sail thou with the Unwearied Stars. . . . Live thou this pleasant life which the lord of the horizon lives." . . . "This king Pepi goes to the Field of Life, the birthplace of Re in the sky. He finds Kebehet approaching him with these her four jars with which she refreshes the heart of the Great God (Re) on the day when he awakes (or 'by day when he awakes'). She refreshes the heart of this king Pepi therewith to life, she purifies him, she cleanses him. He receives his provision from that which is in the granary of the Great God; he is clothed by the Imperishable Stars." To Re and Thoth (the sun and the moon) the voice cries: "Take ye this king Unis with you that he may eat of that which ye eat, and that he may drink of that which ye drink, that he may live on that whereon ye live, that he may sit in that wherein ye sit, that he may be mighty by that whereby ye are mighty, that he may sail in that wherein ye sail. The booth of King Unis is plaited (erected) in the reeds, the pool of King Unis is in the Field of Offerings. His offering is among you, ye gods. The water of King Unis is wine like (that of) Re. King Unis circles the Sky like Re, he traverses the sky like Thoth." The voice summons the divine nourishment of the king: "Bring the milk of Isis for King Teti, the flood of Nephthys, the circuit of the lake, the waves of the sea, life, prosperity, health, happiness, bread, beer, clothing, food, that King Teti may live therefrom." "Lo, the two who are on the throne of the Great God (Re), they summon this king Pepi to life and satisfaction forever; they (the two) are Prosperity and Health." Thus "it is better with him today than yesterday," and we hear the voice calling to him: "Ho! King Pepi, pure one! Re finds thee standing with thy mother Nût (the sky). She leads thee in the path of the horizon and thou makest thy abiding place there. How beautiful it is together with thy ka for ever and ever."

Over and over again the story of the king's translation to the sky is brought before us with an indomitable conviction and insistence which, it must be concluded, were thought to make the words of inevitable power and effect. Condensed into a paragraph the whole sweep of the king's celestial career is presented to us in a few swift strokes, each like a ray of sunshine touching for but an instant the prominences of some far landscape across which we look. Long successions of such paragraphs crowd one behind another like the waves of the sea, as if to overwhelm and in their impetuous rush to bear away as on a flood the insistent fact of death and sweep it to utter annihilation. It is difficult to convey to the modern reader the impression made by these thousands of lines as they roll on in victorious disregard of the invincibility of death, especially in those epitomisations of the king's celestial career which are so frequent, the paragraphs here under discussion. In so far as they owe their impressiveness to their mere bulk, built up like a bulwark against death, we can gain the impression only by reading the whole collection through.

Perhaps the finest fragment of literature preserved in the Pyramid Texts is a sun-hymn in which the king is identified with the Sun-god. The hymn addresses Egypt in a long and imposing enumeration of the benefits which she enjoys under the protection and sovereignty of the Sun-god. Hence Egypt offers him her wealth and produce. Now in view of the fact that the Pharaoh is identified with the Sun-god, the Pharaoh consequently confers the same benefits on Egypt, and must therefore receive the same gifts from Egypt. The entire hymn is therefore repeated with the insertion of the Pharaoh's name wherever that of Re or Horus occurs in the original hymn, and thus the king appropriates to himself all the homage and offerings received by the Sun-god from Egypt.

But the imagination of the priests does not stop here. Equality or identity with Re is not enough, and we behold the translated Pharaoh a cosmic figure of elemental vastness, even superior to the Sun-god in the primæval darkness. The mysterious voice cries: "Father of King Teti! Father of King Teti in darkness! Father of King Teti, Atum in darkness! Bring thou King Teti to thy side that he may kindle for thee the light; that he may protect thee, as Nun (the primæval ocean) protected these four goddesses on the day when they protected the throne, (even) Isis, Nephthys, Neit, and Serket." The dead king sweeps the sky as a devouring fire as soon as "the arm of the sunbeams is lifted with King Unis." Again we see him towering between earth and sky: "This his right arm, it carries the sky in satisfaction; this his left arm, it supports the earth in joy." The imagination runs riot in figures of cosmic power, and the king becomes "the outflow of the rain, he came forth at the origin of water"; or he gains the secret and the power of all things as "the scribe of the god's book, which says what is and causes to be what is not." He came forth before the world or death existed. "The mother of King Pepi became pregnant with him, O Dweller in the ⌜nether sky⌝; this king Pepi was born by his father Atum before the sky came forth, before the earth came forth, before men came forth, before gods were born, before death came forth. This king Pepi escapes the day of death as Set escaped the day of death. This king Pepi belongs to your ⌜company⌝, ye gods of the nether sky, who cannot perish by their enemies; this king Pepi perishes not by his enemies. (Ye) who die not by a king, this king Pepi dies not by a king; (ye) who die not by any dead, King Pepi dies not by any dead." When in process of time the gods were born, the king was present at their birth.

The mergence of the king into the very body and being of Re is analogous to his assimilation by the gods as a group. One of the most remarkable passages in the Pyramid Texts employs the ceremony and the suggestiveness of incense-burning as a sympathetic agency by which, as the odorous vapour arises from earth to the gods, it bears aloft the fragrance of the king to mingle with that of the gods, and thus to draw them together in fellowship and association. The passage is of importance as a very early priestly interpretation of the significance of incense as fellowship with the gods, a conception which eventually spread to Europe and still survives in some branches of the Christian Church today. The passage reads:

"The fire is laid, the fire shines;
The incense is laid on the fire, the incense shines.
Thy fragrance comes to King Unis, O Incense;
The fragrance of King Unis comes to thee, O Incense.
Your fragrance comes to King Unis, O ye gods;
The fragrance of King Unis comes to you, O ye gods.
King Unis is with you, ye gods;
Ye are with King Unis, ye gods.
King Unis lives with you, ye gods;
Ye live with King Unis, ye gods.
King Unis loves you, ye gods;
Love ye him, ye gods."

This fellowship thus mystically symbolised is in sharp contrast with a dark and forbidding picture, surviving from vastly remote prehistoric days, in which we see the savage Pharaoh ferociously preying upon the gods like a blood-thirsty hunter in the jungle, as if in continuation of the prehistoric hunting life, or even a reminiscence of early cannibalistic practices, of which, however, we have no other evidence. The passage begins with the terrifying advent of the Pharaoh in the sky:

"Clouds darken the sky,
The stars rain down,
The Bows (a constellation) stagger,
The bones of the hell-hounds tremble,
The [porters] are silent,
When they see King Unis dawning as a soul,
As a god living on his fathers,
Feeding on his mothers.
King Unis is lord of wisdom,
Whose mother knows not his name.
The honour of King Unis is in the sky,
His might is in the horizon,
Like Atum his father who begat him.
When he begat him, he was stronger than he.
. . . .[1]

King Unis is one who eats men and lives on gods,
Lord of messengers, who despatches his messages;
It is[2] 'Grasper-of-Forelocks' living in *Kehew*
Who binds them for King Unis.
It is the serpent, 'Splendid-Head'
Who watches them for him and repels them for him.
It is 'He-who-is-upon-the-Willows'

[1] The passage omitted is an obscure description of the equipment of the dead king, which, however, contains an important statement that the king "lives on the being of every god, eating their organs who come with their belly filled with charms."

[2] The following four composite names are those of demons or genii who assist the king in capturing and slaying the prey, that is, men and gods.

Who lassoes them for him.
It is 'Punisher-of-all-Evil-doers'
Who stabs them for King Unis.
He takes out for him their entrails,

. . . .

Shesmu cuts them up for King Unis
And cooks for him a portion of them
In his evening kettles (or 'as his evening kettles' meaning 'meal').
King Unis is he who eats their charms,
And devours their glorious ones (souls).
Their great ones are for his morning portion,
Their middle-sized ones are for his evening portion,
Their little ones are for his night portion.
Their old men and their old women are for his incense-burning.
It is the 'Great-Ones-North-of-the-Sky'
Who set for him the fire to the kettles containing them,
With the legs of their oldest ones (as fuel).
The 'Dwellers-in-the-Sky' revolve for King Unis (in his service).
⌜The kettles are replenished⌝ for him with the legs of their women.
He has encircled all the Two Skies (corresponding to the Two Lands),
He has revolved about the two regions.
King Unis is the 'Great Mighty-One'
Who overpowers the 'Mighty Ones'

. . . .

He has taken the hearts of the gods;
He has eaten the Red,
He has swallowed the Green.
King Unis is nourished on satisfied organs,
He is satisfied, living on their hearts and their charms.

. . . .

Their charms are in his belly.
The dignities of King Unis are not taken away from him;
He hath swallowed the knowledge of every god.

The lifetime of King Unis is eternity,
His limit is everlastingness in this his dignity of:
'If-he-wishes-he-does,
If-he-wishes-not-he-does-not,'[3]
Who dwells in the limits of the horizon for ever and ever.
Lo, their (the gods') soul is in the belly of King Unis,
Their glorious ones are with King Unis.
The plenty of his portion is more than (that of) the gods.

. . . .

Lo, their soul is with King Unis."

In this remarkable picture the motive of the grotesque cannibalism is perfectly clear. The gods are hunted down, lassoed, bound, and slaughtered like wild cattle, that the king may devour their substance, and especially their internal organs, like the heart where the intelligence had its seat, in the belief that he might thus absorb and appropriate their qualities and powers. When "he has taken the hearts of the gods," "he has swallowed the knowledge of every god," and "their charms are in his belly"; and because the organs of the gods which he has devoured are plentifully satisfied with food, the king cannot hunger, for he has, as it were, eaten complete satiety.

This introduces us to a subject to which the Pyramid Texts devote much space—the question of the food supply in the distant realm of the Sun-god. To explain the apparently aimless presentation of food at the tomb, where, in the Solar belief the dead no longer tarried, it was assumed that the food offered there was transmitted to the dead in various ways.

More commonly the celestial region where he tarries furnishes all his necessities. As son of Re, born of the Sky-goddess, he is frequently represented as suckled by one

[3] This is a name or rank expressed in a couplet.

of the Sky-goddesses or some other divinity connected with Re, especially the ancient goddesses of the prehistoric kingdoms of South and North. These appear as "the two vultures with long hair and hanging breasts; . . . they draw their breasts over the mouth of King Pepi, but they do not wean him forever." We hear the voice, "O mother of this king Pepi . . . give thy breast to this king Pepi, suckle this king Pepi therewith." To this the goddess responds: "O my son Pepi, my king, my breast is extended to thee, that thou mayest suck of it, my king, and live, my king, as long as thou art little." This incident exhibits more of the naturally and warmly human than anything else in the Solar theology. Besides this source of nourishment, and the very bodies of the gods themselves, there were also the offerings of all Egypt, as in the ancient sun-hymn, where the dead king receives all that is offered by Egypt to Re. It is taken for granted that the celestial revenues belong to the king, and that they will meet all his wants.

Finally one of the most, if not the most, important of the numerous sources from which the departed Pharaoh hoped to draw his sustenance in the realm of Re was the tree of life in the mysterious isle in the midst of the Field of Offerings, in search of which he sets out in company with the Morning Star. The Morning Star is a gorgeous green falcon, a Solar divinity, identified with "Horus of Dewat." He has four faces, corresponding to the four Horuses of the East, with whom he is doubtless also identified. We find him standing in the bow of his celestial barque of 770 cubits in length, and there the voice addresses him: "Take thou this king Pepi with thee in the cabin of thy boat. . . . Thou takest this thy favourite harpoon, thy staff which ⌜pierces⌝ the canals, whose points are the rays of the sun, whose barbs are the claws of Mafdet. King Pepi cuts off therewith the heads of the adversaries, dwelling in the Field of Offerings, when he has descended to the sea. Bow thy head, decline thy arms, O Sea! The children of Nût (the Sky-goddess) are these (Pepi and the Morning Star) who have descended to thee, wearing their garlands on their heads, wearing their garlands at their throats." Here the homage of the sea is claimed because Pepi and the Morning Star are bent upon a beneficent errand for Isis and Horus. The story then proceeds: "This king Pepi opened his path like the fowlers, he exchanged greetings with the lords of the kas, he went to the great isle in the midst of the Field of Offerings over which the gods make the swallows fly. The swallows are the Imperishable Stars. They give to this king Pepi this tree of life, whereof they live, that ye (Pepi and the Morning Star) may at the same time live thereof."

Many details might be added to this picture of the celestial hereafter, but the above sketch suggests at least the main outlines of the beliefs held by the Egyptian of the Old Kingdom (roughly 3000–2500 B.C.) concerning the Solar hereafter. There can be no doubt that at some time they were a fairly well-defined group, having no immediate connection as a group with those of the Osirian faith. To the Osirian faith, moreover, they were opposed, and evidences of their incompatibility, or even hostility, have survived. We find it said of the Sun-god that "he has not given him (the king) to Osiris, he (the king) has not died the death; he has become a Glorious One in the horizon"; and still more unequivocal is the following: "Re-Atum does not give thee to Osiris. He (Osiris) numbers not thy heart, he gains not power over thy heart."

It is evident that to the devotee of the Solar faith, Osiris once represented the realm and the dominion of death, to which the follower of Re was not delivered up. In harmony with this is the apprehension that the entire Osirian group might enter the pyramid with evil intent. As a great Solar symbol it was necessary to protect the pyramid from the possible aggressions of Osiris, the Osirian Horus, and the other divinities of the Osirian group. Some reconciliation of Solar and Osirian beliefs was inevitable, and in following that reconciliation later we shall discern how the process eventually involved the triumph of Osiris.

CHAPTER VII

THE NATURE GODS AND HUMAN SOCIETY: OSIRIS

We have followed the Sun-god from his earlier domain in which he was conceived simply as a great power of nature, through the transition by which he entered human society as an earthly sovereign and arbiter of the life of men. His arena thus became that of human affairs. Moving in unapproachable magnificence and impenetrable mystery his daily round left no region in which his movements or his operations could be shared by man. There was another realm of nature, however, in which man had begun to *co-operate* with the elusive functions of a divinity, and, guiding its mysterious powers, could share in its beneficent operations. This more tractable power of nature, with which man could carry on a kind of partnership, was that of vegetable life. We have referred to the fact that the domestication of wild wheat and barley completely transformed the life of prehistoric man, as he shifted from the wandering existence of a hunter to a settled life of agriculture, probably some eight or ten thousand years ago. It was a transformation which created a new world in Egypt and Western Asia far back in the Late Stone Age. When cultivation at length covered extensive tracts throughout the whole Near East and thus created the first agricultural region in the long course of human development, there arose a widespread realisation of the fact that everywhere men were dependent on the fruits of the green earth for life. This realisation stimulated emotions which we may compare with those that prompted our fathers to ordain an autumn day of thanksgiving for the bounty of the fields. In the life of early man as he shifted from hunting to agriculture this feeling of dependence on the fruitfulness of the earth became the ultimate religious expression of the profound change in his manner of life. The imperishable life of the fruitful earth, which died and ever rose again many times multiplied, was personified as a dying and ever rising god. Hence not only Osiris, the most beloved god of Egypt, but also many of the local gods of Western Asia, where he was known as Tammuz or Adonis, were believed to have lived, died, and risen again. In Egypt the enormously ancient association with Asia in this faith was never forgotten and eventually found expression in the Osiris myth, which recounts how the dead body of the god floated ashore at Byblos on the Phœnician coast of Asia and there revived as a green tree. A tree thus became the symbol of this reviving life, and gave rise to a beautiful feast each year when a fallen tree was erected and with much ceremony planted, and, having thus been restored to life, it was beautifully decorated and clothed with green leaves. This tree has descended to us in the form of the Maypole, which we still continue to erect and to decorate, accompanied by feasting and dancing, to celebrate the return of spring.

While a prehistoric event like the introduction of agriculture ages before the advent of writing has necessarily left no written record, we must undoubtedly recognise in the Osiris faith an echo of the great change that created the earliest tillers of the soil. In the Osiris faith we hear the early world's religious response to the possession of agriculture. This revelation of the mind of man, thus coming for the first time into close and sensitive contact and actual friendly co-operation with the green life of the earth, is one of the earliest glimpses of human thinking now discernible. It had a profound influence on the ideas of life after death. It passed into the Greek mysteries, where the initiation of the neophyte included his presentation with a sheaf or head of grain; and it is reflected even in the New Testament: "Except a grain of wheat fall into the earth and die it abideth by itself alone; but if it die, it beareth much fruit" (John 12:24). In Egypt the idea was eventually merged with the whole group of beliefs regarding rewards and punishments beyond the grave and hence modified essentially Egyptian moral ideas.

Before we can discuss the Osirian morality, however, we must probe somewhat further into the question of the significance of Osiris as a nature god. While there is no question whatever regarding the natural phenomenon of which Re, Atum, Horus, and the other Sun-gods were personifications, there has been much uncertainty and discussion of the same question in connection with Osiris. Exactly what phenomenon of nature did he personalise?

The clearest statement of the nature of Osiris is that contained in the incident of the finding of the dead god by his son Horus, as narrated in the Pyramid Texts: "Horus comes, he recognises his father in thee, youthful in thy name of 'Fresh Water.'" Equally unequivocal are the words of King Ramses IV, who says to the god: "Thou art indeed the Nile, great on the fields at the beginning of the seasons; gods and men live by the moisture that is in thee." In these two ancient sources Osiris is identified with water, and specifically with that of the Nile.

While water, even the great fountains of water, are identified with Osiris, it is evidently a particular function of the waters with which he was associated. It was water as a source of fertility, water as a life-giving agency with which Osiris was identified. It is water which brings life to the soil, and Osiris is therefore closely associated with the soil likewise. This view of him is carried so far in a hymn of the Twelfth Century B.C. as to identify Osiris not only with the soil but even with the earth itself. This hymn says of him: "As for thee, the Nile comes forth from the sweat of thy hands. Thou spewest out the wind that is in thy throat into the nostrils of men, and that whereon men live is divine. It is alike in thy nostrils, the tree and its verdure, reeds—plants, barley, wheat, and the tree of life. When canals are dug, . . . houses and temples are built, when monuments are transported and fields are cultivated, when tomb-chapels and tombs are excavated, they rest on thee, it is thou who makest them. They are on thy back, although they are more than can be put into writing. [Thy] back hath not an empty place, for they all lie on thy back. . . ." The writer of this hymn regarded Osiris as the earth, but especially the verdure-producing earth.

The earliest references to Osiris known to us, therefore, associate him with vegetable life or identify him with it. In the early days of the Second Union, when the leadership of the nation was at Memphis, we recall that in the Memphite drama (see page 36) Memphis was called the "granary of the god." Thereupon the Memphite thinkers introduced Osiris into their sacred drama in order to explain how it was that Memphis became the "granary of the god." Still thinking of the naturalistic aspect of Osiris, they say that this designation of Memphis arose "because he was drowned in his water" at Memphis, which thus became the "granary of the god." The earlier views of the Pyramid Texts also represent him as intimately associated with vegetable life. In the earliest versions of the Book of the Dead, Osiris is identified with grain, as the deceased says of himself: "I am Osiris, I live as 'Grain,'[1] I grow as 'Grain.' . . . I am barley." With these early statements we should compare the frequent representations showing grain sprouting from the prostrate body of Osiris, or a tree growing out of his tomb or his coffin, or the effigies of the god as a mummy moulded of bruised corn and earth and buried with the dead, or in the grainfield to insure a plentiful crop.

It is evident from the earliest sources, therefore, that Osiris was identified with the *waters,* especially the inundation, the *soil,* and with *vegetation.* This is a result of the Egyptian tendency always to think in graphic and concrete forms. The god was doubtless in Egyptian thought the imperishable principle of life wherever found, and this conception not infrequently appears in representations of him, showing him even in death as still possessed of generative power. The ever-waning and reviving life of the earth, sometimes associated with the life-giving waters, sometimes with the fertile soil, or again discerned in vegetation itself—that was Osiris. The fact that the Nile, like the vegetation which its rising waters nourished and supported, waxed and waned every year, made it more easy to see him in the Nile, the most important feature of the Egyptian's landscape, than in any other form.[2]

[1] Here personified as god of Grain (*Npr.*). The passage is from the Middle Kingdom Coffin Texts.

[2] The later classical evidence from Greek and Roman authors is in general corroborative of the above conclusions. This later evidence is, however, of only secondary importance as compared with the early sources employed above. The most important passages from the classic sources will be found in Frazer's *Adonis, Attis, Osiris,* pp. 330–345 (London, 1907). The treatment in Frazer's book suffers from lack of adequate acquaintance with the early Egyptian sources, especially the Pyramid Texts.

As a matter of fact the Nile was but the source and visible symbol of that fertility of which Osiris was the personification.

The functions of Osiris in themselves early involved him in the domain of human affairs so that he was rapidly humanised and socialised. This ever-dying, ever-reviving god, who seemed to be subjected to human destiny and human mortality, was inevitably the inexhaustible theme of legend and saga. Like the Sun-god, after kings appeared in the land, Osiris also became an ancient king of Egypt. He was commonly called "the heir of Geb," the Earth-god, who "assigned to him the leadership of the lands for the good of affairs. He put this land in his hand, its water, its air, its verdure, all its herds, all things that fly, all things that flutter, its reptiles, its game of the desert, legally conveyed to the son of Nût[3] (Osiris)."

Thus Osiris began his beneficent rule as king of Egypt, and "Egypt was content therewith, as he dawned upon the throne of his father, like Re when he rises in the horizon." But long after he had become king, as the above evidence shows, his domain was chiefly the control of the fruitfulness of the earth. Gradually he entered the political realm also, and the same hymn says of him, "He overthrew his enemies, and with a mighty arm he slew his foes, setting the fear of him among his adversaries, and extending his boundaries."

The humanisation of Osiris is especially marked in the family relations which the Osiris myth wove about him. His sister Isis, who was at the same time his wife, stood loyally at his side; she "protected him, driving away enemies, warding off [danger]." Nevertheless his assailants at last prevailed against him, if not openly then by strat-

[3] Nût, the Sky-goddess, was the mother of Osiris.

agem, as narrated by Plutarch, although there is no trace in the Egyptian sources of Plutarch's story of the chest into which the doomed Osiris was lured by the conspirators and then shut in to die. The arch enemy of the good Osiris was his brother Set, who, however, feared the good king. One of the oldest sources, the Pyramid Texts, indicated assassination: "his brother Set felled him to the earth in *Nedyt,*" or "his brother Set overthrew him upon his side, on the further side of the land of *Gehesti*"; but the Memphite drama, which is even older than the Pyramid Age, says: "Osiris was drowned in his new water (the inundation)."

When the news reached the unhappy Isis, she wandered in great affliction seeking the body of her lord, "seeking him unweariedly, sadly going through this land, nor stopping until she found him." The oldest literature is full of references to the faithful wife unceasingly seeking her murdered husband: "Thou didst come seeking thy brother Osiris, when his brother Set had overthrown him." The Plutarch narrative even carries her across the Mediterranean to Byblos, where, as we have already mentioned, the body of Osiris had drifted in the waters. The Pyramid Texts refer to the fact that she at last found him "upon the shore of *Nedyt,*" where he had been slain by Set, and it may be indeed that Nedyt is an ancient name for the region of Byblos, although it was later localised at Abydos in Egypt, and one act of the Osirian passion play was presented at the shore of Nedyt, near Abydos.

The goddess Nephthys frequently accompanies her sister Isis in the long search, both of them being in the form of birds. "Isis comes, Nephthys comes, one of them on the right, one of them on the left. . . . They have found Osiris, as his brother Set felled him to the earth in

Nedyt." "'I have found (him),' said Nephthys, when they saw Osiris (lying) on his side on the shore. . . . 'O my brother, I have sought thee; . . . Weep for thy brother, Isis! Weep for thy brother, Nephthys! Weep for thy brother." The lamentations of Isis and Nephthys became the most sacred expression of sorrow known to the heart of the Egyptian, and many were the varied forms which they took until they emerged in the Osirian mysteries of Europe, three thousand years later. Then the two sisters embalm the body of their brother to prevent its perishing, and when they have laid him in his tomb a sycamore grows up and envelops the body of the dead god, like the *erica* in the story of Plutarch. This sacred tree is the visible symbol of the imperishable life of Osiris, which in the earliest references was already divine and might be addressed as a god.

Such were the life and death of Osiris. His career, as picturing a cycle of nature, could not of course end here. It is continued in his resurrection, and likewise in a later addition drawn from the Solar theology, the story of his son Horus and the Solar feud of Horus and Set, which was not originally Osirian. Even in death the life-giving power of Osiris did not cease. The faithful Isis drew near her dead lord, "making a shadow with her pinions and causing a wind with her wings . . . raising the weary limbs of the silent-hearted (dead), receiving his seed, bringing forth an heir, nursing the child in solitude, whose place is not known, introducing him when his arm grew strong in the Great Hall" (at Heliopolis?).

The imagination of the common people loved to dwell upon this picture of the mother concealed in the marshes of the Delta, and there bringing up the youthful Horus, that "when his arm grew strong" he might avenge the murder of his father. All this time Set was, of course, not idle, and many were the adventures and escapes which befell the child at the hands of Set. These are too fragmentarily preserved to be reconstructed clearly, but even after the youth has grown up and attained a stature of eight cubits (nearly fourteen feet), he is obliged to have a tiny chapel of half a cubit long made, in which he conceals himself from Set. Grown to manhood, however, the youthful god emerges at last from his hiding-place in the Delta, and "comes purified that he may avenge his father."

The filial piety of Horus was also a theme which the imagination of the people loved to contemplate, as he went forth to overthrow his father's enemies and take vengeance upon Set. The battle of Horus with Set, which, as we recall, was a Solar incident, waged so fiercely that the young god lost his eye at the hands of his father's enemy. When Set was overthrown, and the eye was finally recovered by Thoth, this wise god spat upon the wound and healed it. This method of healing the eye, which is, of course, folk-medicine reflected in the myth, evidently gained wide popularity, passed into Asia, and seems to reappear in the New Testament narrative, in the incident which depicts Jesus doubtless deferring to recognised folk-custom in employing the same means to heal a blind man.

Horus now seeks his father, even crossing the sea in his quest, that he may raise his father from the dead and offer to him the eye which he has sacrificed in his father's behalf. This act of filial devotion, preserved to us in the Pyramid Texts, made the already sacred Horus-eye doubly revered in the tradition and feeling of the Egyptians. It became the symbol of all sacrifice; every gift or offering might be called a "Horus-eye," especially if offered to the dead (see p. 49). Excepting the sacred beetle, or scarab, it became the commonest and the most revered symbol known to Egyptian religion, and the myriads of eyes, wrought in blue or green glaze, or even cut from costly stone, which fill our museum collections and are brought home by thousands by modern tourists, are survivals of this ancient story of Horus and his devotion to his father.

A chapter of the Pyramid Texts tells the whole story of the resurrection of the dead god. Over and over again the rising of Osiris is reiterated, as the human protest against death found insistent expression in the invincible fact that he rose. We see the tomb opened for him: "The brick are drawn for thee out of the great tomb," and then "Osiris awakes, the weary god wakens, the god stands up, he gains control of his body." "Stand up! Thou shalt not end, thou shalt not perish."

The malice of Set was not spent, however, even after his defeat by Horus and the resurrection of Osiris. He entered the tribunal of the gods at Heliopolis and lodged with them charges against Osiris. We have no clear account of this litigation, nor of the nature of the charges, except that Set was using them as a means of gaining the throne of Egypt. There must have been a version in which the subject of the trial was Set's crime in slaying Osiris. But Osiris was triumphantly vindicated, and the throne was restored to him against the claim of Set.

The verdict rendered in favour of Osiris really means "true, right, just, or righteous of voice." It must have been a legal term already in use when this episode in the myth took form. It is later used in frequent parallelism with "victorious" or "victory," and possessed the essential meaning of "triumphant" or "triumph," both in a moral as well as a purely material and physical sense. The later development of the Osirian litigation shows that it gained a moral sense in this connection, if it did not possess it in the beginning. We shall yet have occasion to observe the course of the moral development involved in the wide popularity of this incident in the Osiris myth.

The risen and victorious Osiris then finally receives his kingdom. Nevertheless Osiris does not really belong to the kingdom of the living. His dominion is the gloomy Nether World beneath the earth, to which he at once descends. The Memphite drama says of him after his death, "He entered the secret gates in the splendour of the lords of eternity, in the footsteps of him who rises in the horizon, even the paths of Re in the Great Throne (Memphis).... Thus came Osiris into the Earth in the 'King's castle,' on the north side of this land at which he had arrived (Memphis), and his son Horus dawned as King of Upper Egypt and dawned as King of Lower Egypt, in the arms of his father Osiris."[4] The son of Osiris was thus his successor in the land of the living, but it was a subterranean kingdom of the dead over which Osiris himself reigned, and it was especially as champion and friend of the dead that he gained his great position in Egyptian religion.

[4] The malicious Set continued to assert his claims to the throne in opposition to the youthful Horus. A recently discovered papyrus, published in 1931 by Doctor Alan H. Gardiner, recounts in the form of a market-place tale, the interminable stages of this *cause célèbre*. See *The Library of A. Chester Beatty: Description of a Hieratic Papyrus with a Mythological Story, Love-Songs, and Other Miscellaneous Texts,* by Alan H. Gardiner (London, The Oxford University Press, and Emery Walker, Ltd., 1931).

CHAPTER VIII

SUNSHINE AND VERDURE: THE COMMINGLING OF RE AND OSIRIS AND THE TRIUMPH OF OSIRIS

"THAT which thou thyself sowest is not quickened, except it die."

These words of Saint Paul[1] are but a late hint of the profound impression made by the annual cycle of dying and reviving vegetable life on the minds of ancient men. We recall that the Greek mysteries were saturated with the same ideas, and the Mediterranean world was everywhere keenly responsive to oriental conceptions of this kind. Their influence on the New Testament is unmistakable. The *oldest* revelation of the effect of the verdure on the thoughts of men regarding death is found most fully in the sweeping triumph of the Osirian beliefs over other early Egyptian ideas of the hereafter. The *latest* manifestation of the persistent power of this earliest surviving impression of nature on the soul of man is of course modern devotion to the Easter festival.

We have already had occasion to refer to the fact that the beliefs of both the Solar and the Osirian faiths merged at a very early age. While the nucleus of each group of myths is fairly distinguishable from the other, the coalescence of the Solar and Osirian conceptions of the hereafter has left us a very difficult process of analysis if we undertake to separate them. The sunshine and the verdure were as indissolubly interfused in Egyptian religion as they are in nature. There is a certain body of beliefs

[1] I Cor. 15:36.

regarding the hereafter which we may designate as Solar, and another group which is unquestionably Osirian, but the two faiths have so interpenetrated each other that there is much neutral territory which we cannot assign to either to the entire exclusion of the other. In organisation, however, the two faiths are more clearly distinguishable. It is clear that in the Solar faith we have a state theology, with all the splendour and the prestige of its royal patrons behind it; while in that of Osiris we are confronted by a religion of the people, which made a strong appeal to the individual believer. It is not impossible that the history of the early sequence of these beliefs was thus: At a very early period the prehistoric Egyptians had gained a primitive belief in a subterranean kingdom of the dead which claimed all men. As an exclusive privilege of *kings,* at first, and then of the great and noble, the glorious *celestial* hereafter, which we have been discussing, finally emerged as a Solar kingdom of the dead. When the growing prestige of Osiris had displaced the older mortuary gods, he became the great lord of the Nether World. Thereupon Osiris and his realm entered into competition with the Solar and celestial hereafter. In the mergence of these two faiths we discern for the first time in history the age-long struggle between a state form of religion and a more popular faith of the masses. We must now proceed to disengage, as far as may be, the nucleus of the Osirian teaching of the after-life, and to trace the still undetermined course of its struggle with the imposing celestial theology whose doctrine of the royal dead we have been following.

Probably nothing in the life of the ancient Nile-dwellers commends them more appealingly to our sympathetic consideration than the fact that when the Osirian faith had once developed it so readily caught the popular imagination as to spread rapidly among all classes. It thus came into active competition with the Solar faith of the court and the state priesthoods. This was especially true of its doctrines for the afterlife, in the progress of which we can discern the gradual Osirianisation of Egyptian religion, and especially of the Solar teaching regarding the hereafter.

There is nothing in the Osiris myth, nor in the character or later history of Osiris, to suggest a celestial hereafter. Indeed we recall that clear and unequivocal survivals from a period when he was hostile to the celestial and Solar dead are still discoverable in the Pyramid Texts, which contain exorcisms intended to restrain Osiris and his kin from entering the pyramid, a Solar tomb, with evil intent. The prehistoric Osiris faith, once local to the Delta, involved a forbidding hereafter which was dreaded and at the same time was opposed to celestial blessedness beyond. When Osiris migrated up the Nile from the Delta to Abydos, his kingdom was conceived as situated in the West, or below the western horizon, where it merged into the Nether World. He became king of a realm of the dead below the earth, and hence his frequent title, "Lord of the Nether World" which occurs even in the Pyramid Texts. It is as lord of a subterranean kingdom of the dead that Osiris finally gained his universal triumph.

As there was nothing in the myth or the offices of Osiris to carry him to the sky, so the simplest of the Osirian Utterances in the Pyramid Texts do not carry him thither. There are as many varying pictures of the Osirian destiny as in the Solar theology. But the verdure always survives its death and Osiris inevitably rises from the dead. The resurrection of Osiris was a triumph over death of irresistible power in Egyptian mortuary beliefs. It resulted in the identification of the king with Osiris. The dead king does all that Osiris did, receiving heart and limbs as did Osiris, or becoming Osiris himself. This was the favourite belief of the Osiris faith. The king *became Osiris and rose from the dead as Osiris had done.* This identity began at birth and is described in the Pyramid Texts with all the wonders and prodigies of a divine birth. It is not the mere assumption of the form of Osiris, but complete identity with him, which is set forth in this doctrine of the Pyramid Texts. Osiris himself under various names is adjured, "Thy body is the body of this king Unis, thy flesh is the flesh of this king Unis, thy bones are the bones of this king Unis. As he (Osiris) lives, this king Unis lives; as he dies not, this king Unis dies not; as he perishes not, this king Unis perishes not." Thus the dead king receives the throne of Osiris, and becomes, like him, king of the dead. "Ho! King Neferkere (Pepi II)! How beautiful is this! How beautiful is this, which thy father Osiris has done for thee! He has given thee his throne, thou rulest those of the hidden places (the dead), thou leadest their august ones, all the glorious ones follow thee."

The supreme boon which this identity of the king with Osiris assured to the dead Pharaoh was the good offices of the son of Osiris, Horus, the personification of filial piety. All the pious attention which Osiris had once enjoyed at the hands of his son Horus now likewise became the king's portion. A long series of Utterances in the Pyramid Texts sets forth this championship of the dead king as Osiris by his valiant son Horus. In all this there is little or no trace of the celestial destiny, or any indication of the place where the action occurs. While it was evidently at first the Heliopolitan priests who Solarised and celestialised the Osirian mortuary doctrines, notwithstanding their essentially terrestrial origin and character, these Solar theologians were in their turn unable to resist the powerful influence which the popularity of the Osirian faith brought to bear upon them. The Pyramid Texts were eventually Osirianised, and the steady progress of this process, exhibiting the course of the probably long struggle between the Solar faith of the state temples and the popular beliefs of the Osirian religion thus discernible in the Pyramid Texts, is one of the most remarkable survivals from the early world, preserving as it does the earliest example of such a spiritual and intellectual conflict between state and popular religion. It suggests an interesting parallel with the later struggle in the Roman Empire between the devotion of the common folk to the risen Jesus, a popular faith, and the organised state worship of Cæsar as *Sol invictus,* "the invincible Sun." Early Christianity carried with it echoes of the ancient struggle on the Nile between the ever-reviving verdure and the Sun-god. With the people, the Verdure-god, the human Osiris, made the stronger appeal, and even the wealthy and subsidised priesthoods of the Solar religion could not withstand the power of this appeal.

We can watch this process of Osirianisation going on in the Pyramid Texts, as the priests edited them from reign to reign during five successive reigns, now represented by a series of five pyramids containing five recensions of the Pyramid Texts. A few examples may suffice to make the evidence and the process more clear.

The ladder leading to the sky was originally an element of the Solar faith. That it had nothing to do with Osiris is evident, among other things, from the fact that one version of the ladder episode represents it in charge of Set, traditional enemy of Osiris. The Osirianisation of the ladder episode is clearly traceable in four versions of it, which are but variants of the same ancient original. The four represent a period of nearly a century, at least of some eighty-five years. In the oldest form preserved to us the ladder barely emerges and the climber is the Pharaoh himself. A generation later the ladder is more developed and the original climber is Atum, the Sun-god; but the Osirian goddesses, Isis and Nephthys, are introduced. Finally in the latest form eighty-five years later than the earliest, the opening acclamation of the old gods as they behold the ascent of the Pharaoh is put into the mouths of Isis and Nephthys, and *the climber has become Osiris.* Thus did Osiris take possession of the old Solar episode of the ladder and appropriate the old Solar text. It is interesting to notice that this has taken place in spite of embarrassing complications. In harmony with the common co-ordination of Horus and Set in the service of the dead, an old Solar doctrine represented them as assisting him at the ascent of the ladder which Re and Horus set up. But when the ascending king becomes Osiris, the editor seems quite unconscious of the incongruity, as Set, the mortal enemy and slayer of Osiris, assists him to reach his celestial abode!

Nowhere is the intrusion of Osiris in the Pyramid Texts more striking than in the Utterances devoted to the services on behalf of the dead rendered by four Solar genii, known as the four Eastern Horuses. A favourite means of ascension, of opening the sky-gates, of ferrying over, of purification and the like, was to have all these things first done for each of the four Horuses in succession, and then by sympathetic inevitability also for the dead king.

Four considerable "Utterances" are built up in this way, each containing an account of the things done by each of the four Horuses, and then likewise by the king.

In the oldest form of these Utterances, this quartette of gods are all Solar divinities, namely:

1. Horus of the Gods.
2. Horus of the Horizon (Harakhte).
3. Horus of the Shesmet.
4. Horus of the East.

Two generations afterwards, we find the same four Horuses, first unaltered, and then with a further development of the group exhibiting an intruder; it appears thus:

1. Horus of the Gods.
2. Horus of the East.
3. Horus of the Shesmet.
4. Osiris!

Osiris has thus pushed his way into this Solar group to the displacement of the most unequivocally Solar of them all, Horus of the Horizon (Harakhte). The intrusion of Osiris here is the most convincing example of his power, and the most clearly discernible in the whole range of the process which Osirianised the Pyramid Texts. This example is strikingly parallel with the history of the birthday of the Sun, celebrating his halt in his southward march and the beginning of his return northward. In early Christian times this birthday of the Sun had become that of the Roman Emperor identified with the Sun-god. The appropriation by Christianity of this old Solar feast held on the 25th of December is exactly parallel with the displacement of the Sun-god in the Pyramid Texts three thousand years earlier.

The ladder, the ferry-boat, the reed floats—in fine all the instrumentalities for reaching the skies, a place with which Osiris had properly nothing to do—were thus early Osirianised. We cannot wonder therefore that the sky itself and its denizens were likewise appropriated by Osiris till the "Imperishable Stars" are called "followers of Osiris." In the same way, when the king is born, like Osiris, as Nile, we may find him transferred to the sky and flooding the heavens as the Nile inundation; he makes all the sky fresh and verdant. "King Unis comes to his pools that are in the region of the flood at the great inundation, to the place of peace with green fields, that is in the horizon. Unis makes the verdure to flourish in the two regions of the horizon."

Now, while all this resulted in Osirianising the celestial and Solar mortuary teachings, they still remained celestial. When the dead Osiris is taken up by the Sun-god, it is evident that the Sun-god's position in these composite mortuary doctrines is still the chief one. The fact remains, then, that the *celestial* doctrines of the hereafter dominate the Pyramid Texts throughout, and the later *subterranean* kingdom of Osiris, and the Sun-god's nightly voyage through it, are still entirely in the background in these royal mortuary teachings. Among the *people* the Sun-god is later, as it were, dragged into the Nether World to illumine there the subjects of Osiris in his mortuary kingdom, and this is one of the most convincing evidences of the power of Osiris among the lower classes. In the *royal* and *state temple* theology, Osiris is lifted to the sky, and while he is there Solarised, he also tinctures the Solar teaching of the celestial kingdom of the dead with Osirian doctrines. The result was thus inevitable confusion, as the two faiths interpenetrated.

In both faiths we recall that the king is identified with the god, and hence we find him unhesitatingly called Osi-

FIG. 8. AN EGYPTIAN GENTLEMAN AND HIS WIFE WORSHIPPING OSIRIS ENTHRONED

This beautiful vignette from a mortuary papyrus represents the deceased coming forth from his house (*at right*) and passing through his garden into the presence of the great god (*at left*), who is attended by Maat the goddess of truth. In the other world the Egyptian expected a home and an estate like the one he had owned in this world; the house, rectangular lake, and surrounding trees are all features of the typical ancient Egyptian home. The gradual assimilation by Osiris of the Sun-god's attributes is well illustrated by the sun-disk above the head of Maat and the sun-hymn which is written in the vertical columns above the vignette. (*British Museum.*)

ris and Re in the same passage. There are extensive passages in the Pyramid Texts which illustrate the often inextricable confusion resulting from the interweaving of these unharmonised elements. The fact that in such passages both Re and Osiris appear as supreme kings of the hereafter cannot of course be reconciled, and such mutually irreconcilable beliefs caused the Egyptian no more discomfort than was felt by any early civilisation in the maintenance of a group of religious teachings side by side with others involving varying and totally inconsistent suppositions. Even Christianity itself has not escaped this experience, nor did it wholly escape the influence of Egyptian notions of the hereafter. Egyptian ideas of the Nether World, with its fiery gates and seas of flame, contributed to embellish the fiery Christian hell; and the celestial realm of the Sun-god with its tree of life was probably the origin of our Western conception of a paradise in the skies later so vividly pictured in the Christian painting of Europe.

There is, however, a marked difference between Osiris and Re. Osiris is exclusively a king of the *dead* and he is in function passive. Rarely does he become an active agent even on behalf of the dead. The blessedness of the Osirian destiny consisted largely in the enjoyment of the good offices of Horus, who appears as the son of the dead man as soon as the latter is identified with Osiris. It is the services of *others* on behalf of Osiris (not *by* Osiris) which the dead man (as Osiris) enjoys. Osiris remains a god of the dead. On the other hand, Re is king of the *living,* as a mighty sovereign. Although often directly interposing in favour of the dead, Re is the great power in the affairs of living men, and there we behold his sovereignty expanding and developing to hold sway in a more exalted realm of moral values—a realm of which we shall gain the earliest glimpses anywhere vouchsafed us as we endeavour to discover more than the merely material agencies, and the materials ends, which we have seen thus far dominating the Egyptian conception of the hereafter.

CHAPTER IX

CONDUCT, RESPONSIBILITY, AND THE EMERGENCE OF A MORAL ORDER

It has been the purpose of the preceding chapters to furnish a background which will enable us to resume more intelligently our survey of the developing moral life of the Egyptians in the period of the Second Union as they stood at the culmination of Old Kingdom civilisation after 3000 B.C. We have already observed that as early as the First Union, before the middle of the Fourth Millennium, human conduct was under consideration, and might be "loved" or "hated," that is, approved or disapproved, by society (pp. 38 ff.). We recall that this fact is disclosed by a document dating from the beginning of the Second Union, the Memphite Drama, which reflects to us echoes from the earlier period before the end of the First Union. The scanty fragments of written records from the first four centuries of the Second Union contribute little to our knowledge of Egyptian beliefs; but after 3000 B.C., as the Pyramid Age began, we find that the colossal tombs in the magnificent cemeteries of Gizeh and Memphis (Sakkara), so familiar to modern travellers in Egypt, begin to disclose the new society of the Old Kingdom and afford some glimpses of their beliefs regarding human conduct and its motives.

These glimpses of course reveal primarily outward developments, for the life of the Egyptians was absorbed in unprecedented material triumphs. Nowhere in ancient times has the capacity of a race to control the material world been so fully expressed in impressive surviving remains as in the Nile Valley. In the abounding fulness of their energies they built up a fabric of material civilisation, the monuments of which it would seem time can never wholly sweep away. But *conduct* is the drift of that manifold and intangible substance of life, interfused of custom and tradition, of individual traits fashioned among social, economic, and governmental forces, ever developing in the daily operations and functions of life. These things, which create the attitude of the individual and impel the inner man as he is called upon to make momentary decisions, constitute an elusive higher atmosphere of the ancient world, of which tomb masonry and pyramid orientation have transmitted but fragmentary glimpses to us. Save in a few scanty references in the inscriptions of the Pyramid Age, and the remarkable Maxims of Ptahhotep, it has vanished forever; for even the inscriptions, as we have seen, are concerned chiefly with the *material* welfare of the departed in the hereafter. What the surviving sources disclose, however, is of unique interest, revealing as it does the next stage in the ethical evolution that followed the Memphite Drama, together with which it forms the earliest chapter in the moral development of man as known to us—a chapter marking the most important fundamental step in the evolution of civilisation. Moreover, these materials from the Pyramid Age have never been put together,[1] and in gathering them together for this book I have been not a little surprised not only to find them as numerous as they are, but also to discern how unmistakably they disclose the family as

[1] A first attempt to put them together was made in 1912 in the author's *Development of Religion and Thought in Ancient Egypt* (pp. 166 *ff.*), where, however, the Old Kingdom date of the Maxims of Ptahhotep had not yet been recognised.

the primary influence in the rise and development of moral ideas.

The Egyptian of the Pyramid Age had become so aware of a mandatory moral atmosphere, that the Pyramid Texts disclose him to us already looking back upon a time when sin and strife did not exist, to "that first body" of "the company of the just," "born before occurred," "strife," "voice," "blasphemy," "conflict," or the frightful mutilations inflicted upon each other by Horus and Set. With this belief in an ideal age of innocence, or at least of righteousness and peace, we must associate also the time to which the Pyramid Texts refer, "before death came forth."

In this early age, in the earliest society thus revealed to us, it was recognised that the individual's claim to worthy character might be based on his spirit and conduct in his relations with his own family, father, mother, brothers, and sisters. This is a fact of profound interest and one of fundamental importance to this investigation. In the Twenty-seventh Century B.C. a noble of Upper Egypt affirms in his tomb inscription, after telling of his good deeds, "I speak no lie, for I was one beloved of his father, praised of his mother, excellent in character to his brother, and amiable to [his sister]." A little later a royal favourite of the far south avers, "The king praised me. My father made a will in my favour, (for) I was excellent . . . [one beloved] of his father, praised of his mother, whom all his brothers loved." Repeatedly the nobles of the Pyramid Age sum up their deserving qualities with the statement, "I was one beloved of his father, praised of his mother, whom his brothers and sisters loved."

In the inscriptions of the Pyramid Age the most common virtue discernible is filial piety. Over and over again we find that the massive tombs of the pyramid cemeteries were erected by the son for the departed father, and that a splendid interment was arranged by the son. Indeed one of the sons of this age even surpasses the example of all others, for he states in his tomb inscription: "Now I caused that I should be buried in the same tomb with this Zau (his father), in order that I might be with him in the same place; not, however, because I was not in a position to make a second tomb; but I did this in order that I might see this Zau every day, in order that I might be with him in the same place."

A still more remarkable case of a son's devotion to his father is that of Sebni, "warden of the southern gate," that is, guardian of the Egyptian frontier towards the Sudan at the First Cataract of the Nile. Sebni's father Mekhu had made a venturesome journey far into the Sudan for purposes of traffic and was there set upon by savages and slain. When Sebni heard of his father's death he made the dangerous journey into the hostile region without hesitation and at the risk of his life rescued his father's body and brought it back for embalmment. His tomb at Assuan still contains the inscription recording a son's heroic rescue of his father's body in the far-off Pyramid Age.

The testimony of the tomb inscriptions left by this earliest known aristocratic society is corroborated by the beautiful painted wall reliefs with which these noble families were accustomed to adorn the chapel chambers of their tombs, especially as they are found surviving today in the vast cemetery of Memphis, commonly called the cemetery of Sakkara. These remarkable wall sculptures, sometimes with the bright hues of their original colouration remarkably well preserved, are a charmingly realistic revelation of the daily life of the nobles of the Pyramid Age.

Today they form a very appealing picture and one often beheld by modern globe-trotters and Nile tourists who throng to Egypt every winter. But I doubt very much whether any of these travellers as they ride on their donkeys through the palm groves that now cover the streets and houses of ancient Memphis—I doubt very much whether any one of them realises that what they are about to see is the earliest known revelation of family life. As the modern visitor issues from these Memphite palm groves he looks out upon the sandy slopes that lead to the top of the sand-covered Sahara plateau—the cemetery of ancient Memphis. Thence he may look down upon the far-spreading but scanty remains of the magnificent ancient city, now covered with waving fields and bowing palm groves. There lived those earlier generations of men in a noble city which they raised thousands on thousands of years ago. And when life was finished they were carried up to this plateau to which the modern visitor ascends. Here they were laid away in vast tombs of massive limestone masonry. These ancient tomb structures of nearly five thousand years ago are now silent and in ruins, sand-covered and desolate, but we may still enter the open doors of the tomb chapels and pass from room to room. The walls are covered with sculptures and brightly coloured scenes of ancient life.[2] In these relief pictures, we behold the lordly owner of one of the great estates that surrounded Memphis, depicted there upon the wall in heroic stature towering over the smaller figures of the people of his estate as he inspects them sowing the grain

[2] The Oriental Institute of the University of Chicago is maintaining an epigraphic expedition at this great cemetery under the direction of Professor Prentice Duell, charged with the work of making the first complete copies of these Old Kingdom reliefs both in line drawings and in colour and publishing them in a series of plates of folio size. The project is made possible by the generous support of John D. Rockefeller, Jr.

or harvesting the fields; driving the flocks and herds to and from their pastures; fording the irrigation canals; busily occupied as craftsmen in the boat yards, carpenter shops, copper-smiths' shops, potters' booths, and a hundred other activities. Here then is pictured the whole wide range of their life in agriculture, cattle-breeding, and industry, on the basis of which this ancient civilisation had grown up. Now on all these excursions about the broad estate the Egyptian noble is shown accompanied by his wife, and when he enters the gate that leads to the beautiful garden in the midst of which his luxurious villa is embowered, she moves by his side; she shares with him all his life and all his work, and is his hourly companion. Their children are ever with them. One of the most charming scenes among these tomb chapel pictures shows us a little boy trotting about beside his father, clutching in one hand a tiny hoopoe bird. When the lord of the manor hunts in the marshes, which were the ancient Egyptian's hunting preserves, we see his wife and child beside him in the little raft-like reed boat with which he pushes about among the tall papyrus blossoms, where the child leans down and plucks the water lilies. Or when he is shown resting in his garden, we see his children playing at ball or splashing about in the garden pool chasing the fishes.

These tomb reliefs of the Memphite cemetery, representing roughly half a millennium, from nearly 3000 B.C. to about 2500 B.C. or after, form the first graphic revelation of family life which has survived to us from the ancient world. Their significance has heretofore been considered to be chiefly as monuments of art, and sources for our knowledge of agricultural, pastoral, industrial, and to some extent of social, life. It is, however, obvious that the delightfully amiable family relations disclosed by these tomb reliefs are a revelation of fundamental value in the *history of morals,* for combined with the tomb inscriptions and the Maxims of Ptahhotep, which we have still to explore, they furnish us with conclusive *historical* evidence that moral discernment had its roots in the life of the family.

Here then in the Egyptian sources of the first half of the Third Millennium B.C. is a body of evidence demonstrating for the first time *historically* what the modern social psychologists have concluded from their observations of the life of man as it is found in modern times. I am referring to their conclusion that the moral impulses in the life of man have grown up out of the influences that operate in family relationships. McDougall says, "From this emotion [parental tenderness] and its impulse to cherish and protect, spring generosity, gratitude, love, pity, true benevolence, and altruistic conduct of every kind; in it they have their main and absolutely essential root, without which they would not be."[3] Discussing the ensuing development of such emotions, McDougall refers to the fact that any wrong towards a child, the object of parental tenderness, inevitably produces anger and resentment, and then continues, "This intimate alliance between tender emotion and anger is of great importance for the social life of man, and the right understanding of it is fundamental for a true theory of the moral sentiments; for the anger evoked in this way is the germ of all moral indignation, and on moral indignation justice and the greater part of public law are in the main founded. Thus, paradoxical as it may seem, be-

[3] W. McDougall, *An Introduction to Social Psychology,* p. 74 (rev. ed., Boston, 1926).

neficence and punishment alike have their firmest and most essential root in the parental instinct."[4]

Both the tomb monuments of the Pyramid Age, therefore, and, as we shall see, also the Maxims of Ptahhotep, notwithstanding the fact that they all represent a secondary stage in the moral evolution of man in the ancient world, evidently throw an instructive light backward upon the primary stage of human development in these respects, as we observe how unmistakably they disclose the emotions of family affection as closely associated with moral feeling. Our knowledge of primitive human life as found today is very significant just at this point. Westermarck well sums up the observations of the anthropologists in studying surviving primitive life, when he says, "Innumerable facts might indeed be quoted to prove that parental affection is not a late product of civilisation, but a normal feature of the savage mind as it is known to us."[5] Ages ago in the days when the desiccation of the North African Plateau was forcing the savage hunters down into the Nile Valley, such feelings were doubtless already present, and were developing all through the prehistoric evolution which led to the First Union not later than 4000 B.C. Then, five hundred years later, in the Thirty-fifth Century B.C., the earliest written evidence, the Memphite Drama, and just after 3000 B.C., the cemetery of Memphis, combined with the wisdom of Ptahhotep, disclose to us a much more highly developed stage of man's unfolding moral life.

In these Old Kingdom sources, therefore, we are dealing with the *earliest* surviving body of evidence disclosing historically that man's moral ideas are the product of so-

[4] *Ibid.*, p. 75.

[5] E. Westermarck, *Origin and Development of Moral Ideas,* vol. I, p. 531 (London, 1912).

cial conditions and form part of a social process. As we have already noted in respect of the family, this historical conclusion is in complete harmony with modern social observation. Green has well said that "no individual can make a conscience for himself. He always needs a society to make it for him."[6]

In this period, therefore, we are watching the higher aspects of an evolutionary process which cannot be observed at so early a stage anywhere else in the career of man. We are contemplating the emergence of a sense of moral responsibility as it was gradually assuming an increasing mandatory power over human conduct, a development which was moving towards the assertion of conscience as an influential social force.

This is evident in the fact that while the range of good conduct may at first have been confined to the family, it had in the Pyramid Age long since expanded to become a neighbourhood or community matter. Thus, on the base of a mortuary statue set up in his tomb, the deceased represented by the portrait statue says: "I had these statues made by the sculptor and he was satisfied with the pay which I gave him." In a tomb inscription of the Fourth Dynasty (*ca.* 2900–2750 B.C.), now in the Glyptothek at Munich, the steward of an estate named Meni, says: "As for every man who has done this for me (that is, has worked on this tomb), he was never dissatisfied; whether craftsman or quarryman, I satisfied him." Both of these men very evidently wished it known that their mortuary equipment was honestly gotten, and every service fully paid. A nomarch (baron) of the Twenty-seventh Century B.C. left the following record of his upright life: "I gave

[6] T. H. Green, *Prolegomena to Ethics*, p. 387 (5th ed., Oxford University Press, 1924).

bread to all the hungry of the Cerastes-Mountain (his domain); I clothed him who was naked therein. I filled its shores with large cattle and its [lowlands] with small cattle. I satisfied the wolves of the mountain and the fowl of the sky with [flesh] of small cattle. . . . I never oppressed one in possession of his property so that he complained of me because of it to the god of my city; [but] I spake and told that which was good. Never was there one fearing because of one stronger than he, so that he complained because of it to the god. . . . I was a benefactor to it (his domain) in the folds of the cattle, in the settlements of the fowlers. . . . I speak no lie, for I was one beloved of his father, praised of his mother, excellent in character to his brother, and amiable to [his sister]."

Over and over these men of four thousand five hundred to five thousand years ago affirm their innocence of evil doing. "Never did I do anything evil towards any person," says the chief physician of King Sahure in the middle of the Twenty-eighth Century before Christ, while a priest a little later says essentially the same thing: "Never have I done aught of violence towards any person." A century later a citizen of little or no rank places the following address to the living upon the front of his tomb: "O ye living, who are upon earth, who pass by this tomb . . . let a mortuary offering of that which ye have, come forth for me, for I was one beloved of the people. Never was I beaten in the presence of any official since my birth; never did I take the property of any man by violence; I was a doer of that which pleased all men." Another man's tomb inscription was obviously of interest to his neighbours, as he says: "I did that which men loved and the gods approved, that they may make my eternal house (meaning his tomb) endure and my name flourish in the mouth of men." It is evident from such addresses to the living as this that one motive for these affirmations of estimable standing in the community was the hope of maintaining the good-will of one's surviving neighbours, that they might present mortuary offerings of food and drink at the tomb.

To answer for any wrong or injustice of which a man had been guilty during his earthly life he might be summoned by the injured party in the next world to stand before the Sun-god, who sat as the supreme judge over a court of justice like those on earth. The steward Meni, whom we found so punctilious about paying the workmen who built his tomb, placed the following warning on the door-post: "The crocodile shall be against him in the water! The serpent shall be against him on land! Even him who does anything against it (my tomb). It is the great god, who shall judge (him)." It is clear, therefore, that moral worthiness was deemed of value in the sight of the gods and might materially influence the happiness of the dead in the hereafter. Both the motives mentioned are found combined in a single address to the living on the front of the tomb of the greatest of early African explorers, Harkhuf of Elephantine, who penetrated the Sudan in the Twenty-sixth Century B.C. His tomb, cut in the western cliffs, overlooking modern Assuan, where any tourist with the necessary sturdy legs may climb to visit it, bears carved upon its front the story of his adventurous life. Among other things, he says: "I was . . . [beloved] of his father, praised of his mother, whom all his brothers loved. I gave bread to the hungry, clothing to the naked, I ferried him who had no boat. O ye living who are upon earth, [who shall pass by this tomb] whether going down-stream or going up-stream, who shall say, 'A thousand loaves, a thousand jars of beer for the owner of this tomb!' I will intercede for their sakes in the Nether World. I am a worthy and equipped Glorious One, a ritual priest whose mouth knows. As for any man who shall enter into [this] tomb as his mortuary possession, I will seize him like a wild fowl; he shall be judged for it by the Great God. I was one saying good things and repeating what was loved. Never did I say aught evil to a powerful one against anybody. I desired that it might be well with me in the Great God's presence. Never did I [judge two brothers] in such a way that a son was deprived of his paternal possession." Here the threat of judgment is not only used to deter the lawless who might take possession of the dead man's tomb, but the thought of that judgment, meaning moral responsibility beyond the grave, is affirmed to have been the motive of the great explorer's exemplary life. That motive is thus carried back to the actual course of his daily, earthly life as when he says: "I desired that it might be well with me in the Great God's presence." Throughout his life, then, he looked forward to the possibility of being summoned to stand in that dread presence to answer for any wrongdoing while on earth. As the earliest evidence of moral responsibility beyond the tomb, such utterances in the cemeteries of the Pyramid Age, nearly five thousand years ago, are not a little impressive. In other lands, for over two thousand years after this, good and bad alike were consigned to the same realm of the dead, and no distinction whatever was made between them. It is, as it were, an isolated moral vista down which we look, penetrating the early gloom as a shaft of sunshine penetrates the darkness.

The moral mandate was not exclusively a personal influence confined to a man's relations with his family and neighbourhood or community; it was already beginning to be felt in high places and to affect the obligations of government towards the people as a whole, even at the cost of complete disregard of the claims of family. Already in the Pyramid Age the just vizier Kheti had become proverbial because of a decision he had made when he had presided over a lawsuit to which his own relatives were a party. Without reference to the merits of the case he decided against his kin, lest he should be accused of partial judgment in favour of his own family. The ancient inscription of later days which recounts the incident adds, "When one of them appealed against the judgment . . . he (the vizier Kheti) persisted in his discrimination." Fifteen hundred years later the name of Kheti was proverbially cited in Egyptian governmental life as an example of leaning over backward which was not to be emulated; and the viziers of the Fifteenth Century B.C. were told by the Pharaoh that Kheti's famous decision was "more than justice."

The Pyramid Texts contain unequivocal evidence that the demands of justice and righteousness were mightier than the king himself. He was not exempt from the requirement which the tombs of his nobles disclose them as so anxious to fulfil, and the god whom he satisfied, as in the case of his subjects, was Re. "There is no evil which King Pepi has done. Weighty is this word in thy sight, O Re." In a typical Solar Utterance, we find Re's ferryman thus addressed: "O thou who ferriest over the just who is without a ship, ferryman of the Field of Rushes, King Merire (Pepi I) is just before the sky and before the earth." Or again: "This king Pepi is justified, this king Pepi is praised." Similarly, the Morning Star, a Solar deity, takes due note of the moral status of the dead Pharaoh. "Thou (O Morning Star) makest this Pepi to sit down because of his righteousness and to rise up because of his reverence."

The moral worthiness of the deceased must of course, in accordance with the Egyptian's keen legal discernment, be determined in legal form and by legal process. We have seen that the nobles refer to judgment in their tombs, and that even the king was subject to such judgment. Indeed not even the gods escaped it; for it is stated that every god who assists the Pharaoh to the sky "shall be justified before Geb (the Earth-god)."

The translated Pharaoh, who is thus declared just, continues to exhibit the same qualities in the exercise of the celestial sovereignty which he receives. "He judges justice before Re on that day of the feast, (called) 'First of the Year.' The sky is in satisfaction, the earth is in joy, having heard that King Neferkere (Pepi II) has placed justice [in the place of injustice]. They are satisfied who sit with King Neferkere in his court of justice with the just utterance which came forth from his mouth." It is significant that the king exercises this just judgment in the presence of Re the Sun-god. Similarly in a Solar Utterance we find it affirmed that "King Unis has set justice therein (in the isle where he is) in the place of injustice."

In the Twenty-eighth Century B.C. one of the state names of King Userkaf was "Doer of Righteousness (Maat)." It was therefore in continuation of the moral order which he had maintained on earth that the translated Pharaoh was conceived as administering it (Maat) in the hereafter. The Pyramid Texts say of him "King Unis comes forth to righteousness (Maat) that he may take it (Maat) with him." And again: "King Unis goes forth on this day, that he may bring righteousness (Maat) with him."

As we contemplate the royal name of Userkaf it is not a little interesting to observe that a famous Grand Vizier of the same dynasty concluded a collection of his wise maxims with these words: "I have attained one hundred and ten years of life, while the king gave to me rewards above (those of) the ancestors because *I did righteousness* for the king even unto the grave." The great prime minister who made this statement was Ptahhotep, who retired as Grand Vizier under the Pharaoh Isesi of the Fifth Dynasty in the Twenty-seventh Century B.C. He was evidently already a mature man in the reign of Userkaf, and we may therefore see some connection between the sage vizier's assertion "I did righteousness" and Userkaf's state name "Doer of Righteousness."

The Maxims of Ptahhotep furnish us with the earliest formulation of right conduct to be found in any literature.[7] While we have heretofore gained only scattered glimpses of moral conduct and the surprising advance in moral discernment achieved by the civilisation of the Second Union, Ptahhotep's seasoned wisdom summarises for us much of the moral insight of the age. According to the introduction the aged vizier, feeling the infirmity of advancing years, requested the sovereign to permit him to instruct his (the vizier's) son, in preparation for the duties of an official career as his father's assistant and successor. The king consented and thereupon the old vizier admonished his son not to misuse the wisdom he was about to receive, but to practice all modesty: "Be not

[7] The Maxims of Ptahhotep were long supposed to be of Twelfth Dynasty (Middle Kingdom) date, that is, sometime after 2000 B.C. The accumulation of evidence for its Old Kingdom (Second Union) origin is now conclusive, and the Horus name of Userkaf, cited above, is an additional indication that we may regard Ptahhotep himself as the author.

proud because of thy learning. Take counsel with the unlearned as with the learned, for the limit of a craft is not fixed and there is no craftsman whose worth is perfect. Worthy speech is more hidden than greenstone, being found even among slave-women at the mill-stone." Then follow forty-three paragraphs of miscellaneous instruction without any effort at order or arrangement, but seemingly just as the random items of his long experience might occur to an old man merely laying down his responsibilities.

There is much emphasis on common sense and the use of the mind, which is as usual called the "heart." A youth's ability to heed or obey (literally "hearken") is his most valuable quality. "A hearkener is one whom the god loves, one whom the god hates is one who hearkens not. It is the understanding (literally "heart") which makes its possessor a hearkener or one not hearkening. The good fortune of a man is his understanding. . . . How worthy it is when a son hearkens to his father! If the son of a man receives what his father says, none of his projects will miscarry. Instruct as thy son one who hearkens, who shall be successful in the opinion of the princes, who directs his mouth according to that which is said to him. . . . How many mishaps befall him who hearkens not! The wise man rises early to establish himself, but the fool is in trouble. As for the fool who hearkens not there is none who has done anything for him. He regards wisdom as ignorance, and what is profitable as useless. A son who hearkens . . . reaches old age, he attains reverence. He speaks likewise to his own children, renewing the instruction of his father. . . . He speaks with his children, then they speak to their children." As far back as the Twenty-seventh Century B.C., therefore, conduct had already become a traditional matter, the maxims of which were standard and were being handed down from father to son.

Worldly success loomed large, and the measures for ensuring it were highly important. They occupy about one third, that is fourteen out of the forty-three paragraphs of the old vizier's wisdom. Some of them merely inculcate circumspect conduct in the presence of the great, and include even deportment at dinner with a superior. "Take when he gives to thee what he puts before thee, but do not look at what is before *him,* look at what is before *thee,* and bombard him not (literally "shoot him not") with many glances (that is, don't stare at him!) . . . Turn thy face downward until he addresses thee, and speak only when he has addressed thee. Laugh when he laughs, so shalt thou be very agreeable to his heart and what thou doest will be very pleasant to the heart. One knows not what is in the heart." It is very important on any occasion not to be over-communicative and noticeably aggressive conduct or bearing is to be avoided.

Much more space is devoted to shrewd wisdom in guiding one's official activity. If your chief is one who was formerly of very humble station, "have no knowledge of his former low estate, . . . be respectful towards him because of what he has achieved; for substance cometh not of itself." Never repeat injudicious words uttered in heat by some one else. "Be silent, for it (silence) is better than *teftef*-flowers. Speak thou when thou knowest that thou solvest difficulties. It is a craftsman who speaks in council and speech is more difficult than any craft." Give helpful advice to the prince, for "thy food hangs upon his mood, the belly of one loved is filled, thy back shall be clothed thereby." . . . "Let thy mind be deep and thy speech scanty. . . . Let thy mind be steadfast as long as thou speakest. May the princes who shall hear it say, 'How seemly is that which comes out of his mouth!' "

The obvious motive of such counsel is shrewd and worldly diplomacy with surprisingly little Machiavellianism for an age so remote. It is clear that this old statesman had a keen eye for the main chance, but he was not without discernment of much higher values. Realisation of the uncertainties of human life had taught him humility. He admonishes his son: "If thou hast become great after thou wert little, and hast gained possessions after thou wert formerly in want, . . . be not unmindful of how it was with thee before. Be not boastful of thy wealth, which has come to thee as a gift of the god. Thou art not greater than another like thee to whom the same has happened." Moreover the career of a civil servant is hazardous, therefore, "beware of the days that may come hereafter." It is well to make large investments in good will. Therefore "satisfy thy intimate associates with that which has come to thee, which comes to one whom the god (that is the king) favours. . . . There is none who knows his (future) fortune when he thinks of tomorrow. When something happens in (royal) favour, it is the intimate associates who (still) say 'Welcome!' " But, as we shall see, "when thy fortunes are evil, thy virtue shall be above thy friends."

A man should give attention to the character of his friends. "If thou searchest the character of a friend, ask no questions, (but) approach him and deal with him when he is alone. . . . Disclose his heart in conversation. If that which he has seen come forth from him, (or) he do aught that makes thee ashamed for him, . . . do not answer."

More important than friends, however, are family responsibilities. "If thou art a successful man establish thy household. Love thy wife in the house as is fitting." After this book had gone to the printer a Luxor *fellah* who had been digging fertiliser among the ancient ruins brought me a flake of limestone which he had found there and on which a scribe of more than three thousand years ago had scribbled in ink a few lines quoted from the Maxims of Ptahhotep, then over fifteen hundred years old. The ink was still black and legible and the lines proved to be a variant text of the old vizier's admonitions about a wife. It was as if the ancient wise man had suddenly entered my rooms at Luxor to tell me something more of his thoughts, for one of the variants was attractive. It read: "If thou art a successful man establish [thy house and take] to thyself a wife as the heart's mistress." In the more prosaic and less romantic older text, the love that is "fitting" is defined as involving practical demonstrations of husbandly affection: "Fill her body, clothe her back." No luxury is too good for her. What the modern woman prizes in perfumes and "compact" her ancient sister on the Nile found in costly perfumed unguents, which the wise old statesman does not forget to include for his son's wife: "The recipe for her limbs is ointment." Thus with affection which the sagacious old vizier puts first, then with bodily necessities of food and wardrobe, and luxuries like cosmetics, the good husband is to make his wife happy: "Make her heart glad as long as thou livest. She is a profitable field for her lord." This last remark anticipates the same statement made by Mohammed in the Koran nearly thirty-five hundred years later.

Of fatherhood Ptahhotep had very definite views, "If

thou art a successful man and establishest thy household and begettest a son having the favour of the god (meaning the king), if he lives correctly, inclines to thy character, hearkens to thy instruction, while his purposes are worthy in thy house, and he conserves thy possessions as should be, then seek for him every good thing. He is thy son, whom thy ka has begotten for thee. Separate not thy affection from him. . . . If he errs and transgresses thy purposes, and does not observe thy instruction, (if) his purposes are evil and he opposes all that thou sayest, his mouth is defiled with evil speech, . . . thou shalt drive him away; he is not thy son, for he has not been born to thee."

While the old vizier recognises fully the desirability of worldly advancement and wealth, they must not be permitted to destroy family relationships. "Be not avaricious in a division, nor greedy (even) for thy (own) goods. Be not avaricious towards thy own kin. Greater is the appeal of the gentle than that of the strong. Impoverished is he who overreaches his kin; he is lacking in effective speech. A little for which one practices guile engenders enmity even in the cool tempered." Avarice is the greatest enemy of wholesome family relationships. "If thou desirest that thy conduct be worthy, withhold thee from all evil, and beware of avarice. It is an ill and incurable disease, wherein is no intimate association. It makes bitter the sweet friend, it alienates the intimate friend from his lord, it estranges fathers and mothers and the mother's brothers, it sunders wife and husband. It is a bale of evil things, it is a bundle of all unworthiness. . . . There is no tomb for the avaricious."

This recognition of the high value of family associations in one's own household is accompanied by respect for those of other households, where the greatest circumspection in a visitor's bearing towards the women is enjoined. "If thou desirest to establish friendship in a house into which thou enterest, whether as lord, as brother, or as friend, wheresoever thou enterest in, beware of approaching the women. The place where they are is not seemly, and it is not wise to intrude upon them. A thousand men are undone for the enjoyment of a brief moment like a dream. Men gain only death for knowing them." A later manuscript of this admonition is more picturesque: "When one is intoxicated with shining limbs (literally 'limbs of glass'), then they become but *herset*-stone. A little, an instant, like a dream, and the end is death." From other sources we know that in later times the penalty of conjugal infidelity was death, and it was presumably so in the Old Kingdom. In the matter of concubines the old vizier was of course a child of his age and he devotes a short paragraph to admonition that such a woman be kindly treated. In the same connection he charges his son never to practice the corruption of boys.

A spirit of tolerant kindliness pervades all of the aged statesman's wisdom. It begins in a man's home and family, the relations in which are regarded as of supreme value, but it extends also to those with whom one has official and business relations. Such feeling seems to be involved in the atmosphere of cheerfulness which the old man commends to his son: "Let thy face be cheerful as long as thou livest," and he continues with a sentiment which seems to be the ancestor of our own proverb, "There's no use crying over spilt milk." This benevolent cheerfulness is in keeping with the old vizier's insistence on relaxation and diversion. It is probable that in the following he refers to little more than good dinners, music, dancing, draughts, the diversions of his charming gardens, the delights of hunting in the marshes, or a pleasant jaunt about his estate borne in a palanquin on the shoulders of his servants, while they disclose their affection for their lord as they sing,

> "Happy are the bearers of the palanquin!
> It is pleasanter (for them) when it is occupied,
> Than when it is empty."

In any case Ptahhotep enjoins his son: "Follow thy desire (literally 'thy heart') as long as thou livest. Do not more than is told thee. Shorten not the time of following desire. It is an abomination to encroach upon the time thereof. Take no care daily beyond the maintenance of thy house. When possessions come, follow desire, for possessions are not complete when he (the owner) is harassed."

A man of this spirit must have found kindness easy; the old vizier charges his son: "If thou art an administrator, be gracious when thou hearest the speech of the petitioner. Do not assail him until he has cleaned out (literally 'swept out') his belly of what he thought to say to thee. He who is suffering wrong desires that his heart be cheered to accomplish that on account of which he has come. . . . It is an ornament of the heart to hear kindly."

It can hardly be doubted that this kindliness is close kin to fair and just treatment, and it is therefore not surprising to find that righteousness and justice are lifted above everything else in this Wisdom of Ptahhotep. He says, "If thou art an administrator issuing ordinances for the multitude, seek for thee every excellent precedent, that thy ordinance may endure without error therein. Great is righteousness; its dispensation endures, nor has it been overthrown since the time of its maker;[8] for punishment is inflicted on the transgressor of its laws. . . . *Although misfortune may carry away wealth, . . . the power of righteousness is that it endures,* so that a man may say, 'It is a possession of my father (which I have inherited).'" Hence in carrying out any commission the youth is charged, "Hold fast the truth (or 'righteousness') and transgress it not, even though the report (which thou art delivering) be not one pleasing the heart." The young man is to deliver the facts even though he is obliged to tell his chief some unwelcome truth.

Obviously this line demands strength of character and this is the old man's hope for his son, as he says, "Attain character . . . make righteousness to flourish and thy children shall live." He reminds the youth, "Precious to a man is the virtue of his son, and good character is a thing remembered." "If thou hearkenest to this which I have said to thee, all the fashion of thee will be according to the ancestors. *As for the righteousness thereof, it is their worth;* the memory thereof shall not vanish from the mouths of men, because their maxims are worthy. Every word will be carried on, it shall not perish in this land forever, and it will make worthy the utterance according to which the princes speak. . . . When a worthy reputation arises with him who is thy chief, it shall be excellent forever and all its wisdom shall be for eternity. As for the wise man, his soul rejoiceth to make his worth enduring thereby on earth. A wise man is recognised by that which he knows. His heart is the balance for his tongue, his lips are correct when he speaks, and his eyes in seeing; his ears to-

[8] It is important to note that the Middle Kingdom manuscript of Ptahhotep has "Osiris" at this point, while the Empire manuscript preserves what is evidently the older reading, "its maker," obviously meaning the Sun-god, Re.

gether hear what is profitable for his son, *who does righteousness and is free from lying."* Perhaps the ethical spirit of the old vizier is best summarised in his warning against avarice, when without too obvious relevancy he bursts out almost triumphantly with the assurance, *"Established is the man whose standard is righteousness, who walketh according to its way."* This has decidedly the ring of Hebrew wisdom as preserved to us in the Old Testament, but it is over two thousand years older.

It is on the note of righteousness that the old vizier closes his admonitions to his son: "Behold a worthy son, whom the god gives, renders more than his lord says to him. *He does righteousness,* his heart acts according to his way. According as thou attainest me (what I have attained), shall thy flesh be sound, the king shall be satisfied with all that happens and thou shalt attain (my) years of life. They are not few that I have spent on earth. I have attained one hundred and ten years of life, while the king gave to me rewards above those of the ancestors because *I did righteousness* for the king even unto the grave." We have already observed (p. 128) that the Pharaoh Userkaf had made one of his royal names: "Doer of Righteousness," a fact which suggests that Ptahhotep's wisdom was regarded in high places even in his youth.

Over half of Ptahhotep's admonitions deal with personal character and conduct, while the remainder have to do with administration and official conduct. We have seen that in general they inculcate gentleness, moderation, and discretion without lack of self-assertion, displaying indeed the soundest good sense in the poise and balance to which they commend the young man. Life is abundantly worth while. A wholesome amount of pleasure is to be taken, and official or other burdens are not to be allowed to curtail the hours of relaxation. Moreover, a man should always wear a cheerful face, for "there is no use in crying over spilt milk." Finally the dominant note is a commanding moral earnestness which pervades the whole homely philosophy of the old vizier's wisdom. The most prominent imperative throughout is "do right," and "deal justly with all."

The supreme, indeed the imperishable, quality in human life is repeatedly asserted by this ancient sage to be "righteousness" and worthy character, as something which lives after a man has passed on, so that the memory of such a character survives eternally. It is no accident that such convictions find expression in an ancient papyrus roll which reflects to us at the same time an atmosphere of kindliness, of family affection, and of reverence for father and mother, and especially warns against such a defect as "avarice" which destroys family harmony. All these sentiments belong in the same social world and grew up in the same environment: the family first and the rest as the obvious fruit of family relationships. In the Wisdom of Ptahhotep therefore we find full confirmation of the evidence from the tomb inscriptions and relief pictures that it was family life which first made man conscious of moral responsibilities.

It was in this age, too, that such responsibilities became the subject of reflection. Here began also reflective contemplation of human nature: the wise man and the fool were contrasted, traits good and bad were balanced against each other, and a world of new values was emerging. In such an age the consciousness of personality was born, and human society became an arena consciously new, where new forces and new weapons clashed. It was in this age of the earliest recognition of character that the first individuals emerged, rising above the nameless masses submerged in the immemorial ages of the remoter past. The strong man made his impression on society because of his outstanding traits of mind and character. The monuments of this first great historic age have preserved to us the names of some of these men. In the Thirtieth Century B.C. Imhotep, a Grand Vizier of the Third Dynasty, transmuted the clay and wood and wattle buildings of his age into massive stone and created the first stone architecture. He is the first outstanding individual in human history. His wise maxims and his medical lore made his a household name for thousands of years, and once revered as a great physician, he still lives as the Asclepios of the Greeks, the Æsculapius of the Romans, the patron god of medical science throughout the ages. His wise sayings, although they have now perished, were quoted by his descendants for at least fifteen centuries after his death.

Kagemni, another wise vizier who flourished in the Thirtieth Century B.C. not long after Imhotep, was known to have delivered wise instruction to his sons, but these too have not survived to us. About a century later than Imhotep, lived Hardedef, son of Khufu, the builder of the Great Pyramid of Gizeh, whose proverbial wisdom was preserved in the mouths of men along with that of Imhotep for a millennium and a half. Of all these sages of the Pyramid Age, Ptahhotep is the only one whose wisdom has survived to the present day as part of the scanty wreckage of this first great age of the human mind. With these we must place the unknown first scientist, the author of the oldest known scientific treatise, a disquisition on surgery which arose possibly as early as the time of Imhotep himself. The author of this treatise, the earliest known scientist, was the first man to make the distinction between the forces of nature and those attributed to the gods, when he discusses an injury of the head due to an external cause, or as he called it, "something entering from outside," the accident from without. Although thus recognised as the natural or physical external cause, it was at the same time a blow involved in the mystery of good or ill-fortune which the archaic surgeon says "means the breath of an outside god, or death, *not the intrusion of something which his (the patient's) flesh engenders.*" The domain of natural causes in the internal economy of the human body is here distinguished from the realm of good or ill-fortune controlled by the gods—a profound observation occurring, in so far as I know, for the first time in the surviving records of human thought.[9]

The power of personality, the forces that we recognise as those of character, were now beginning to find expression, not only in the written works of thoughtful and contemplative men, like Ptahhotep, but were consciously felt in the art of the time especially by the most gifted of the sculptors in the earliest known portrait sculpture. The long-established order had resulted in the creation of an Old Kingdom type of sculptured portrait which is almost if not entirely lacking in individualistic character. It is possible that in these portraits the sculptors of the age are revealing to us the earliest "standardisation" of human types and thus disclosing the uniformity in the effects of a long-enduring moral order which obliterated differences. This *typical* character, however, has been overemphasised by modern art critics; the greatest work

[9] See the author's *The Edwin Smith Surgical Papyrus,* Vol. I, pp. 212–214 (2 vols., Chicago, 1930).

of the Old Kingdom sculptors shows us that they had begun to discern the power and individuality of the supreme personality, as it was for the first time emerging in the imposing figure of the Pharaoh himself. It is very impressively expressed in such powerful portraits as that of Khafre, the builder of the second pyramid of Gizeh, and must have profoundly influenced conceptions of divinity. Furthermore, a whole series of portraits convey to us remarkable impressions of the group of great men who surrounded the Pharaoh in the Pyramid Age, the statesmen and sages, artists, architects and engineers who five thousand years ago made Egypt a land of architectural marvels which even at the present day it continues to be; while the chiefly mud-brick buildings of Western Asia, throughout the whole period preceding the imperial palaces of Persia, have been almost entirely swept away. The contrast is not without significance and enhances the impression of Egypt as having brought forth the first great age of personality.

These great men were not a mushroom growth; they were the product of a millennium of human experience with organised life, and they were the first men who could look back into such a deep vista of the earlier life of man. In so doing they must long have groped for a term which would best express their idea of the human order, and focus in its meaning the achievements of which they were the heirs. They eventually found it in a single remarkable word, which summed up for them all that was highest in human life. It was the word "*Mat*" or "*Maat,*" one of the earliest abstract terms preserved in human speech, the word which we have been translating "righteousness," "justice," "truth," for all of these conceptions were finally represented in Egyptian speech, by

FIG. 9. HEAD OF DIORITE STATUE OF KING KHAFRE (TWENTY-NINTH CENTURY B.C.)

Probably the most impressive portrait of the Pyramid Age, illustrating the powerfully individualistic portrayals of the supreme personality, the sovereign, in an age when character and individuality were first emerging. *After von Bissing.* (*Cairo Museum.*)

this single word, Maat. For their ancestors it had at first meant merely "right," in the sense of "correct," just as we use our own word "right" both in a mathematical and an ethical sense. At the advent of the Old Kingdom Maat had gradually expanded in meaning to include a wide and important range of significance. It was the opposite not only of falsehood, but also of moral wrong in general. When this development began we do not know; but it is interesting to observe that the word Maat is not found in the preserved portions of the Memphite Drama. This may of course be the result of accident.

After 3000 B.C. the great men of the Old Kingdom began to discern the meaning of Maat in terms of their impressive national experience. While not divested of its significance as a word designating personal qualities, it became in the minds of Old Kingdom thinkers a term expressing a sense of the national order, the moral order of the nation, the national cosmos under the dominion of the Sun-god. Let us now recall for a moment the past upon which the sages of the Old Kingdom were able to look back—the past which for them had expanded the word Maat and given it more spacious meaning. They had lists of hoary kings who had ruled even before the foundation of the First Union; they knew that after ages of small and local city kingdoms, there had been a preliminary unification, the First Union. They were acquainted with the story of this preparatory union, and how after its course was run Egypt had been consolidated in a Second Union, which endured for a thousand years, from about the Thirty-fifth to about the Twenty-fifth Century B.C. It is fundamentally important for us to realise that this thousand years was man's first uninterrupted millennium of national experience, that is, of human development in unified national form—a steadily moving evolution in which a nation of some millions of souls for the first time on our globe rose to the creation of an imposing structure of organised human life capable of enduring a thousand years. It was this impressive vision of an enduring state and its ever-functioning organisation, which contributed substantially to the larger, more comprehensive meaning of the Egyptian word "Maat," till it had come to signify not only "justice," "truth," "righteousness," which the men of the Pyramid Age discerned as something practiced by the individual, but also an existent social and governmental reality, a moral order of the world, identified with the rule of the Pharaoh. The chief judge in the Egyptian courts of justice wore on his breast a lapis lazuli image of the goddess Maat and to indicate the winning litigant, the judge was accustomed to turn this symbol towards the winner as the two litigants stood before him.[10] Ptahhotep glories in the supremacy of Maat, as a thing established for eternity: "Great is Maat; its dispensation endures, nor has it been overthrown since the time of its maker." Over and over again in the ancient monuments Maat is the thing which the Pharaoh personifies and enforces, as against anarchy, injustice, and deceit practiced by his rivals for the throne, who afflict the people with disorganisation. It was a thousand years of such organised government which gave the Egyptian sages of the Old Kingdom a majestic picture of the actual operation and beneficence of Maat, and imbued it with a historical meaning which it could not otherwise have gained.

It will be seen that both society and government, both

10 There are three of these lapis lazuli images in the Berlin Museum. See G Moeller, *Zeitschrift für ægyptische Sprache,* Vol. 56 (1920), pp. 67–68.

social influences and the state, had brought forth the order which the Egyptian sages summed up in the word Maat. Having arisen as an individual and personal matter, as a designation of right conduct in the family or immediate community, Maat had then gradually passed into a larger arena as the spirit and method of a *national* guidance and control of human affairs, a control in which orderly administration is suffused with moral conviction. There was thus created for the first time a realm of universal values, and in conceiving the divine ruler of such a realm the Egyptians were moving on the road towards monotheism. This divine ruler was the Sun-god, the spirit of whose rule they picturesquely suggested by personifying Maat as a goddess and making her the Sun-god's daughter. It was along this road, as we shall see, that the Egyptians eventually attained monotheism, and it was no accident that they reached it long before any other people; nor is it an accident that the next people to gain monotheism were Egypt's nearest neighbours across the borders of Asia in Palestine, one of whose prophets said: "Unto you that fear my name shall the sun of righteousness arise with healing in his wings,"[11] obviously referring to the Egyptian Sun-god so commonly depicted as a winged sun-disk.

As we thus look forward and our eyes are inevitably drawn Asiaward it becomes clear at once why Western Asiatic civilisation lagged behind in such development. In the Egyptian conception of a great administrative and moral order, designated by Maat, we must recognise the highest manifestation of ancient oriental civilisation. Here is a conception which, as we have seen, was obviously the product of a millennium of social and governmental evo-

[11] Malachi 4:2.

lution in a great unified, continuous, orderly, and ever more highly organised national life. This conception of an administrative and moral order, although vaguely adumbrated in beautiful pictures of a righteous king two thousand years later by the Hebrew prophets, did not clearly emerge in Western Asia until the advent of Zoroaster and his great moral system after the rise of the Persian Empire under Cyrus and his successors. The history of Western Asia shows quite clearly why it was earlier impossible. In Egypt, developing through the Second Union and the Old Kingdom, we have civilisation as the product of more than a thousand years of social experience within the guiding forms of a stable, stimulating, and vigorous national organisation, possessed of the vitality to endure for over a millennium; whereas Babylonia, the earliest outstanding Western Asiatic state, continued throughout that thousand years to suffer constant disorganisation in the petty wars between the insignificant city-states of which it was made up during the greater part of that millennium. Even before its beginning Egypt had already left the struggles of the local city-kingdoms far behind. *Material* civilisation is doubtless as old in Western Asia, as it is in Egypt, but civilisation in its broadest aspects is the product of a long social evolution. Hence the arguments of the archæologists, who, on the basis of such things as copper axes and the craft of the goldsmith, would place Babylonian civilisation, which had had no opportunity for an uninterrupted social evolution, at an earlier date than that of Egypt, are too superficial to be worthy of refutation. Without question the political, social, and, in general, the civilised development of mankind along the Nile was many centuries older than in Western Asia. Indeed, in religious, social, and political experience Babylonia was at least a thousand years later than Egypt.

The fact is important, for it places us in a position to realise the unique significance of Egypt's great millennium of civilised development. It is along the Nile that we are watching the vanguard of the human advance—man for the first time dimly realising the nature of the conquest he has begun, and out of a thousand years of national experience girding himself for a struggle in the arena of social forces, which were to assail him *from within*. During all that millennium he had gained the most impressive triumphs over his *outward* adversaries in the world of material forces; but now the voices *within* were beginning to challenge him to enter a new and higher arena of which he had been little conscious before.

There is conclusive evidence to show that the earliest moral ideas of the Egyptians developed in association with the Sun-god rather than with Osiris. The Maxims of Ptahhotep explicitly designate the Sun-god as "its (righteousness') maker," in a passage where the partisans of Osiris have inserted his name in the Middle Kingdom manuscript—interesting evidence of the Osirian crusade of that period. Unfortunately the earliest god whom the Egyptians conceived as the moral judge in the hereafter is not mentioned by name, but an epithet, "Great God," is employed instead. This is expanded in one tomb to "Great God, lord of the sky." It is therefore hardly possible that any other than the Sun-god can be meant. This conclusion is confirmed by all that we find in the Pyramid Texts, where the Sun-god is over and over again the lord of the judgment. It is he who is meant when Inti, a noble of Deshasheh, says: "But as for all people who shall do evil to this (tomb), who shall do anything destructive to this (tomb), who shall damage the writing therein, judgment shall be had with them for it by the Great God, the lord of judgment in the place where judgment is had." The later rapid growth of ethical teaching in the Osiris faith and the assumption of the rôle of judge by Osiris is not yet discernible in the Pyramid Age, for the development which made these elements so prominent in the Middle Kingdom took place in the obscure period after the close of the Pyramid Age. Contrary to the common conclusion, it was the Sun-god, therefore, who was the earliest champion of moral worthiness and the great judge in the hereafter. A thousand years later Osiris, as the victorious litigant at Heliopolis, as the champion of the dead who had legally triumphed over all his enemies, emerged as the great moral judge. In the usurpation of this rôle by Osiris we have another evidence of the irresistible process which Osirianised Egyptian religion. To these later conditions from which modern students have drawn their impressions, the current conclusion regarding the early moral supremacy of Osiris is due. The greater age of the Solar faith in this as in other particulars is, however, perfectly clear.

These early moral aspirations had their limitations. Let us not forget that we are dealing with an age lying between fifty-five and forty-five hundred years ago. We have seen that the chief conquests of man in this remote age had been gained in a struggle with material forces. In this struggle he had issued a decisive victor, but nevertheless it was amid the distractions of a host of obscuring influences that early man had caught some vision of new values surpassing merely material achievements. Without any doubt the reign of Maat remained for the most part a lofty vision of the sages, which official corruption had rendered impossible of realisation, just as it continues to hamper government in the Orient at the present day. Let us not imagine, then, that the obligations which this vision imposed were all-embracing or that it could include all that we discern in it. For example, the requirements of the great judge in the hereafter were not incompatible with the grossest sensuality. Not only was sensual pleasure permitted in the hereafter as depicted by the Pyramid Texts, but positive provision was made for supplying it. The king is assured of sensual gratification in the grossest terms, and we hear it said of him that he "is the man who takes women from their husbands whither he wills and when his heart desires."

Nevertheless that was a momentous step which regarded felicity after death as in any measure dependent upon the ethical quality of the dead man's earthly life; and it must indeed have been a commanding moral consciousness which made even the divine Pharaoh, who was above the mandates of earthly government, amenable to the celestial judge and subject to moral requirements. This step could not have been taken at once. It is possible that even in the brief century and a half covered by the Pyramid Texts we may discern some trace of the progress of ethical consciousness as it was involving even the king in its imperious demands. In one passage in the Pyramid Texts is found this statement regarding the king, "This king Pepi is justified." Now, it happens that the Utterance in which this statement occurs is found in a variant form in the pyramids of Unis and Teti, two kings earlier than Pepi. Neither of these earlier forms contains this statement of justification, and within a period of sixty to eighty years the editors deemed it wise to insert it.

It is not easy to read the spiritual and intellectual progress of a race in monuments so largely material as contrasted with literary documents. It is easy to be misled and to misinterpret the meagre indications furnished by purely material monuments. Behind them lies a vast complex of human forces and of human thinking which for the most part eludes us. Nevertheless it is impossible to contemplate the colossal tombs of the Fourth Dynasty, so well known as the Pyramids of Gizeh, and to contrast them with the comparatively diminutive royal tombs which follow in the next two dynasties, without, as we have before hinted, discerning more than exclusively political causes behind this sudden and startling change. As we have said before, the great Pyramids of Gizeh represent the struggle of titanic material forces in the endeavour by purely material agencies to immortalise the king's physical body, enveloping it in a vast and impenetrable husk of masonry, there to preserve forever all that linked the spirit of the king to material life. The great Pyramids of Gizeh, while they are today the most imposing surviving witnesses to the earliest emergence of organised man and the triumph of concerted effort, are likewise the silent but eloquent expression of a supreme endeavour to achieve a blessed immortality by sheer physical force.

For merely physical reasons such a colossal struggle with the forces of decay could not go on indefinitely; with these reasons political tendencies too made common cause; but combined with all these we must not fail to see that the mere insertion of the Pyramid Texts in the royal tombs of the last century and a half of the Pyramid Age was in itself almost an abandonment of the titanic struggle with material forces and an evident resort to less tangible agencies. The recognition of a judgment and the requirement of moral worthiness in the hereafter was a still more momentous step in the same direction. It marked a transition from reliance on agencies external to the personality of the dead to dependence on inner values. For the first time immortality dawned upon the mind of man as a thing achieved in a man's own soul. It was the beginning of a shift of emphasis from objective advantages to subjective qualities. It was thus also one of the important steps in the long process which we have been watching—the process by which the individual personality begins to emerge as contrasted with the mass of society. The vision of the possibilities of individual character had dawned upon the minds of these men of the early world; their own moral ideals were passing into the character of their greatest god, his dominion had been recognised as a great moral order benevolently administered on earth by the sovereign for the good of the Egyptian nation, and with this supreme achievement the development of the thousand years which began with the Second Union reached its close not long after 2500 B.C.

CHAPTER X

THE COLLAPSE OF MATERIALISM AND THE EARLIEST DISILLUSIONMENT

THE pyramids of Gizeh are impressive evidence of the centralised power and wealth which the Pharaohs of the Fourth Dynasty held in their hands. The survival of these imposing structures for nearly five thousand years is strong reinforcement of their testimony. A sovereign who could converge the wealth and labour of his several million subjects upon a mausoleum 481 feet high, and which still covers 13 acres of solid masonry, must have held in his grasp a powerfully centralised government. Without any doubt he must have used it with much indifference to human suffering in forced labour. We now know that the officials who operated this great administrative machine gradually gained wealth, especially lands presented to them by the sovereign, and thus built up large estates until they were living like feudal lords on their landed baronies, and after a few centuries they gained a great degree of independence. Thus the once closely centralised government, reflected to us in the vast royal tombs of Gizeh, gradually suffered complete decentralisation and, by 2500 B.C., had become a loosely co-ordinated group of feudal states forming a nation which threatened to lose all coherence and to fall to pieces. In a period of probably something less than two thousand years the first civilisation had thus made the complete revolution from the coalescence of the prehistoric local chieftainships into a unified state, through the completest degree of centralisation, and thence by steady decentralisation had fallen back again into local units of power. It was the first such cycle of human experience, and we have seen that it made a profound impression upon the minds of thinking men who were able by the end of the Old Kingdom to look back for the first time upon such a long-continued process of advancing human organisation. Under the influence of this majestically moving panorama of the earliest organised human life, their ancestors had gradually shifted the old nature gods into the realm of human affairs, and we are now to watch the growing effect of social experience upon their ideas of man, of human conduct, and of God.

Probably not very long after 2500 B.C. the Old Kingdom state, the Second Union, collapsed and fell to pieces. Some time in the course of the ensuing conflict among the local nobles the head of a family of barons living at Heracleopolis, some twenty-five leagues south of Memphis, seized the power so long wielded by the Memphite sovereigns, and made himself Pharaoh. This politically feeble Heracleopolitan Dynasty has left little to tell us of the period. The southern half of Upper Egypt fell away and gained its independence and there was fighting at times along the border in middle Upper Egypt. The tremendous impression produced by this final break-up of the Second Union, after it had endured for a thousand years, did not yet find full expression but like the fall of Rome it wrought powerfully upon the minds of the men who saw it. Thinking men were thrown back from the consideration of outward splendours to the contemplation of inner values. Civilised life in the Old Kingdom centres of power and culture like Memphis and Heliopolis must have continued, and at Heracleopolis itself at least one of the rulers was a sage of sagacious and thoughtful mind. His name is unfortunately unknown, but as he approached the end of his reign he wrote, for the instruction of his son Merikere, a treatise on the conduct of a king which we may call the "Instruction Addressed to Merikere."

This remarkable document, preserved on a papyrus now in the Museum of Leningrad, bears conclusive internal evidence of having been produced in the age from which it purports to come, and we may regard it as the authentic voice of the old Heracleopolitan king. As he addresses his son he looks back upon the Old Kingdom with profound respect for the wisdom which it produced. As for the wise man, says the old statesman, "Truth (Maat) comes to him well-brewed, after the manner of the ancestors. Imitate thy fathers, thy ancestors, . . . for lo, their words abide in writing. Open, that thou mayest read and imitate knowledge. Thus shall the craftsman become instructed." In these words we may recognise the influence of Ptahhotep, who called speech a "craft," and a skilled speaker a "craftsman." It is a roll of Ptahhotep's maxims which the Heracleopolitan prince is bidden to open and read, that he may ponder the wisdom which was then doubtless over four hundred years old. "Be a craftsman in speech," says the old king, "that thou mayest be strong, for the strength of one is the tongue, and speech is mightier than all fighting." This is not so far from our own, "the pen is mightier than the sword"; but the Egyptian statesman, as Ptahhotep has showed us, knew very well that an effective tongue needs wise guidance, for he adds, "None thwarts him who is sagacious, nor do those who know he is wise oppose him. Thus no misfortune occurs in his time." It was of course impossible to ignore the difficulties of the existent political situation. The young prince is therefore admonished to maintain peaceful relations with the independent South, and much attention is given to the exposed frontiers towards Asia on the east and the Libyans on the west.

It is in *internal* politics, however, that the old Heracleopolitan demonstrates especially his political wisdom. He frankly recognises the power of the great noble families, and like many a later sovereign in European history, he adopts a policy of conciliation and co-operation. At the same time he shows great shrewdness in recognising the necessity of discovering unrecognised ability in humble quarters and creating new men whom he can use against the old coteries. He says, "Raise up the new generation that the Residence may love thee. . . . Thy city is full of newly trained youth of twenty years. Increase the new generations of thy followers, equipped with possessions, endowed with fields, and entrusted with herds. Exalt not the son of an important man above an humble one, but take for thyself a man because of his ability." Nevertheless it will not do to neglect the old noble families. "Make great thy nobles," he adds, "that they may execute thy laws." For unless they are in affluent circumstances they will not carry on a just administration. "He who is wealthy in his house does not show partiality, for he is a possessor of property and is without need. But the poor man (in office) does not speak according to his righteousness (Maat), for he who says 'Would I had,' is not impartial; he shows partiality to the one who holds his reward. Great is he whose nobles are great, and mighty is the king who possesses a court. August is he who is rich in nobles. If thou speakest the truth (Maat) in thy house, the nobles who are over the land will fear thee. It shall go well with an impartially minded sovereign, for it is the inside (of the palace) which conveys respect to the outside."

Besides responsibility for secular justice, the old king admonishes his son that a sovereign has important duties in the temple, and that he must give every attention to all the sacred observances which evince his full recognition of his dependence on divine favour. The quality of a king, however, is not disclosed by such outward and external observances alone; neither are they a sufficient insurance of divine approval. The character of the giver is more important than the gift. In one of the noblest observations in ancient Egyptian moral thinking, the old Heracleopolitan then bids his son remember: *"More acceptable is the virtue of the upright man than the ox of him that doeth iniquity."* When the youth gains the throne, therefore, he must carry on his rule in accordance with inner, moral qualities. "Do righteousness that thou mayest be established on earth. Comfort the mourner, afflict not the widow, deprive not a man of the possessions of his father, injure not the nobles in their positions. Do not chastise (probably meaning, 'personally'), that is not profitable for thee, but punish thou by beaters with restraint and this land shall be established by it. . . . God knoweth the rebellious man and God smiteth his iniquity in blood. . . . Slay not a man whose worth thou knowest, with whom thou hast chanted the writings (doubtless in school)." The mildness which was so commended by Ptahhotep is then carried much further by the old sage of Heracleopolis. He adjures his son, "Be not harsh, kindness is seemly. Establish thy monument in the love of thee. . . . Men shall thank God for thy reward, . . . giving praise for thy kindness and praying for thy health."

We recall that Ptahhotep was much concerned about

the future *in this world,* because of the uncertainties that beset a man's position in life. Merikere is admonished by his royal father to think of the future *in the next world.* "The court of judges who judge the unworthy, thou knowest that they are not lenient on that day of judging the wretched, in the hour of executing the writ. . . . Set not thy mind on length of days, for they (the judges) view a lifetime as an hour. A man surviveth after death and his deeds are placed beside him like mountains. For it is eternity, abiding yonder (in the next world), and a fool is he who disregards it. As for him who reacheth it without having committed sin, he shall abide there like a god, striding on like the lords of eternity (the justified dead)." This old king sees a good life *here* as the chief reliance *yonder,* for he says, "The soul goeth to the place which it knoweth and swerveth not from its path of yesterday," presumably meaning its wonted path of worthy conduct. At the same time a tomb is important: "Adorn thy dwelling (thy tomb) of the West and embellish thy seat in the necropolis, as one who hath been upright, as one who hath done righteousness (Maat); for this it is upon which their heart resteth."

The most important fact in a man's life is his relation with his god, whether here or hereafter. "One generation passeth on to another among men, and God, who knoweth character, hath hidden himself, . . . He is one who confoundeth by what is seen of the eyes. Let God be served in his fashion, whether made of precious stones, or fashioned of copper, like water replaced by water. There is no stream that suffereth itself to be hidden; it bursteth the dyke by which it was hidden." This remarkable utterance of an Egyptian thinker of over four thousands years ago is obviously an effort to distinguish between the god and the conventional temple image which comes forth in the temple procession and is acclaimed by the multitude. But, as water bursts the dyke, so the being of God cannot be confined within the visible image, which is a thing that "confounds by what is seen of the eyes," while the invisible god "who knoweth character hath hidden himself," as elusive as one body of water merging into another. Such figures are exceedingly difficult to follow, especially in a language so very lacking in abstract terms; but it is obvious that we have in this papyrus a series of reflections on the Sun-god in which the Egyptian thinker is close to monotheism.[1] He recognises a group of gods serving as judges in the hereafter, and obviously relapses therefore from an exclusive acceptance of a sole god; but he is so close to a recognition of the moral dominion of a sole deity, that I have in places, perhaps with some inconsistency, capitalised the word *God* to indicate more nearly its real significance. The monotheistic character of these reflections is further noticeable in the following picture in which the old Heracleopolitan sage, as the conclusion of his reflections, depicts the benevolent creator and ruler: "Well bestead are men, the flocks of God; for he made heaven and earth according to their desire, he quenched the thirst for water, he made the air that their nostrils might live. They are his likenesses which came forth from his limbs. He rises in the sky according to their desire, he made for them plants and animals, fowl and fish, to nourish them. He slew his enemies, he chastised his children, because of their plots in making rebellion. He made the light according to their desire, that he might ⌜sail⌝ the sky to see them. He raised

[1] This fact was noted by Gardiner in his courageous translation of the whole document. I am inclined to think that the complete significance of the above extraordinary passage has not yet been fully grasped by any of us.

a protection around them; when they weep he heareth. He made for them rulers in the egg (rulers predestined before birth) to support the back of the feeble."

The reference to the fact that the god "slew his enemies" is an allusion to the myth of the Sun-god's earthly reign as Pharaoh, when his subjects plotted against him and he was obliged to destroy them. There was an ethical aspect of man's fall from divine favour in this myth, and in it the ethical dominion of the Sun-god is fully recognised. In the mind of our old Heracleopolitan king there is evidently an effort to balance his high conception of ethical requirements with the inherited tradition regarding the value of material agencies. He says to his son, "Make enduring monuments for the god, for it maketh live the name of the maker thereof. Let a man do what is profitable for his soul, the monthly purification, taking the white sandals and visiting the temple, unveiling the mysteries, entering the holy-of-holies and eating bread in the temple. Make the offering to flourish, multiply the loaves, increase the permanent offerings, for it is profitable to him who does it. Make enduring thy monuments according to thy fortune, for a single day is wont to yield eternity, and an hour may be enduring for the future. God knows of the one who does any service for him." The effort to balance materialism and ethical requirements is very marked in connection with the remarkable utterance already quoted above, when the old king says: "More acceptable is the virtue of the upright man than the ox of him that doeth iniquity. (Nevertheless) offer to God, that he may do the like for thee, with offerings for replenishing the offering table and with inscription, for that is what perpetuates thy name. God takes knowledge of him that offers to him."

Here is full recognition of the value of a worthy life in the sight of God, who will not accept gifts in lieu of character—a recognition which has advanced far beyond the highest ideals of the Pyramid Age. Nevertheless the ancestral tradition regarding the value of material means, both in buildings and in offerings, is still accepted by the old king. Without being aware of it, perhaps, he was drawing an issue which could not be left thus balanced and undecided. The centuries were inexorably revealing the futility of reliance on material agencies for the future welfare of the human soul. The march of time was mercilessly disclosing the collapse of materialism, and the sombre shadows of the earliest disillusionment were beginning to darken the Egyptian sky.

The wisdom of the royal sage of Heracleopolis was not without its effect long after his dynasty had disappeared. We hear an echo of it in an autobiography on the tombstone of an Eleventh Dynasty noble, who significantly says, "I have heard the mouth of men, in that saying that is in the mouths of the great, 'A man's virtue is his monument (but) forgotten is the man of evil repute.' "[2] Some centuries later, indeed, we find reminiscences of the Heracleopolitan king's admonitions almost in the same words, in the tomb autobiographies of two nobles who lived under Sesostris I a generation after 2000 B.C.[3] One of them, a wealthy lord of Siut, is proud to boast that he was "one who judged two (litigants) without partiality, for I was wealthy, my abomination was lying, right-minded, without swerving." In the autobiography of the

[2] See Griffith, *Proceedings of the Society of Biblical Archæology,* XVIII (1896), 195 ff. (Plate, ll. 15–16); and Gunn, *Journal of Egyptian Archæology,* XII (1926), p. 282.

[3] The connection of these two quotations with the Instruction Addressed to Merikere was first noticed by H. Kees (*Zeitschrift für ægyptische Sprache,* Vol. 63 (1928), pp. 76–78).

other, inscribed on a beautiful stone tablet now in the Metropolitan Museum of Art, the noble, whose name was Mentuwoser, says, "I was one who heard (legal) cases according to the facts without showing partiality in favour of him who held the reward, for I was wealthy and goodly in luxury."

There is here almost an attitude of endeavouring to justify wealth as an aid in dealing righteously with men in the dispensation of justice. But the futility of reliance on material agencies became more and more evident after the end of the Second Union. Relying on just such means the great sovereigns of the Pyramid Age had for centuries carried on a hopeless struggle with death—a struggle whose decaying monuments were daily demonstrating the failure of material means. That struggle of titans which had gone on for five hundred years was impressively demonstrated before their eyes in a sixty-mile rampart of pyramids sweeping along the margin of the western desert. There they stretched like a line of silent outposts on the frontiers of death. It was nearly a thousand years since the first of them had been built, and centuries had elapsed since the architects had rolled up their papyrus drawings of the latest and the last group of workmen had gathered up their tools and departed. The priesthoods too, left without support, had long forsaken the sumptuous temples and monumental approaches that rose on the valley side. The sixty-mile pyramid cemetery lay in silent desolation, deeply encumbered with sand half hiding the ruins of massive architecture, of fallen architraves and prostrate colonnades, a solitary waste where only the slinking figure of the vanishing jackal, long sacred to Anubis, an archaic god of the dead, suggested the futile protection of the old mortuary gods of the desert. Even at the present day no such imposing spectacle as the pyramid cemeteries of Egypt is to be found anywhere in the ancient world, and we easily recall something of the reverential awe with which they oppressed us when we first looked upon them. Do we of the modern world ever realise that this impression was felt by their descendants only a few centuries after the Pyramid Builders had passed away? and that they were already ancient to the men of 2000 B.C.? On the minds of the Egyptian sages who arose after the end of the Second Union the Pyramid cemetery made a profound impression. If already in the Pyramid Age there had been some relaxation in the conviction that by sheer material force man might make conquest of immortality, the spectacle of these colossal ruins now quickened such doubts into open scepticism, a scepticism which ere long found effective literary expression.

It is a ripe age which has passed beyond the unquestioning acceptance of traditional beliefs as bequeathed by the fathers. Scepticism means a long experience with inherited beliefs, much rumination on what has heretofore received unthinking acquiescence, a conscious recognition of personal power to believe or disbelieve, and thus a distinct step forward in the development of self-consciousness and personal initiative. It is only a people of ripe civilisation which develops scepticism. It is never found under primitive conditions. It was a momentous half millennium of intellectual progress, therefore, of which these sceptics who followed the fall of the Second Union represented the culmination. Their mental attitude finds expression in a song of mourning, often sung at a kind of Feast of All Souls, which was celebrated in the cemetery, when the relatives gathered in the tomb of their departed ancestor. We possess two fragmentary versions of the song, one on papyrus, the other on the walls of a Theban tomb. But the papyrus version was also copied from a tomb, for the superscription reads: "Song which is in the house (tomb-chapel) of King Intef[4] the justified, which is in front of the singer with the harp." It is an extraordinary fact that an Eleventh Dynasty king, about 2100 B.C. should have had this song engraved on the wall of his tomb-chapel. As we follow the lines we might conclude that, as he sang, the singer stood on some elevated point overlooking the pyramid cemetery of the Old Kingdom. The song reads:

THE SONG OF THE HARP-PLAYER

"How prosperous is this good prince![5]
The goodly destiny has come to pass,
The generations pass away,
While others remain,
Since the time of the ancestors,
The gods who were aforetime,
Who rest in their pyramids,
Nobles and the glorious departed likewise,
Entombed in their pyramids.
Those who built their (tomb)-temples,
Their place is no more.
Behold what is done therein.
I have heard the words of Imhotep and Hardedef,
Words greatly celebrated as their utterances.

Behold the places thereof;
Their walls are dismantled,
Their places are no more,
As if they had never been.

None cometh from thence
That he may tell us how they fare;

[4] This is one of the Eleventh Dynasty Intefs.
[5] Meaning the dead king in whose tomb the song was written.

That he may tell us of their fortunes,
That he may content our heart,
Until we too depart
To the place whither they have gone.

Encourage thy heart to forget it,
Making it pleasant for thee to follow thy desire,
While thou livest.
Put myrrh upon thy head,
And garments on thee of fine linen,
Imbued with marvellous luxuries,
The genuine things of the gods.

Increase yet more thy delights,
And let [not] thy heart languish.
Follow thy desire and thy good,
Fashion thine affairs on earth
After the mandates of thine own heart.
Till that day of lamentation cometh to thee,
When the silent-hearted hears not their lamentation,
Nor he that is in the tomb attends the mourning.

Celebrate the glad day,
Be not weary therein.
Lo, no man taketh his goods with him.
Yea, none returneth again that is gone thither."

Such were the feelings of some of the Egyptian thinkers of the new age as they looked out over the tombs of their ancestors and contemplated the colossal futility of the vast pyramid cemeteries of the Old Kingdom. Even the names of some of the wise men of a thousand years before, like Imhotep and Hardedef, whose sayings had become proverbial, and who thus had attained more than a sepulchral immortality in some colossal tomb, arose in the recollection of the singer. It can hardly be a matter of chance that Imhotep, the first of the two whom the singer commemorates, was the earliest architect in stone

FIG. 10. BLIND HARPIST SINGING WITH ORCHESTRA THE SONG OF THE HARP-PLAYER

While a priest officiates before the nobleman (cut off at left) the orchestra plays the accompaniment to the Song of the Harp-Player, the words of which are written on the wall above their heads. The upper portion of the song is gone, but enough is left to tell us that it was a copy of the papyrus version; see p. 163. (*Leyden Rijksmuseum.*)

The other version of the song, from the tomb of the "divine father (priest) of Amon, Neferhotep," at Thebes, is hardly as effective as the first, and unhappily is very fragmentary. It contains, however, some valuable lines which should not be overlooked.

"How rests this just prince!
The goodly destiny befalls,
The generations pass away
Since the time of the god (Re),
And generations come into their places.

Re shows himself at early morn,
Atum goes to rest in Manu.[7]
Men beget and women conceive,
Every nostril breathes the air.
Morning comes, they bear numerously,
They (the new-born) come to their (appointed) places.

Celebrate the glad day, O divine father.
Put the finest spices together at thy nose,
Garlands of lotus flowers at thy shoulder, at thy neck.
Thy sister who dwells in thy heart,
She sits at thy side.
Put song and music before thee,
Behind thee all evil things,
And remember thou (only) joy.
Till comes that day of mooring,
At the land that loveth silence,

. . . .

I have heard all that befell
Those . . .
Their houses are dismantled,
The place of them is no more,
They are as if they had never been,
Since the time of the god,
Those lords . . .

[7] These two lines merely recall the ceaseless rising and setting of Manu is the mountain of the west.

masonry on a large scale, the father of architect
stone. As the architect of King Zoser of the Thirtieth
tury B.C., he was the builder of the oldest superstru
of stone masonry still surviving from the ancient w
the so-called "terraced pyramid" of Sakkara. It was a
culiarly effective stroke to revert to the tomb of this fi
great architect, and to find it in such a state of ruin th
the places thereof were "as if they had never been." In
deed, to this day its place is unknown. Hardedef, too, the
other wise man whom the poem recalls, was a son of
Khufu, and therefore connected with the greatest of the pyramids. The fact, too, that these two ancient sages had survived only in their wise sayings was another illustration of the futility of material agencies as a means of immortality. At the same time the disappearance of such souls as these to a realm where they could no longer be discerned, whence none returned to tell of their fate, strikes the sombrest and most wistful note in all these lines. It is a note of which we seem to hear an echo in the East three thousand years later in the lines of Omar Khayyam:

> "Strange, is it not? that of the myriads who
> Before us passed the door of Darkness through,
> Not one returns to tell us of the Road
> Which to discover we must travel too."[6]

Here is bared a scepticism which doubts *all* means, material or otherwise, for attaining felicity or even survival beyond the grave. To such doubts there is no answer; there is only a means of sweeping them temporarily aside, a means to be found in sensual gratification which drowns such doubts in forgetfulness. "Eat, drink, and be merry, for tomorrow we die."

[6] Fitzgerald, *Rubaiyat,* 64.

Wilt thou plant for thee pleasant trees
Upon the shore of thy pool,
That thy soul may sit under them,
That he may drink their water?
Follow thy desire wholly,

. . . .

Give bread to him who hath no field.
So shalt thou gain a good name
For the future forever.[8]

. . . ."

The song continues with reflections on the vanity of riches, as if in expansion of the single line in the other version referring to the fact that no man may take his goods with him when he departs. Wealth is fruitless, for the same fate has overtaken

"Those who had granaries,
Besides bread for offerings,
And those [who had none] likewise."

Hence the rich man is admonished:

"Remember thou the day
When thou shalt be dragged (in the funeral sledge)
To the land of . . .
[Follow thy desire] wholly.
There is none that returns again."

The singer of this second version finds no hope in the contemplation of death, but suggests that it is well in any case to leave an enduring good name behind; not because it necessarily insures the good man anything in the world to come, but rather that it may abide in the minds of those who remain behind. Indeed, the obligation to a moral

[8] While a tomb and the grove attached to it are fruitless trouble, moral worthiness, kindness to the poor, and the resulting good name shall endure.

life imposed by the "Great God" whose judgment is yet to come, as well as the benefits in the world of the dead, resulting from the fulfillment of this obligation, play no part in this sceptic's thought. The gods are largely ignored. The only one mentioned is the Sun-god (Re or Atum), who appears even in connection with the mummy, where we should have expected the appearance of Osiris. Self-indulgence and a good name *on earth* hereafter may be said to summarise the teaching of these sceptics, who have cast away the teaching of the fathers.

The beginnings of reflective morals doubtless go back to the Memphite Drama but it is not until fifteen hundred years later in the Feudal Age, especially after 2000 B.C., that the Egyptians gained the detachment which enabled them for the first time to discern human *society* as a whole, so that it became a realm which might be thoughtfully contemplated. The result of such contemplation was for some men hopeless pessimism. Was not the character of society so iniquitous that even the "good name" might be less desirable than the singer of the Song of the Harp-Player had discerned? Suppose that a man's good name be innocently and unjustly forfeited, and the opportunities for self-indulgence cut off by disease and misfortune? It is exactly this situation which is presented to us in a papyrus preserved in the Berlin Museum, perhaps the most remarkable document surviving from this remote age. We may term it "The Dialogue of a Misanthrope with his Own Soul," though no ancient title has survived. The general subject is the despair resulting from the situation mentioned, a despair which turns to death as the only escape. It is perhaps hardly necessary to call attention to the remarkable choice of such a subject in so remote an age, a subject which is essentially a *state of mind,* the inner experience of an afflicted soul unjustly suffering. It is thus the earliest known literary composition of which the subject is a spiritual experience. It is our earliest Book of Job, written some fifteen hundred years before a similar experience brought forth a similar book among the Hebrews.

The introduction narrating the circumstances which brought about this spiritual convulsion is unhappily lost. The prologue of the book is therefore lacking, but some of the facts which it must have contained, setting forth the reasons for the reflections offered by the book, can be drawn from these reflections themselves. Our unfortunate (we never learn his name) was a man of gentle spirit who nevertheless was overtaken by blighting misfortunes. He fell sick only to be forsaken by his friends, and even by his brothers, who should have cared for him in his illness. No one proved faithful to him, and in the midst of his distress his neighbours robbed him. The good that he had done yesterday was not remembered, and although a wise man, he was repulsed when he would have pleaded his cause. He was unjustly condemned, and his name, which should have been revered, became a stench in the nostrils of men.

At this juncture, when in darkness and despair he determines to take his own life, the portion of the document preserved to us begins. We see him as he stands on the brink of the grave, while his soul shrinks back from the darkness in horror and refuses to accompany him. In a long dialogue which now sets in, we discern the unfortunate man discoursing with himself, that is, conversing with his soul as with another person. The first reason for his soul's unwillingness is apprehension lest there should be no tomb in which to dwell after death. This, at first, seems strange enough in view of the scepticism with which such material preparation for death was viewed by just such men as our unfortunate proved himself to be. We soon discover, however, that this, like another which follows, was but a literary device intended to offer opportunity for exposing the utter futility of all such preparations. It would seem that the soul itself had previously advised death by fire; but that it had then itself shrunk back from this terrible end. As there would be no surviving friend or relative to stand at the bier and carry out the mortuary ceremonies, the misanthrope then proceeded to adjure his own soul to undertake this office. The soul, however, now refuses death in any form and paints the terrors of the tomb. "My soul opened its mouth and answered what I had said: 'If thou rememberest burial it is mourning, it is a bringer of tears, saddening a man; it is taking a man from his house and casting him forth upon the height (the cemetery plateau). Thou ascendest not up that thou mayest see the sun. Those who build in red granite, who erect the sepulchre in the pyramid, those beautiful in this beautiful structure, who have become like gods, the offering-tables thereof are as empty as those of these weary ones who die on the dike without a survivor, (when as he lies half immersed on the shore) the flood has taken (one) end of him, the heat likewise; those to whom the fish along the shore speak (as they devour the body). Hearken to me—lo, it is seemly for men to hearken—follow the glad day and forget care.' "

This then is the reply of the soul when the conventional view of death has been held up before it. The misanthrope has affirmed that he is fortunate "who is in his pyramid over whose coffin a survivor has stood," and he has besought his soul to be the one "who shall be my burier, who shall make offering, who shall stand at the tomb on the day of burial, that he may prepare the bed in the cemetery." But like the harp-player in the two songs we have read, his soul remembers the dismantled tombs of the great, whose offering-tables are as empty as those of the wretched serfs dying like flies among the public works, along the vast irrigation dikes, and who lie there exposed to heat and devouring fish as they await burial. There is but one solution: to live on in forgetfulness of sorrow and drown it all in pleasure.

Up to this point the Dialogue, with its philosophy of "Eat, drink, and be merry, for tomorrow we die," has gone no further than the Song of the Harp-Player. It now proceeds to a momentous conclusion, going far beyond that song. It undertakes to demonstrate that life, far from being an opportunity for pleasure and unbridled indulgence, is more intolerable than death. The demonstration is contained in four poems which the unhappy man addresses to his own soul. These constitute the second half of the document, and are fortunately much more intelligible than the first half. The first poem portrays the unjust abhorrence in which our unfortunate's name is held by the world. Each three-line strophe begins with the refrain, "My name is abhorred," and then, to enforce this statement, adduces for comparison some detestable thing from the daily life of the people, especially the notorious stench of fish and fowl so common in the life of the Nile-dweller.

THE UNJUST ABHORRENCE OF HIS NAME

"Lo, my name is abhorred,
Lo, more than the odour of birds
On summer days when the sky is hot.

Lo, my name is abhorred,
Lo, more than a fish-receiver
On the day of the catch when the sky is hot.

Lo, my name is abhorred,
Lo, more than the odour of fowl
On the willow-hill full of geese.

Lo, my name is abhorred,
Lo, more than the odour of fishermen
By the shores of the marshes when they have fished."

Six more strophes in the same vein follow. While this poem is but a rather monotonous reiteration of the fact that the unhappy man's name has become a stench in the nostrils of his fellows, in the second poem he turns from himself to characterise those who are responsible for his misery. He looks out over the society of his time and finds only corruption, dishonesty, injustice, and unfaithfulness even among his own kin. It is a fearful indictment, and as he utters it he asks himself in an ever-recurring refrain which opens each strophe, "To whom do I speak today?" His meaning probably is, "What manner of men are those to whom I speak?" and the answer following each repetition of this question is a new condemnation.

THE CORRUPTION OF MEN

"To whom do I speak today?
Brothers are evil,
Friends of today are not of love.

To whom do I speak today?
Hearts are thievish,
Every man seizes his neighbour's goods.

To whom do I speak today?
The gentle man perishes,
The bold-faced goes everywhere.

To whom do I speak today?
He of the peaceful face is wretched,
The good is disregarded in every place.

To whom do I speak today?
When a man should arouse wrath by his evil conduct,
He stirs all men to mirth, although his iniquity is wicked.

To whom do I speak today?
Robbery is practised,
Every man seizes his neighbour's goods.

To whom do I speak today?
The pest is faithful,
(But) the brother who comes with it becomes an enemy.

. . . .

To whom do I speak today?
There are no righteous,
The land is left to those who do iniquity."

The soul of the sufferer had shrunk back from death, and, like the Song of the Harp-Player, had proposed a life of pleasure as a way of escape. Deeply moved by the terror of death, and recognising the hopelessness of material preparations to meet it, the unhappy man had recoiled for a moment and turned to contemplate life. The two poems we have just read depict what he saw as he thus turned. What follows is the logical rebound from any faint hope that life may be possible, to the final conviction that death alone is the release from the misery in which he is involved. The third poem is therefore a brief hymn in praise of death. It is not an exalted contemplation of the advantages of death, such as we find fifteen hundred years later in Plato's story of the death of Socrates; nor is it comparable to the lofty pessimism of the afflicted Job; but as the earliest utterance of the unjustly afflicted, as the first cry of the righteous sufferer echoing to us from the early ages of the world, it is of unique interest and not without its beauty and its wistful pathos. It is remarkable that it contains no thought of God; it deals only with glad release from the intolerable suffering of the past and looks not forward. It is characteristic of the age and the clime to which the poem belongs, that this glad release should appear in the form of concrete pictures drawn from the daily life of the Nile-dweller.

DEATH A GLAD RELEASE

"Death is before me today
Like the recovery of a sick man,
Like going forth into a garden after sickness.

Death is before me today
Like the odour of myrrh,
Like sitting under the sail on a windy day.

Death is before me today
Like the odour of lotus flowers,
Like sitting on the shore of drunkenness.

Death is before me today
Like the course of the freshet,
Like the return of a man from the war-galley to his house.

Death is before me today
Like the clearing of the sky,
Like a man fowling towards that which he knows not.

Death is before me today
As a man longs to see his house
When he has spent many years in captivity."

In spite of the fact that these pictures are drawn from the life of a distant world, for the most part unfamiliar to us, they do not altogether fail of their effect. Life as a long sickness from which we recover at death as the convalescent enters a beautiful garden; death as the odour of myrrh borne on the fresh Nile wind, while the voyager sits beneath the bellying sail; death as the return of a war-worn wanderer in far waters approaching his home, or the glad restoration of the captive from foreign exile—these are figures of universal appeal in any age or clime.[9]

The forward glance into the ultimate future, which is so noticeably lacking in the preceding song, is the theme of the fourth poem. Each of its three strophes begins with the refrain, "He who is yonder," a common phrase, especially in the plural, "those who are yonder," for "the dead," which we have already met in the Instruction Addressed to Merikere. "He who is yonder" shall himself be a god and "inflict the punishment of wickedness on the doer of it," *not,* as in the life of our misanthrope, on the innocent. "He who is yonder" embarks with the Sun-god in his celestial ship, and shall see that the best of offerings are presented to the temples of the gods, and not (by implication) be spent in corrupt rewards or diverted by thieving officials. "He who is yonder" is a respected sage, not repelled as he appeals to the corrupt officials, but directing to the Sun-god (Re) his appeals for which his daily presence with the god affords him opportunity.

Earlier in the struggle with his soul, the sufferer had expressed the conviction that he should be justified hereafter. He now returns to this conviction in this fourth poem, with which the remarkable document closes. It

[9] Two of the figures are obscure: "the course of the freshet" is perhaps a reference to the dry water-course comparable with life, while its sudden filling by the waters of the freshet is the welcome refreshing corresponding to death. "A man fowling towards that which he knows not" may perhaps refer to the approach of the hunter to unfamiliar regions. "Sitting on the shore of drunkenness" is a picture of sensual pleasure in a drinking-booth on the dike or highway, here called "the shore."

therefore concludes with a solution likewise found among those discerned by Job—an appeal to justification hereafter (although Job does not necessarily make this a reason for seeking death), thus making death the vestibule to the judgment-hall and therefore to be sought as soon as possible.

THE HIGH PRIVILEGES OF THE SOJOURNER YONDER

"He who is yonder
Shall seize (the culprit) as a living god,
Inflicting punishment of wickedness on the doer of it.

He who is yonder
Shall stand in the celestial barque,
Causing that the choicest of the offerings there be given to the temples.

He who is yonder
Shall be a wise man who has not been repelled,
Praying to Re when he speaks."

Thus longing for the glad release which death affords and seeming to have regained some confidence in the high privileges he shall enjoy beyond, the soul of the unhappy man at last yields, he enters the shadow and passes on to be with "those who are yonder." It is not without some feeling that we watch this unknown go, the earliest human soul, into the inner chambers of which we are permitted a glimpse across a lapse of four thousand years.

The men of the Feudal Age took great pleasure in such literary efforts. This particular Berlin papyrus was copied by a book-scribe, whose concluding remark is still legible at the end of the document: "It is finished from beginning to end like that which was found in writing." He copied it therefore from an older original, and doubtless many such copies were to be found on the shelves of the thinking men of the time. The story of the Misanthrope was one which owed its origin to individual experiences through which the men of this time were really passing, and they found profit in perusing it. It is a distinct mark in the long development of self-consciousness, the slow process which culminated in the emergence of the individual as a moral force, an individual aware of conscience as an ultimate authority at whose mandate he may confront and arraign society. Such an attitude, taken by men conscious of a great moral responsibility, is familiar to us of the modern world from numerous historical examples, like the Hebrew prophets, Mohammed, Jesus, and a long line of European prophets from Savonarola to John Wesley; but human experience at the rise of the Feudal Age, over four thousand years ago, had never yet brought forth any such men. Their appearance on the Nile at this time was an epoch-making event, and the recognition of a new arena of human thought and human responsibility. Let us notice their rise a little more fully.

The story of the Misanthrope, although that of an *individual* experience, nevertheless involved scrutiny of society to whose failings this individual experience of the writer was largely due. In the Maxims of Ptahhotep, throughout the Old Kingdom, and as late as the Instruction Addressed to Merikere, the Egyptian social thinkers found great satisfaction in placidly discussing ideals of worthy conduct, of which they gained really high and noble conceptions; but they did not turn to contrast these with the actually low moral level of society. In Merikere we find the "ox of him that doeth iniquity," and some consciousness that a man's sins may be piled up beside him like mountains at the judgment, but there is no realisation of the moral unworthiness of society. We are now approaching an age in which the Egyptian sages have become fully aware of the glaring contrast between the inherited ideals of worthy character and the appalling reality in the society around them. In similar experiences of our own at the present day there is nothing new, but in that of the Misanthrope the subject himself had remained the chief or exclusive concern. On the other hand, deep concern for social degradation, combined with the ability to contemplate and discern the unworthiness of men, also appears as the subject of dark and pessimistic reflections in this remarkable age of growing self-consciousness and earliest disillusionment.

A priest of Heliopolis, in this age, a man named Khekheperre-soneb, gave expression to his sombre musings on society in a composition which was still circulating centuries later, when a scribe of the Eighteenth Dynasty copied it upon a board now preserved in the British Museum. It is of especial interest, as indicating at the outset that such men of the Feudal Age were perfectly conscious that they were thinking upon new lines, and that they had departed far from the traditional complacency which characterised the wisdom of the fathers. The priest of Heliopolis begins his little tractate as follows:

"Would that I had unknown utterances, sayings that are unfamiliar, even new speech that has not occurred (before), free from repetitions, not the utterance of what has long passed, which the ancestors spake. . . .

"I have spoken this in accordance with what I have seen, beginning with the first men down to those who shall come after. . . . Righteousness is cast out, iniquity is in the midst of the council-hall. The plans of the gods are violated, their dispositions are disregarded. The land is in distress, mourning is in every place, towns and districts are in lamentation. All men alike are under wrongs; as for respect, an end is made of it. . . .

. . . .

"When I would speak thereof, my limbs are heavy laden. I am distressed because of my heart, it is suffering to hold my peace concerning it. Another heart would bow down, (but) a brave heart in distress is the companion of its lord. Would that I had a heart able to suffer. Then would I rest in it. . . . Come then, my heart, that I may speak to thee and that thou mayest answer for me my sayings and mayest explain to me that which is in the land. . . . I am meditating on what has happened. Calamities come to pass today, tomorrow afflictions are not past. All men are silent concerning it, (although) the whole land is in great disturbance. Nobody is free from evil; all men alike do it. Hearts are sorrowful. He who gives commands is as he to whom commands are given; the heart of both of them is content. Men awake to it in the morning daily, (but) hearts thrust it not away. The fashion of yesterday therein is like today. . . . There is none so wise that he perceives, and none so angry that he speaks. Men awake in the morning to suffer every day. Long and heavy is my malady. *The poor man has no strength to save himself from him that is stronger than he.* It is painful to keep silent concerning the things heard, (but) it is suffering to reply to the ignorant man. . . ."

Here is a man deeply stirred by the corruption of his fellows. He contemplates society as a whole, and while he constantly gives expression to his own misery in view of such a prospect, it is not his own suffering which is the chief burden of his utterance. His concern is for society, shackled by its own inertia, incapable of discerning its own misery, or, if at all conscious of it, without the initiative to undertake its own regeneration. Many of his reflections might find appropriate place in the mouth of a morally sensitive social observer of our own times. It is evident, then, that an age had been reached when for the first time in history men were awakened to a deep sense of the moral unworthiness of society.

The new attitude of these social thinkers was in some measure due to an increasingly sensitive moral discernment, but other causes also contributed to their disillusionment. These men were profoundly moved by contemplation both of human life here and human destiny hereafter. We have already observed something of the tragic disillusionment with which they had discovered the futility of purely material agencies for ensuring a human soul felicity in the next world. Here was an immemorially ancient tradition of the ancestors, which had broken down, and with its collapse had gone all sense of security in the hereafter. Probably the traditional, unquestioned confidence in the wisdom of the ancestors was seriously undermined. If this had been their experience with inherited tradition regarding the life *hereafter,* they were now faring worse in their experience with life *here.* For a thousand years there had stood unshaken a national order personified and maintained by the Pharaoh and its name was Maat, "Truth-Justice-Righteousness." But this, too, was now breaking down. Already in the Instruction Addressed to Merikere, we find the nation divided into North and South, and the king betraying concern for the defense of the North against foreign invasion. Gradually the organised power, that had endured so long, disintegrated, the foreign invaders discovered the feebleness of the once great nation, and they poured into the Delta from Asia in the east and Libya on the west. Complete anarchy ensued. It must be this catastrophe that our Heliopolitan priest, whose lamentations we have just read, is describing.

The serene optimism of the Old Kingdom sages as expressed in the Maxims of Ptahhotep was darkened by a two-fold catastrophe: *first,* the complete eclipse of hope in the hereafter as based on elaborate material provision for eternal life; and *second,* the tragic collapse of a seemingly eternal administrative and moral order which had been the very framework of human society. For thinking men like our Heliopolitan priest, all hope, both for this life and the life to come, had gone down in universal darkness which not even the Sun-god could ever again dispel. In the course of possibly two thousand years of national life organised humanity had built up some seemingly imperishable values, and those which men had prized most had been completely swept away. It was the earliest known age of social disillusionment. Such apparently complete shipwreck of human hopes has happened several times since then, and the latest, following upon the World War, still overshadows us. Was lamentation to be the only response of the Egyptians, as these chilling shadows settled around them? To us who are still battling with corruption and mal-administration in human government, it is not a little interesting to follow the thoughts and the courageous response of these men of four thousand years ago as they found themselves involved in the first such catastrophe which the written documents of mankind have preserved to us.

CHAPTER XI

THE EARLIEST SOCIAL PROPHETS AND THE DAWN OF MESSIANISM

THE unrelieved pessimism of the Misanthrope, and of our Heliopolitan priest, Khekheperre-soneb, was not universal. There were contemplative men, who, while fully recognising the corruption of society and the terrible consequences of governmental disorganisation—the eclipse of Maat—nevertheless dared dream of better days. The very fact that the administrative collapse was so largely responsible for the social catastrophe led some of the optimists to believe that *better government* could restore the lost order and usher in a brighter day—even the dawn of a Golden Age. Better government! Out with corruption! That has a familiar ring. Had they been able to look down the ages that were to follow, these men of four thousand years ago, in so far as we know the first men to try it, might have lost some courage as they contemplated our Tammany investigations or our Capone trials. How was better government to be secured? To the Egyptian social thinker, the answer was obvious. Some of them were convinced that a new age might be ushered in by a generation of honest and just officials; others believed that it could be done by a righteous king as the saviour and regenerator of society. The men of the first school, as they scanned life, held wholesome and practical principles of right living applicable to the daily situation of the average member of the official class. They still believed in the imperishable supremacy of righteousness, the old Maat, and they continued to cling to the hope that it could be restored as the controlling order of Egyptian life. These views have found expression in a tractate which we may call: "The Eloquent Peasant." We are fortunate in the fact that this composition has not descended to us in a late and corrupt copy, like so many literary documents of this age, but is preserved in a stately papyrus roll, written in the Feudal Age and now in the Berlin Museum. The author, whose name, as so commonly in this impersonal age, we do not know, has cast his discussion into the form of a picturesque oriental tale, conceived solely to furnish a dramatic setting for a series of disquisitions on the proper character and spirit of the just official, and the resulting social and administrative justice towards the poor. We recall the despairing words of Khekheperre-soneb, "The poor man has no strength to save himself from him who is stronger than he." We remember how Merikere was told by his royal father that an official "who says, 'Would I had' is not impartial, he shows partiality to the one who holds his reward," that is, a bribe. The remedy recommended to Prince Merikere at Heracleopolis was plentiful incomes for all his officials.

We are now to see that this remedy had not of itself proved sufficient. Within sight of the palace, on the outskirts of Heracleopolis, we are now to witness a deed of cruel oppression by a corrupt official on the estate of the king's own Grand Steward—a deed of cruelty demonstrating quite conclusively that liberal official incomes will not save the poor from official oppression. It is not a little interesting to discern this ancient thinker who wrote The Eloquent Peasant four thousand years ago, wrestling with a difficulty which has since then continued to be one of the most refractory problems of all administrators in the East, a problem which has not been wholly solved even under the skilled and experienced administration of England in modern Egypt. A peasant of the Faiyum region in the Natron district of the western desert, living in a village called the Salt-Field, finds the family granary nearly empty. He therefore loads a small train of donkeys with the produce of his village and goes down to Heracleopolis, near the mouth of the Faiyum, to trade for grain. On the way thither he is obliged to pass the house of one Thutenakht, a subordinate official among the people of Rensi, who was no less a noble than the Grand Steward of the Pharaoh himself, whose royal residence was at Heracleopolis. Now, when Thutenakht sees the donkeys of the peasant approaching, he at once devises a plan for seizing them. Sending a servant hastily into the house, he secures thence a chest filled with linen, which he takes out of the chest and spreads out in the highway so as to cover it entirely from the edge of a grain-field on the upper side of the road to the water of the canal on the lower. The unsuspecting peasant approaches, as the tale, with a discernible touch of the writer's indignation, states, "on the way belonging to every one," which Thutenakht has thus blocked. Fearing the water below, the peasant turns upward to skirt the edge of the grain-field. As the donkeys pass, one of them nips a mouthful of the tempting grain, at once affording the wily Thutenakht the opportunity he desired. The peasant pathetically maintains the attitude and the speech of deprecatory but not servile courtesy, until with loud complaint Thutenakht seizes the asses. Thereupon the peasant repeats his former courteous remonstrance, but adds a bold protest. "My way is right. One side is blocked. I bring my donkey along the edge thereof, and thou seizest him because he has plucked a mouthful of the grain. Now, I know the lord of this domain. It belongs to the Grand Steward, Meru's son, Rensi. Now, it is he who drives off every robber in this whole land. Shall I then be robbed in his domain!" Infuriated by the peasant's boldness, Thutenakht seizes a branch of green tamarisk, mercilessly beats his victim, and, in spite of the peasant's cries and protests, drives off all the asses to his own quarters. After four days of fruitless pleading for the return of the asses, the unhappy peasant, all the time knowing that his family at home is on the verge of starvation, determines to apply to the Grand Steward himself, on whose domain the outrage occurred. He is the more encouraged in so doing by the proverbial reputation for justice which the Grand Steward enjoys. As the peasant approaches the city, he fortunately meets the Grand Steward issuing from the shoregate of his estate and going down to embark in his state barge on the canal. By the most ceremonious politeness and complete command of the current diplomacy of address, the peasant gains the ear of the great man for a moment as he passes, so that he sends a body-servant to hear the peasant's story. When the servant has returned and communicated Thutenakht's theft to Rensi, the Grand Steward lays the affair before his suite of officials. Their reply is the author's skilfully created occasion for bringing before the reader, without comment, the current and conventional treatment of such complaints of the poor in official circles. The colleagues of the Grand Steward at once range themselves on the side of their subordinate, the thievish Thutenakht. They reply to Rensi, with much indifference, that the case is probably one of a peasant who has been paying his dues to the wrong superior officer, and that Thutenakht has merely seized dues which rightfully belonged to him. They ask with indignation, "Shall Thutenakht be punished for a little natron and a little salt? (Or at most) let it be commanded him to replace it and he will replace it." It is characteristic of their class that they quite ignore the asses, the loss of which means starvation to the peasant and his family.

Meantime the peasant stands by and hears his fatal loss thus slurred over and ignored by those in authority. The Grand Steward meanwhile sits musing in silence. It is a tableau which epitomises ages of social history in the East: on the one hand, the brilliant group of the great man's sleek and subservient suite, the universal type of the official class; and, on the other, the friendless and forlorn figure of the despoiled peasant, the pathetic personification of the cry for social justice. This scene is one of the earliest examples of that oriental skill in setting forth abstract principles in concrete situations, so wonderfully illustrated later in the parables of Jesus. Seeing that the Grand Steward makes no reply, the peasant makes another effort to save his family and himself from the starvation which threatens them all. He steps forward and with amazing eloquence addresses the great man in whose hands his case now rests, promising him a fair voyage as he embarks on the canal and voicing the fame of the Grand Steward's benevolence on which he had reckoned. "For thou art the father of the orphan, the husband of the widow, the brother of the forsaken, the kilt of the motherless. Let me put thy name in this land above every good law, O leader free from avarice, great man free from littleness, who destroyest unrighteousness and establishest righteousness. Respond to the cry which my mouth utters, when I speak, hear thou. Do justice, thou who art praised, whom the praised praise. Relieve my misery. Behold me, I am heavy laden; prove me, lo I am in loss."[1]

The Grand Steward is so pleased with the peasant's extraordinary readiness in speech, that he leaves him without giving any decision in his case, and proceeds at once to the court, where he says to the king: "My lord, I have found one of these peasants who is verily beautiful of speech." The king, greatly pleased, charges the Grand Steward to lead the peasant on without giving him a decision, in order that he may deliver himself of further addresses. The king likewise commands that what the peasant says shall be carefully written down, that meantime he shall be supplied with food and maintenance, and that a servant be sent to his village to see that his family suffers no want in the interval. As a result of these arrangements, the peasant then proceeds to make no less than eight successive appeals to Rensi. At this point we have reached the end of the dramatic introduction, which was intended to give a social treatise the form of a tale and we begin the eight speeches which together form a social tractate.

These addresses to the Grand Steward at first reflect the grievous disappointment of the peasant in view of the great man's reputation for unswerving justice. He therefore begins his *second* address with reproaches, which Rensi interrupts with threats. The peasant is undaunted and continues his reproof. The *third* speech reverts to praises like those of his first appeal to Rensi. "O Grand Steward, my lord! Thou art Re, lord of the sky together with thy court. All the sustenance of men is from thee,

[1] In the older Berlin papyrus the conclusion reads: "Count me (or 'prove me'), lo, I am few."

as from the flood (inundation); thou art the Nile that maketh green the fields and furnisheth the waste lands. Ward off the robber, protect the wretched, become not a torrent against him who pleads. Take heed, (for) eternity draws near. Prefer acting as it is (proverbially) said, 'It is the breath of the nostrils to do justice' (or 'right,' Maat). Execute punishment on him to whom punishment is due, and none shall be like thy uprightness. Do the balances err? Does the scale-beam swerve to one side? . . . Speak not falsehood, (for) thou art great (and therefore responsible). Be not light, (for) thou art weighty. Speak not falsehood, for thou art the balances. Swerve not, for thou art uprightness. Lo, thou art at one with the balances. If they deflect thou deflectest (falsely). . . . Thy tongue is the plummet (of the balances), thy heart is the weight, thy two lips are the beam thereof."

These comparisons of the Grand Steward's character and functions with the balances appear repeatedly in the speeches of the peasant.[2] Their lesson is evident. The norm of just procedure is in the hands of the ruling class. If they fail, where else shall it be found? It is expected that they shall weigh right and wrong and reach a just decision with the infallibility of accurate balances. The balances thus form a symbol which became widely current in Egyptian life, till the scales appear as the graphic means of depicting the judgment of each soul in the hereafter. They appear here for the first time in the history of morals, and in the hands of blind Justice they have survived even into our own day. But this symbol had its origin among these social thinkers of the Feudal Age in Egypt four thousand years ago. Not only the balances as

[2] It is a comparison which the great nobles of the Feudal Age were fond of using on their tomb stelæ.

a whole but also its parts appear constantly as symbols of rectitude in the Feudal Age. We find the supporting "post," the "scale-beam" borne upon it, and especially the "plumb-line" and the "weight" attached to it, which hung from a projecting peg at the top of the supporting post. An index pointer, extending vertically downward from the centre of the scale-beam and firmly attached at right angles to it, moved with the scale-beam and when weighing, it could be constantly compared with the plumb-line hanging behind it. When the tip of the pointer was exactly in line with the plumb-line, the beam of the balances was level and the scales were in exact balance. The unswerving plumb-line was thus an infallible test of the balances. It should be noticed at this point that the peasant reminds the Grand Steward of his own appearance before the judgment of the impartial balances. "Take heed," says he "(for) eternity draws near." This is one of few appeals against injustice to the future responsibility of the oppressor. It is found once more also in this document, in the second speech of the peasant.

The threats of the peasant now prove too keen for the Grand Steward as he stands before the palace, and he despatches two servants to flog the unhappy man. Nevertheless the peasant undauntedly awaits Rensi's coming, as he issues from the state temple of the residence, and having addressed him in a *fourth* speech, then proceeds in a *fifth,* which, though the shortest of them all, is even sharper in denunciation. "Thou art appointed," he says, "to hear causes, to judge two litigants, to ward off the robber. But thou makest common cause with the thief. Men love thee, although thou art a transgressor. Thou art set for a dam for the poor man to save him from drowning, but behold thou art his moving flood."

Still there is no response from Rensi, and the peasant begins a *sixth* address with renewed appeal to the great man's sense of justice and his reputation for benevolence. "O Grand Steward, my lord! Destroy injustice, bring about justice. Bring about every good thing, destroy every evil thing; like the coming of satiety, that it may end hunger; (or) clothing, that it may end nakedness; like the peaceful sky after the violent tempest, that it may warm those who suffer cold; like fire that cooks what is raw; like water that quenches thirst."

As Rensi remains unresponsive to this appeal, the wretched peasant is again goaded to denunciation. "Thou art instructed, thou art educated, thou art taught, but not for robbery. Thou art accustomed to do like all men and thy kin are (likewise) ensnared. (Thou), the rectitude of all men, art the (chief) transgressor of the whole land. The gardener of evil waters his field with iniquity that his fields may bring forth falsehood, in order to flood the estate with wickedness." Even such denunciation seems now to leave the Grand Steward entirely indifferent and the peasant approaches for his *seventh* speech. He begins with the usual florid encomium in which the Grand Steward is the "rudder of the whole land according to whose command the land sails," but turns soon to his own miserable condition. "My belly[3] is full, and my heart is burdened," he complains; "there is a break in the dam and the waters thereof rush out. (Thus) my mouth is opened to speak." Then as the indifference of this man of just and benevolent reputation continues, the unhappy peasant's provocation is such that the silence of the Grand Steward appears as something which would have aroused

[3] "Belly" as the seat of emotions. The same idea, describing an anxious petitioner, is found in Ptahhotep's admonitions to treat a petitioner kindly. See p. 136.

the speech of the most stupid and faltering of pleaders. "There is none silent whom thou wouldst not have roused to speech. There is none sleeping whom thou wouldst not have wakened. There is none depressed whom thou wouldst not have aroused. There is no closed mouth which thou wouldst not have opened. There is none ignorant whom thou wouldst not have made wise. There is none foolish whom thou wouldst not have taught." Unable to restrain the tide of his indignation, therefore, the peasant goes on to his *eighth* speech and continued denunciation. "Thy heart is avaricious; it becomes thee not. Thou robbest; it profiteth thee not. . . . The officials who were installed to ward off iniquity are a refuge for the unbridled, (even) the officials who were installed to prevent injustice." The appeal to justice, however, is not abandoned, and the peasant returns to it in the most remarkable utterances of this remarkable tractate. "Do justice for the sake of the lord of justice whose justice has indeed become justice, thou (who art) Pen and Roll and Writing Palette, (even) Thoth,[4] being far removed from doing evil; when right is (really) right, then is it (indeed) right. *For justice (Maat) is for eternity. It descendeth with him that doeth it into the grave, when he is placed in the coffin and laid in the earth. His name is not effaced on earth, but he is remembered because of right. Such is the uprightness of the word of God.*" Upon these impressive words follows naturally the question whether, in spite of this, injustice is still possible; and so the peasant asks: "Is he a (hand) balance, not swerving? Is he a standing balance, not deflecting?" Or is it merely that no decision at all has been reached to right the shameful wrong which he has suffered? And yet the

[4] God of writing and legal procedure.

just magistrate who might have righted it has been present from the beginning. "Thou hast not been sick, thou hast not fled, thou hast not perished! (But) thou hast not given me requital for this good word which came out of the mouth of Re himself: 'Speak the truth, do the truth.[5] For it is great, it is mighty, it is enduring. The reward thereof shall find thee, and it shall follow thee unto revered old age.' "

No response from Rensi follows these noble words. The peasant lifts up his voice again in a final despairing plea, his *ninth* address. He reminds the Grand Steward of the dangers of consorting with deceit; he who does so "shall have no children and no heirs on earth. As for him who sails with it (deceit), he shall not reach the land, and his vessel shall not moor at her haven. . . . There is no yesterday for the indifferent. There is no friend for him who is deaf to justice. There is no glad day for the avaricious. . . . Lo, I make my plea to thee, but thou hearest it not. I will go and make my plea because of thee to Anubis." In view of the fact that Anubis is a god of the dead, the peasant doubtless means that he goes to take his own life. The Grand Steward sends his servants to bring him back as he departs, and some unintelligible words pass between them. Meantime, Rensi had committed "to a new papyrus roll every petition (of the peasant) according to its day." It is supposably a copy of this roll which has descended to us; but, unfortunately, the conclusion is much mutilated. We can only discern that the roll prepared by Rensi's secretaries is taken by him to the king, who found "it more pleasant to his heart than anything in this whole land."

[5] In such an utterance as this it is important to remember that "truth" (Maat) is always the same word which the Egyptian employs for "right, righteousness, justice," according to the connection in which it is used. In such an injunction as this we cannot distinguish any particular one of these concepts to the exclusion of the rest.

The king commands the Grand Steward to decide the peasant's case; the attendants bring in the census-rolls, which determine where he officially belongs, his exact legal and social status, the number of people in his household, and the amount of his property. Less than a dozen broken words follow, from which it is probable that Thutenakht was punished, and that the possessions of that greedy and plundering official were bestowed upon the peasant.

It is remarkable, indeed, to find the aristocrats of the Pharaoh's court four thousand years ago sufficiently concerned for the welfare of the lower classes to have given themselves the trouble to issue treatises like these, which were very evidently propaganda for a régime of justice and kindness towards the poor. Such men were pamphleteers in a crusade for social justice. They have made this particular pamphlet, too, pleasant reading for the patrician class to whom it was directed. In spite of the constant obscurity of the language, the florid style, and the bold and extreme figures of speech, which make much of the peasant's eloquence unintelligible to the modern scholar, this treatise enjoyed a place as literature of a high order in its day. It is evidently in the approved style of its age, and the pungent humour which here and there reaches the surface could but enhance the literary reputation of the tractate in the estimation of the humour-loving Egyptians. But it was literature with a moral purpose.

The tale of the Eloquent Peasant is a good illustration of the helplessness of honest officials if not supported by a just and benevolent sovereign. There were social thinkers of the time who recognised this need of a righteous ruler. Among the sages who looked forward to the advent of such a righteous king was Ipuwer, a social prophet of this great age, who has put into dramatic setting not only his passionate arraignment of the times, but also constructive admonitions looking towards the regeneration of society and a golden age which he dared to hope might follow. This, one of the most remarkable documents of this whole group of social and moral tractates of the Feudal Age, may be called the "Admonitions of Ipuwer."[6] The beginning of the papyrus, containing the narrative introduction setting forth the circumstances under which the sage utters his reflections, is unfortunately lost. The situation in its chief externals is, however, clear, and the document may be summarised as follows. The wise man Ipuwer, in the presence of an unknown, unidentified king and of some others, possibly the assembled court, delivers a long and impassioned arraignment of the times concluding with counsel and admonition. A brief rejoinder by the king follows, and a few words of reply by the sage conclude the pamphlet. Of the long principal oration by the wise man, constituting the bulk of the treatise, over two-thirds is occupied by this arraignment; that is, nearly ten out of nearly fourteen pages. This indictment displays no logical arrangement of content, though there has been evident effort to dispose the utterances of the sage in strophic form, each strophe beginning with the same phrase, just as in the poem of the Misanthrope. In the following paragraphs we shall endeavour to summarise by subjects the chief content of the arraignment, with brief quotation to indicate the character of the wise man's utterances. The fragmentary condition of the papyrus and the extreme difficulty of the language employed make a

[6] So Gardiner, in what will remain the standard edition. See Alan H. Gardiner, *The Admonitions of an Egyptian Sage* (Leipzig, 1909).

continuous translation, even with copious commentary, quite out of the question.[7]

With searching vision the sage sweeps his eye over the organised life of the Nile-dwellers and finds all in confusion. Government is practically suspended, "the laws of the judgment-hall are cast forth, men walk upon [them] in the public places, the poor break them open in the midst of the streets."[8] This disorganisation of government is due to a state of violence and warfare within the land. "A man smites his brother of the same mother. What is to be done?" . . . "Behold a man is slain by the side of his brother, while he (the brother) forsakes him to save his own limbs." . . . "A man regards his son as his enemy. . . ." "A man goes to plough bearing his shield. . . ."

To this condition of disorganisation and revolt within are added the terrors of foreign invasion. A prey to internal disorder and revolt, helpless before the raids of the Asiatics on the eastern frontiers of the Delta, the property of Egypt is destroyed and the economic processes of the land cease. "Behold, all the craftsmen, they do no work; the enemies of the land impoverish its crafts. [Behold, he who reaped] the harvest knows naught of it; he who has not ploughed [fills his granaries]. . . ." "Behold, cattle are left straying; there is none gathering them together. Every man brings for himself those that are branded with his name. . . ." "Civil war pays no taxes. . . . For what is a treasury without its revenues?"

[7] The translations are chiefly those of Gardiner, who has been commendably cautious in his renderings.

[8] This was particularly heinous from the orderly Egyptian's point of view; the withdrawing of writings and records from the public offices for purposes of evidence or consultation was carefully regulated. The regulations governing the vizier's office have survived; see Breasted, *Ancient Records of Egypt*, Vol. II, p. 276.

Under such economic conditions at home, foreign commerce decays and disappears. "Men sail not northward to [Byb]los[9] today. What shall we do for cedars for our mummies, with the tribute of which priests are buried; and with the oil of which [princes] are embalmed as far as Keftyew (Crete). They return no more." Such conditions might be expected, for the public safety of men and merchandise has vanished. "Although the roads are guarded, men sit in the thickets until the benighted traveller comes, in order to seize his burden. That which is upon him is taken away. He is beaten with blows of a stick and wickedly slain." "Indeed, the land turns around (the order of things is overturned) as does a potter's wheel. He who was a robber is lord of wealth, [the rich man] is (now) one plundered." Thus, as the figure of the "potter's wheel" suggests, all is overturned. Social conditions have suffered complete upheaval. In the longest series of utterances in the document, all similarly constructed, the sage sets forth the altered conditions of certain individuals and classes of society, each utterance contrasting what *was* with what *now is.* "Behold, he who had no yoke of oxen is (now) possessor of a herd; and he who found no plough-oxen for himself is (now) owner of a herd. Behold, he who had no grain is (now) owner of granaries; and he who used to fetch grain for himself (now) has it issued (from his own granary)."

In the general ruin moral decadence is, of course, involved, though it is not emphasised as the cause of the universal misery. "The man of virtues walks in mourning by reason of what has happened in the land"; others say, "If I knew where God is, then would I make offerings to him." "Indeed, [righteousness] is in the land

[9] At that time the greatest commercial port of Phœnicia.

(only) in this its name; what men do, in appealing to it, is iniquity."[10] Little wonder that there is universal despair. "Indeed, mirth has perished, it is no longer made; it is sighing that is in the land, mingled with lamentations." "Indeed, great and small [say], 'I would that I might die.' Little children say, 'Would there were none to keep me alive.'" . . . "Indeed, all the flocks, their hearts weep; the cattle sigh by reason of the state of the land." The sage cannot view all this dispassionately; he, too, is deeply affected by the universal calamity and prays for the end of all. "Would that there might be an end of men, that there might be no conception, no birth. If the land would but cease from noise, and strife be no more." He even chides himself that he has not endeavoured to save the situation before. "Would that I had uttered my voice at that time, that it might save me from the suffering wherein I am. . . . Woe is me for the misery in this time!"

Such is the dark picture painted by the Egyptian sage. This arraignment, occupying, as we have said, nearly two thirds of the document as preserved, must be regarded as setting forth the conditions in Egypt at a very definite time. The close relationship in language, thought, and point of view between this tractate of Ipuwer and the other social pamphlets known to belong to the Feudal Age, leaves little question as to the date of our document. The unhappy state of Egypt depicted by the sage is obviously the situation which we must recognise as having followed the complete collapse of government and the foreign invasions subsequent to the fall of the Old

[10] The restoration of "righteousness" (Maat) is due to Sethe, and in view of its frequent occurrence, as the opposite of the word here used as "iniquity" (*ysft*), from the Pyramid Texts on, the restoration fits the context admirably, but Gardiner states that the traces in the lacuna do not favour the restoration. The original hieratic of the passage is not included in his publication.

Kingdom, the end of the Pyramid Age, and the dissolution of the Second Union.

As might be imagined from the intense grief with which Ipuwer views the misery of the time, he is not content to leave his generation in this hopeless state and eventually he discerns reason for hope. Out of a large lacuna in the fragmentary papyrus there emerges at last the most important passage in the entire speech of the sage, and one of the most important in the whole range of Egyptian literature.

In this remarkable utterance the sage looks forward to the restoration of the land, doubtless as a natural consequence of the admonitions to reform which he has just laid upon the hearts of his countrymen. He sees the ideal ruler for whose advent he longs. That ideal king once ruled Egypt as the Sun-god Re, and as the sage recalls his divine sovereignty as a golden age, he contrasts it with the iniquitous reign under which the land now suffers. "He brings cooling to the flame (of the social conflagration). It is said he is the shepherd[11] of all men. There is no evil in his heart. When his herds are few, he passes the day to gather them together, their hearts being fevered.[12] Would that he had discerned their character in the first generation. Then would he have smitten evil. He would have stretched forth his arm against it. He would have smitten the seed thereof and their inheritance. . . . Where is he today? Doth he sleep perchance? Behold his might is not seen."

Here is a picture of the ideal sovereign, the righteous

[11] Or "herdman." The Sun-god is called "a valiant herdman who drives his cattle" in a sun-hymn of the Eighteenth Dynasty, and in Merikere men are called "the flocks of God," shown by the context to be the Sun-god.

[12] This probably means thirsty, perhaps a symbol for afflicted. Compare the hearts of the "flocks (small cattle) weeping" above, p. 197.

ruler with "no evil in his heart," who goes about like a "shepherd" gathering his reduced and thirsty herds. Such a righteous reign, like that of David in Hebrew tradition, has been, and may be again. The element of hope, that the advent of the good king is imminent, is unmistakable in the final words: "Where is he today? Doth he sleep perchance? Behold his might is not seen." With this last utterance one involuntarily adds, "as yet." The peculiar significance of the picture lies in the fact that, if not the social programme, at least the social ideals, the golden dream of the thinkers of this far-off age, already included the ideal ruler of spotless character and benevolent purposes who would cherish and protect his own and crush the wicked. Whether the coming of this ruler is definitely predicted or not, the vision of his character and his work is here unmistakably lifted up by the ancient sage—lifted up in the presence of the living king and those assembled with him, that they may catch something of its splendour. This is, of course, Messianism nearly fifteen hundred years before its appearance among the Hebrews.

In the mind of the sage the awful contrast between the rule of the ideal king and that of the living Pharaoh, in whose presence he stands, now calls forth the fiercest denunciation of his sovereign. Like Nathan[13] with his biting words to David, "Thou art the man," he places the responsibility for all that he has so vividly recalled, upon the shoulders of the king. "Royal Command, Knowledge, and Righteousness (Maat) are with thee," he says, (but) "it is strife which thou puttest in the land, together with the sound of tumult. . . . Thou hast (so) done as to bring forth these things. Thou hast spoken unrighteousness." When the sage had completed his long address, the

[13] The similarity was noticed by Gardiner.

king actually made a reply, though we are unable to recover it from the broken fragments of the tattered page on which it was written.

The wise man's reproaches culminated in a scathing reference to the Pharaoh's traditional character endowed with "royal command, knowledge, and Maat," the ancient administrative and moral order, which the sovereigns of the Second Union had maintained for a thousand years, and which had now given way to anarchy. It is therefore clear enough that the situation of public disorder described by Ipuwer arose at some juncture in the period following the fall of the Old Kingdom. It is now impossible to discern the position of the remarkable kings of Heracleopolis who produced such extraordinary idealistic treatises, or to determine their relation to the collapse of the State. Was their social idealism, in such an age, one of the causes of political weakness? We have observed that in the midst of the national desolation, thus pictured without reserve, the prophet Ipuwer still maintained some hope of saving the wreck. Did he have some able man in mind among the survivors of the old princely families? In view of the utterances of another sage of the same period, to whom we shall presently listen, it is not unlikely that his hopes were already fixed upon a leader, "whose might is not seen," as he asks the wistful questions, "Where is he today? doth he sleep perchance?" Another social prophet of the time, as we shall now see, actually has very definitely in mind the identity of the coming king who is to usher in the New Age, and does not hesitate to mention his name.

In a papyrus discovered by Golénischeff and now in the museum at Leningrad, we have the prophetic utterances of a priestly lector, named Neferrohu, alleged to have been delivered in the presence of King Snefru, well nigh a thousand years before the time with which they deal. This is simply the dramatic setting to give effect to Neferrohu's significant utterances. Fortunately for us, a scribe of the Egyptian Empire in the Fifteenth Century B.C. found them of interest, and lacking fresh paper for copying them, he took some old accounts from his files and copied them on the backs of these account sheets. In this casual form, and obscured by innumerable mistakes which slipped in as they were being thus casually copied, the prophecies of Neferrohu have survived to us.

After the alleged historical introduction, Neferrohu pictures the desolation and anarchy which he finds around him. Like Khekheperre-soneb he speaks to his own heart, "Give heed, my heart, and weep for this land whence thou art sprung. . . . Ruined is this land, while none is concerned for it, none speaks, and none sheds tears. How fares this land? The sun is veiled and he shines not that the people may see." Because the great public works of irrigation have stopped "The river of Egypt is dry, one may cross it on foot. When one shall seek water for the ships for sailing it (the river), his way becomes shore and shore becomes water. All good things have passed away, the land is prostrate in wretchedness by reason of that food of the Bedouin who invade the land. Enemies have arisen in Egypt, the Asiatics have descended into Egypt. . . . I will show thee the land invaded and suffering. What never had happened has happened. . . ."

"A man sits in his corner turning his back while one slays another.

"I will show thee a son as an enemy, a brother as a foe, and a man slaying his own father. Every mouth is filled with 'Love me!' (a beggar's cry?) and all good things have passed away. The land is perishing . . . the property of a man is taken from him and given to an outsider.

"I will show thee the possessor in want and the outsider satisfied. . . . The land is diminished while its rulers are multiplied. . . . Scanty is the grain, while the grain-measure is large and it is measured (by the tax-gatherer) running over. . . .

"I will show thee the land invaded and suffering. . . . The district of Heliopolis shall no longer be the birth-land of every god."

Then without hesitation or uncertainty Neferrohu turns away from this picture of a land lying desolate and in the following remarkable words proclaims the coming of the king who is to save it.

"There shall be a king of the South to come, whose name is Ameni. He is the son of a woman of Nubia, born of [Upper Egypt]. He shall take the White Crown, he shall put on the Red Crown, uniting the double diadem; he shall pacify the Two Lands (Egypt) with what they desire. . . .

"The people of his time shall rejoice, the son of man shall make his name forever and ever. Those who plotted evil and devised rebellion, they have stilled their mouths for fear of him. The Asiatics shall fall by his sword and the Libyans shall fall by his flame. The revolters shall yield to his counsels and the rebellious to his might. The uræus serpent-crest on his brow shall subdue for him the rebellious.

"They shall build the 'Wall of the Ruler,' so that the Asiatics shall not be suffered to go down into Egypt. They shall beg for water after their traditional manner, in order to give their flocks to drink.

"Righteousness (*Maat*) *shall return to its place, un-*

righteousness shall be cast out. Let him rejoice who shall see it and who shall be serving the king."

Here we have the actual advent of the saviour-king, whose coming was the hope of Ipuwer. Neferrohu knows him by name. Ameni, the form of the name which Neferrohu employs, is a well-known informal abbreviation of the fuller form, "Amenemhet." This is obviously the great founder of the Twelfth Dynasty, the restorer who re-established the power of Egypt in the Feudal Age about 2000 B.C., and is significantly stated in an historical inscription of three generations later, to have "cast out unrighteousness, . . . because he so greatly loved righteousness (Maat)."[14] Our seer is confident that his hero will assume the two crowns of the double diadem that symbolises the united sovereignty of both Upper and Lower Egypt and usher in a new day. He places the great restoration for the most part still in the future. This raises an interesting question. Was this bold assertion merely a *vaticinium post eventum,* a prediction after the event, or was it a triumphant proclamation of a victorious champion who had already accomplished so much in the restoration of the South that his ultimate triumph and restoration of all Egypt could be foreseen? Was Neferrohu perhaps actually dispatched by Amenemhet to the North to proclaim his coming? Or was he merely a partisan of Amenemhet, who glorifies the restoration by picturing it against the background of the preceding ruin and desolation? It is impossible to furnish a conclusive answer to these questions, but there seems to be greater reason for concluding that Neferrohu was really surrounded by the desolation which he so vividly pictured, and that Amenemhet's vic-

[14] See Breasted, *Ancient Records of Egypt,* Vol. I, p. 283. Nile tourists may recall having seen this great inscription running around the base of the wall in the impressive rock-hewn chapel of the tomb of Khnumhotep at Benihasan.

torious career in the South had already made it evident that he would succeed in reuniting all Egypt and restoring its ancient glory. In this connection it is at first very surprising that Neferrohu frankly discloses the fact that the new Pharaoh was not a son of the old royal line. There had doubtless been so many claimants and pretenders that the advent of another such pretender would not have made any impression. The designation employed by the seer, the "son of man," is striking and at once suggests connections where perhaps we should see none. The term is employed in the Instruction Addressed to Merikere to designate the son of a man of importance. A similar term was also used in ancient Babylonia.

The seer's proclamation includes two coming achievements of his king, which were of vital importance to the unhappy people of prostrate Egypt. These were: first, the extermination of the invaders and protection against future invasion; and second, the restoration of internal order. The "Wall of the Ruler" was an ancient fortress of the eastern Delta on the Asiatic frontier, which had been built to guard the road from Asia into Egypt in the days of the Pyramid Builders, and Neferrohu announces that the new king will build it as before. The seer's picture of the resulting situation of the Asiatics reminds us strikingly of the Hebrew tradition regarding the journeys of their ancestors into Egypt. The announcement of the restoration of internal order is remarkable for its brevity and simplicity: "Righteousness shall return to its place, and unrighteousness shall be cast out." It is the old "Maat"[15] which the new king will restore as the established order by which the life of the Egyptian people is again to be governed and controlled. "Maat," that ancient order which for a thousand years had been the guide of ruler and gov-

[15] See above, pp. 144–147.

ernment, was again to resume its sway, and presumably the rejoicing, which the old seer announces, signified the return of the old ideals of worthy conduct and the old happiness.

Such was, alas, far from the actual reality. Amenemhet was indeed one of the great administrators of the ancient world and gifted with remarkable sagacity. He undoubtedly restored the ancient order in so far as it was at all possible to do so; but he was unavoidably obliged to use as his servants and officials in the administration of the nation's affairs, the men produced and fashioned by the generations of decadence which had followed the Pyramid Age. They had not escaped the devastating effect of lawlessness and degradation into which the Egyptian people had fallen during generations, perhaps centuries of anarchy from which Amenemhet had now saved them. The moral vision of such men as the Misanthrope, Khekheperre-soneb, the Heliopolitan priest, and, not least, of Ipuwer, has revealed to us an appalling condition of social degradation. Old Ptahhotep's serene conviction that all was well, had vanished forever, and Amenemhet, the king himself, was fully aware of the fact.

After a long and successful reign, lasting for a generation, the distrust of men, which had afflicted the old king all his life, received a final confirmation. He suffered a base attempt upon his life. As he began to feel the burden of years he addressed to his son, the first to bear the great name of Sesostris, a brief word of counsel, after the manner of Prince Merikere's father, but in a very different spirit.

> "He saith, while distinguishing righteousness,
> For his son . . .
>
> . . . .

Hearken to that which I say to thee,
That thou mayest be king of the land,
That thou mayest be ruler of the shores,
That thou mayest increase good.
Harden thyself against all subordinates.
The people give heed to him who terrorises them.
Approach them not alone,
Fill not thy heart with a brother,
Know not a friend,
Nor make for thyself intimates,
Wherein there is no end.
When thou sleepest, guard for thyself thine own heart;
For a man has no people
In the day of evil.
I gave to the beggar, I nourished the orphan;
I admitted the insignificant as well as him who was of great account.
(But) he who ate my food made insurrection;
He to whom I gave my hand aroused fear therein."

This picture of pessimistic distrust of men is followed by the story of the attempt on his life, an incident which accounts to some extent for the disillusionment of the embittered old king.

These views of human society, the profound distrust of men, were so deeply felt that they cast their shadow on the greatest art of the time, the portrait sculpture of the Feudal Age. In the noble portraits of these Middle Kingdom Pharaohs we find the same sombre shadows with which they looked out upon the life of their time. As we look upon these heroic and undaunted faces, darkened by indefinable shadows of hopelessness and despair, we realise that these portraits themselves are a striking social revelation in the field of art, disclosing to us unmistakably the spirit of this earliest age of disillusionment.

CHAPTER XII

THE EARLIEST CRUSADE FOR SOCIAL JUSTICE AND THE DEMOCRATISATION OF MORAL RESPONSIBILITY

Not all of the social thinkers at the court of the Pharaoh in the Feudal Age shared the unqualified pessimism of the sovereign himself. We have seen how some of them recognised the fact that the righteous king, the hope of Messianic dreamers, would be helpless without a body of just officials, and the treatise we have called the Eloquent Peasant was intended to aid in creating a body of worthy and honest officials who should usher in the era of social justice.

The question now arises whether these social treatises of the Feudal Age really became social forces. In 1922 I purchased from a native antiquity dealer in Luxor a sizeable flake of limestone, covered on both sides with hieratic writing, a piece such as scholars commonly call an *ostrakon*. My friend Doctor Gardiner noticed that, among other things, the writing contained a quotation from the Eloquent Peasant. The piece evidently dated from the Twelfth or Thirteenth Century B.C. and showed that the peasant's eloquence was still esteemed in the late Egyptian Empire.

Do the surviving sources disclosing the government and the society of the Feudal Age itself, however, indicate that this crusade for social justice achieved any results? Or did the Messianic hopes and the high ideals of social justice so unequivocally expressed by the social prophets of this age remain only dreams? Did the gloomy and depressing pictures which we have found in the writings of such pessimists as the Misanthrope, Khekheperre-soneb, and King Amenemhet I continue to be the actual reality? Did the awakening of the Feudal Age to what seemed to be the real character of human society and the resulting terrible disillusionment remain without any fruitful constructive results?

We have seen that the hopes of the Messianists were based on the advent of a righteous *king,* while more practical social reformers sought the transformation of society in a new generation of *just officials.* In spite of the pessimism of Amenemhet I, we have very conclusive evidence that the sovereign himself made carefully conceived efforts and plans for ensuring a righteous reign. The Pharaoh's mouthpiece and the chief organ of government under the king was the prime minister, the grand vizier. Preserved only in Empire copies some centuries later than the Feudal Age is an address orally delivered to the vizier by the king in person whenever a new incumbent was inducted into the vizierial office. This remarkable address shows that the dreams of such Messianists as Ipuwer and Neferrohu had been realised, in so far as the character of the sovereign was concerned. Their spirit of social justice had reached the throne itself and pervaded even the very structure of the state. The address is as follows:

"Regulation laid upon the Vizier X.[1] The council was conducted into the audience hall of Pharaoh, Life! Prosperity! Health! One (meaning the king) caused that there be brought in the Vizier X, newly appointed."

[1] Here of course was the name of the vizier, varying from incumbent to incumbent.

"Said his majesty to him, 'Look to the office of the vizier; be watchful over all that is done therein. Behold it is the established support of the whole land.

" 'Behold, as for the vizierate, it is not sweet; behold, it is bitter. . . . He (the vizier) is copper enclosing the gold of his [lord's] house. Behold it (the vizierate) is not to show respect-of-persons to princes and councillors; it is not to make for himself slaves of any people. . . .

" 'Behold, when a petitioner comes from Upper or Lower Egypt (even) the whole land, . . . see thou to it that everything is done in accordance with law, that everything is done according to the custom thereof, [giving] to [every man] his right. Behold a prince is in a conspicuous place, water and wind report concerning all that he does. For, behold, that which is done by him never remains unknown. . . .' "

The Pharaoh then stipulates in detail the methods by which the vizier shall deal with causes brought before him, and cites a case, wrongly decided by Kheti, a famous old vizier of the Pyramid Age.

" 'Behold, it is a saying which was in the vizierial installation of Memphis in the utterance of the king in urging the vizier to moderation . . . "[Bewar]e of that which is said of the vizier Kheti. It is said that he discriminated against some of the people of his own kin [in favour of] strangers, for fear lest it should be said of him that he [favoured] his [kin dishon]estly. When one of them appealed against the judgment which he thought [to make] him, he persisted in his discrimination." Now that is more than justice (Maat).

" 'Forget not to judge justice. It is an abomination of the god to show partiality. This is the teaching. Therefore do thou accordingly. Look upon him who is known to thee like him who is unknown to thee; and him who is near the king like him who is far from [his house]. Behold, a prince who does this, he shall endure here in this place. . . .

"'Be not wroth against a man wrongfully; (but) be thou wroth at that at which one should be wroth.

"'Cause thyself to be feared. Let men be afraid of thee. A prince is a prince of whom one is afraid. Behold, the dread of a prince is that he does justice. Behold, if a man causes himself to be feared too many times, there is something wrong in him in the opinion of the people. They do not say of him, "He is a man (indeed)." Behold, the [fear] of a prince [deters] the liar, when he (the prince) proceeds according to the dread of him. Behold, this shalt thou attain by administering this office, doing justice.

"'Behold, men expect the doing of justice in the procedure [of] the vizier. Behold, that is its (justice's) customary [law] since the earthly reign of the god. Behold, it is said concerning the scribe of the vizier: "A just scribe," is said of him. . . . Now, as for "him who shall do justice before all the people," it is the vizier.

"'Behold, when a man is in his office, let him act according to what is commanded him. [Behold] the success of a man is that he act according to what is said to him. Make no [delay] at all in justice, the law of which thou knowest. Behold, it becomes the arrogant that the king should love the timid more than the arrogant. . . .

"'[Behold the regulation] that is laid up[on] thee.'"

The chief emphasis throughout this remarkable state document is on social justice. The vizierate is not for the purpose of showing any preference "to princes and councillors" nor to enslave any of the people. All justice administered shall be according to law in every case, not forgetting that the vizier's position is a very conspicuous one, so that all his proceedings are widely known among the people. Even the waters and the winds report his doings to all. Nor does justice mean that any injustice shall be shown those who may be of high station, as in the famous case of the ancient Memphite vizier Kheti, who made a decision against his own kin in spite of the inherent merits of their case. This is not justice. On the other hand, justice means strict impartiality, treating without distinction, known and unknown, him who is near the king's person and him who enjoys no connection with the royal house. Such administration as this will secure the vizier a long tenure of office. While the vizier must display the greatest discretion in his wrath, he must so demean himself as to ensure public respect and even fear, but this fear shall have its sole basis in the execution of impartial justice; for the true "dread of a prince is that he does justice." Hence he will not find it necessary repeatedly and ostentatiously to excite the fear of the people, which produces a false impression among them. The administration of justice will prove a sufficient deterrent. Men expect justice from the vizier's office, for justice has been its customary law since the reign of the Sun-god on earth. The Egyptian of the Feudal Age was here looking back through the thousand years of the Second Union to the First Union at the Sun-city of Heliopolis. Since then he whom they proverbially call "him who shall do justicc before all the people" is the vizier. A man's success in office depends upon his ability to follow instructions. Therefore let there be no delay in the dispensation of justice, remembering that the king loves the timid and defenceless more than the arrogant. Then with a reference to the lands which probably formed the royal fortune, and the inspection of the officials in charge of them, the king concludes this veritable magna charta of the poor with the words: "Behold the regulation that is laid upon thee."

Was it the vision of the ideal king held up at the court by Ipuwer, the sombre picture of the corruption of men painted by the Misanthrope, or the picturesque scene of official oppression disclosed in the story of the Eloquent Peasant, which finally so enveloped the throne in an atmosphere of social justice, that the installation of the prime-minister and chief-justice of the realm, for such the vizier was, called forth from the king a speech from the throne, an official expression by the head of the state to its highest executive officer, embodying the fundamental principles of social justice? We might now of course put forward the claim that this state document, so deeply imbued with the spirit of social justice, was the product and direct consequence of the social tractates which we have been reading. There is some evidence for this conclusion. The same regard for the "timid" in preference to "arrogant" or "violent-hearted," which the king displays in these instructions to the vizier is also found in Ipuwer's Admonitions. In general the Installation of the Vizier is in full accord with the teachings of the social tractates. Whether the king's social policy is specifically his response to these writings or not is a question of no real consequence; for in any case it is quite clear that in the Feudal Age conscience had become something more than an influence on the conduct of the individual. It had become for the first time in human history a powerful social force. The king had quite obviously become responsive to the influence of the moral thinkers of the time, and a policy of social justice had become part of the very framework of government. The old days when a man's conduct was satisfactory if it received the approval of father, mother, brothers, and sisters, were passed, there had arisen what may be called a social conscience, and with it the *Age of Character* had dawned.

As far as the *righteous king* is concerned the Messianists had seen their dream fulfilled in the accession of Amenemhet I. How was it with the more prosaic reformers whose hopes were based on a new generation of *just officials?* As a matter of fact the two programmes cannot be separated, for the reign of a righteous king is almost wholly ineffective without a body of just officials to carry out the royal policy. Amenemhet I was fully conscious of this fact, and having no confidence in men, he had little hope that his own rectitude would avail anything. But the unknown author of such a tale as the Eloquent Peasant was expecting results from such writings. There is some evidence that he was not disappointed.

Few documents which might disclose to us the operations of the Egyptian State have survived, but the social doctrines of the barons and officials of the Feudal Age are disclosed in the mortuary inscriptions engraved in their tombs. Travellers on the Nile will recall the visit made by the tourist steamers at the tombs of Benihasan. Perhaps the tomb of Ameni, the feudal baron and head of the local government, makes but a slight impression on such travellers, but it is a notable monument in social history, and enables us to discern at least one instance in which the campaign of the social crusaders was having some effect on the new official generation. On the doorpost of his tomb-chapel Ameni says:

"There was no citizen's daughter whom I misused, there was no widow whom I afflicted, there was no peasant whom I evicted, there was no herdman whom I expelled, there was no overseer of five whose people I took away for (unpaid) taxes. There was none wretched in my community, there was none hungry in my time. When years of famine came, I ploughed all the fields of the Oryx barony (his estate) as far as its southern and its northern boundary, preserving its people alive, furnishing its food so that there was none hungry therein. I gave to the widow as to her who had a husband. I did not exalt the great (man) above the small (man) in anything that I gave. Then came great Niles (inundations), rich in grain and all things, but I did not collect the arrears of the field."

In this record we seem to hear an echo of the Installation of the Vizier, especially in the statement, "I did not exalt the great man above the small man in anything that I gave." It is easy to believe that such a baron as this had been present at court and had heard the instructions of the Pharaoh at the vizier's inauguration. If the administration of Ameni was in any measure what he claims for it, we must conclude that the social teachings of the wise at the court were widely known among the great throughout the kingdom. Even though we may conclude that he has idealised his rule to a large extent, we have still to account for his desire to create such an impression as we gain from his biography. The same is true of the records of other feudal barons of the same age carved in the alabaster quarry of Hatnub, which contain a number of similar assurances. They tell us that the noble was one "who rescued the widow and supported the suffering, who buried the aged and nourished the child, who sustained alive his city in famine, who fed it when there was nothing, who gave to it without discrimination therein, (so that) its great ones were like its little ones." We have already noted that under Amenemhet I's son Sesostris I, two nobles boast in their mortuary autobiographies that they exercised with justice and without partiality or thought of reward their functions as judges. They make this boast in the very language of the Instruction Addressed to Merikere (see pp. 155 and 160 f.) and thus reveal that centuries later the social idealism of the old royal sage of Heracleopolis was still influential in the Feudal Age. It is evident that the ideals of social justice, so insistently set forth in the literature of this age, had not only reached the king, but they had also exerted a profound influence among the ruling class everywhere.

Herein, then, we may discern a great transformation. The pessimism with which the men of the early Feudal Age contemplated the hereafter or beheld the desolated cemeteries of the Pyramid Age and the hopelessness with which some of them regarded the earthly life were met by a persistent counter-current in a gospel of righteousness and social justice set forth in the hopeful teachings of more optimistic social thinkers—men who saw hope in positive effort toward better conditions. We must regard the Admonitions of Ipuwer, the prophecies of Neferrohu, and the Tale of the Eloquent Peasant as striking examples of such efforts, and we must recognise in their writings the weapons of the earliest known group of moral and social crusaders. What more could such a man as Ipuwer have wished than the address delivered by the king at the installation of the vizier? A king capable of delivering such an address approaches the stature of that ideal king of whom Ipuwer dreamed and whom Neferrohu believed he had found. Similarly there is reason to believe that Ameni of Benihasan would have represented very well the new generation of just officials whom the author of the Eloquent Peasant hoped to see carrying on the government of Egypt.

We have already remarked that family approval of a man's conduct is no longer sufficient. An age of reflection has developed ideals of conduct that involve whole classes of society—conduct which is subject to a social verdict, and this social verdict has now been put into the mouth of the Sun-god. The Eloquent Peasant said to the Grand Steward, "Do justice for the sake of the lord of justice," and again he referred to "this good word which came out of the mouth of Re himself, 'Speak the truth, do the truth,'" in which we remember that "truth" is, likewise, justice and righteousness (Maat). In the instructions of the vizier we have found that this programme of social kindness and justice, in which the king loves the timid and defenceless more than the powerful and the arrogant, has become distinctly religious in motive and is attributed to God. "It is an abomination of the god," says the king, "to show partiality." We see then that ideas of social justice, as they found practical expression first in the idealised kingship, and then in the actual character of its incumbent, were thereupon quickly reflected into the character and activities of the Sun-god, the ideal king. The obligation to maintain social justice, which men felt within them, became a fiat of the god, their own abomination of injustice was soon believed to be that of the god, and their own moral ideals, thus becoming likewise those of the god, gained new mandatory power.

It was, then, furthermore easy to believe that justice had been the traditional law of the vizier's office since the time when the Sun-god ruled in Egypt. The rule of Pharaoh, inherited through some two thousand years since the establishment of the First Union, and supposed to continue the blood and the line of Re, was likewise continuing the justice of the Sun-god's ancient régime on earth. The king lays his mandate unequivocally upon the vizier, but at the same time he does not hesitate to appeal to a higher court. The vizier must do justice because the great god of the state abhors injustice, and not solely because the king enjoins it.

Twelve to thirteen hundred years later we find the Hebrew prophets boldly proclaiming the moral sovereignty of their Yahveh as over that of the king, but how many generations of seemingly fruitless ministry were required before this contention of the prophets found expression in the spirit of the Hebrew government, much less in royal pronouncements such as this of the Feudal Age in Egypt. We have not been accustomed to associate such principles of government with the early East, nor even with the modern Orient.

The influence of such lofty ideals of social justice, which thus found expression in government, was no doubt in large measure due to the form in which they circulated among all classes. Such doctrines, had they been enunciated as abstract principles, would have attracted little attention and exerted little or no influence. The Egyptian, moreover, always thought in concrete terms and in graphic forms. He thought not of theft but of a thief, not of love but of a lover, not of poverty but of a poor man: he saw not social corruption but a corrupt society. Hence Ptahhotep, a *man* meeting the obligations of office with wholesome faith in righteous conduct and just administration to engender happiness, and passing on this experience to his son; hence the Misanthrope, a *man* in whom social injustice found expression in the picture of a despairing soul who tells of his despair and its causes;

hence Ipuwer, a *man* in whom dwelt the vision to discern both the deadly corruption of society and the golden dream of an ideal king restoring all; hence the Eloquent Peasant, a *man* suffering official oppression and crying out against it; hence even the Instruction of Amenemhet, a *king* suffering shameful treachery, losing faith in men, and communicating his experience to his son. The result was that the doctrines of these social thinkers were placed in a dramatic setting, and the doctrines themselves found expression in dialogue growing out of experiences and incidents represented as actual.

In the East, and doubtless everywhere, such teachings, we repeat, make the most universal and the most powerful appeal in this form. It was the form into which the problem of suffering, as graphically exemplified in the story of Job, most naturally fell. The Story of Aḥiḳar, recently recovered in its ancient Aramaic form, is unquestionably a discourse on the folly of ingratitude which belongs in the same class; while the most beautiful of all such tales, the parables of Jesus, adopt the method and the form for ages current in the East. When Plato wished to discourse on the immortality of the soul, he assumed as his dramatic setting the death of Socrates, and the doctrines which he wished to set forth took the form of conversation between Socrates and his friends.[2] It is worth considering whether this form of moralising and philosophising in dialogue after an introduction which throws the whole essentially into the form of a tale, a form adopted for so many treatises in Egypt, had some influence on the emergence of the dialogue form in Asia and Europe. The wide international circulation of the Aḥiḳar tale

[2] The analogy of the Platonic dialogues was noticed by Gardiner, *Admonitions*, p. 17.

Fig. 11. PORTRAIT OF KING AMENEMHET III OF THE FEUDAL AGE OF EGYPT

The stern, self-repressed expression and the somber lines of the face disclose a sovereign keenly conscious of his grave responsibilities in an age of moral awakening. *After Evers.* (*Cairo Museum.*)

Fig. 12. OBSIDIAN HEAD OF AMENEMHET III

A fine personification of earliest disillusionment, the somber face showing how the royal portrait sculptors felt the pessimism of the social sages and expressed it with masterful power in the face of the sovereign. (*Gulbenkian Collection.*)

demonstrates how such literary products could travel, and it is perhaps significant that the oldest form of the Aḥiḳar tale was found in Egypt.

We have already observed that the social idealism of the Feudal Age was given divine authority and attributed to divine sources. It is important to scan the evidence for this fact and to establish beyond doubt the identity of the god to whose authority the social idealists made their appeal. This earliest social idealism was unmistakably associated with the Sun-god's earthly reign. We have observed before that he was a god of the affairs of men, in the world of the living, whereas Osiris was god of the *dead*. There can be no doubt that the ideal king was Re, the Sun-god, the moral glories of whose reign were to be renewed in his Pharaonic representative on earth. It was to the approval and to the traditional character of the reign of the Sun-god that the king appealed as the final basis for his instruction to the vizier. It is Re who is dominant in the thinking of these social philosophers of the Feudal Age. In the Song of the Harp-Player even the mummy of the dead is set up before the Sun-god. It is to him that the Misanthrope looks for justification in the hereafter, and Khekheperre-soneb was a priest of the Sun-city of Heliopolis. Ipuwer's vision of the future ideal king emerges from reminiscence of the blessedness of Re's earthly reign among men; while the summary of the whole appeal of the Eloquent Peasant is contained in "that good word which came out of the mouth of Re himself: 'Speak truth, do truth (or "righteousness"), for it is great, it is mighty, it is enduring.'" The moral obligations emerging in the Solar theology are thus a reflection of the earliest social regeneration of which we know anything in history. One of the most important consequences of the idealised kingship of the Sun-god was the hope of a recurrence of such a beneficent rule. It was this hope which had brought with it golden visions of a Messianic kingdom yet to come.

It is evident here also, as in the Pyramid Texts, that the connection of Osiris with ideals of righteousness and justice is secondary. He was tried and found innocent in the great hall at Heliopolis, that is, before the *Solar* bar of justice recognised, at the time when the Osiris myth was forming, as the tribunal before which he must secure acquittal; and his later exaltation as judge is but the Solarisation of the Osirian functions on the basis of the Solar judgeship so common in the Pyramid Texts. In the Pyramid Texts, Osiris had already climbed upon the celestial throne of Re; we shall see him now also appropriating Re's judgment-seat. The Sun-god, Re, thus became the great moral arbiter before whom all might receive justice, not excepting even Osiris. It is not necessary to deny to early Osirian belief some ethical content, of which we found indications likewise in the local faiths of a number of Egyptian gods of the Pyramid Age; but here again it should not be forgotten that the Pyramid Texts have preserved traces of a view of Osiris which, far from making him the ideal king and the friend of man, discloses him as an enemy of the dead and hostile to men.[3] It is not until the Feudal Age that Osiris unmistakably emerges as the champion of righteousness. We shall now observe Osiris and Re, side by side, in the moral thinking of the age.

It was now not only religious belief and social axiom, but also formally announced royal policy, that before the bar of justice the great and the powerful must expect the

[3] See above, pp. 92–93.

same treatment and the same verdict accorded to the poor and the friendless. It can hardly be doubted that such doctrines of social justice as we have found in this age contributed powerfully to develop the conviction that not the man of power and wealth, but the man of justice and righteousness, would be acceptable before the great god's judgment-seat. The theologising priests of the time were strongly affected by this tendency of democratisation. A fundamentally important utterance of the Sun-god in the Coffin Texts clearly discloses this influence, when he says:

"I have made the four winds *that every man might breathe thereof like his brother* during his time. (See especially B6C, ll. 506–507.)

"I have made the great waters that *the pauper like the lord* might have use of them.

"I have made *every man like his brother,* and I have forbidden that they do evil, (but) it was their hearts which undid that which I had said.

"I have made their hearts not to forget the West (death and the grave) that they may present offerings to the district gods!"[4]

It is not a little interesting to find here complete human equality: "I have made every man like his brother," a statement which is at once viewed in its moral aspects: "I have forbidden that they do evil, (but) it was their hearts which undid that which I had said." The emergence of such a view of humanity as this, in which all social distinctions are levelled in the creator's intention at the time of creation, placing all men likewise on the same

[4] I first saw this passage in the coffin of S't-ḥḏ-ḥtp (Cairo 28085) designated in the Oriental Institute publication B3C (Bersheh 3, Cairo). I am indebted to De Buck's kindness for calling my attention to the parallel texts, one in Cairo and one in Boston. The last is the best text, but the corrupt B6C furnishes a valuable fuller text. All three have been employed in the above translation.

level of moral responsibility, is the more extraordinary nearly two thousand years before Christ, when we notice that it is practically contemporary with the reign of Hammurapi, in whose great code of laws all penalties and legal decisions are graded according to the social station of the culprits or the rank of the litigants. This fact explains at once why Babylonian civilisation contributed little or nothing to our moral heritage in Western Asia.

Here then ends the special and peculiar claim of the great and powerful to consideration and to felicity in the hereafter, and the democratisation of blessedness beyond the grave begins. We must now endeavour to discern the effect of the ideas of social justice which arose in the Feudal Age, on the growing beliefs of the Egyptians regarding the destiny of the human soul in the hereafter.

CHAPTER XIII

POPULAR APPROPRIATION OF THE OLD ROYAL HEREAFTER AND THE GROWTH OF MAGIC

THE scepticism towards preparations for the hereafter involving a massive tomb and elaborate mortuary furniture, the pessimistic recognition of the futility of material equipment for the dead, pronounced as we have seen these tendencies to be in the Feudal Age, were, nevertheless, but an eddy in the broad current of Egyptian life. These tendencies were undoubtedly the accompaniment of unrelieved pessimism and hopelessness, on the one hand, as well as of a growing belief in the necessity of moral worthiness in the hereafter on the other; they were revolutionary views which did not carry with them any large body of the Egyptian people. As the felicity of the departed was democratised, the common people, grasping eagerly at their new privilege of sharing the glorious celestial destiny long ago the exclusive privilege of the Pharaohs—the common people took up and continued the old mortuary usages; and the development and elaboration of such customs went on without heeding the eloquent silence and desolation that reigned on the pyramid plateau and in the cemeteries of the fathers.

Merikere's royal father, while feeling strongly the vital importance of a worthy life, cannot recommend to his son that he dispense with a tomb. He says: "Adorn thy dwelling (thy tomb) of the West and embellish thy seat in the necropolis"; but he cannot refrain from adding "as one who hath been upright, as one who hath done righteousness; for this it is, upon which their heart resteth." Evidently the old king did not regard an enduring tomb alone as sufficient provision for happiness in the next world. On the other hand, even Ipuwer had said to the king, "It is moreover good when the hands of men build pyramids, lakes are dug, and groves of sycamores of the gods are planted." In the opinion of the prosperous official class the loss of the tomb was the direst possible consequence of unfaithfulness to the king, and a wise man said to his children:

> "There is no tomb for one hostile to his majesty;
> But his body shall be thrown to the waters."[1]

By the many, therefore, tomb-building and tomb equipment were carried on by the nobles as of old. To be sure, the kings no longer held such absolute control of the state that they could make it merely a highly organised agency for the construction of the gigantic royal tomb; but the official class in charge of such work did not hesitate to compare it with Gizeh itself. Meri, an architect of Sesostris I, displays noticeable satisfaction in recording that he was commissioned by the king "to execute for him an eternal seat, greater in name than Rosta (Gizeh) and more excellent in appointments than any place, the excellent district of the gods. Its columns pierced heaven; the lake which was dug reached the river, the gates, towering heavenward, were of limestone of Troja. Osiris, First of the Westerners, rejoiced over all the monuments of my lord (the king). I myself rejoiced and my heart was

[1] The Misanthrope refers to the similar fate of an abandoned body. See p. 170 and also p. 160.

glad at that which I had executed."[2] The "eternal seat" is the king's tomb, including, as the description shows, also the chapel or mortuary temple in front.

While the tombs of the feudal nobles were no longer grouped about the royal pyramid, as had been those of the administrative nobles of the Pyramid Age, and were now scattered in the baronies throughout the land, they continued to enjoy to some extent the mortuary *largesses* of the royal treasury. The familiar formula, "an offering which the king gives," so common in the tombs about the pyramids, is still frequent in the tombs of the nobles. It is, however, no longer confined to such tombs. With the wide popularisation of the highly developed mortuary faith of the upper classes it had become conventional custom for every man to pray for a share in royal mortuary bounty, and all classes of society, down to the humblest craftsman buried in the Abydos cemetery, pray for "an offering which the king gives," although it was out of the question that the masses of the population should enjoy any such privilege.

It is not until this Feudal Age that we gain any full impression of the picturesque customs for carrying on the maintenance of the dead in the hereafter—customs now so deeply rooted in the life of the people. The tombs still surviving in the baronies of Upper Egypt have preserved some memorials of the daily and ordinary, as well as of the ceremonial and festival, usages with which the people thought to brighten and render more attractive the life of those who had passed on. We find the same precautions taken by the nobles which we observed in the Pyramid Age.

[2] The excavations of the Metropolitan Museum of New York have indeed revealed the unusually sumptuous character of the surroundings of this pyramid of Sesostris I at Lisht.

The rich noble Hepzefi of Siut, who flourished in the Twentieth Century before Christ, had before death erected a statue of himself in both the leading temples of his city, that is, *one* in the temple of Upwawet, an ancient Wolf-god of the place, from which it later received its name, Lycopolis, at the hands of the Greeks, and the *other* in the temple of Anubis, a well-known Dog- or Jackal-god, once one of the mortuary rivals of Osiris. The temple of Upwawet was in the midst of the town, while that of Anubis was farther out on the outskirts of the necropolis, at the foot of the cliff, some distance up the face of which Hepzefi had excavated his imposing cliff tomb. In this tomb likewise he had placed a third statue of himself, under charge of his mortuary priest. He had but one priest for the care of his tomb and the ceremonies which he wished to have celebrated on his behalf; but he had secured assistance for this man by calling in the occasional services of the priesthoods of both temples, and certain of the necropolis officials, with all of whom he had made contracts, as well as with his mortuary priest, stipulating exactly what they were to do, and what they were to receive from the noble's revenues in payment for their services or their oblations, regularly and periodically, after the noble's death.

These contracts, ten in number, were placed by the noble in bold inscriptions on the inner wall of his tomb-chapel, and they furnish today a very suggestive picture of the calendar of feasts celebrated in this provincial city of which Hepzefi was lord—feasts in all of which living and dead alike participated. On the basis of these contracts the following imaginative reconstruction endeavours to correlate them with the life which they suggest. The most important celebrations were those which took place in connection with the new year, before its advent, as well as at and after its arrival. They began five days before the end of the old year, on the first of the five intercalary days with which the year ended. On this day we might have seen the priests of Upwawet in procession winding through the streets and bazaars of Siut, and issuing at last back of the town as they conducted their god to the temple of Anubis at the foot of the cemetery cliff. Here a bull was slaughtered for the visiting deity. Each of the priests carried in his hand a large conical loaf of white bread, and as they entered the court of the Anubis temple, each deposited his loaf at the base of Hepzefi's statue.

Five days later, as the day declined, the overseer of the necropolis, followed by the nine men of his staff, climbed down from the cliffs past many an open tomb-door, which it was the duty of these men to guard, and entered the shades of the town below, now quite dark as it lay in the shadows of the lofty cliffs that overhung it. It is New Year's Eve, and in the twilight here and there the lights of the festival illumination begin to appear in doors and windows. As the men push on through the narrow streets in the outskirts of the town, they are suddenly confronted by the high enclosure wall of the temple of Anubis. Entering at the tall gate they inquire for the "great priest," who presently delivers to them a bale of torches. With these they return, slowly rising above the town as they climb the cliff again. As they look out over the dark roofs shrouded in deep shadows, they discover two isolated clusters of lights, one just below them, the other far out in the town, like two twinkling islands of radiance in a sea of blackness which stretches away at their feet. They are the courts of the two temples, where the illumination is now in full progress. Hepzefi, their ancient lord, though buried in far-off Nubia,[3] is, nevertheless, present yonder in the midst of the joy and festivity which fill the temple courts. Through the eyes of his statue rising above the multitude which now throngs those courts, he rejoices in the beauty of the bright colonnades, he revels, like his friends below, in the sense of prodigal plenty spread out before him, as he beholds the offering loaves arrayed at his feet, where we saw the priests depositing them; and his ears are filled with the roar of a thousand voices as the rejoicings of the assembled city, gathered in their temples to watch the old year die and to hail the new year, swell like the sound of the sea far over the dark roofs, till its dying tide reaches the ears of our group of cemetery guards high up in the darkness of the cliffs as they stand silently looking out over the town.

Just above is the great façade of the tomb which was prepared for their departed lord, Hepzefi. The older men of the party remember him well, and recall the generosity which they often enjoyed at his hands; but their juniors, to whom he is but an empty name, respond but slowly and reluctantly to the admonitions of the gray-beards to hasten with the illumination of the tomb, as they hear the voice of Hepzefi's priest calling upon them from above to delay no longer. The sparks flash from the "friction lighter" for an instant and then the first torch blazes up, from which the others are quickly kindled. The procession passes out around a vast promontory of the cliff and

[3] Hepzefi was later sent to Nubia as governor. There he died and was buried in a tumulus, which Reisner excavated at Kerma in 1913. Thus he never occupied the tomb prepared at Siut. However, his contracts with his mortuary priests and the endowments to support them were still in force, and the ceremonies at Siut continued as though Hepzefi's body rested in his cliff-tomb there.

then turns in again to the tall tomb door, where Hepzefi's priest stands awaiting them, and without more delay they enter the great chapel. The flickering light of the torches falls fitfully upon the wall, where gigantic figures of the dead lord rise so high from the floor that his head is lost in the gloom far above the waning light of the torches. He seems to admonish them to punctilious fulfilment of their duties towards him, as prescribed in the ten contracts recorded on the same wall. He is clad in splendid raiment, and he leans at ease upon his staff. Many a time the older men of the group have seen him standing so, delivering judgment as the culprits were dragged through the door of his busy bureau between a double line of obsequious bailiffs; or again watching the progress of an important irrigation canal which was to open some new field to cultivation. Involuntarily they drop in obeisance before his imposing figure, like the scribes and artisans, craftsmen and peasants who fill the walls before him, in gayly coloured reliefs vividly portraying all the industries and pastimes of Hepzefi's great estates and forming a miniature world, where the departed noble, entering his chapel, beholds himself again moving among the scenes and pleasures of the provincial life in which he was so great a figure. To him the walls seem suddenly to have expanded to include harvest-field and busy bazaar, workshop and ship-yard, the hunting-marshes and the banquet-hall, with all of which the sculptor and the painter have peopled these walls till they are indeed alive.

The torches are now planted around the offerings, thickly covering a large stone offering-table, behind which sits Hepzefi's statue in a niche in the wall; and then the little group slowly withdraws, casting many a furtive glance at a false door in the rear wall of the chapel, through which they know Hepzefi may at any moment issue from the shadow world behind it, to re-enter this world and to celebrate with his surviving friends the festivities of New Year's Eve.

The next day, the first day of the new year, is the greatest feast-day in the calendar. There is joyful exchange of gifts, and the people of the estate appear with presents for the lord of the manor. Hepzefi's descendants are much absorbed in their own pleasure, but his cautious contracts, as still recorded in the town archives, ensure him from neglect. While the peasants and the leaseholders of the barony are crowding the gates of the manor-house, bringing in their gifts to their living lord and thinking little, if at all, of his departed predecessor, we discover the little knot of ten necropolis guards, headed by their chief, again entering the outskirts of the town and proceeding to one of the treasuries of the estate where they are entitled to draw supplies. Presently they march away again, bearing 550 flat cakes, 55 white loaves, and 11 jars of beer. Pushing their way slowly through the holiday crowds they retrace their steps to the entrance of the cemetery at the foot of the cliffs, where they find a large crowd already gathered, every one among them similarly laden. Amid much shouting and merry-making, amid innumerable picturesque scenes of oriental folk-life, such as are still common in the Mohammedan cemeteries of Egypt at the Feast of Bairam, the good townspeople of Siut carry their gifts of food and drink up the cliff to the numerous doors which honeycomb its face, that their dead may share the joyous feast with them. It is, indeed, the earliest Feast of All-Souls. The necropolis guards hasten up to Hepzefi's chapel with their supplies, which they quickly deliver to his priest, and are off again to preserve order among the merry crowds now everywhere pushing up the cliff.

As the day wears on there are busy preparations for the evening celebration, for the illumination, and the "glorification of the blessed," who are the dead. The necropolis guards, weary with a long day of arduous duty in the crowded cemetery, descend for the second time into the town to the temple of Upwawet. Here they find the entire priesthood of the temple waiting to receive them. At the head of the line the "great priest" delivers to the ten guards of the necropolis the torches for Hepzefi's "illumination." These are quickly kindled from those which the priests already carry, and the procession of guards and priests together moves slowly out of the temple court and across the sacred enclosure "to the northern corner of the temple," as the contract with Hepzefi prescribes, chanting the "glorification" of Hepzefi.[4] As they go the priests carry each a large conical loaf of white bread, such as they had laid before the statue of Hepzefi in the temple of Anubis five days before. Arrived at the "northern corner of the temple," the priests turn back to their duties in the crowded sanctuary, doubtless handing over their loaves to the necropolis guards, for, as stipulated, these loaves were destined for the statue of Hepzefi in his tomb. Threading the brightly lighted streets of the town, the little procession of ten guards pushes its way with considerable difficulty through the

[4] The nature of this ceremony, which was performed by the living, at the New Year's and other feasts, on behalf of their dead, while not clear in its details, must have been what its name technically defines it to have been. It means "the act of making glorious," and, as we have seen above, one of the epithets applied to the dead was "the glorious." It was therefore a ceremony for accomplishing the transformation of the deceased into a "glorious one," precisely as he was transformed also into a "soul" (ba) by an analogous ceremony performed by the living, a ceremony indeed which may have been much the same as that of glorification.

throngs, passing at length the gate of the Anubis temple, where the illumination is in full progress, and the statue of Hepzefi is not forgotten. As they emerge from the town again, still much hampered by the crowds likewise making their way in the same direction, the dark face of the cliff rising high above them is dotted here and there with tiny beacons moving slowly upward. These are the torches of the earlier townspeople, who have already reached the cemetery to plant them before the statues and burial-places of their dead. The guards climb to Hepzefi's tomb as they had done the night before and deliver torches and white bread to Hepzefi's waiting priest. Thus the dead noble shared in the festivities of the New Year's celebration as his children and former subjects were doing.

Besides these and other great feasts which were thus enjoyed by the dead lord, he was not forgotten on any of the periodic minor feasts which fell on the first of every month and half-month, or on any "day of a procession." His *daily* needs were met by the laymen serving in successive shifts in the temple of Anubis. As this sanctuary was near the cemetery, these men, after completing their duties in the temple, went out *every day* with a portion of bread and a jar of beer, which they deposited before the statue of Hepzefi "which is on the lower stairs of his tomb." There was, therefore, not a day in the year when Hepzefi failed to receive the food and drink necessary for his maintenance.[5] Such beliefs and practices demonstrate how persistent were the ancient materialistic notions of

[5] The preceding account has attempted to indicate to some extent the place of the dead in the celebration of the calendar of feasts as they were in the life of the people. Perhaps imagination has been too liberally drawn upon. The bare data as furnished by the contracts of Hepzefi will be found in the author's *Development of Religion and Thought in Ancient Egypt* (pages 268 and 269); the contracts themselves may be found translated in the author's *Ancient Records,* Vol. I, pp. 258–271.

the hereafter: elaborate insurance of physical survival, in the face of new light on the indispensability of good character in the next world.

That such materialistic provision for the dead noble should continue indefinitely was, of course, quite impossible. Khnumhotep, one of the powerful barons of Benihasan, says regarding his mortuary endowments: "Now, as for the mortuary priest, or any person who shall disturb them, he shall not survive, his son shall not survive in his place." The apprehension of the noble is evident, and such apprehensions are common in documents of this nature. We have seen Hepzefi equally apprehensive. Even we of today are not greatly moved by pious concern for the grave of a departed grandfather; in a new land like ours few of us even know where our great-grandfathers are interred. The priests of Anubis and Upwawet and the necropolis guards at Siut will have continued their duties only so long as Hepzefi's mortuary priest received his income and was true to his obligations in reminding them of theirs, and in seeing to it that these obligations were met. We find such an endowment surviving a change of dynasty (from the Fourth to the Fifth), and lasting at least some thirty or forty years, in the middle of the Twenty-eighth Century before Christ. In the Twelfth Dynasty, too, there was in Upper Egypt great respect for the ancestors of the Old Kingdom. The nomarchs of El-Bersheh, in the Nineteenth and Twentieth Centuries before Christ, repaired the tombs of their ancestors of the Pyramid Age, tombs then over six hundred years old and therefore in a state of ruin. The pious nomarch used to record his restoration in these words: "He (the nomarch) made (it) as his monument for his fathers, who are in the necropolis, the lords of this promontory; restoring what was found in ruin and renewing what was found decayed, the ancestors who were before not having done it." We find the nobles of this province using this formula five times in the tombs of their ancestors. In the same way, Intef, a baron of Hermonthis, says: "I found the chapel of the prince Nekhtyoker fallen to ruin, its walls were old, its statues were shattered, there was no one who cared for them. It was built up anew, its plan was extended, its statues were made anew, its doors were built of stone, that its place might excel beyond that of other august princes." Such piety towards the departed fathers, however, was very rare, and even when shown could not do more than postpone the evil day. The marvel is that with their ancestors' ruined tombs before them they nevertheless still went on to build for themselves sepulchres which were inevitably to meet the same fate. The tomb of Khnumhotep, the greatest of those left us by the Benihasan lords of four thousand years ago, bears on its walls, among the beautiful paintings which adorn them, the scribblings of 120 generations in Egyptian, Coptic, Greek, Arabic, French, Italian, and English. The earliest of these scrawls is that of an Egyptian scribe who entered the tomb-chapel over three thousand years ago and wrote with reed pen and ink upon the wall these words: "The scribe Amenmose came to see the temple of Khufu and found it like the heavens when the sun rises therein." The chapel was some seven hundred years old when this scribe entered it, and its owner, although one of the greatest lords of his time, was so completely forgotten that the visitor, finding the name of Khufu in a casual geographical reference among the inscriptions on the wall, mistook the place for a chapel of Khufu, the builder of the Great Pyramid. All knowledge of the noble and of the endowments which were to support him in the hereafter had disappeared in spite of the precautions which he has recorded in his tomb. How vain and futile now appear the imprecations on these time-stained walls!

But the Egyptian was not wholly without remedy even in the face of this dire contingency. He endeavoured to meet the difficulty by engraving on the front of his tomb prayers believed to be efficacious in supplying all the needs of the dead in the hereafter. All passers-by were solemnly adjured to utter these prayers on behalf of the dead.

Such prayers illustrate the belief in the effectiveness of the uttered word on behalf of the dead which had developed enormously since the Pyramid Age. This is a development which accompanies the popularisation of the mortuary customs of the upper classes. In the Pyramid Age, as we have seen, such utterances were confined to the later pyramids. These concern exclusively the destiny of the Pharaoh in the hereafter. They were now largely appropriated by the middle and the official class. At the same time there emerges another body of mortuary literature which we now call the "Coffin Texts." These are similar utterances, identical in function but evidently more suited to the needs of common mortals, and now used by the *people* of the Feudal Age; however, some fragments of them are much older than this age. Later the Book of the Dead was made up of selections from the Coffin Texts. Built up out of copious extracts from the Pyramid Texts and more popular mortuary literature, the Coffin Texts were now written on the inner surfaces of the heavy cedar coffins, in which the better burials of this age are found. The number of such mortuary texts is still increasing as additional coffins from this age are found. Every local coffin-maker was furnished by the priests of his town with copies of these utterances or spells. Before the coffins were put together, the scribes in the maker's employ filled the inner surfaces with pen-and-ink copies of such texts as he had available. It was all done with great carelessness and inaccurary, the effort being to fill up the planks with writing as fast as possible. They often wrote the same chapter over twice or even three times in the same coffin, and in one instance a chapter is found no less than five times in the same coffin.[6]

In so far as these Coffin Texts are identical with the Pyramid Texts we are already familiar with their general function and content. The hereafter to which these citizens of the Feudal Age looked forward was still largely celestial and Solar as in the Pyramid Age. The Coffin Texts disclose a surprising predominance of the celestial hereafter. There is the same identification with the Sun-god which we found in the Pyramid Texts. There is a chapter of "Becoming Re-Atum," and several of "Becoming a Falcon," the bird sacred to the Sun-god.

Just as in the Pyramid Texts, however, so in these Coffin Texts, the Osirian theology has intruded and has indeed taken possession of them. The best example is the text which afterwards became the famous seventeenth chapter of the Book of the Dead, which was already a favour-

[6] The Coffin Texts form the most important and the largest body of Egyptian sources still unpublished. There are nearly 100 such coffins in the Cairo Museum, besides those in the European and American museums, making altogether 138 coffins. In 1921 the Oriental Institute of the University of Chicago undertook to rescue this great body of Egyptian religious literature and is now about to publish a complete corpus of them. The work of copying was begun in 1922 by Doctor Alan H. Gardiner and the present author. It was then continued by Doctor Gardiner and Doctor A. De Buck. The work of copying has consumed ten years and is now complete. The copies contain nearly 30,000 lines, 6825 pages of manuscript, which fill 37 loose-leaf volumes. The publication in four to six volumes will require several years more. A full statement of the old bibliography will be found in the author's *Religion and Thought*, pp. 273 *f*.

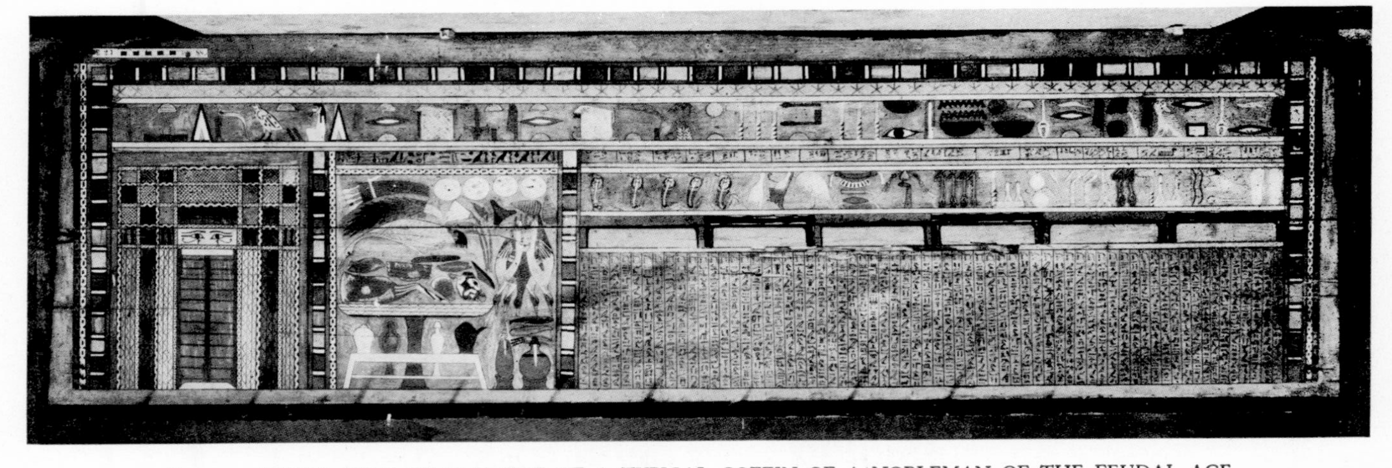

Fig. 13. INSIDE VIEW OF ONE SIDE OF A TYPICAL COFFIN OF A NOBLEMAN OF THE FEUDAL AGE

At right below in vertical lines are written portions of the mortuary literature known as "Coffin Texts." At the extreme left is the false door through which the spirit of the dead man might come and go. These subjects are all painted on a heavy cedar plank forming one side of the coffin. (*Cairo Museum.*)

ite chapter in this age, and begins the texts on a number of coffins. It is largely an identification of the deceased with the Sun-god, although other gods also appear. The dead man says:

> "I am Atum, I who was alone:
> I am Re at his first appearance.
> I am the Great God, self-generator,
> Who fashioned his names, lord of gods,
> Whom none approaches among the gods.
> Mine is yesterday, I know tomorrow."

Already in the Feudal Age this ancient Solar text had been supplied with an explanatory commentary, which adds to the line, "Mine is yesterday, I know tomorrow," the words, "that is Osiris," although it is quite clear that the text concerns exclusively the Sun-god. The result of this Osirianisation was the intrusion of the Osirian *subterranean* hereafter, even in Solar and celestial texts. In the Coffin Texts we thus have not only the commingling of Solar and Osirian beliefs which now more completely coalesce than before, but the result is that Re is intruded into the *subterranean* hereafter. The course of events may be stated in somewhat exaggerated form if we say that in the Pyramid Texts Osiris was lifted skyward, while in the Coffin Texts and the Book of the Dead, Re was dragged earthward. The resulting confusion is even worse than in the Pyramid Texts. This interfusion of a bright and glorious celestial destiny with a sombre hereafter in the gloomy Nether World reminds one of a sojourn somewhere "over Jordan" in the "Promised Land" side by side with a home in the skies, in the "spirituals" of the American negroes; or a subterranean purgatory preliminary to a celestial Paradise.

It is difficult to gain any coherent conception of the hereafter which the men of this age thus hoped to attain. There are the composite Solar-Osirian pictures which we have already found in the Pyramid Texts, and in which the priests to whom we owe these Coffin Text compilations allow their fancy to roam at will. The deceased Egyptian, now sharing the destiny of Osiris and called such by Horus (son of Osiris), hears himself receiving words of homage and promises of felicity addressed to him by his divine son. Such Osirian pictures shift abruptly to Solar privileges:

"Thou goest around the countries with Re; he lets thee see the pleasant places, thou findest the valleys filled with waters for washing thee and for cooling thee, thou pluckest marsh-flowers and *heni*-blossoms, lilies and lotus-flowers. The bird-pools come to thee by thousands, lying in thy path; when thou hast hurled thy boomerang against them, it is a thousand that fall at the sound of the wind thereof. They are *ro*-geese, green-fronts, quails, and *ḳunuset*-birds. I cause that there be brought to thee the young gazelles, bullocks of white bulls; I cause that there be brought to thee males of goats and grain-fed males of sheep. There is fastened for thee a ladder to the sky. Nût gives to thee her two arms. Thou sailest in the Lily-lake." In this picture we behold the deceased hunting in the marshes, the favourite pastime of the Pharaoh and his nobles; but thereupon he is abruptly shifted to a celestial lake in the sky.

While the destiny, everywhere so evidently royal in the Pyramid Texts, has thus become the portion of any one, the simpler life of the humbler citizen which he longed to see continued in the hereafter is quite discernible also in these Coffin Texts. As he lay in his coffin he could read a spell which concerned "Building a house for a man in the Nether World, digging a garden-pool and planting fruit-trees." Once supplied with a house, surrounded by a garden with its pool and its shade-trees, the dead man must be assured that he shall be able to occupy it, and hence a "chapter of a man's being in his house." The lonely sojourn there without the companionship of family and friends was an intolerable thought, and hence a further chapter entitled "Sealing of a Decree concerning the Household, to give the Household [to a man] in the Nether World." In the text the details of the decree are five times specified in different forms. Geb, the Earth-god, "has decreed that there be given to me my household, my children, my brothers, my father, my mother, my slaves, and all my establishment." Lest they should be withheld by any malign influence the second paragraph asserts that "Geb has said to release for me my household, my children, my brothers and sisters, my father, my mother, all my slaves, all my establishment at once, rescued from every god, from every goddess, from every death (or dead person)." To assure the fulfilment of this decree there was another chapter entitled "Uniting of the Household of a Man with Him in the Nether World," which effected the "union of the household, father, mother, children, friends, connections, wives, concubines, slaves, servants, everything belonging to a man, with him in the Nether World." The rehabilitation of a man's home and household in the hereafter was a thought involving the old-time belief in the necessity of food. Hence, another "Chapter of Eating Bread in the Nether World," or "Eating of Bread on the Table of Re, Giving of Plenty in Heliopolis." The very next chapter shows us how "the sitter sits to eat bread when Re sits to eat bread.

. . . Give to me bread when I am hungry. Give to me beer when I am thirsty."

A tendency which later came fully to its own in the Book of the Dead is already very prominent in these Coffin Texts. It regards the hereafter as a place of innumerable dangers and ordeals, most of them of a physical nature, although they sometimes concern also the intellectual equipment of the deceased. The weapon to be employed and the surest means of defence available to the deceased was some magical agency, usually a charm to be pronounced at the critical moment. This tendency then inclined to make the Coffin Texts, and ultimately the Book of the Dead which grew out of them, more and more a collection of charms, which were regarded as inevitably effective in protecting the dead or securing for him any of the blessings which were desired in the life beyond the grave. There was, therefore, a spell for "Becoming a Magician," addressed to the august ones who are in the presence of Atum the Sun-god. It is, of course, itself a charm and concludes with the words, "I am a magician." Lest the dead man should lose his magic power, there was a ceremony involving the "attachment of a charm so that the magical power of a man may not be taken away from him in the Nether World." The simplest of the dangers against which these charms were supplied doubtless arose in the childish imagination of the common folk. They are frequently grotesque in the extreme. We find a spell "preventing that the head of a man be taken from him." There is the old charm found also in the Pyramid Texts to prevent a man from being obliged to eat his own foulness. He is not safe from the decay of death; hence there are two charms that "a man may not decay in the Nether World."

Implicit confidence in such charms offered the priests unlimited opportunity for gain. Their imagination grew increasingly fertile in the issuance of ever new spells, which of course they sold to increasing numbers of credulous buyers. This practice undoubtedly contributed much to heighten the popular dread of the dangers of the hereafter and spread the belief in the usefulness of such means for meeting them. We should doubtless recognise the work of the priests in the figure of a mysterious scribe named Gebga, who is hostile to the dead, so that a charm was specially devised to enable the dead man to break the pens, smash the writing outfit, and tear up the rolls of the malicious Gebga. That menacing danger which was also feared in the Pyramid Texts, the assaults of venomous serpents, must likewise be met by the people of the Feudal Age. The dead man, therefore, finds in his roll charms for "Repulsing Serpents and Repulsing Crocodiles." The way of the departed was furthermore beset with fire, and he would be lost without a charm for "Going Forth from the Fire," or of "Going Forth from the Fire Behind the Great God." When he was actually obliged to enter the fire he might do so with safety by means of a "Spell for Entering into the Fire and of Coming Forth from the Fire Behind the Sky." Indeed, the priests had devised a chart of the journey awaiting the dead, guiding him through the gate of fire at the entrance and showing the two ways by which he might proceed, one by land, the other by water, with a lake of fire between them. This chart was painted on the floor, that is on the bottom of the inside of the coffin, where it was *under* the body of the deceased, the appropriate place for a diagram of the Nether World. It was accompanied by a kind of magical guide-book called the "Book of the Two

Ways" which was likewise recorded in the coffin. In spite of such guidance it might unluckily happen that the dead man wander into the place of execution of the gods; but from this he was saved by a spell of "Not Entering Into the Place of Execution of the Gods"; and lest he should suddenly find himself condemned to walk head downward, he was supplied with a "Spell for Not Walking Head Downward." These unhappy dead who were compelled to walk in this inverted posture were one's most malicious enemies in the hereafter. Protection against them was vitally necessary. It is said to the deceased: "Life comes to thee, but death comes not to thee. . . . They (Orion, Sothis, and the Morning Star) save thee from the wrath of the dead who go head downward. Thou art not among them. . . . Rise up for life, thou diest not; lift thee up for life, thou diest not."

The belief in the efficacy of magic as an infallible agent in the hand of the dead man was thus steadily growing, and we shall see it ultimately dominating the whole body of mortuary belief as it emerges a few centuries later in the Book of the Dead. It cannot be doubted that the popularity of the Osirian faith had much to do with this increase in the use of mortuary magical agencies. The Osiris myth, now universally current, made all classes familiar with the same agencies employed by Isis in raising her husband, Osiris, from the dead, and which every Egyptian believed would be equally efficacious in his own case.

Powerful as the Osiris faith had been in the Pyramid Age, its wide popularity now surpassed anything before known. We see in it the triumph of folk-religion as opposed to or contrasted with the state cult of Re, which was not unlike an established church. The supremacy of

Re was a political triumph; that of Osiris, while unquestionably fostered by an able priesthood probably practising constant propaganda, was a triumph of popular faith among all classes of society, a triumph which not even the court and the nobles were able to resist. The blessings which the Osirian destiny in the hereafter offered to all proved an attraction of universal power. If they had once been an exclusively royal prerogative, as the Solar destiny in the Pyramid Texts had been, we have seen that even the royal Solar hereafter had now been appropriated by all.

One of the venerable tombs of the First Dynasty kings at Abydos, a tomb by this time thirteen or fourteen hundred years old, had now come to be regarded as the tomb of Osiris. It rapidly became the Holy Sepulchre of Egypt, to which all classes made pilgrimage. The greatest of all blessings was to be buried in the vicinity of this sacred tomb, and more than one functionary took advantage of some official journey or errand to erect a tomb there. If a real tomb was impossible, it was nevertheless beneficial to build at least a false tomb there bearing one's name and the names of one's family and relatives. Failing this, great numbers of pilgrims and visiting officials each erected a memorial tablet or stela bearing prayers to the Great God on behalf of the visitor and his family. Thus an official under Sesostris I says: "I have made this tomb at the stairway of the Great God, in order that I may be among his followers, while the soldiers who follow his majesty give to my ka of his bread and his provision, just as every royal messenger does who comes inspecting the boundaries of his majesty." The enclosure and the approach to the temple of Osiris were filled with these memorials, which as they survive today form an important part of our documentary material for the history of this age. The body of a powerful baron might even be carried to Abydos to undergo certain ceremonies there, and to bring back certain sacred things to his tomb at home, as the Arab takes home water from the well of Zemzem, or as Roman ladies brought back sacred water from the sanctuary of Isis at Philæ. Khnumhotep of Benihasan has depicted on the walls of his tomb-chapel this voyage on the Nile, showing his embalmed body resting on a funeral barge which is being towed northward, accompanied by priests and lectors. The inscription calls it the "voyage up-stream to know the things of Abydos." A pendent scene showing a voyage down-stream is accompanied by the words, "the return bringing the things of Abydos."[7] Just what these sacred "things of Abydos" may have been we have no means of knowing, but it is evident that on this visit to the Great God at Abydos, it was expected that the dead might personally present himself and thus ensure himself the favour of the god in the hereafter.

The visitors who thus came to Abydos, before or after death, brought so many votive offerings that the modern excavators of the alleged Osiris tomb found it deeply buried under a vast accumulation of broken pots and other gifts left there by the pilgrims of thousands of years. There must eventually have been multitudes of such pilgrims at this Holy Sepulchre of Egypt at all times, but especially at that season when the incidents of the god's

[7] Both scenes are stated to depict the voyage to Abydos. It is clear, both from the inscriptions ("voyage up-stream" and "return") and from the scenes themselves, that the voyage *to Abydos and return* are depicted. The vessel going up-stream shows canvas set as it should for sailing up-stream, while the other (the "return") shows the mast unstepped, as customary in coming down-stream at the present day. *Moreover, both boats actually face to and from Abydos as they now stand on the tomb wall.* This device is not unknown elsewhere, *e.g.,* the ships of Hatshepsut, on the walls of the Deir el-Bahri temple, face to and from Punt.

myth were dramatically re-enacted in what may properly be called a "passion play." Although this play is now completely lost, the memorial stone of Ikhernofret, an officer of Sesostris III, who was sent by the king to undertake some restorations in the Osiris temple at Abydos, a stone now preserved in Berlin, furnishes an outline from which we may draw at least the titles of the most important acts. These show us that the drama must have continued for a number of days, and that each of the more important acts probably lasted at least a day, the multitude participating in much that was done. In the brief narrative of Ikhernofret we discern eight acts. The *first* discloses the old mortuary god Upwawet issuing in procession that he may scatter the enemies of Osiris and open the way for him. In the *second* act Osiris himself appears in his sacred barque, into which ascend certain of the pilgrims. Among these is Ikhernofret, as he proudly tells us in his inscription. There he aids in repelling the foes of Osiris who beset the course of the barque, and there is undoubtedly a general mêlée of the multitude, such as Herodotus saw at Papremis fifteen hundred years later, some in the barque defending the god, while others, acting as his enemies in the crowd below, are proud to carry away a broken head on behalf of the celebration. Ikhernofret, like Herodotus, passes over the death of the god in silence. It was a thing too sacred to be described. He only tells us that he arranged the "Great Procession" of the god, a triumphal celebration of some sort, when the god met his death. This was the *third* act. In the *fourth,* the god of wisdom, Thoth, goes forth and doubtless finds the body, though this is not stated. The *fifth* act is made up of the sacred ceremonies by which the body of the god is prepared for entombment, while in the *sixth* we behold the multitude moving out in a vast throng to the Holy Sepulchre in the desert behind Abydos to lay away the body of the dead god in his tomb. The *seventh* act must have been an imposing spectacle. On the shore or water of Nedyt, near Abydos, the enemies of Osiris, including of course Set and his companions, are overthrown in a great battle by Horus, the son of Osiris. The raising of the god from the dead is not mentioned by Ikhernofret, but in the *eighth* and final act we behold Osiris, restored to life, entering the Abydos temple in triumphal procession. It is thus evident that the drama presented the chief incidents in the myth.

Such a popular festival as this gained a great place in the affections of the people, and over and over again, on their Abydos tablets, the pilgrims pray that after death they may be privileged to participate in this celebration, just as Hepzefi arranged to share in those at Siut. Thus presented in dramatic form the incidents of the Osiris myth made a powerful impression upon the people. The "passion play" in one form or another caught the imagination of more than one community, and just as Herodotus found it at Papremis, so now it spread from town to town, to take the chief place in the calendar of festivals. Osiris thus gained a place in the life and the hopes of the common people held by no other god. The royal destiny of Osiris and his triumph over death, thus vividly portrayed in dramatic form, rapidly disseminated among the people the belief that this destiny, once reserved for the king, might be shared by all. As we have said before, it needed but the same magical agencies employed by Isis to raise her dead consort, the slain Osiris, to bring to every man the blessed destiny of the departed god. Such a development of popular mortuary belief, as we have already seen, inevitably involved also a constantly growing confidence in the efficacy of magic in the hereafter.

It is difficult for the modern mind to understand how completely the belief in magic penetrated the whole substance of life, dominating popular custom and constantly appearing in the simplest acts of the daily household routine, as much a matter of course as sleep or the preparation of food. It constituted the very atmosphere in which the men of the early oriental world lived. Without the saving influence of such magical agencies constantly invoked, the life of an ancient household in the East was unthinkable. The destructive powers would otherwise have annihilated all. While it was especially against disease that such means must be employed, the ordinary processes of domestic and economic life were constantly placed under its protection. The mother never hushed her ailing babe and laid it to rest without invoking unseen powers to free the child from the dark forms of evil, malice, and disease that lurked in every shadowy corner, or, slinking in through the open door as the gloom of night settled over the house, entered the tiny form and racked it with fever. Such demons might even assume friendly guise and approach under pretext of soothing and healing the little sufferer. We can still hear the mother's voice as she leans over her babe and casts furtive glances through the open door into the darkness where the powers of evil dwell.

"Run out, thou who comest in darkness, who enterest by stealth, his nose behind him, his face turned backward, who loses that for which he came.

"Run out, thou who comest in darkness, who enterest by stealth, her nose behind her, her face turned backward, who loses that for which she came.

"Comest thou to kiss this child? I will not let thee kiss him.

"Comest thou to soothe him? I will not let thee soothe him.

"Comest thou to harm him? I will not let thee harm him.

"Comest thou to take him away? I will not let thee take him away from me.

"I have made his protection against thee out of *Efet*-herb, it makes pain; out of onions, which harm thee; out of honey which is sweet to (living) men and bitter to those who are yonder (the dead); out of the evil (parts) of the *Ebdu*-fish; out of the jaw of the *meret;* out of the backbone of the perch."

The apprehensive mother employs not only the uttered charm as an exorcism, but adds a delectable mixture to be swallowed by the child. It is made of herbs, honey, and fish and designed to drive out the malignant demons, male and female, which afflict the baby with disease or threaten to carry it away. A hint as to the character of these demons is contained in the description of honey as "sweet to men (meaning the living) and bitter to those who are yonder (the dead)." It is evident that the demons dreaded were some of them the disembodied dead. At this point the life of the living throughout its course impinged upon that of the dead. The malicious dead must be bridled and held in check. Charms and magical devices which had proved efficacious against them during earthly life might prove equally valuable in the hereafter. This charm which prevented the carrying away of the child might also be employed to prevent a man's heart from being taken away in the Nether World. The dead man need only say: "Hast thou come to take away this my living heart? This my living heart is not given to thee"; whereupon the demon that would seize and flee with it must inevitably slink away. In this way the magic of daily life was more and more brought to bear on the hereafter and placed at the service of the dead.

We have seen that in the Pyramid Age it was not yet the belief that an inevitable and universal judgment in the hereafter awaited *all* men. For some particular misdeed a wrong-doer might be summoned to justice in the next world, and the Sun-god held court there in order to try such cases. In the Feudal Age, however, as the Coffin Texts reveal to us (p. 221), the Sun-god avers that *all* men are equally responsible: "I have made every man like his brother, and I have forbidden that they do evil, (but) it was their hearts which undid that which I had said." Already in the Instruction Addressed to Merikere we recall that in the presence of the dread judges in the hereafter a man's sins are piled up beside him like mountains (see p. 157). However blameless a man's life might be, in the belief of the Feudal Age, he must expect the ordeal of an ethical judgment in the hereafter. This consciousness of moral responsibility after death had become a powerful influence in the life of the Egyptian people, but there were two strong forces which were undermining it. There was, *first,* the still surviving belief of the common people in the efficacy of material agencies such as the tomb and its equipment, to ensure the happiness of the dead in the next world; and, *second,* the increasing reliance on magic in the hereafter, a belief fostered by the priests who eventually went so far as the endeavour even to produce magical charms believed to ensure the ethical acceptability of the dead in the judgment.

CHAPTER XIV

THE JUDGMENT HEREAFTER AND MAGIC

WE have followed a long development of the belief in moral responsibility hereafter, which we recall was already present in the minds of the Pyramid Builders, although it then involved only a man's liability to be summoned before the Sun-god as judge by some one whom the deceased had wronged, rather than a general judgment. At that time it was presumably believed that unless so summoned a man might never be subjected to any judgment in the next world. Some centuries later, but as far back as the Instruction Addressed to Merikere, this belief had taken more definite form. The old king who delivered these wise words to his son was deeply impressed with the fact that even a king must look forward to responsibility beyond the grave for the moral quality of his earthly life. We recall his remarkable admonition: "The court of judges who judge the unworthy, thou knowest that they are not lenient on that day of judging the wretched, in the hour of executing the writ. . . . Set not thy mind on length of days, for they (the judges) view a life-time as an hour. A man surviveth after death and his deeds are placed beside him like mountains. For it is eternity, abiding yonder (in the next world), and a fool is he who disregards it. As for him who reacheth it without having committed sin, he shall abide there like a god, striding on like the lords of eternity (the justified dead)." If a man is preparing his tomb in the cemetery, Merikere is reminded that he should do so "as one who hath been upright, as one who hath done righteousness (Maat); for this it is, upon which their heart resteth."

The friendless peasant, pleading with the Grand Steward for justice, says: "Beware! Eternity approaches." Ameni, the great lord of Benihasan, placed upon his tomb door, as we have seen, his record of social justice in dealing with his people, as the best passport he could devise in preparation for the journey into the realms of the hereafter. The alabaster quarry called Hatnub ("House of Gold"), in the eastern desert behind Amarna, is filled with inscriptions recording in endless iteration the just and benevolent lives of the neighbouring lords in the Feudal Age (see p. 214). Over and over again these men of the Feudal Age reiterate also in their tombs their claims to righteousness of character. "Sesenebnef has done righteousness, his abomination was evil, he saw it not," says an official of the time on his sarcophagus. The Coffin Texts (see p. 221) show clearly that the consciousness of moral responsibility in the hereafter has greatly deepened since the Pyramid Age. The balances of justice to which the peasant appealed so often and so dramatically are now really finding place in the drama of justification hereafter. "The doors of the sky are opened to thy beauty," says one to the deceased; "thou ascendest . . . thy evil is expelled, thy iniquity is wiped away, by those who weigh with the balances on the day of reckoning." Just as the peasant so often called the Grand Steward the "balances of justice," so the deceased may be possessed of character as true and unswerving as the scales themselves. Hence we find the Coffin Texts saying, "Lo, this X (name of the deceased) is the balances of Re, wherewith he weighs truth" (or righteousness). It is evident also whose are the balances of truth and who the judge who presides over them. It is as before the Sun-god, before whom even Osiris had been tried. A similar connection of the judgment with Re places it in the cabin of the Solar barque.

The moral requirement of the great judge has become a matter of course. The dead says: "He loves righteousness and hates evil, upon his favourite ways of righteousness whereon the gods lead." When the dead man entered those righteous paths of the gods, it was with a sense of moral unworthiness left behind. "My sin is expelled," he said, "my iniquity is removed. I have cleansed myself in those two great pools which are in Heracleopolis." Those ceremonial washings which were so common in the Pyramid Texts have now become distinctly moral in their significance. "I go upon the way where I wash my head in the Lake of Righteousness," says the dead man. Again and very often the deceased claims that his life has been blameless: "I am one who loved righteousness, my abomination was evil." "I sit down justified, I rise up justified." "I have established righteousness, I have expelled evil."

We have seen that the judge before whom all souls were to appear was originally Re, but Osiris also early discloses himself as the judge. We hear in the Coffin Texts of "the Great Council (or court of justice) of Osiris" as early as the Ninth or Tenth Dynasty (Twenty-fourth to Twenty-second Centuries) in the days of Merikere. Doubtless the growing popularity of Osiris had much to do with the spread of the conviction, now universal, that *every* soul must meet this ethical ordeal in the hereafter. At the advent of the Middle Kingdom it had become the custom to append to the name of *every* deceased person the epithet "justified." It was this appellation which had been received by Osiris, as a victorious litigant in the court of the Sun-god. At first, as the Pyramid Texts show us, this epithet had been applied only to the Pharaoh, but it gradually became the privilege of every soul, at least of every morally worthy soul.

Similarly, after the Osirian doctrine had gained acceptance at the royal court, the king was identified with the justified Osiris and the priests prefixed "Osiris" to the deceased king's name. We remember that in the Pyramid Texts King Pepi is called "Osiris Pepi," and King Teti becomes "Osiris Teti." As a result of the growing popularity of Osiris, the process which was democratising the splendid royal hereafter now began to identify *every* deceased person, man or woman, with Osiris, so that the deceased not only entered the kingdom of Osiris as of old to enjoy the god's protection and favour, but he (or she!) now *became* Osiris and was conceived as king. Even in burials of simple folk, the mummy was fashioned and laid on the back like the mummy of Osiris and amulets representing the royal insignia of the Pharaoh were painted on the inside of the coffin or laid beside the body. The popular power of the ancient god was strikingly demonstrated in the new custom of prefixing the name of Osiris to that of the dead man; for while he might be and was frequently identified with the Sun-god too, nevertheless, it was by the name of Osiris that he was designated, whereas the Sun-god's name Re was never prefixed to the name of the deceased.

With the rise of the Egyptian Empire after 1600 B.C. the evidences disclosing the long ethical evolution which we are following increased in number and importance, especially as they reveal to us the Egyptian's growing sense of his own personal responsibility for the quality of his character. The reflective stage of moral development had substantially advanced, for he had by this time pondered deeply on his own nature, and as a result thoughtful Egyptians were placing each man's moral responsibility squarely on his own understanding. For this last important concept, *"understanding,"* we remember that he had no designation other than his old word "heart." Already as far back as the Pyramid Age the wise old vizier, Ptahhotep, had some intimation of the "heart" as the seat of responsibility and guidance. We recall his statement, "A hearkener (to good advice) is one whom the god loves, one whom the god hates is one who hearkens not. It is the heart which makes its possessor a hearkener or one not hearkening. The good fortune of a man is his heart." In Ptahhotep the "heart" of a man had become his mentor—in effect his conscience. In the Empire, however, the human heart was to become much more than a responsive listener to good advice, or even a guide to "good fortune." To be sure, Ptahhotep's ideas of the heart as a wise guide continued, and in the fifteenth century B.C. a court herald of the conqueror Thutmose III, in recounting his services for the king, says regarding them: "It was my heart which caused that I should do them, by its guidance of my affairs. It was . . . as an excellent witness. I did not disregard its speech, I feared to transgress its guidance. I prospered thereby greatly, I was successful by reason of that which it caused me to do, I was distinguished by its guidance. 'Lo, . . .' said the people, 'it is an oracle of God in every body. Prosperous is he whom it has guided to the good way of achievement.' Lo, thus I was." The relatives of Pahri, a prince of El-Kab, addressing him after his death, pray thus: "Mayest thou spend eternity in gladness of heart, in the favour of the god that is in thee," and another dead man similarly declares, "The heart of a man is his own god, and my heart was satisfied with my deeds." To this inner voice of the heart, which with surprising insight was even termed a man's god, the Egyptian had now become more sensitive than ever before; for the heart had now gained a much more discriminating and mandatory voice than in Ptahhotep's day, announcing its approval or disapproval of a man's conduct. Having thus become so fully aware of this voice, the Egyptian had also begun to give the word "heart" a meaning which made it more fully the equivalent of our word *conscience* than it had been in the Pyramid Age.

We are now in a position to understand the significance of the increasing definiteness and elaboration with which the Egyptian pictured his growing conception of the judgment hereafter as the Empire dawned. These more detailed ideas of the judgment have come down to us in the Book of the Dead. Three different versions of the judgment, doubtless originally independent, have been combined in the fullest and best rolls. The first is entitled, "Chapter of Entering Into the Hall of Truth (or Righteousness),"[1] and it contains "that which is said on reaching the Hall of Truth, when X (the deceased's name) is purged from all evil that he has done, and he beholds the face of the god. 'Hail to thee, great god, lord of Truth.[2] I have come to thee, my lord, and I am led (hither) in order to see thy beauty. I know thy name, I know the names of the forty-two gods who are with thee in the Hall of Truth, who live on evil-doers and devour their blood, on that day of reckoning character

[1] The word "truth" here is commonly written in the dual, which grammatically equals "the two truths." This curious usage is merely an idiom of intensification, as "morning" is written in the dual for "early morning," or as "happy" (in "Happy New Year") is dualised for "very happy."

[2] In the dual as above, and for the most part throughout this chapter.

before Wennofer (Osiris). Behold, I came to thee, I bring to thee righteousness and I expel for thee sin. I have committed no sin against people. . . . I have not done evil in the place of truth. I knew no wrong. I did no evil thing. . . . I did not do that which the god abominates. I did not report evil of a servant to his master. I allowed no one to hunger. I caused no one to weep. I did not murder. I did not command to murder. I caused no man misery. I did not diminish food in the temples. I did not decrease the offerings of the gods. I did not take away the food-offerings of the dead. I did not commit adultery. I did not commit self-pollution in the pure precinct of my city-god. I did not diminish the grain measure. I did not diminish the span.[3] I did not diminish the land measure. I did not load the weight of the balances. I did not deflect the index of the scales. I did not take milk from the mouth of the child. I did not drive away the cattle from their pasturage. I did not snare the fowl of the gods. I did not catch the fish in their pools. I did not hold back the water in its time. I did not dam the running water.[4] I did not quench the fire in its time.[5] I did not withhold the herds of the temple endowments. I did not interfere with the god in his payments.' "

A second scene of judgment is now enacted. The judge, Osiris, is assisted by forty-two gods who sit with him in judgment on the dead. They are terrifying demons, each bearing a grotesque and horrible name, which the deceased claims that he knows. He therefore addresses them one after the other by name. They are such names as these: "Broad-Stride-that-Came-out-of-

[3] A measure of length.

[4] This refers to diverting the waters of the irrigation canals at time of inundation at the expense of neighbors, still one of the commonest forms of corruption in Egypt.

[5] The text is clear, but the meaning is quite obscure.

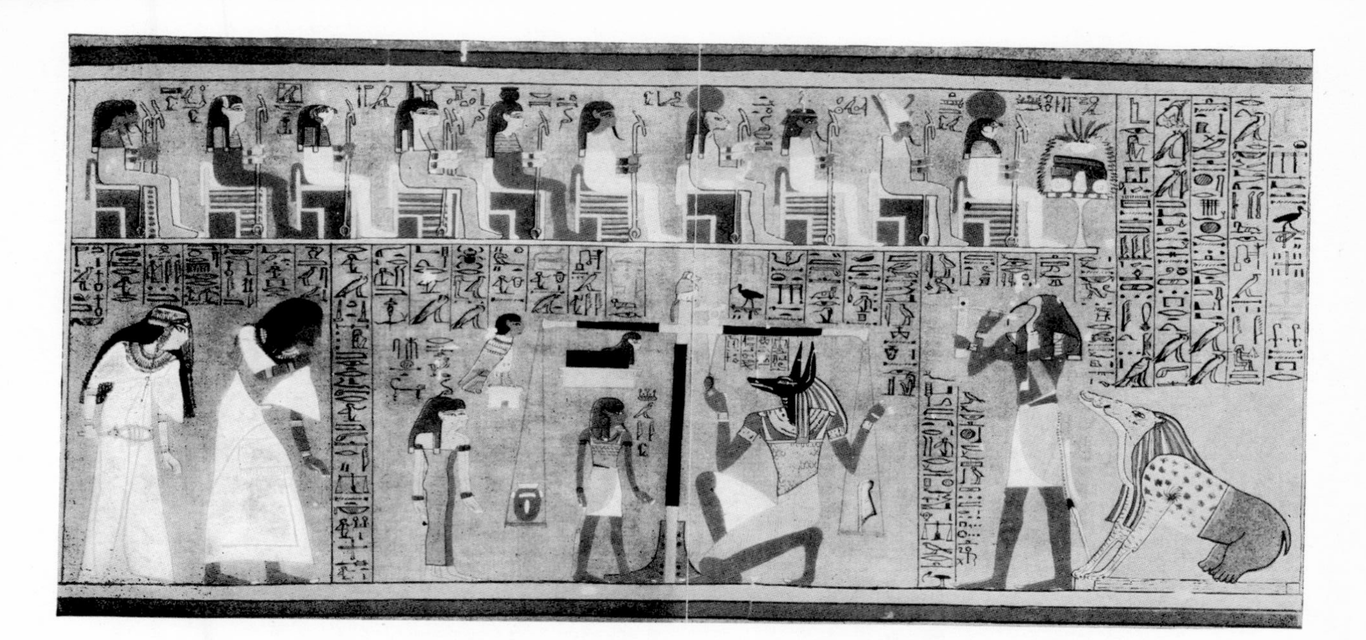

FIG. 14. THE JUDGMENT SCENE IN THE BOOK OF THE DEAD: WEIGHING THE HEART

The balances (*in the middle*) are operated by the jackal-headed Anubis (*at right of balances*). Behind him we see the Ibis-headed scribal god Thoth recording the verdict, while at extreme right squats the grotesque "Devouress" waiting to devour the unjust soul. At the left of the balances stand Shay ("Destiny") and behind him two goddesses of birth. Ani and his wife entering at the left bow humbly as Ani fixes his eye on his own heart in the left scale-pan as it is being weighed over against a feather, the symbol of "truth" or "righteousness" in the other (*right*) scale-pan. Over the balances is written Ani's prayer to his heart not to betray him and at the top is a line of ancient gods who witness the judgment. (*British Museum Papyrus.*)

Heliopolis," "Flame-Hugger-that-Came-out-of-Troja," "Shadow-Eater-that-Came-out-of-the-Cave," "Two-Eyes-of-Flame-that-Came-out-of-Letopolis," "Bone Breaker that-Came-out-of-Heracleopolis," "Blood-Eater-that-Came-out-of-the-Place-of-Execution." These and other equally edifying creations of priestly imagination the deceased calls upon, addressing to each god in turn a declaration of innocence of some particular sin.

It is evident that these forty-two gods are an artificial creation. As was long ago noticed, they represent the forty or more nomes, or administrative districts, of Egypt. The priests doubtless built up this court of forty-two judges in order to control the character of the dead from all quarters of the country. The deceased would find himself confronted by one judge at least who, having come from the deceased's "home town," was acquainted with his local reputation up and down "Main Street," and who therefore could not be deceived.

These forty-two declarations cover much the same ground as those we have already rendered in the first address. The priestly editors had some difficulty in finding enough sins to make up a list of forty-two, and there are several verbatim repetitions, not to mention essential repetitions with slight changes in the wording. The crimes which may be called those of violence are these: "I did not slay men (5), I did not rob (2), I did not steal (4), I did not rob one crying for his possessions (18), my fortune was not great but by my (own) property (41), I did not take away food (10), I did not stir up fear (21), I did not stir up strife (25)." Deceitfulness and other undesirable qualities of character are also disavowed: "I did not speak lies (9), I did not make falsehood in the place of truth (40), I was not deaf to truthful words (24), I did not diminish the grain-measure (6), I was not avaricious (3), my heart devoured not (coveted not?) (28), my heart was not hasty (31), I did not multiply words in speaking (33), my voice was not over loud (37), my mouth did not wag (lit.: go) (17), I did not wax hot (in temper) (23), I did not revile (29), I was not an eavesdropper (16), I was not puffed up (39)." The dead man is free from sexual immorality: "I did not commit adultery with a woman (19), I did not commit self-pollution (20, 27)"; and ceremonial transgressions are also denied: "I did not revile the king (35), I did not blaspheme the god (38), I did not slay the divine bull (13), I did not steal temple endowment (8), I did not diminish food in the temple (15), I did not do an abomination of the gods (42)." These denials, and some that are unintelligible, make up this declaration of innocence.

This section of the Book of the Dead is commonly called the "Confession." It would be difficult to devise a term more opposed to the real character of the dead man's statement, which as an obvious declaration of innocence is, of course, the reverse of a confession. The ineptitude of the designation has become so evident that some editors have added the word negative, and thus call it the "negative confession," which means nothing at all. The Egyptian does *not* confess at this judgment, and this is a fact of the utmost importance in his religious development, as we shall see. To mistake this section of the Book of the Dead for "confession" it totally to misunderstand the development which was now slowly carrying the ancient Egyptian towards that complete acknowledgment and humble disclosure of his sin which is nowhere found in the Book of the Dead.

Having thus vindicated himself before the entire great

FIG. 15. THE JUDGMENT SCENE CONTINUED: THE JUSTIFIED DECEASED LED BEFORE THE JUDGMENT SEAT OF OSIRIS

The verdict of the balances (see preceding figure) has been favorable, and Ani is seen twice: first, led by Horus, the son of Osiris, into the presence of the great god; and second, kneeling in reverence before the throne of Osiris. As a Verdure-god the body of Osiris is here painted bright green and he sits in a green kiosk. As a god who had died he is represented as a mummy figure. Behind him stand Isis and Nephthys. As Horus leads in Ani, he announces that "His (Ani 's) heart is righteous." (*British Museum Papyrus.*)

court, the deceased confidently addresses them: "Hail to you, ye gods! I know you, I know your names. I fall not before your blades. Report not evil of me to this god whom ye follow. My case does not come before you. Speak ye the truth concerning me before the All-Lord; because I did the truth (or righteousness) in the land of Egypt. I did not revile the god. My case did not come before the king then reigning. Hail to you, ye gods who are in the Hall of Truth, in whose bodies are neither sin nor falsehood, who live on truth in Heliopolis . . . before Horus dwelling in his sun-disk.[6]. . . . Behold, I come to you without sin, without evil, without wrong. . . . I live on righteousness, I feed on the righteousness of my heart. I have done that which men say, and that wherewith the gods are content. I have satisfied the god with that which he desires. I gave bread to the hungry, water to the thirsty, clothing to the naked, and a ferry to him who was without a boat. I made divine offerings for the gods and food-offerings for the dead. Save ye me; protect ye me. Enter no complaint against me before the Great God. For I am one of pure mouth and pure hands, to whom was said 'Welcome, welcome' by those who saw him." With these words the claims of the deceased to moral worthiness merge into affirmations that he has observed all ceremonial requirements of the Osirian faith, and these form more than half of this concluding address to the gods of the court.

The third record of the judgment was doubtless the version which made the deepest impression upon the Egyptian. Like the drama of Osiris at Abydos it is graphic and depicts the judgment as effected by the bal-

[6] It should be noted that this is another evidence of the Solar origin of this court.

ances (see Fig. 14). In the sumptuously illustrated papyrus of Ani we see Osiris sitting enthroned at one end of the judgment hall, with Isis and Nephthys standing behind him. Along one side of the hall are ranged the nine gods of the Heliopolitan Ennead, headed by the Sun-god. *They* afterwards announce the verdict, showing the originally Solar origin of this third scene of judgment, in which Osiris has now assumed the chief place. In the midst stand "the balances of Re wherewith he weighs truth," as we have seen them called in the Feudal Age; but the judgment in which they figure has now become Osirianised. The balances are manipulated by the ancient mortuary god, the jackal-headed Anubis, behind whom stands Thoth, the scribe of the gods, who presides over the weighing, pen and writing palette in hand, that he may record the result. Behind him crouches a grotesque monster called the "Devouress," with the head of a crocodile, fore quarters of a lion and hind quarters of a hippopotamus, waiting to devour the unjust soul. Beside the balances in subtle suggestiveness stands the figure of "Destiny" accompanied by Renenet and Meskhenet, the two goddesses of birth, about to contemplate the fate of the soul at whose coming into this world they had once presided. Behind the enthroned divinities sit the gods "Command" and "Intelligence." In other rolls we not infrequently find standing at the entrance the goddess "Truth, daughter of Re," who ushers into the hall of judgment the newly arrived soul. Ani and his wife, with bowed heads and deprecatory gestures, enter the fateful hall, and Anubis at once calls for the heart of Ani. Looking much like a tiny vase, the Egyptian hieroglyph for heart, representing here the heart of Ani, appears on one side of the balances, while on the other side appears a feather, the symbol and hieroglyph for Truth, Righteousness, Justice (Maat). At the critical moment Ani addresses his own heart: "O my heart that came from my mother! O my heart belonging to my being! Rise not up against me as a witness. Oppose me not in the council (court of justice). Be not hostile to me before the master of the balances. . . . Let not my name be of evil odour with the court, speak no lie against me in the presence of the god."

Evidently this appeal has proven effective, for Thoth, "envoy of the Great Ennead, that is in the presence of Osiris," at once says: "Hear ye this word in truth. I have judged the heart of Osiris [Ani].[7] His soul stands as a witness concerning him, his character is just by the great balances. No sin of his has been found." The Nine Gods of the Ennead at once respond: "How good it is, this which comes forth from thy just mouth. Osiris Ani, the justified, witnesses. There is no sin of his, there is no evil of his with us. The Devouress shall not be given power over him. Let there be given to him the bread that cometh forth before Osiris, the domain that abideth in the field of offerings, like the Followers of Horus."

Having thus received a favourable verdict, the fortunate Ani is led forward by "Horus, son of Isis," who presents him to Osiris, at the same time saying: "I come to thee, Wennofer (Osiris); I bring to thee Osiris Ani. His righteous heart comes forth from the balances and he has no sin in the sight of any god or goddess. Thoth has judged him in writing; the Nine Gods have spoken concerning him a very just testimony. Let there be given to him the bread and beer that come forth before Osiris-Wennofer like the Followers of Horus." With his hand in that of Horus, Ani then addresses Osiris: "Lo, I am be-

[7] Omitted by the scribe.

fore thee, Lord of the West. There is no sin in my body. I have not spoken a lie knowingly nor (if so) was there a second time. Let me be like the favourites who are in thy following." Thereupon he kneels before the great god, and as he presents a table of offerings, he is received into the kingdom of Osiris (see Fig. 15).

These three accounts of the judgment, in spite of the grotesque appurtenances with which the priests of the time have embellished them, are not without impressiveness even to the modern beholder as he contemplates these rolls of three thousand five hundred years ago, and realises that these scenes are the graphic expression of the same feeling of moral responsibility, of the same admonishing voice within, to which we still feel ourselves amenable. Ani importunes his heart, which is his word for "conscience," not to betray him, and his cry finds an echo down all the ages in such words as those of Richard:

> "My conscience hath a thousand several tongues,
> And every tongue brings in a several tale,
> And every tale condemns me for a villain."

The Egyptian heard the same voice, feared it, and *endeavoured to silence it.* He strove to still the voice of the heart; he did not yet confess, but insistently maintained his innocence. The next step in his higher development was humbly to disclose the consciousness of guilt to his god. That step he later took. But another force intervened and greatly hampered the complete emancipation of his conscience. There can be no doubt that this Osirian judgment thus graphically portrayed and the universal reverence for Osiris in the Empire had much to do with spreading the belief in moral responsibility beyond the grave, and in giving general currency to those ideas of the supreme value of moral worthiness which we have seen among the moralists and social philosophers of the Pharaoh's court several centuries earlier, in the Feudal Age. The Osiris faith had thus become a great power for righteousness *among the people*. While the Osirian destiny was open to all, nevertheless all must prove themselves morally acceptable to him.

Had the priests left the matter thus, all would have been well. Unhappily, however, the growth of belief in the efficacy of magic in the next world continued. It was believed that all *material* blessings might infallibly be attained by the use of the proper charm. Even the less tangible *mental* equipment, the "heart," meaning the understanding, might also be restored by magical agencies. We have seen that the same charm by which an apprehensive mother prevented a malicious demon from carrying away her child, might likewise be used to prevent a man's "heart," that is his understanding, from being taken away (p. 248). Already in the Feudal Age the priests inserted in the Coffin Texts a charm for this purpose entitled: "Chapter of not Permitting a Man's Heart to be Taken Away from Him in the Nether World." This charm was now included in the Book of the Dead. Here magic entered a new realm—that of conscience, personal qualities, and character. The unlimited possibilities of gain made it inevitable that the priests should now take the momentous step of permitting such agencies thus to enter the world of moral values. Magic might become an agent for moral ends. As we shall see, the Book of the Dead is chiefly a book of magical charms, and the section pertaining to the judgment did not continue to be an exception. The poignant words addressed by Ani to his heart as it was weighed in the balances, "O my heart, rise not up against me as a witness," were now written upon a stone image of the sacred beetle, the scarabæus, and placed over the heart as a mandate of magical potency preventing the heart from betraying the character of the deceased. The words of this charm became a chapter of the Book of the Dead, where they bore the title, "Chapter of Preventing that the Heart of a Man Oppose Him in the Nether World." The scenes of the judgment and the text of the Declaration of Innocence were multiplied on rolls by the scribes and sold to all the people. In these copies the places for the name of the deceased were left vacant, and the purchaser filled in the blanks after he had secured the document. The words of the verdict, declaring the deceased had successfully met the judgment and acquitting him of evil, were not lacking in any of these rolls. Any citizen, whatever the character of his life, might thus secure from the scribes a certificate declaring that Blank was a righteous man before it was known who Blank would be. He might even obtain a formulary so mighty that the Sun-god, as the real power behind the judgment, would be cast down from heaven into the Nile, if he did not bring forth the deceased fully justified before his court. Thus the earliest moral development which we can trace in the life of ancient man was suddenly arrested, or at least seriously checked, by the detestable devices of a corrupt priesthood eager for gain.

It is needless to point out the confusion of distinctions involved in this last application of magic. It is the old failure to perceive the difference between "that which goeth in" and "that which cometh out" of the man. A justification mechanically applied from without, and freeing the man from punishments coming from without, cannot, of course, heal the ravages that have taken place within. The voice within, to which the Egyptian was more sensitive than any people of the earlier East, and to which the whole idea of the moral ordeal in the hereafter was due, could not be quieted by any such means. The general reliance upon such devices for escaping ultimate responsibility for an unworthy life must have seriously poisoned the life of the people. While the Book of the Dead discloses to us more fully than ever before in the history of Egypt the character of the moral judgment in the hereafter and the reality with which the Egyptian clothed his conception of moral responsibility, it is likewise a revelation of ethical decadence. In so far as the Book of the Dead had become a magical agency for securing moral vindication in the hereafter, irrespective of character, it had become a positive force for evil.

This priestly product, the Book of the Dead, was further an evil influence because it was a body of magical charms and spells believed to be infallible in procuring for the deceased the satisfaction of all material and physical needs in the hereafter. In the Egyptian Empire these charms had increased in number, and each had its title indicating just what it was intended to accomplish for the deceased. Combined with some of the old hymns of praise to Re and Osiris, some of which might be recited at the funeral, and usually including also some account of the judgment, these mortuary texts were now written on a roll of papyrus and deposited with the dead in the tomb. It is these papyri which have now commonly come to be called the Book of the Dead. As a matter of fact, there was in the Empire no such book. Each roll contained a random collection of such mortuary texts as the scribal copyist happened to have at hand, or those which he found enabled him best to sell his rolls; that is, such as enjoyed the greatest popularity. There were sumptuous and splendid rolls, sixty to eighty feet long and containing from seventy-five to as many as a hundred and twenty-five or thirty chapters or charms. On the other hand, the scribes also copied small and modest rolls but a few feet in length, bearing but a meagre selection of the more important chapters. No two rolls exhibit the same collection of charms and chapters throughout, and it was not until the Ptolemaic period, some time after the Fourth Century B.C., that a more nearly canonical selection of chapters was gradually introduced. It will be seen, then, as we have said, that, properly speaking, there was in the Empire no *Book* of the Dead, but only various groups of mortuary chapters filling the mortuary papyri of the time. The entire body of chapters or charms from which these rolls were made up, were upwards of two hundred in number, although even the largest rolls did not contain them all. The independence or identity of each chapter was now evident in the custom of prefixing to every chapter a title—a custom which had begun in the case of many chapters in the Coffin Texts. Groups of chapters forming the most common nucleus of the Book of the Dead were frequently called "Chapters of Ascending by Day," a designation also in use in the Coffin Texts; but there was no current title for a roll of the Book of the Dead as a whole.

While a few scanty fragments of the Pyramid Texts have survived in the Book of the Dead, it may nevertheless be said that they have almost disappeared. The Coffin Texts reappear, however, in increasing numbers and contribute largely to the various collections which make up the Book of the Dead. An innovation of which only indications are found in the CoffinTexts is the insertion in the

Empire rolls of gorgeous vignettes illustrating the career of the deceased in the next world. Great confidence was placed in their efficacy, especially, as we have seen, in the scene of the judgment, which was now elaborately illustrated. It may be said that these illustrations in the Book of the Dead are another example of the elaboration of magical devices designed to ameliorate the life beyond the grave. Indeed, the Book of the Dead itself, as a whole, is but a far-reaching and complex illustration of the increasing dependence on magic in the hereafter.

The benefits to be obtained in this way were unlimited, and it is evident that the ingenuity of a mercenary priesthood now played a large part in the development which followed. To the luxurious nobles of the Empire, the old peasant vision of the hereafter where the dead man might plough and sow and reap in the happy fields, and where the grain grew to be seven cubits (about twelve feet) high,[8] did not appear an attractive prospect. To be levied for labour and to be obliged to go forth and toil, even in the fields of the blessed, no longer appealed to the pampered grandees of an age of wealth and luxury. Already in the Middle Kingdom wooden figures of the servants of the dead were placed in the tomb, that they might labour for him in death as they had done in life. This idea was now carried somewhat further. Statuettes of the dead man bearing sack and hoe were fashioned, and a cunning charm was devised and written upon the breast of the figure: "O statuette,[9] counted for X (name of deceased), if I am called, if I am counted to do any work that is done in the Nether World, . . . thou shalt

[8] Book of the Dead, Chap. CIX.

[9] The word used is that commonly written "Ushebti," or "Shawabti" and translated "respondent." It is, however, of very obscure origin and of uncertain meaning.

count thyself for me at all times, to cultivate the fields, to water the shores, to transport sand of the east to the west, and say, 'Here am I.' " This charm was placed among those in the roll, with the title, "Chapter of Causing that the Statuette Do the Work of a Man in the Nether World."[10] The device was further elaborated by finally placing one such little figure of the dead in the tomb for each day in the year, and they have been found in the Egyptian cemeteries in such numbers that museums and private collections all over the world, as has been well said, are "populated" with them.

With such means of gain so easily available, we cannot wonder that the priests and scribes of this age took advantage of the opportunity. The dangers of the hereafter were now greatly multiplied, and for every critical situation the priest was able to furnish the dead with an effective charm which would infallibly save him. Besides many charms which enabled the dead to reach the world of the hereafter, there were those which prevented him from losing his mouth, his head, his heart, others which enabled him to remember his name, to breathe, eat, drink, avoid eating his own foulness, to prevent his drinking-water from turning into flame, to turn darkness into light, to ward off all serpents and other hostile monsters, and many others. The desirable transformations, too, had now increased, and a short chapter might in each case enable the dead man to assume the form of a falcon of gold, a divine falcon, a lily, a Phœnix, a heron, a swallow, a serpent called "son of earth," a crocodile, a god, and, best of all, there was a chapter so potent that by its use a man might assume any form that he desired. It is such productions as these which form by far the larger proportion of the mass

[10] Book of the Dead, Chap. VI.

of texts which we term the Book of the Dead. To call it the "Bible of the Egyptians," then, is quite to mistake the function and content of these rolls.[11]

The tendency which brought forth this mass of charms or spells, commonly called "chapters," is also characteristically evident in two other books each of which was in itself a coherent and connected composition. The Book of the Two Ways, as old, we remember, as the Middle Kingdom,[12] had already contributed much to the Book of the Dead regarding the fiery gates through which the dead gained entrance to the world beyond and to the two ways by which he was to make his journey. On the basis of such fancies as these, the imagination of the priests now put forth a "Book of Him Who is (or 'What is') in the Nether World," describing the subterranean journey of the sun during the night as he passed through twelve long cavernous galleries beneath the earth, each one representing a journey of an hour, the twelve caverns leading the sun at last to the point in the east where he rises. The other book, commonly called the "Book of the Gates," represents each of the twelve caverns as entered by a gate and concerns itself with the passage of these gates.[13] While these compositions never gained the popularity enjoyed by the Book of the Dead, they are magical guide-books devised for gain, just as was much of the material which made up the Book of the Dead.

That which saves the Book of the Dead itself from

[11] The designation "Bible of the old Egyptians" is at least as old as the report of the Committee of the Oriental Congress, which sat in London in 1874 and arranged for publishing the Book of the Dead. See Naville, *Todtenbuch,* Einleitung, p. 5 (Berlin, 1886).

[12] See above, pp. 241 ff.

[13] Nile travellers will perhaps recall having seen this great composition in the royal tombs at Luxor, *e.g.,* in the Tomb of Ramses VI just above that of Tutenkhamon.

being exclusively a magical *vade-mecum* for use in the hereafter is its elaboration of the ancient idea of the moral judgment, and its evident appreciation of the burden of conscience. We have seen that before the Feudal Age, the relation with God had become something more than merely the faithful observance of external rites. It had now become a matter of the heart and of character.

So strong was the moral sense of the Egyptian that he did not limit the value of a worthy life to its availability in rendering him acceptable to Osiris in the next life. Herein lies the limitation of the Osirian ethics which bade a man think only of moral consequences beyond the grave. After all, as we have so often said, Osiris was a god of the dead. The old social philosophers of the Feudal Age had preached the righteousness of Re, the Sun-god, and demanded social justice *here* because Re demanded it. They were not without their descendants in the Empire—men who found in the Solar faith an obligation to righteous living here and now, and who discerned earthly rewards in so living. The Sun-god was not chiefly a god of the dead. He reigned in the earthly affairs of men, and during the earthly life men felt the moral obligation which he placed upon them hourly. About 1400 B.C. one of the architects of Amenhotep III, addressing a hymn of praise to the Sun-god, says: "I was a valiant leader among thy monuments, doing righteousness for thy heart. I know that thou art satisfied with righteousness. Thou makest great him who doeth it on earth. I did it and thou didst make me great." Similarly, when the Pharaoh made oath he swore, "As Re loves me, as my father Amon (long since identified with Re) favours me"; and the conqueror Thutmose III in making this oath to the truth of what he says, and affirming his respect for the truth in the sight of his god, refers to the Sun-god's presence thus: "For he knoweth heaven and he knoweth earth, he seeth the whole earth hourly." While it is true that the subterranean hereafter of the Osiris faith depicts the Sun-god as journeying from cavern to cavern beneath the earth, passing through the realm of Osiris and bringing light and joy to the dead who dwell there, this is a conception unknown to the early Solar theology as found in the Pyramid Texts. In the Empire the Sun-god was pre-eminently a god of the world of living men, in whose affairs he was constantly present and active. Men felt their responsibility to him here and now, and that dominion as it deepened in the hearts of men was now also to expand with the expanding horizon of the imperial age until, for the first time in history, there dawned upon the eyes of these early Nile-dwellers the vision of the world-god.

CHAPTER XV

UNIVERSAL DOMINION AND EARLIEST MONOTHEISM

In the Feudal Age the *social* realm had made its deepest impression upon religion and morals as in the Pyramid Age the Egyptian state, the *political* realm, had earlier done. Both of these were limited to the territory of Egypt. To be sure, the Pyramid Age had gained a dim vision of the vast extent of the Sun-god's dominion, and in the Pyramid Texts he is once addressed by the sounding title, "Limitless." We have seen also that the Pyramid Age, in the social discernment of such men as Ptahhotep, had created a realm of universal ethical values, and in giving the Sun-god the sovereignty of such a realm the Egyptians were already moving on the road towards monotheism (see p. 145). We recall that the instruction of the unknown Heracleopolitan king had likewise carried the Egyptians a long way on that road. Through the conception of a great administrative and moral order, for which they had already developed a word, the Egyptians might have advanced to full recognition of monotheism as later philosophers and theologians have done. Nevertheless, in the Pyramid Age this moral order had remained a *national* conception and it was not extended to embrace the world as a whole.

The Sun-god ruled only Egypt, and in the great sun-hymn of the Pyramid Texts he stands guardian on the Egyptian frontiers, where he builds the gates which restrain all outsiders from entering his inviolable domain.

In the Pyramid Age, too, the Sun-god had already begun the process of absorbing the other gods of Egypt, a process resulting even at so remote a date in a form of national pantheism, in which all the gods ultimately coalesced into forms and functions of one. But even this process, though it did not cease, had left the supreme god's dominion still restricted to Egypt. He was very far from being a world-god. The Egyptians indeed had not as yet gained the world-idea, the world-empire over which they might install the world-ruler. The influences of an environment restricted to the limits of the Nile Valley had now, however, gone as far as they could, when a career of imposing foreign expansion of national power enlarged the theatre of thought and action. The Solar theology had been sensitively responsive to conditions in the Nile-Valley world. It proved to be not less sensitive to the larger world, to include which the Egyptian horizon had now expanded.

Egypt's imperial expansion northward and southward until the Pharaoh's power had united the contiguous regions of Asia and Africa into the first stable Empire in history is the commanding fact in the history of the East in the Sixteenth Century B.C. The consolidation of that power by Thutmose III's twenty years' campaigning in Asia is a stirring chapter of military imperialism in which for the first time in the East we can discern the skilfully organised and mobile forces of a great state as they are brought to bear with incessant impact upon the nations of Western Asia, until the Egyptian supremacy is undisputed from the Greek Islands, the coasts of Asia Minor, and the highlands of the Upper Euphrates on the north to the Fourth Cataract of the Nile on the south. This great military leader himself made the remark which we have quoted above regarding his god: "He seeth the whole earth hourly." If this was true it was because the sword of the Pharaoh had carried the power of Egypt's god to the limit of Egypt's Empire. Fifty years earlier, indeed, Thutmose I proclaimed his kingdom as far as "the circuit of the sun." In the Old Kingdom the Sun-god was conceived as a Pharaoh, whose kingdom was Egypt. With the expansion of the Egyptian kingdom into a world-empire it was inevitable that the domain of the god should likewise expand. As the kingdom had long since found expression in religion, so now the Empire was to make a powerful impression upon religious thought.

While this was a more or less mechanical and unconscious process, it was accompanied by an intellectual awakening which shook the old Egyptian traditions to the foundations and set the men of the age to thinking in a larger world. The Sun-god had been an Egyptian Pharaoh for two thousand five hundred years, a Pharaoh ruling Egypt; but after 1600 B.C. the Pharaoh became lord of the civilised world. The conqueror Thutmose III was the first character of universal aspects in human history, the first world-hero. As such he made a profound impression upon his age. The idea of universal power, of a world-empire, was visibly and tangibly bodied forth in his career. There is a touch of universalism now discernible in the theology of the Empire which is directly due to such impressions as he and his successors made. Egypt is forced out of the immemorial isolation of her narrow valley into world-relations, with which the theology of the time must reckon—relations with which the Sun-god, as we have seen, was inextricably involved. Commercial connections, maintained from an immemorially remote past, had not sufficed to bring the great outside world effectively into the purview of Egyptian thinking. The limits of the dominion of the Egyptian gods had been fixed as the outer fringes of the Nile Valley long before the outside world was familiar to the Nile-dwellers; and merely commercial intercourse with a larger world had not been able to shake the tradition. Many a merchant had seen a stone fall in distant Babylon and in Egyptian Thebes alike, but it had not occurred to him, or to any man in that far-off age, that the same natural force, pulling down the falling stone, reigned in both these widely separated countries. The world was far indeed from the lad lying beneath the apple-tree and discovering a universal force in the fall of an apple. Many a merchant of that day, too, had seen the sun rise behind the Babylonian tower-temples as it did among the clustered obelisks of Thebes, but the thought of the age had not yet come to terms with such far-reaching facts as these, even though the Conqueror himself had said of the Sun-god, "He seeth the whole earth hourly." It was universalism expressed in terms of imperial power which first caught the imagination of the thinking men of the Empire, and disclosed to them the universal sweep of the Sun-god's dominion as a physical fact. Monotheism was but imperialism in religion.

It is no accident, therefore, that about 1400 B.C., in the reign of Amenhotep III, the most splendid of the Egyptian emperors, we find the first of such impressions. Two architects, Suti and Hor, twin brothers, whom Amenhotep III was employing at Thebes, have left us a sun-hymn on a stela now in the British Museum, which discloses the tendency of the age and the widening vision with which these men of the Empire were looking out upon the world and discerning the unlimited scope of the Sun-god's realm. This sun-hymn contains such significant lines as these:

" . . . .

Thou art a craftsman shaping thine own limbs;
Fashioner without being fashioned;
Unique in his qualities, traversing eternity;
Over ways with millions under his guidance.

. . . .

When thou sailest across the sky all men behold thee,
(Though) thy going is hidden from their sight.

. . . .

Thou traversest a journey of leagues,
Even millions and hundred-thousands of time.
Every day is under thee.
When thy setting comes,
The hours of the night hearken to thee likewise.
When thou hast traversed it
There comes no ending to thy labours.
All men, they see by means of thee.

. . . .

Creator of all and giver of their sustenance,

. . . .

A mother, profitable to gods and men,
A craftsman of experience, . . .
Valiant herdman who drives his cattle,
Their refuge and giver of their sustenance,

. . . .

Who beholds that which he has made,
Sole lord taking captive all lands every day,
As one beholding them that walk therein;
Shining in the sky, a being as the sun.
He makes the seasons by the months,
Heat when he desires,
Cold when he desires,

. . . .

Every land is in rejoicing
At his rising every day, in order to praise him."

It is evident in such a hymn as this that the vast sweep of the Sun-god's course over all the lands and peoples of the earth has at last found consideration, ... and the momentous step has been taken of extending the sway of the Sun-god over all lands and peoples. No earlier document left us by the thought of Egypt contains such unequivocal expression of this thought as we find here:

> "Sole lord, taking captive all lands every day,
> As one beholding them that walk therein."

It is important to observe also that this tendency is connected directly with the social movement of the Feudal Age. Such epithets applied to the Sun-god as

> "Valiant herdman who drives his cattle,
> Their refuge and the giver of their sustenance,"

of course carry us back to the Instruction Addressed to Merikere, in which men are called "the flocks of God," and the thoughts of Ipuwer and his "shepherd of all men." The other remarkable epithet,

> "A mother, profitable to gods and men,"

carries with it the idea of similar solicitude for mankind. The humane aspects of the Sun-god's sway, to which the social thinkers of the Feudal Age chiefly contributed, have not disappeared among the powerful political motives of this new universalism.

When Amenhotep III's son, Amenhotep IV, succeeded his father, about 1375 B.C., a keen struggle arose between the royal house, on the one hand, and the sacerdotal organisation dominated by Amon, on the other. It is evident that the young king favoured the claims of the old Sun-god as opposed to those of Amon, whose powerful Theban priesthood had begun calling their once obscure local god by a composite name "Amon-Re," thus indicating his identity with the Sun-god Re. Early in his reign we find Amenhotep IV ardently supporting a new form of the old Solar faith, which may have been the result of a compromise between the two. At a time when the Asiatic situation was exceedingly critical, and the Pharaoh's supremacy there was threatened, he devoted himself with absorbing zeal to the new Solar universalism which we have discerned under his father. The Sun-god was given a designation which freed the new faith from the compromising polytheistic tradition of the old Solar theology. He was now called "Aton," an ancient name for the physical sun, and probably designating his disk. It occurs twice in the hymn of the two architects of Amenhotep III, quoted above, and it had already gained some favour under this king, who named one of his royal barges "Aton-Gleams." Not only did the Sun-god receive a new name, but the young king now gave him a new symbol also. We recall that the most ancient symbol of the Sun-god was a pyramid, and as a falcon the figure of that bird was also used to designate him. These, however, were intelligible only in Egypt, and Amenhotep IV had a wider arena in view. The new symbol depicted the sun as a disk from which diverging beams radiated downward, each ray terminating in a human hand (see Fig. 16). It was a masterly symbol, suggesting a power issuing from its celestial source, and putting its hand upon the world and the affairs of men. As far back as the Pyramid Texts the rays of the Sun-god had been likened to his arms and had been conceived as an agency on earth: "The *arm* of the sunbeams is lifted with King Unis," raising him to the skies. Such a symbol was suited to be understood throughout the world which the Pharaoh controlled. Its meaning was so clear that an Asiatic on the Euphrates or a Nubian on the Sudanese Nile would discern its significance at once. It was not only a symbol of universalism, but was supremely fitted to be a universal symbol.

There was also some effort to define the Solar power thus symbolised. The full name of the Sun-god was "Harakhte (Horizon-Horus), rejoicing in the horizon in his name 'Heat which is in Aton.'" It was enclosed in two royal cartouches, like the double name of the Pharaoh, a device suggested by the analogy of the Pharaoh's power, and another clear evidence of the impression which the Empire as a state had now made on the Solar theology. But the name enclosed in the cartouches roughly defined the actual physical force of the sun in the visible world, and was no political figure. The word rendered "heat" sometimes means also "light." It is evident that what the king was deifying was the force by which the Sun made himself felt on earth. In harmony with this conclusion are the numerous statements in the Aton hymns, which, as we shall see, represent Aton as everywhere active on earth by means of his "rays." While it is evident that the new faith drew its inspiration from Heliopolis, so that the king assuming the office of High Priest of Aton called himself "Great Seer," the title of the High Priest of Heliopolis, nevertheless most of the old lumber which made up the externals of the traditional theology was rejected. We look in vain for the sun-barques, and in the same way also later accretions, like the voyage through the subterranean caverns of the dead, are completely shorn away.

If the Aton movement was intended as a compromise with the priests of Amon, it failed. The bitterest enmities soon broke out, culminating finally in the determination on the king's part to make Aton sole god of the Empire and to annihilate Amon. The effort to obliterate all trace of the existence of the upstart Amon resulted in the most extreme measures. The king changed his own name from "Amenhotep" ("Amen rests" or "is satisfied") to "Ikhnaton," which means "Aton is satisfied," and is a translation of the king's old name into a corresponding idea in the Aton faith. The name of Amon, wherever it occurred on the great monuments of Thebes, was expunged, and in doing so not even the name of the king's father, Amenhotep III, was respected. These erasures were not confined to the name of Amon. Even the word "gods" as a compromising plural was expunged wherever found, and the names of the other gods, too, were treated like that of Amon.

Finding Thebes embarrassed with too many theological traditions, in spite of its prestige and its splendour, Ikhnaton forsook it and built a new capital about midway between Thebes and the sea, at a place now commonly known as Tell el-Amarna. He called it Akhetaton, "Horizon of Aton." A similar Aton city was founded in Nubia, and in all likelihood there was another in Asia. The three great portions of the Empire, Egypt, Nubia, and Syria, were thus each given a centre of the Aton faith. Besides these, sanctuaries of Aton were also built at various other places in Egypt.

This was, of course, not accomplished without building up a powerful court party, which the king could oppose to the evicted priesthoods, especially that of Amon. The resulting convulsion undoubtedly affected seriously the power of the royal house. The life of this court party, which now unfolded at Akhetaton, centred about the propagation of the new faith, and as preserved to us in the wall reliefs which fill the chapels of the cliff tombs, excavated by the king for his nobles in the face of the low cliffs of the eastern plateau behind the new city, it forms, perhaps, the most interesting and picturesque chapter in the story of the early East. It is to the tombs of these partisans of the king that we owe our knowledge of the content of the remarkable teaching which he was now propagating. They contain a series of hymns in praise of the Sun-god, or of the Sun-god and the king alternately, which afford us at least a glimpse into the new world of thought, in which we behold this young king and his associates lifting up their eyes and endeavouring to discern God in the illimitable sweep of his power—God no longer of the Nile Valley only, but of all men and of all the world. We can do no better at this juncture than to let these hymns speak for themselves. The longest and most important is as follows:[1]

UNIVERSAL SPLENDOUR AND POWER OF ATON

"Thou dawnest beautifully in the horizon of the sky,
O living Aton who wast the Beginning of life!
When thou didst rise in the eastern horizon,
Thou didst fill every land with thy beauty.
Thou art beautiful, great, glittering, high over every land,
Thy rays, they encompass the lands, even to the end of all that
thou hast made.
Thou art Re, and thou penetratest to the very end of them;[2]
Thou bindest them for thy beloved son (the Pharaoh).

[1] Some changes in the above translation, as compared with that in the author's *History,* are due to a few new readings in Davies's carefully copied text (*Rock Tombs of El Amarna,* Vol. VI, pl. XXVII, London), as well as to further study of the document also. A translation by Sethe has added some interesting new interpretations of which I have adopted several (see H. Schäfer, *Amarna in Religion und Kunst,* pp. 63–70 [Leipzig, 1931]). The divisions into strophes are not in the original, but are indicated here for the sake of clearness. Titles of the strophes have been inserted to aid the modern reader.

[2] There is a pun here on the word Re, which is the same as the word used for "end."

Though thou art far away, thy rays are upon earth;
Though thou art in the faces of men, thy footsteps are unseen.

NIGHT AND MAN

"When thou settest in the western horizon of the sky,
The earth is in darkness like death.
They sleep in their chambers,
Their heads are wrapped up,
Their nostrils are stopped,
And none seeth the other,
While all their things are stolen,
Which are under their heads,
And they know it not.

Thou makest darkness, and it is night,
Wherein all the beasts of the forest creep forth.
(Psalm 104:20.)

NIGHT AND ANIMALS

"Every lion cometh forth from his den,
All serpents, they sting.
Darkness broods,
The world is in silence,
He that made them resteth in his horizon.

The young lions roar after their prey,
And seek their food from God.
(Psalm 104:21.)

DAY AND MAN

"Bright is the earth when thou risest in the horizon;
When thou shinest as Aton by day
Thou drivest away the darkness.
When thou sendest forth thy rays,
The Two Lands (Egypt) are in daily festivity.
Men waken and stand upon their feet
When thou hast raised them up.
Their limbs bathed, they take their clothing,
Their arms uplifted in adoration to thy dawning.
Then in all the world they do their work.

The sun ariseth, they get them away,
And lay them down in their dens.
Man goeth forth unto his work
And to his labour until the evening.
(Psalm 104:22–23.)

DAY AND THE ANIMALS AND PLANTS

"All cattle rest upon their pasturage,
The trees and the plants flourish,
The birds flutter in their marshes,
Their wings uplifted in adoration to thee.
All the antelopes dance upon their feet,
All creatures that fly or alight,
They live when thou hast shone upon them.

DAY AND THE WATERS

"The barques sail up-stream and down-stream alike.	Yonder is the sea, great and wide,
Every highway is open because thou dawnest.	Wherein are things creeping innumerable,
The fish in the river leap up before thee.	Both small and great beasts.
	There go the ships;
Thy rays are in the midst of the great green sea.	There is leviathan, whom thou hast formed to play therein. (Psalm 104:25–26.)

CREATION OF MAN

"Creator of the germ in woman,
Who makest seed into men,
Making alive the son in the body of his mother,
Soothing him that he may not weep,
Nurse even in the womb,
Giver of breath to sustain alive every one that he maketh!
When he descendeth from the body (of his mother) on the day of his birth,
Thou openest his mouth altogether,
Thou suppliest his necessities.

CREATION OF ANIMALS

"When the fledgling in the egg chirps in the shell,
Thou givest him breath in the midst of it to preserve him alive.
Thou hast made for him his term in the egg, for breaking it.
He cometh forth from the egg to chirp at his term;
. . . .

He goeth about upon his two feet
When he cometh forth therefrom.

UNIVERSAL CREATION

"How manifold are thy works!	O lord, how manifold are thy works!
They are hidden before men	
O sole God, beside whom there is no other.	In wisdom hast thou made them all:
Thou didst create the earth according to thy heart.[3]	The earth is full of thy riches. (Psalm 104:24.)

While thou wast alone:
Even men, all herds of cattle and the antelopes;
All that are upon the earth,
That go about upon their feet;
They that are on high,
That fly with their wings.
The highland countries, Syria and Kush,
And the land of Egypt;
Thou settest every man into his place,
Thou suppliest their necessities,
Every one has his food,
And his days are reckoned.
The tongues are divers in speech,
Their forms likewise and their skins are distinguished,
For thou makest different the strangers.

WATERING THE EARTH IN EGYPT AND ABROAD

"Thou makest the Nile in the Nether World,
Thou bringest it as thou desirest,
To preserve alive the people of Egypt[4]
For thou hast made them for thyself,
Thou lord of them all, who weariest thyself for them;
Thou lord of every land, who risest for them,
Thou Sun of day, great in glory,
All the distant highland countries,

[3] The word "heart" may mean either "pleasure" or "understanding" here.
[4] The word is one used only of the people of Egypt.

Thou makest also their life,
Thou didst set a Nile in the sky.
When it falleth for them,
It maketh waves upon the mountains,
Like the great green sea,
Watering their fields in their towns.

How benevolent are thy designs, O lord of eternity!
There is a Nile in the sky for the strangers
And for the antelopes of all the highlands that go about upon their feet.
But the Nile, it cometh from the Nether World for Egypt.

THE SEASONS

"Thy rays nourish[5] every garden;
When thou risest they live,
They grow by thee.
Thou makest the seasons
In order to make develop all that thou hast made.
Winter to bring them coolness,
And heat that they may taste thee.

UNIVERSAL DOMINION

"Thou didst make the distant sky in order to rise therein,
In order to behold all that thou hast made,
While thou wast yet alone
Shining in thy form as living Aton,
Dawning, glittering, going afar and returning.
Thou makest millions of forms
Through thyself alone;
Cities, villages, and fields, highways and rivers.
All eyes see thee before them,
For thou art Aton of the day over the earth.
When thou hast gone away,
And all men, whose faces thou hast fashioned
In order that thou mightest no longer see thyself alone,
[Have fallen asleep, so that not] one [seeth] that which thou hast made,
Yet art thou still in my heart.

[5] The word used implies the nourishment of a mother at the breast.

REVELATION TO THE KING

. . . .

"There is no other that knoweth thee
Save thy son Ikhnaton.
Thou hast made him wise
In thy designs and in thy might.

UNIVERSAL MAINTENANCE

"The world subsists in thy hand,
Even as thou hast made them.
When thou hast risen they live,
When thou settest they die;
For thou art length of life of thyself,
Men live through thee

The eyes of men see beauty
Until thou settest.
All labour is put away
When thou settest in the west.
When thou risest again
[Thou] makest ⌈every hand⌉ to flourish for the king
And ⌈prosperity⌉ is in every foot,
Since thou didst establish the world,
And raise them up for thy son,
Who came forth from thy flesh,
The king of Upper and Lower Egypt,
Living in Truth, Lord of the Two Lands,
Nefer-khepru-Re, Wan-Re (Ikhnaton),
Son of Re, living in Truth, lord of diadems,
Ikhnaton, whose life is long;
(And for) the chief royal wife, his beloved,
Mistress of the Two Lands, Nefer-nefru-Aton, Nofretete,
Living and flourishing for ever and ever."

This great Royal Hymn probably represents an excerpt, or a series of fragments excerpted, from the ritual of

Aton, as it was celebrated from day to day in the Aton temple at Amarna. Unhappily, it was copied in the cemetery in but one tomb, where about a third of it has perished by the vandalism of the modern natives, leaving us for the lost portion only a very hasty and inaccurate moddern copy made fifty years ago (1883). The other tombs were supplied, with their devotional inscriptions, from the current paragraphs and stock phrases which made up the knowledge of the Aton faith as understood by the scribes and painters who decorated these tombs. It should not be forgotten, therefore, that the fragments of the Aton faith which have survived to us in the Amarna cemetery, our chief source, have thus filtered mechanically through the indifferent hands, and the starved and listless minds of a few petty bureaucrats on the outskirts of a great religious and intellectual movement. Apart from the Royal Hymn, they were elsewhere content with bits and snatches copied in some cases from the Royal Hymn itself, or other fragments patched together in the form of a shorter hymn, which they then slavishly copied in whole or in part from tomb to tomb. Where the materials are so meagre, and the movement revealed so momentous, even the few new contributions furnished by the short hymn are of great value.[6] In four cases the hymn is attributed to the king himself; that is, he is represented as reciting it to Aton. The lines are as follows:

"Thou risest beautifully, O living Aton, Lord of Eternity;
Thou art glittering, beautiful, strong;
Thy love is great and mighty,

6 The short hymn was put together in a composite text of all versions in the second (unpublished) portion of the author's *De hymnis in solem,* and this was later supplemented by my own copies. Davies has also put together a composite text from five tombs in his *Amarna,* Vol. IV, pls. XXXII–XXXIII. The above translation is based on both sources.

Thy rays furnish vision to every one of thy creatures,
Thy glowing hue brings life to the hearts of men,
When thou hast filled the Two Lands with thy love.
O God, who himself fashioned himself,
Maker of every land,
Creator of that which is upon it:
Even men, all herds of cattle and the antelopes,
All trees that grow in the soil,
They live when thou dawnest for them,
Thou art the mother and the father of all that thou hast made.
As for their eyes, when thou dawnest,
They see by means of thee.
Thy rays illuminate the whole earth,
And every heart rejoices because of seeing thee,
When thou dawnest as their lord.

"When thou settest in the western horizon of the sky,
They sleep after the manner of the dead,
Their heads are wrapped up,
Their nostrils are stopped,
Until thy rising comes in the morning,
In the eastern horizon of the sky.
Then their arms are uplifted in adoration of thee,
Thou makest the hearts of men to live by thy beauty,
For men live when thou sendest forth thy rays,
Every land is in festivity:
Singing, music, and shouting of joy
Are in the hall of the Benben[7]-house,
Thy temple in Akhetaton, the seat of Truth (Maat),
Wherewith thou are satisfied.
Food and provision are offered therein;
Thy pure son performs thy pleasing ceremonies,
O living Aton, at his festal processions.
All that thou hast made dance before thee,
Thy august son rejoices, his heart is joyous,

[7] The "Benben" was a pyramidal stone like the pyramidion crowning an obelisk. It was held supremely sacred and originally occupied a special sanctuary or "house" in the Sun-temple at Heliopolis. This passage shows that Ikhnaton had introduced a similar Benben sanctuary at Amarna.

O living Aton, born in the sky every day.
He begets his august son Wanre (Ikhnaton)
Like himself without ceasing,
Son of Re, wearing his beauty, Nefer-khepru-Re, Wan-Re
(Ikhnaton),
Even me, thy son, in whom thou art satisfied,
Who bears thy name.
Thy strength and thy might abide in my heart,
Even thine, O Aton, living forever . . .
Thou hast made the distant sky to rise therein,
In order to behold all that thou didst make,
While thou wast yet alone.
Myriads of life are in thee to sustain them alive,
For it is the breath of life in the nostrils to behold thy radiance.[8]
All flowers live and what grows in the soil
Is made to grow because thou dawnest.
They are drunken before thee.
All cattle skip upon their feet;
The birds in the marsh fly with joy,
Their wings that were folded are spread,
Uplifted in adoration to the living Aton,
Thou maker. . . ."[9]

In these hymns there is an inspiring universalism not found before, either in the thought of Egypt or in that of any other country. It is world-wide in its sweep. The king claims that the recognition of the Sun-god's universal supremacy is also universal, and that all men acknowledge his dominion. On the great boundary stela likewise he says of them, that Aton made them "for his own self; all lands, the Ægeans bear their dues, their tribute is upon their backs, for him who made their life, him by whose rays men live and breathe the air." It is clear that Ikhnaton was projecting a world religion, and

[8] Variant: "Breath, it enters the nostrils when thou showest thyself to them."
[9] The remainder of the line is lost. Only one of the five texts which exist from the beginning goes as far as this point. It also stopped at this place.

endeavouring to displace by it the nationalism which had preceded it for twenty centuries.

Along with this universal power, Ikhnaton is also deeply impressed with the eternal duration of his god; and although he himself calmly accepts his own mortality, and early in his career at Amarna makes public and permanently records on the boundary stelæ instructions for his own burial, nevertheless he relies upon his intimate relation with Aton to insure him something of the Sun-god's duration. His official titulary always contains the epithet after his name, "whose lifetime is long."

But in the beginning of all, Aton called himself forth out of the eternal solitude, the author of his own being. On one of the great boundary stelæ at Amarna the king calls him "My rampart of a million cubits, my reminder of eternity, my witness of the things of eternity, who himself fashioned himself with his own hands, whom no artificer knew." In harmony with this idea, the hymns love to reiterate the fact that the creation of the world which followed was done while the god was yet alone. The words "while thou wert alone" are almost a refrain in these hymns. He is the universal creator who brought forth all the races of men and distinguished them in speech and colour of skin. His creative power still goes on calling forth life, even from the inanimate egg. Nowhere do we find more marked the naïve wonder of the king at the Sun-god's life-giving power than in this marvel, that within the egg-shell, which the king calls the "stone" of the egg—within this lifeless stone, the sounds of life respond to the command of Aton, and, nourished by the breath which he gives, a living creature issues forth.

FIG. 16. TUTENKHAMON AND HIS QUEEN IN A PALACE CHAMBER

The young king sits in a free and careless posture, violating all tradition for a royal portrait, and illustrating the *emancipation of the Aton revolution in art.* The girlish queen (Ikhnaton's third daughter) leans graciously forward, holding a perfume vase in one hand, and with the other adjusting her husband's elaborate collar or touching it with perfume—a scene of personal relations suggested with wonderful grace and charm of line and contour. Above is the symbol of Ikhnaton's god, the sun-disk with rays terminating in human hands, a new symbol illustrating *the emancipation of the Aton revolution in religion.* The background is heavy sheet gold, the garments of silver, the flesh of reddish glass, the ornamental details are incrustation of brightly colored costly stones, like carnelian, all producing a brilliance once dazzlingly gorgeous, now softened by age. From the back of a chair, found in the tomb of Tutenkhamon. *By courtesy of Mr. Howard Carter.* (*Cairo Museum.*)

This lifegiving power is the constant source of life and sustenance, and its immediate agency is the rays of the Sun, bringing light and heat to men. This extraordinary recognition of the Sun's energy as the source of all earthly life is constantly reiterated. The hymns love to dwell upon his rays as an ever-present universal power. "Thou art in the sky, but thy rays are on earth"; "Though thou art far away, thy rays are on earth"; "Thy rays are in the midst of the great green sea"; "Thy rays are on thy beloved son"; "He who makes whole the eyes by his rays"; "It is the breath of life in the nostrils to behold thy rays"; "Thy child (the king), who came forth from thy rays"; "Thou didst fashion him (the king) out of thine own rays"; "Thy rays carry a million royal jubilees"; "When thou sendest forth thy rays, the Two Lands are in festivity"; "Thy rays embrace the lands, even all that thou hast made"; "Whether he is in the sky or on earth, all eyes behold him without ceasing; he fills [every land] with his rays, and makes all men to live."

The obvious dependence of Egypt upon the Nile also made it impossible to ignore this source of life, and there is nothing which discloses more clearly the surprising rationalism of Ikhnaton than the fact that without hesitation he strips off the venerable body of myth and tradition which had for ages deified the Nile as Osiris, and thereupon attributes the inundation to natural forces controlled by his god, who in like solicitude for other lands has made a Nile for them in the sky. *Osiris is completely ignored.* He is never mentioned in any record of Ikhnaton or in any of the tombs at Amarna.

It is at this point that Ikhnaton's thought passes beyond a purely materialistic recognition of the Sun's activity on earth, and discerns the fatherly solicitude of

Aton for all creatures. It is this thought which lifts the movement of Ikhnaton far above all that had before been attained in the religion of Egypt or of the whole East before this time. To Ipuwer the Sun-god was a kindly shepherd, and to Merikere's royal father men were his "flocks" for which he made air and water and food; but Ikhnaton goes further, and says to the Sun-god: "Thou art the father and the mother of all that thou hast made." This teaching is one which anticipates much of the later development in religion even down to our own time. To the sensitive soul of this Egyptian dreamer, the whole animate world seems alive with consciousness of the presence of Aton, and filled with recognition of his fatherly kindness. The picture of the lily-grown marshes, where the flowers are "drunken" in the intoxicating radiance of Aton, where the birds unfold their wings and lift them "in adoration of the living Aton," where the cattle dance with delight in the sunshine, and the fish in the river beyond leap up to greet the light, the universal light whose beams are even "in the midst of the great green sea"—all this discloses a discernment of the universal presence of God in nature, and a mystic conviction of the recognition of that presence by all creatures. There is here an appreciation of the revelation of God in the visible world such as we find seven or eight hundred years later in the Hebrew psalms, and in our own poets of nature since Wordsworth.

It is evident that, in spite of the political origin of this movement, the deepest sources of power in the remarkable revolution lay in this appeal to nature, in this admonition to "consider the lilies of the field." Ikhnaton was a "God-intoxicated man," whose mind responded with marvellous sensitiveness and discernment to the visible evidences of God about him. He was fairly ecstatic in his sense of the beauty of the eternal and universal light. Its beams enfold him on every monument of his which has survived, and *only* him and his queen and the royal children, for he claims a unique relationship with his god. He prays, "May my eyes be satisfied daily with beholding him, when he dawns in this house of Aton and fills it with his own self by his beams, beauteous in love, and lays them upon me in satisfying life for ever and ever." In this light—which more than once, as here, he identifies with love, or again with beauty, as the visible evidence of the presence of God—he revels with an intoxication rarely to be found, and which may be properly compared to the ecstatic joy felt by such a soul as Ruskin in the contemplation of light. Ruskin, as he sees it playing over some lovely landscape, calls it "the breathing, animated, exulting light, which feels and receives and rejoices and acts—which chooses one thing and rejects another—which seeks and finds and loses again—leaping from rock to rock, from leaf to leaf, from wave to wave, glowing or flashing or scintillating according to what it strikes, or in its holier moods absorbing and enfolding all things in the deep fulness of its repose, and then again losing itself in bewilderment and doubt and dimness, or perishing and passing away, entangled in drifting mist, or melted into melancholy air, but still—kindling or declining, sparkling or still—it is the living light, which breathes in its deepest, most entranced rest, which sleeps but never dies."[10] Here is modern ecstasy in the joyousness of light, a veritable gospel of the beauty of light, of which the earliest disciple was this lonely idealist of the Fourteenth Century before

[10] Ruskin, *Modern Painters,* Vol. I, p. 250 (New York, 1873).

Christ. To Ikhnaton, too, the eternal light might sleep, when he that made the world has "gone to rest in his horizon," but to him also as with Ruskin it "sleeps but never dies." A badly broken passage in the great hymn has been successfully interpreted by Sethe as indicating that although the darkness had fallen and men slept, Ikhnaton could feel: "Yet art thou still in my heart."[11]

In this aspect of Ikhnaton's movement, then, it is a gospel of the beauty and beneficence of the natural order, a recognition of the message of nature to the soul of man, which makes it the earliest of those revivals which we call in the case of such artists as Millet and the Barbizon school, or of Wordsworth and his successors, "a return to nature." The painters depict the wild life of the marshes with a new spirit different from the quiet pleasure of the mastaba painters of the Pyramid Age, whose serene pictures of the nobleman's excursions into the papyrus thickets adorn the walls of the tomb chapels in the Memphite cemetery at Sakkara. The frescoes which adorned the floor of Ikhnaton's colonnaded palace hall at Amarna are filled with a new joy of life, and we feel something of the passion which quickened the hand of the artist as in his mind's eye he saw the wild bull leaping in the papyrus thicket and tossing his head at the timorous birds twittering above the marsh reeds and scolding the ponderous intruder who is endangering their nests. Alas, that this noble painting, quivering with life and *movement* which long delighted the eyes of modern visitors at Amarna has now perished forever at the hands of modern native vandals from the neighbouring village!

This new spirit which drew its inspiration from the

[11] See above, p. 285.

beauty and beneficence of *nature* was at the same time deeply sensitive to the life of *man* and to human relations as they actually were, undisturbed by convention or tradition. Ikhnaton's charmingly natural and unrestrained relations with his family were now depicted even on public monuments without reserve. A statuette found unfinished in a royal sculptor's studio at Amarna not only shows the king seated with his little daughter on his knee, as the royal father embraces the little princess, but depicts the Pharaoh in the very act of kissing the little girl as any normal father might do. It is not difficult to imagine the rage and horror which such a royal portrait excited in the feelings of the traditionalists of Ikhnaton's age, the conventional grandees of the court in whose eyes a Pharaoh should be depicted as he had been for two thousand years, an august presence seated in unbending majesty, a figure of divine immobility, unblemished by any evidence or suggestion of human feeling or human weakness. The lovely chair which came out of the palace at Amarna and has been preserved to us in the tomb of Tutenkhamon is adorned with a scene showing us the youthful king seated in a posture of negligent relaxation, with one arm thrown carelessly over the back of his chair, while the lovely young queen stands before him with a little jar of perfume in her hand, from which with exquisite grace she is touching her husband's costume with drops of fragrance. For the first time in the history of art, we have here a scene the subject of which is a *human relationship,* and interpretative art is here dealing with human life as its subject. These are but two among many examples which might be mentioned, which illustrate Ikhnaton's powerful individuality and his fearless readiness to throw off the shackles of tradition without hesitation in the endeavour to establish a world of things as they are, in wholesome naturalness.

It is important to notice, therefore, that Ikhnaton was a prophet both of nature and of human life. Like Jesus, who, on the one hand, drew his lessons from the lilies of the field, the fowls of the air, or the clouds of the sky, and, on the other, from the human society about him in stories like the Prodigal Son, the Good Samaritan, or the woman who had lost her piece of money, so this revolutionary Egyptian prophet drew his teachings from a contemplation both of nature and of human life. While the interpretative art of this revolutionary movement under Ikhnaton's guidance found *new* content in the life of man, there was much in Egyptian experience with human society which Ikhnaton could not ignore. He fully accepted the inherited Solar doctrine of a great moral order, and if in this brief history of Egyptian morals we have devoted some space to the revolutionary monotheism of Ikhnaton, it is for the reason that this whole monotheistic movement is the culmination of the ancient recognition of a moral order by the Egyptian thinkers of the Pyramid Age, and their creation of a realm of universal ethical values, represented by the inclusive term Maat, brought forth by the Sun-god at Heliopolis. This new monotheism grew up on a threefold basis. The *first,* as we have seen, was *political,* so that even the Sun-god's new name was enclosed in a Pharaonic double cartouche; the *second* was observation of the Sun-god's universal sway as a *physical force,* everywhere present in the sun's heat and light; and the *third* was the logical development of the ancient Heliopolitan doctrine of a *moral order,* a doctrine some two thousand years old in Ikhnaton's day.

We have still to consider the last of these fundamental bases of Ikhnaton's monotheism. It is at this point that we feel the insufficiency of our written sources, which are very meagre. Even the scanty sources which have survived to us, however, disclose progress in the young king's thinking during the half generation of his rule. It is unthinkable that such a growing and progressing movement as that of Ikhnaton should not have produced treatises in which he set forth his doctrines. There is, moreover, good evidence of the existence of such writings. In the Amarna tombs where the nobles of Ikhnaton's court love to depict their relations with their sovereign, they constantly refer to the new faith. They have only one word for it, and that is the "teaching." It is attributed solely to the king, and we cannot doubt that this teaching is the general name for the formal statement of his doctrine in a treatise of some kind, written of course on papyrus. After his fall Ikhnaton's enemies left no stone unturned to obliterate every surviving evidence of his hated rule, and of course they destroyed these papyrus writings of the king. Our knowledge of the movement, as far as its tenets are concerned, is drawn exclusively from a few accidental scraps and fragments, especially the hymns with which the nobles embellished their tombs.

On first reading the great Aton hymn it seems remarkable that as an expression of religious aspiration such a hymn should contain so little reference to character and to human conduct, which as we know had held such a prominent place in the thinking of Solar religion at Heliopolis, and in which the entire Aton movement was deeply rooted. The source of this omission is to be found in the fact that the chief force which moved the soul of Ikhnaton was *emotion*. The Aton revolution was in spirit primarily and powerfully emotional. This fact is unmistakable in the hymns, and it is very prominent also in the art. When an Amarna artist sketches the worshipping figure of Ikhnaton or any of his subjects with arms "uplifted in adoration" to the Sun-god, the emotional quality of the lines with which he represents the uplifted arms is as powerfully appealing as the beseeching arms of Eleonora Duse outstretched to her beloved Armando. It is the beauty and beneficence of the Sun-god which Ikhnaton adores, and it is this emotion of which the Amarna hymns are the vehicle. They therefore contain no theology or social morality. Nevertheless it is quite clear that Ikhnaton fully accepted the highly developed ethics of Heliopolis, and indeed made the ethical system of the old Solar teaching more prominent than it had ever been before his reign.

The close connection of Ikhnaton's revolution with the Heliopolitan theology is evident throughout. The identification of the royal line with that of the Sun-god by the Heliopolitan priests in the Pyramid Age making every Pharaoh a son of the Sun-god had resulted, as we have seen, in transferring to Re the humane qualities of beneficent dominion with which the Pharaohs of the Feudal Age were imbued. At that time the Pharaoh had become the "good shepherd" or "good herdman," and this figure of the paternal and protecting sovereign had been transferred to Re. Re had thus gained wondrously in qualities of humane and paternal sympathy, as a result of this development in the conception of the kingship in the Feudal Age. The social forces which had contributed this high ideal of kingship were thus the ultimate influences, which, through the kingship, enriched and humanised the otherwise rather mechanical and perfunctory political conception of Re's dominion. The human appeal which he now made was thus akin to that of Osiris himself. The teaching of Ikhnaton was entirely in sympathy with this tendency of the Solar faith. Under his father we have found a sun-hymn calling the Sun-god "the valiant herdman driving his herds," a hint clearly connecting the Aton faith with the social and moral movement of the Feudal Age.

Recalling now the Heliopolitan origin of Maat, "justice," "truth," "righteousness," personified as a goddess, the daughter of the Sun-god, it is important to notice that in the Book of the Dead (Chapter CXXV) we find a group of the gods who sit in the "Hall of Maat, in whose bodies are neither sin nor falsehood, who live in truth (Maat)." To these gods the deceased asserts, "I live on truth, I feed on the truth (or "righteousness") of my heart." Now this Solar doctrine maintained by the gods at Heliopolis was so fully accepted by Ikhnaton that he regularly appended to the official form of his royal name in all his great state monuments, the words "Living on Truth" (Maat). This significant epithet attached to Ikhnaton's name proclaimed him the official representative and supporter of the great moral and national order conceived by the Solar priests at Heliopolis as far back as the Pyramid Age, and given ever deeper ethical significance by the social thinkers and prophets of the Feudal Age. When we recall Ikhnaton's unqualified claim to universal dominion, it is evident that by appending these words to his royal name he intended to extend the old *national* moral order to exercise sway over the greater *international* world of which he was lord. The Sun-god's ancient realm of ethical values, expanded to its logical universal limits and the monotheism long ago implicit in the teaching of the priests of Heliopolis, was thus given unequivocal expression by Ikhnaton.

In harmony with this fact Ikhnaton called his new capital at Amarna the "seat of truth" (Maat) in the short hymn. His partisans were fully aware of the king's convictions regarding Maat, and we frequently find the men of his court glorifying "truth." One of his leading supporters, Eye, who later displaced Tutenkhamon as king, says: "He (the king) put truth in my body and my abomination is lying. I know that Wanre (Ikhnaton) rejoices in it (truth)." The same man affirms that the Sun-god is one "(whose) heart is satisfied with truth, whose abomination is falsehood." Another official states in his Amarna tomb: "I will speak to his majesty, (for) I know that he lives therein. . . . I do not that which his majesty hates, (for) my abomination is lying in my body. . . . I have reported truth to his majesty, (for) I know that he lives therein. Thou art Re, begetter of truth . . . I took not the reward of lying, nor expelled the truth for the violent." As important evidence of Ikhnaton's devotion to truth it should be recalled here that he did not confine truth to conduct only, but introduced it also into the realm of *art* with epoch-making results.

In Ikhnaton's revolution, therefore, Re was still the author and sustainer of truth or righteousness (Maat), the moral and administrative order, as he had been for over two thousand years before, and if we hear of no judgment hereafter in the Amarna tombs, it was clearly only the rejection of the cloud of gods and demi-gods, with Osiris at their head, who had been involved in the judgment as we find it in the Book of the Dead. These were now banished, and the dramatic scene of the judgment seems to have disappeared with them, although it is clear that the ethical requirements of the Solar faith, the faith in which they emerged and developed, were not relaxed in Ikhnaton's teaching. The sacerdotal invasion of the moral realm with mechanical magical agencies for insuring justification was also evidently repelled by Ikhnaton. The familiar heart scarab now no longer bears a charm to still the accusing voice of conscience, but a simple prayer, in the name of Aton, for long life, favour and food. The same was true of the Ushebti figures, the little images which performed labour in the deceased's stead in the hereafter (p. 267).

On a moment's reflection, such fundamental changes as these suggest what an overwhelming tide of inherited thought, custom, and tradition had been diverted from its channel by the young king who was guiding this revolution. It is only as this aspect of his movement is clearly discerned that we begin to appreciate the power of his remarkable personality. Before his time religious documents were commonly attributed to ancient kings and wise men, and the power of a belief lay chiefly in its claim to remote antiquity and the sanctity of immemorial custom. Until Ikhnaton the history of the world had largely been merely the irresistible drift of tradition. The outstanding exception was the great physician-architect, Imhotep, who introduced stone architecture and built the first stone masonry pyramidal tomb of the Thirtieth Century B.C. Otherwise men had been but drops of water in the great current. With the possible exception of Imhotep, Ikhnaton was the first individual in history. Consciously and deliberately, by intellectual process he gained his position, and then placed himself squarely in the face of tradition and swept it aside. He appeals to no myths, to no ancient and widely accepted versions of the dominion of the gods, to no customs sanctified by centuries—he appeals only to the present and visible evidences of his god's dominion, evidences open to all, and as for tradition wherever it had left material manifestations of other gods in records which could be reached, he endeavoured to annihilate it. A policy so destructive was doomed to encounter fatal opposition. We shall now examine some of the forces of that opposition.

CHAPTER XVI

THE FALL OF IKHNATON—THE AGE OF PERSONAL PIETY—SACERDOTALISM AND THE END

HERE had been a great people, the onward flow of whose life, in spite of its almost irresistible momentum, had been suddenly arrested and then diverted into a strange channel. Their holy places had been desecrated, the shrines sacred with the memories of thousands of years had been closed up, the priests driven away, the offerings and temple incomes confiscated, and the old order blotted out. Everywhere whole communities, moved by instincts flowing from untold centuries of habit and custom, returned to their holy places to find them no more, and stood dumfounded before the closed doors of the ancient sanctuaries. On feast days, sanctified by memories of earliest childhood, venerable halls that had resounded with the rejoicings of the multitudes, as we have recalled them at Siut, now stood silent and empty; and every day as the funeral processions wound across the desert margin and up the plateau to the cemetery, the great comforter and friend, Osiris, the champion of the dead in every danger, was banished, and no man dared so much as utter his name. Even in their oaths, absorbed from childhood with their mothers' milk, the involuntary names must not be suffered to escape the lips; and in the presence of the magistrate at court the ancient oath must now contain only the name of Aton. All this to them was as if the modern man were asked to worship X and swear by Y. Groups of muttering priests, nursing implacable hatred, must have mingled their curses with the execration of whole communities of discontented tradesmen—bakers who no longer drew a livelihood from the sale of ceremonial cakes at the temple feasts; craftsmen who no longer sold amulets of the old gods at the temple gateway; hack sculptors whose statues of Osiris lay under piles of dust in many a tumbled-down studio; cemetery stone-cutters who found their tawdry tombstones with scenes from the Book of the Dead banished from the necropolis; scribes whose rolls of the same book, filled with the names of the old gods, or even if they bore the word god in the plural, were anathema; actors and priestly mimes who were driven away from the sacred groves on the days when they should have presented to the people the "passion play," and murmuring groups of pilgrims at Abydos who would have taken part in this drama of the life and death and resurrection of Osiris; physicians deprived of their whole stock in trade of exorcising ceremonies, employed with success since the days of the earliest kings, two thousand years before; shepherds who no longer dared to place a loaf and a jar of water under yonder tree, hoping thus to escape the anger of the goddess who dwelt in it, and who might afflict the household with sickness in her wrath; peasants who feared to erect a rude image of Osiris in the field to drive away the typhonic demons of drought and famine; mothers soothing their babes at twilight and fearing to utter the old sacred names and prayers learned in childhood, to drive away from their little ones the lurking demons of the dark. In the midst of a whole land thus darkened by clouds of smouldering discontent, this marvellous young king, and the group of sympathisers who surrounded him, set up their tabernacle to the daily light, in serene unconsciousness of the fatal darkness that enveloped all around and grew daily darker and more threatening.

In placing the movement of Ikhnaton against a background of popular discontent like this, and adding to the picture also the far more immediately dangerous secret opposition of the ancient priesthoods, the still unconquered party of Amon, and the powerful military group, who were disaffected by the king's peace policy in Asia and his lack of interest in imperial administration and maintenance, we begin to discern something of the powerful individuality of this first intellectual leader in history. His reign was the earliest attempt at a rule of ideas, irrespective of the condition and willingness of the people upon whom they were to be forced. As Matthew Arnold has so well said, in commenting on the French Revolution: "But the mania for giving an immediate political application to all these fine ideas of the reason was fatal. . . . Ideas cannot be too much prized in and for themselves, cannot be too much lived with; but to transfer them abruptly into the world of politics and practice, violently to revolutionise the world at their bidding—that is quite another thing." But Ikhnaton had no French Revolution to look back upon. He was himself the world's first revolutionist, and he was fully convinced that he might entirely recast the world of religion, thought, art, and life by the invincible purpose he held, to make his ideas at once practically effective.

And so the fair city of the Amarna plain arose, a fatuous Island of the Blest in a sea of discontent, a vision of fond hopes, born in a mind fatally forgetful that the past cannot be annihilated. The marvel is that such a man should have first arisen in the East, and especially in Egypt, where no man except Ikhnaton possessed the ability to forget. Nor was the great Mediterranean World which Egypt now dominated any better prepared for an international religion than its Egyptian lords. The imperial imagination of Ikhnaton reminds one of that of Alexander the Great, a thousand years later, but it was many centuries in advance of his own age.

The reality around him and the threatening situation, which his partisans were called upon to contemplate every day, are pictured in a description written long after his death by his son-in-law, Tutenkhamon: "The temples of the gods and goddesses were desolated from Elephantine (the First Cataract) as far as the marshes of the Delta. . . . Their holy places were forsaken and had become overgrown tracts, . . . their sanctuaries were like that which has never been, and their houses were foot-worn paths. The land was in an evil pass, and as for the gods they had forsaken this land. If people were sent to Syria to extend the borders of Egypt, they prospered not at all; if men prayed to a god for succour, he came not, . . . if men besought a goddess likewise, she came not at all. Their hearts were deaf in their bodies." Under conditions like these Ikhnaton's followers prayed that his rule might endure "until the swan is become black and the raven white, until the mountains rise up and walk and water flows up-hill!"

The fall of the great revolutionary is shrouded in complete obscurity. The immediate result of his fall was the restoration of Amon and the old gods whom the Amonite priesthood forced upon Ikhnaton's youthful and feeble son-in-law, Tutenkhamon. The old régime returned. Tutenkhamon's account of his restoration of the gods is an interesting revelation of the religious and intellectual attitude of the leading men of affairs when Ikhnaton had passed away. The new king refers to himself as "the good ruler, who did excellent things for the father of all gods (Amon), who restored for him that which was in ruin as everlasting monuments; cast out for him sin in the Two Lands (Egypt), so that righteousness (Maat) endured . . .; and made iniquity to be the abomination of the land, as in the beginning." The overthrow of Ikhnaton was thus regarded by his triumphant enemies as the restoration of the old moral order "righteousness" (Maat) and the expulsion of iniquity. Tutenkhamon then proceeds to describe the conditions he inherited, in a passage just quoted above.

Thus was the memory of the great idealist execrated. In the great royal lists recording on the monuments the names of all the past kings of Egypt, the name of Ikhnaton never appears; and when under later Pharaohs, it was necessary in a state document to refer to him, he was called "the criminal of Akhetaton." The re-established priesthood of Amon rejoiced in the restoration of their power, and a hymn to Amon from this period reveals the exultant triumph of his devotees as they sing to him:

"Thou findest him who transgresses against thee;
Woe to him who assails thee!
Thy city endures;
But he who assails thee falls.

. . . .

The sun of him who knows thee not goes down, O Amon!
But as for him who knows thee, he shines.
The temple of him who assailed thee is in darkness,
But the whole earth is in light."

In this hymn the vindictive malice of Ikhnaton's enemies is unmistakably revealed in the exultant gibe:

"The sun of him (Ikhnaton) who knows thee not goes down,
O Amon!

. . . .

The temple of him (Ikhnaton) who assailed thee is in darkness."

Such was the state of the Amarna Sun-temple, which Ikhnaton's artists always depicted bathed in a flood of sunshine, as the beaming Aton hung over it and enfolded it in his beneficent rays!

Of that once bright sanctuary of the eternal Light, nothing now remains but the scanty foundations. Did anything else survive? Could the earliest revolution of the human mind run its course and leave no enduring results behind? Ikhnaton's revolution had been too violent in its methods to work any lasting transformation. The marvellous art which it brought forth was too refined in conception and power of line to endure. The king's studios at Amarna have revealed to us the amazing virtuosity of the royal artists, and their work left its mark upon the art of the subsequent period, although sculpture and painting never regained the complete emancipation they enjoyed under Ikhnaton, nor felt again the subtle "truth" which breathed in the work of the Amarna studios. In morals the supreme exaltation of truth as it had dawned upon the vision of Ikhnaton passed away. His emotional response to the beauty and beneficence which he beheld in the works of God without doubt made an impression which was never wholly forgotten. We cannot doubt that in some form the Egyptian hymn survived the death of Ikhnaton so that centuries later it was known to the Hebrews and was used by the author of the One Hundred and Fourth Psalm (see pp. 282–284). The spirit of the Aton faith therefore did not wholly disappear, and we shall yet find further evidence of its influence. The fanatical violence of Ikhnaton's assault upon tradition, however, could not but bring down upon him and his movement a retributive vengeance which stopped only with complete annihilation.

We cannot wonder, then, that when the storm broke it swept away almost all traces of this earliest idealist. We have little more to tell us of him than the wreckage of his city, a lonely outpost of idealism, not to be overtaken and passed till many centuries later those Bedouin hordes, who were now drifting into Ikhnaton's Palestinian provinces, had coalesced into a nation of social, moral, and religious aspiration, and had thus brought forth the Hebrew prophets and psalmists to carry on the spirit and the vision of the Egyptian social dreamers.

Ikhnaton's absorption in the abstractions of his great revolution had held him musing and dreaming in his Sun-palace at Amarna, while the Hittites, a formidable new enemy in Western Asia, made rapid conquest of Egypt's Asiatic Empire, and the priests and soldiers among his own people completely undermined the power of the Eighteenth Dynasty, the Pharaoh's venerable family, which had dominated the ancient Orient for two hundred and thirty years. For Egypt a new and different age began with the overthrow of Ikhnaton. The splendour of Egypt's outward greatness, the impressive vision of her age-long stability, still found expression in the pretentious traditional phraseology; but the reality had nevertheless been somewhat dimmed as the end of the Fourteenth Century B.C. approached. Echoes of the Aton faith had not wholly died away, and its connection with old Solar teaching of Heliopolis was still recognised.

The very hymn which contains the malignant triumph of the Amonite priests betrays its connection with the old Solar faith and the paternal interpretation of Re, as it goes on to the praise of Amon as the "good shepherd" and the "pilot," ideas which we recall arose in the social movement of the Feudal Age. Indeed, notwithstanding the restoration of Amon, the ideas and the tendencies which had given birth to the revolution of Ikhnaton did not wholly disappear. It was not possible to carry them on, under a monotheistic form, involving the annihilation of the old gods; but the human and beneficent aspects of Aton, in his care for all men, had taken hold upon the imagination of the thinking classes, and we find the same qualities now attributed to Amon. Men sang of him:[1]

> "Lord of truth, father of gods,
> Maker of men and creator of animals,
> Lord of that which is,
> Creator of the tree of life,
> Maker of herbs, sustaining the cattle alive."

The hymn from which these lines are quoted does not hesitate to call the god thus praised Re or Atum, showing that the Aton movement had left the traditional prestige of the Heliopolitan Sun-god, Re, unblemished. Another passage contains evident echoes of the Aton faith:

> "Hail to thee! Re, lord of Truth,
> . . . .
> Who commanded and the gods became;
> Atum, who made the people,

[1] Great Hymn to Amon in a Cairo papyrus, which is thought by some to be even older than the reign of Ikhnaton.

Who determined the fashion of them,
Maker of their sustenance,
Who distinguished one colour (race) from another;
Who hears the prayer of him who is in captivity,
Who is kindly of heart when one calls upon him,
Who saves the timid from the haughty,
Who separates the weak from the strong,
Lord of Knowledge, in whose mouth is Sovereign Command
For love of whom the Nile comes,
Lord of sweetness, great in love,
At whose coming the people live."

Even the old monotheistic phrases have here and there survived, and this hymn employs them without compunction, though constantly referring to the gods. It says:

"Sole likeness, maker of what is,
Sole and only one, maker of what exists.
From whose eyes men issued,
From whose mouth the gods came forth,
Maker of herbage for the cattle,
And the tree of life for mankind,
Who maketh the sustenance of the fish [in] the stream,
And the birds that traverse the sky,
Who giveth breath to that which is in the egg,
And maketh to live the son of the worm,
Who maketh that on which the gnats live,
The worms and the insects likewise,
Who supplieth the needs of the mice in their holes,
Who sustaineth alive the birds in every tree.
Hail to thee, who hast made all these,
Thou sole and only one, with many arms,
Thou sleeper waking while all men sleep,
Seeking good things for his cattle.

. . . .

'Hail to thee,' say all cattle;
'Jubilation to thee,' says every country,
To the height of heaven, to the breadth of earth,
To the depths of the sea."

A hymn to Osiris of the same age says to him: "Thou art the father and the mother of men, they live from thy breath." There is a spirit of humane solicitude in all this, which, as we have seen, appeared as early as the social teaching of the Feudal Age. The preference for the "timid" as over against the "haughty" and overbearing, and the "sovereign command" and "knowledge" which are the royal and divine prerogatives we have already discovered in social tractates like Ipuwer, and even in a state document like the Installation of the Vizier in the Twelfth Dynasty. That God is the father and mother of his creatures was, of course, a doctrine of the Aton faith. While such hymns also still preserve the universalism, the disregard for national lines, and the spacious, far-reaching vision, which were so prominent in the teaching of Ikhnaton, they nevertheless disclose an individual confidence in the goodness of God which is a significant evidence of personal aspiration and reveals the beginning of a new age of personal religion.

As we look further into the simpler and less ecclesiastical professions of the Thirteenth and Twelfth Centuries before Christ, the two centuries after Ikhnaton, the confidence of the worshipper in the solicitude of the Sun-god for all, even the least of his creatures, has developed into a devotional spirit, and a consciousness of personal relation with the god, which was already discernible in Ikhnaton's declaration to his god: "Yet art thou still in my heart." The surviving influence of the Aton faith and the doctrines of social justice of the Feudal Age now culminated, therefore, in the profoundest expression of the devotional religious spirit ever attained by the men of Egypt. Furthermore, although rooted in the teaching of an exclusive few heretofore, these beliefs in an intimate and personal relation between the worshipper and his god had now, with the lapse of centuries and by slow and gradual process, become widespread among the people.

The result was that an age of personal piety and inner aspiration to God now dawned among the masses. It is a notable development and, like so many of the movements which we have followed in this book, the earliest of its kind as yet discernible in the history of the East, or for that matter in the history of man. We are able to follow it only at Thebes, and it is not a little interesting to be able to look into the souls of the common folk who thronged the streets and markets, who tilled the fields and maintained the industries, who kept the accounts and carried on the official records, the hewers of wood and the drawers of water, the men and women upon whose shoulders rested the great burden of material life in the vast capital of the Egyptian Empire during the Twelfth and Thirteenth Centuries before Christ.

A scribe in one of the treasury magazines of the Theban necropolis prays to Amon, as to him

> "Who cometh to the silent,
> Who saveth the poor,
> Who giveth breath to every one he loveth,
>
> . . . .
>
> Give to me [thy] hand,
> Save me, shine upon me,
> For thou makest my sustenance.
> Thou art the sole god, there is no other,
> Even Re, who dawneth in the sky,
> Atum maker of men,
> Who heareth the prayers of him who calls to him,
> Who saveth a man from the haughty,
> Who bringeth the Nile for him who is among them,
> Who leadeth—for all men,

When he riseth, the people live,
Their hearts live when they see him
Who giveth breath to him who is the egg,
Who maketh the people and the birds to live,
Who supplieth the needs of the mice in their holes,
The worms and the insects likewise."

To a god who, like the God of Jesus, is concerned even for the preservation of the sparrows, these men of Thebes might bring their misfortunes and their daily cares, confident in his kindness and beneficence. A painter of tomb scenes in the Theban necropolis erected a stela in one of the necropolis chapels, telling how Amon, in gracious mercy, had saved his son from sickness. Amon is to him the "august god, who heareth petitions, who cometh at the cry of the afflicted poor, and giveth breath to him who is bowed down," and the story of Amon's goodness he tells thus:

"Praise to Amon!
I make hymns in his name,
I give to him praise,
To the height of heaven,
And the breadth of earth;
I tell of his prowess
To him who saileth down-stream,
And to him who saileth up-stream.

Beware of him!
Repeat it to son and daughter,
To great and small,
Tell it to generation after generation,
Who are not yet born.
Tell it to the fishes in the stream,
To the birds in the sky,
Repeat it to him who knoweth it not
And to him who knoweth it.
Beware of him.

Thou, O Amon, art the lord of the silent,
Who cometh at the cry of the poor.
When I cry to thee in my affliction,
Then thou comest and savest me.
That thou mayest give breath to him who is bowed down,
And mayest save me lying in bondage.

. . . .

When men cry unto thee,
Thou art he that cometh from afar."

"Nebre, painter of Amon in the necropolis, son of Pai, painter of Amon in the necropolis, made this in the name of his lord, Amon, Lord of Thebes, who cometh at the cry of the poor; making for him praises in his name, because of the greatness of his might, and making for him prayers before him and before the whole land, on behalf of the painter Nakht-Amon,[2] when he lay sick unto death, being in the power of Amon, because of his sin.

"I found that the Lord of gods came as the north wind, while fragrant air was before him, that he might save the painter Nakht-Amon, son of the painter of Amon in the necropolis, Nebre, born of the housewife Peshed.

"He saith, 'Though the servant be wont to commit sin, yet is the lord wont to be gracious. The Lord of Thebes spends not the whole day wroth. If he be wroth for the space of a moment, it remaineth not . . . he turns to us in graciousness, Amon turns with his breath.'

. . . .

"He saith, 'I will make this stela in thy name, and I will record this hymn in writing upon it, if thou wilt save for me the painter Nakht-Amon.' Thus I spake to

[2] The son of Nebre, whose life Amon saves.

thee, and thou hearkenedst to me. Now behold I do that which I said. Thou art the lord of the one who calls upon him, who is satisfied with righteousness, the Lord of Thebes.

"Made by the painter, Nebre and [his] son Khai."

The Sun-god, or his supplanter, Amon, has thus become the champion of the distressed, "Who heareth the petition, who heareth the prayers of him who crieth out to him, who cometh at the voice of him who mentions his name," "the loving god who heareth prayers, [who giveth the hand] to the poor, who saveth the weary." So the injured mother, neglected by her son, "raises her arms to the god, and he hears her cry." The social justice which arose in the Middle Kingdom is now a claim which every poor man pleads before the god, who has himself become a "just judge, not accepting a bribe, uplifting the insignificant, [protecting] the poor, not extending thy hand to the rich." And so the poor man prays: "O Amon, lend thine ear to him who stands alone in the court (of justice), who is poor while his [opponent] is rich. The court oppresses him (saying), 'Silver and gold for the scribes! Clothing for the servants!' But Amon transformeth himself into the vizier, that he may cause the poor man to triumph; the poor man is just and the poor man overcometh the rich. Pilot [in] front who knoweth the water, Amon, thou Rudder, . . . who giveth bread to him who hath none, and preserveth alive the servant of his house." For the god is now that "Amon-Re who first became king, O god of the beginning, thou vizier of the poor man, not taking the corrupt reward, not saying, 'Bring witnesses'; Amon-Re who judgeth the earth with his finger, whose words are before the heart, he assigneth him that sinneth against him to the fire, and the just [to] the West." Rich and poor alike may suffer the displeasure of the god aroused by sin. An oath taken lightly or falsely calls down the wrath of the god, and he smites the transgressor with sickness or blindness, from which relief may be obtained as we have seen, if repentance follows and the offender humbly seeks the favour of his god.

Now for the first time conscience is fully emancipated. The sinner pleads his ignorance and proneness to err. "Thou sole and only one, thou Sun-god who hath none other like him, protector of millions, saviour of hundred-thousands, who shieldeth him that calleth upon him, thou lord of Heliopolis; *punish me not for my many sins.* I am one ignorant of his own body, I am a man without understanding. All day I follow after my own dictates as the ox after his fodder." We notice at once that this is in striking contrast with the Book of the Dead, in which the soul admits no sin and claims entire innocence. But now in this posture of acknowledged unworthiness and humility there is inner communion with God night and day. "Come to me, O Re-Harakhte, that thou mayest guide me." As a devout Hebrew loves Jerusalem, the ancestral abiding place of his God, so this ancient Egyptian worshipper turns to the great Sun-city, where the faith of his fathers had been born nearly three thousand years before: "My heart goes out to Heliopolis . . . My heart rejoiceth and my bosom is glad. My petitions are heard, even my daily prayers, and my hymns by night. My supplications shall flourish in my mouth, for they are heard this day."

In the old hymns, made up of objective descriptions, quotations from the myths, and allusions to mythical incidents, all matters entirely external to the life of the worshipper, every man might pray the same prayer; but now prayer becomes a revelation of inner personal experience, an expression of individual communion with God. It is a communion in which the worshipper discerns in his God one nourishing the soul as a shepherd feeds his flock. "O Amon, thou herdman bringing forth the herds in the morning, leading the suffering to pasture; as the herdman leadeth the herds [to] pasture, so dost thou, O Amon, lead the suffering to food, for Amon is a herdman, herding him that leaneth upon him. . . . O Amon-Re, I love thee and I have filled my heart with thee. . . . Thou wilt rescue me out of the mouth of men in the day when they speak lies; for the Lord of Righteousness, he liveth in righteousness. I will not follow the anxiety in my heart, (for) that which Amon hath said flourisheth." There are, to be sure, external and material means which will further this spiritual relation with the god. The wise man sagely admonishes to "celebrate the feast of thy god, repeat his seasons; the god is wroth [with] him who transgresseth [against] him." Nevertheless, even in the opinion of the sages, who are wont to compromise with traditional customs, the most effective means of gaining the favour of God is contemplative silence and inner communion. "Be not of many words, for in silence shalt thou gain good. . . . As for the precinct of God, his abomination is crying out; pray thou with a desiring heart whose every word is hidden, and he will supply thy need, and hear thy speech and receive thy offering." It is in such an attitude as this that the worshipper may turn to his God as to a fountain of spiritual refreshment, saying, "Thou sweet Well for him that thirsteth in the desert; it is closed to him who speaketh, but it is open to him who is silent. When he who is silent cometh, lo, he findeth the Well." This attitude of silent communion, waiting upon the gracious goodness of God, was not confined to the select few, nor to the educated priestly communities. On the humblest monuments of the common people Amon is called the god "who cometh to the silent," or the "lord of the silent," as we have already observed. It is in this final development of devotional feeling, crowning the religious and intellectual revolution of Ikhnaton, and also forming the culmination of the doctrines of social justice emerging in the Feudal Age, that the religion of Egypt reached its noblest development.

In morals and in the attitude towards life the sages continued to maintain a spirit of wholesome regard for the highest practical ideals, an attitude in which we discern a distinct advance upon the teachings of the fathers. Reputation was strictly to be guarded. "Let every place which thou lovest be known," says the sage Ani; and drunkenness and dissolute living are exhibited in all their disastrous consequences for the young. To the young man the dangers of immorality are bared with naked frankness. "Guard thee from the woman from abroad, who is not known in her city; look not on her, . . . know her not in the flesh; (for she is) a flood great and deep, whose whirling no man knows. The woman whose husband is far away, 'I am beautiful,' says she to thee every day. When she has no witnesses, she stands and ensnares thee. O great crime worthy of death when one hearkens, even when it be not known abroad. (For) a man takes up every sin [after] this *one*." As for the good things of life, they are to be regarded with philosophical reserve. It is foolish to count upon inherited wealth as a source of happiness. "Say not, 'My maternal grandfather has a house on the estate of So and So.' Then when thou comest to the division (by will) with thy brother, thy portion is (only) a storage-shed." In such things indeed there is no stability. "So it is forever, men are naught. One is rich, another is poor. . . . He who was rich last year, he is a vagrant this year. . . . The watercourse of last year, it is another place this year. Great seas become dry places, and shores become deeps." We have here that oriental resignation to the contrasts in life which seems to have developed among all the peoples of the early East.[3]

As the Egyptian people passed into the last thousand years B.C. the development of conscience which we have been following for some two thousand years reached its conclusion in a profoundly important transition which had been in preparation for many centuries. The impelling voice within, which had originally grown up out of social influences and had since been further developed by many centuries of contemplative reflection, was now unreservedly recognised by the believer to be the mandate of God himself. We have seen that this idea arose over five hundred years earlier at the beginning of the Empire, but in this new age of personal piety conscience became, as it had never been before, the unmistakable voice of God. Under these circumstances there can of course be no concealment or denial of sin, and the believer, conscious that his whole case is known to his God, places himself without reserve in the hand of God, who guides and controls all his life and fortunes. The approval of society is still important, and the pressure of social influences is still felt, but high above it is responsibility to an all-knowing God.

This new attitude is revealed to us in a remarkable treatise which we may call the "Wisdom of Amenemope." Written by a sage named Amenemope, it is now preserved

[3] See, for example, the song of Sindebad the porter in the court of the rich man's house. Algiers edition of *Sindebad the Sailor,* Arabic text, p. 4.

to us in a papyrus in the British Museum.[4] As so often in such counsel of the Egyptian wise men, these utterances of Amenemope are said to have been delivered by the sage to his son. They are more clearly organised than any such document we have heretofore examined, being systematically divided into thirty chapters; each chapter is devoted to a particular subject, and in external form is divided into strophes, each consisting of four lines, sometimes six or even eight, while there are a few strophes of only two lines each. There is no effort to organise or arrange the succession of chapters in logical order.

Professor Lange of Copenhagen, who has contributed most to the understanding of this extraordinary treatise, in comparing Amenemope with his predecessors, says, "The religious views of Amenemope are much deeper and penetrate much more deeply into his entire world of thought [than his predecessors]. To the other teachers of wisdom piety is a virtue, the thought of death and eternity is a motive for virtuous conduct, it is God who gives riches and fortune. But for Amenemope the consciousness of God is the determining factor in his conception of life and his entire behaviour."[5] To his son, therefore, Amenemope constantly holds up this attitude towards life, that it is to be lived both in personal and official relations, in full realisation of momentary responsibility to God. This ultimate intensity of conscience and God-consciousness in the teachings of an Egyptian thinker in the Tenth Century B.C., before any of the Old Testament was written, is the more remarkable, because we now

[4] Published by *Sir* E. A. Wallis Budge. *Facsimiles of Egyptian Hieratic Papyri in the British Museum, etc.*, Pls. I–XIV, Columns I–XXVII, "The Admonitions of Amenemapt, the Son of Kanekht" (Second Series, London, 1923).

[5] H. O. Lange, *Das Weisheitsbuch des Amenemope,* p. 18 (Copenhagen, 1925).

know that the Wisdom of Amenemope was translated into Hebrew, it was read by Hebrews, and an important part of it found its way into the Old Testament.

In preparing his son for an official career in the Egyptian government, our sage takes up one after another the temptations to corrupt use of his official opportunities for gain, and warns the youth against yielding to such temptations. If he is in the cadastral offices, his father counsels him,

"Remove not the landmark on the boundary of the fields,
. . . .

Be not greedy for a cubit of land,
And trespass not on the boundary of the widow.
. . . .

Mark thou him that doeth so on earth,
. . . .

His house is an enemy of the town,
His granaries are destroyed,
His possessions are taken from the hand of his children,
And his property is given to another.
. . . .

Tread not the furrow of another,
It is profitable for thee to be safe from them.

Plow the fields that thou mayest find thy needs,
And receive thy bread from thine own threshing floor.
Better is a bushel which God giveth to thee,
Than five thousand gained by transgression.
. . . .

Better is poverty in the hand of God
Than riches in the storehouse;
And better are loaves when the heart is joyous,
Than riches in unhappiness."

It is interesting to notice that Amenemope still has regard for social opinion in such situations, for in counselling his son to observe strict honesty in the fiscal records, he says,

> "Better is praise as one whom men love,
> Than riches in the storehouse."

For wealth with a guilty conscience is of no value:

> "Of what advantage are fine clothes,
> When one is a transgressor before God?"

The Egyptian treasury officials had much to do with weights and measures and to this subject Amenemope gives much attention. He says,

> "Shift not corruptly the hand-balances, nor falsify the weights,
> Diminish not the divisions of the grain measure.
> Desire not a field-bushel
> And reject not those of the Treasury.
> . . . .
> Greater is the might of the threshing floor
> Than the (official) oath by the Great Throne."

The obscure comparison at the end is a proverb, probably meaning that the corrupting power of the royal granary is greater than the official oath of fidelity to the throne taken when the incumbent enters upon his office. Official integrity must include both great and small: the sage begins a chapter with the words, "Be not greedy for the goods of an humble man," and follows it immediately by another beginning, "Be not greedy for the goods of a great man."

Amenemope is likewise greatly concerned that his son shall preserve strict uprightness in all legal business and processes at court:

> "Do not force a man to go into court,
> Neither shalt thou bend righteousness (or justice),
> While thy face is inclined towards showy clothing (of a litigant),
> And thou drivest away him who is shabby.
>
> Take not gifts from the strong,
> Neither shalt thou oppress for him the weak.
> Justice is a great gift of God,
> He giveth it to whom he will.
>
> The strength of the one who is like him (God),
> It saveth the afflicted from his (the judge's) blows.
>
> . . . .
>
> Assign property to the owners thereof,
> And (thus) seek for thyself life.
> While thy heart buildeth in their (the owners') house,
> Thy body is condemned to the executioner's block."

Prudent speech and temperate conduct are regarded as very important by our sage. Loud and empty threats take no account of the plans of God for our enemies:

> "Say not, 'I have found a powerful chief,
> Now I can attack a man in thy city.'
> Say not, 'I have found a protector,
> Now I can attack the hated man.'
>
> Verily thou knowest not the plans of God,
> And thou discernest not the morrow.
> Set thyself in the arms of God,
> Until thy silence overthroweth them (his enemies)."

Amenemope continues with warnings against too free speech, and to this dangerous practice he often reverts throughout the treatise:

> "If thou hearest good or evil,
> Leave it outside unheard.
> Put the good report on thy tongue,
> While the evil remaineth concealed in thy belly."

With the same thought in mind the sage warns his son against eavesdropping in great houses, and in this connection he admonishes to modest behaviour at a great man's table. Partially in the same language this same admonition was in Amenemope's time already eighteen centuries old, and had been given to his own son by Ptah-hotep in the Fifth Dynasty. As an important item of discreet deportment towards one's superiors, and after it had been respected by the Egyptians for over two thousand years, it found its way into Hebrew life, and is without doubt the oldest fragment in the Old Testament (see p. 131).

In all relations with the great the youth is adjured to eschew hypocrisy and double dealing:

> "Divorce not thy heart from thy tongue,
> And it shall come to pass that all thy purposes shall be successful,
> And it shall come to pass that thou shalt be a weighty man before the multitude,
> And safe in the hand of God.
>
> For God hateth the man of false speech,
> And his chief abomination is the double-minded."

If association with the great tempts to hypocrisy, relations with the hasty and hot-tempered are also dangerous in leading one to intemperate speech:

> "Fraternise not with the hot-tempered man,
> And press not upon him for conversation."

The treatise is filled with warnings against the quarrelsome and reckless man, and the ideal character, with which the hot-head is contrasted, is that of the man of gentleness, modesty, and self-control. Early in his admonitions Amenemope contrasts the two as two trees, one wild and uncontrolled in the forest and the other adorning a garden:

> "The hot-head serving in the temple,
> He is like a tree growing in the forest.
> In a moment he loseth his branches,
> And findeth his end in the ⌈timber dock⌉.
> He is floated far away from his place,
> And the fire is his grave.
>
> The truly prudent man, who putteth himself aside,
> Is like a tree growing in a garden,
> He flourisheth and multiplieth his fruit,
> He abideth in the presence of his lord,
> His fruit is sweet, his shade is pleasant,
> And he findeth his end in the garden."

Amenemope charges his son:

> "Yoke not up a quarrel with the hot-tongued,"

and urges the youth never to become involved with such men. The sage's word for the reckless, quarrelsome, hothead is simply the substantive adjective "hot," which is clear enough. It is parallel with the Hebrew word rendered "the scornful" in the Book of Proverbs. On the other hand the designation used by the sage for the moderate and self-controlled man is the "truly silent," who treats all with gentleness and modesty. He is closely related to the meditative and silent worshipper whom we have already met and he seems to correspond with the "prudent man" of the Hebrew Proverbs. Such a man treats kindly the widow whom he finds gleaning in his field, for Amenemope reminds his son that:

> "God loveth him that cheereth the humble man
> More than him who honoureth the great man."

It is this gentle and kindly spirit which admonishes that the poor and the afflicted are not to be unkindly treated:

> "Laugh not at a blind man nor mock at a dwarf,
> Injure not a cripple,
> And mock not a man who is in the hand of God,
> Neither be harsh towards him when he transgresseth.
>
> As for men, they are clay and straw (of bricks)
> And God is their builder.
> He pulleth down and buildeth up again daily.
> He maketh a thousand humble as he will,
> And a thousand he maketh overseers,
> When he is in his hour of life.
> Happy is he who reacheth the West (the hereafter),
> While he is safe in the hand of God."

The uncertainty of the human estate and its complete dependence upon God lead Amenemope to warn his son against the fleeting character of riches.

> "Let not thy heart go out after riches,
>
> . . . .
>
> Weary not thyself to seek for more,
> When thy need is (already) secure.

If riches be brought to thee by robbery,
They will not abide the night with thee.

When the morning cometh they are no longer in thy house,

. . . .

They have made themselves wings like geese,
And they have flown to heaven.

. . . .

Pray to Aton the Sun-god when he riseth
And say, 'Give me safety and health';
He will give to thee thy need for life,
And thou art saved from fear."

In the wise conclusion that riches "make themselves wings" and fly away, Amenemope's graphic picture of the uncertainty and perishability of earthly good, we recognise a figure which has come down to us through the editor of the Hebrew Book of Proverbs, and in the life of the Western world has gained proverbial currency after three thousand years. Our sage regards dependence upon such fleeting human resources as futile; the only security is in God, pray to him and "thou art saved from fear." Tranquillity of mind and deliverance from fear are to be had only by reliance on God; and so in the most noble passage of the old Egyptian sage's advice to his son, he says:

"Lie not down to sleep at night fearing the morrow,
For when day dawneth, how is the morrow?
Man knoweth not how the morrow shall be.

God is in his perfection
And man is in his insufficiency,
The words which men speak diverge,
And divergent are the acts of God.

Say not, 'I have no sin,'
And weary not thyself to seek conflict.
As for sin, it belongeth to God,
It is sealed with his finger.

There is no one perfect in the hand of God,
Nor shall insufficiency stand before him.
If one constraineth himself to seek perfection,
In a moment he (himself) destroyeth it.

Be steadfast in thy mind and establish thy heart,
Make not a rudder of thy tongue.
Though the tongue of man be the rudder of the ship,
The Lord-of-All is its pilot."

When Jesus admonished his disciples, "Take no thought for the morrow," was there an echo of old oriental teaching in his words? Perhaps we shall never be able to answer that question, but the Wisdom of Amenemope has contributed essentially to disclose to us the diffusion of Egyptian moral teachings beyond the shores of the Nile and especially in Palestine. The most widely dispersed of Amenemope's wise sayings, however, went much farther than Palestine, and is still in use among us. As Sethe[6] has shown, the seemingly obscure lines regarding the divergence of the words of men and the acts of God can mean nothing else than the wide difference between the words, that is the plans, of men and the subsequent acts of God. Slightly less literally rendered the lines run:

"The words which men speak diverge
And the acts of God diverge."

The contrast is obviously between "the words of men" and "the acts of God," and when it is stated that they

[6] Nachrichten der Gesell. der Wissensch. zu Göttingen, Phil.-Hist. Kl. 1925, pp. 141 *ff*. See also the comments of B. Gunn, *Zeitschrift für ægyptische Sprache,* Vol. 62 (1927), pp. 83–85.

both "diverge" the meaning evidently is "from each other." We thus have here in its oldest form the world-wide proverb, "Man proposes, God disposes." Such a widely distributed ancient Egyptian view of the relation of God and man suggests the whole question of the place of Egyptian moral evolution in the history not only of early man, but of Western civilisation. The discussion of that subject must form the conclusion of this book but before we can enter upon it we must briefly survey the final stages of Egyptian moral reflection before the Nile Valley was drawn into the maelstrom of the Asiatic-Mediterranean empires.

After the fall of the Egyptian Empire in the Twelfth Century B.C. the forces of life both within and without were exhausted and had lost their power to stimulate the moral thinking of Egypt to any further vital development. Stagnation and a deadly and indifferent inertia fell like a stupor upon the once vigorous life of the nation. The development which now ensued was purely institutional and involved no progress in thought. The power of the priesthood as a political influence had led Thutmose III in the Fifteenth Century B.C. to make the High Priest of Amon primate of all the priesthoods of Egypt, the chief sacerdotal official of the state. While this Amonite papacy suffered severely at the hands of Ikhnaton, it later recovered all it had lost and much more. Ramses II even allowed an oracle of Amon to guide him in the appointment of the god's High Priest, and under such circumstances it was easy for the High Priests of Amon to make the office hereditary. Unable to resist the political power of this state within the state, a constant victim of its economic encroachments, Egypt rapidly degenerated into a sacerdotal state, and by 1100 B.C. the Pharaoh had yielded the sceptre to the head of what had become a state church.

It was in the course of this long development which placed the sacerdotal party in control of the throne, that the outward and official manifestations of religion took on those forms of dignity and splendour such as no early religion had before displayed. The sanctuaries of this age will always form one of the most imposing survivals from the ancient world. Not only in their grandeur as architecture, but also in their sumptuous equipment, these vast palaces of the gods lifted the external observances of religion to a plane of splendour and influence which they had never enjoyed before. Enthroned in magnificence which not even the sumptuous East had ever seen, Amon of Thebes became in the hands of his crafty priesthood a mere oracular source for political and administrative decisions. Even routine legal verdicts were rendered by the nod of the god, and such matters as wills and testaments were subject to his oracles. The old prayer of the oppressed, that Amon might become the vizier of the poor man, was receiving a very literal fulfilment, and with results little foreseen by the men who had framed this prayer.

As a personal and moral force, religion survived only in the hearts of poor and lowly believers, such as those whose prayers, breathing the devotion of a personal faith, we have found among the humblest votive tablets of the Theban cemetery (see pp. 313–319). These votive tablets, the advice of Ani, and the Wisdom of Amenemope have revealed to us the spirit of an age of personal piety which brought the development of moral ideas in ancient Egypt to a close within a few generations after 1000 B.C. at the very time when the united monarchy of the Hebrews, which had seen but three kings, collapsed and fell into two kingdoms. It is important to notice that the moral development of Egypt, like her cultural evolution as a whole, after having gone on for some twenty-five hundred years, was nearly ended before the national life of the Hebrews had begun.

When the decadence of Egypt, which had continued for five hundred years, was transformed into a restoration after 700 B.C., the creative age of inner development in religion and morals was forever past. Instead of an exuberant energy expressing itself in the spontaneous development of new forms and new manifestations, as at the beginning of all the great periods of her history, we find that Egypt now fell back upon her great past, and consciously endeavoured to restore and rehabilitate the vanished state of the old days before the changes and innovations introduced by the Empire.[7] Seen through the mist of two thousand years, what was to *them* Ancient Egypt was endowed with the ideal perfection of the divine régime which had preceded it. In the endeavour to reconstitute modern religion, society, and government upon ancient lines, the archaisers must consciously or unconsciously have been constantly thwarted by the inevitable mutability of the social, political, and economic conditions of a race. The two thousand years which had elapsed since the Pyramid Age could not be annihilated. Through the deceptive mantle of antiquity with which they cloaked contemporary conditions, the inexorable realities of the present were discernible. The solution of the difficulty, when perceived, was the same as that later attempted by the Hebrews in a similar dilemma: it was but to attribute to the modern elements

[7] These and the following remarks are adapted largely after the author's *History of Egypt*, pp. 570 *ff*.

FIG. 17. THE GREAT TEMPLE OF AMON AT KARNAK, EGYPT, SEEN FROM THE AIR

The foundations of this temple date from the Twentieth Century B.C. or earlier. Beginning with the first kings of the Empire (Sixteenth Century B.C.), most of the rulers of Egypt thereafter had some part in its enlargement or embellishment. Indeed the extent of the vast temple complex at Karnak discloses the growth of ritual and sacerdotalism which resulted in the decadence of late Egyptian religion. (*Oriental Institute photograph by Reed N. Haythorne.*)

also a hoary antiquity, as the whole body of Hebrew legislation was attributed to Moses. The theoretical revival was thus rescued.

The ancient mortuary writings of the pyramids, which we have called the Pyramid Texts, were revived, and although frequently not understood, were engraved upon the massive stone sarcophagi. The Book of the Dead, still undergoing further redaction, shows plain traces of this influence. In the tomb-chapels we find again the fresh and pleasing pictures from the life of the people in marsh and meadow, in workshop and ship-yard. They are surprisingly accurate reproductions of the relief scenes in the mastaba tombs of the Pyramid Age, so accurate indeed that at the first glance one is not infrequently in doubt as to the age of the monument. Indeed a man named Aba, at Thebes, sent his artists to an Old Kingdom tomb near Siut to copy thence the reliefs for use in his own Theban tomb, because the owner of the ancient tomb was also named Aba.

We recall that the Memphite Drama has been preserved to us because an Ethiopian Pharaoh of the Eighth Century B.C. piously ordered that an ancient papyrus book of the early dynasties, a "work of the ancestors, which was eaten of worms," should be copied on a large black basalt slab now in the British Museum (see pp. 29–32). Thus the writings and sacred rolls of bygone days were now eagerly sought out, and, with the dust of ages upon them, they were collected, sorted, and arranged. The past was supreme. The priest who cherished it lived in a realm of shadows, and for the contemporary world he had no vital meaning. Likewise in Babylon the same retrospective spirit was now dominant in the reviving empire of Nebuchadnezzar. It was soon to take possession of the returning Hebrew exiles. The world seemed to be growing old, and men were dwelling fondly and wistfully on her far-away youth. In this process of conserving the old, the religion of Egypt sank deeper and deeper into decay, to become, what Herodotus found it, a religion of innumerable external observances and mechanical usages, carried out with such elaborate and insistent punctiliousness that the Egyptians gained the reputation of being the most religious of all peoples. But such observances were no longer the expression of a growing and developing inner life, as in the days before the creative vitality of the race was extinct.

We have been tracing in broad lines the development of the moral ideas of a great people, unfolding in the course of over three thousand years, as the forces within and the forces around this ancient man wrought and fashioned his conception of the divine powers and his standards of human conduct. God as discerned everywhere in the ancient oriental world was a human experience. The ancient ideas of God are but the expression of the best that man has felt and thought embodied in a supreme character of which he dreamed. That supreme character was an idealised man. What was intended by Robert G. Ingersoll, I suppose, as a biting gibe, "An honest god is the noblest work of man," is nevertheless profoundly true. We have seen the Egyptian slowly gaining his honest god. We gained ours by inheritance from the Hebrews. We are now in a position to answer the question whether this inheritance of moral and religious ideas was exclusively the product and creation of Hebrew civilisation or whether history discloses our moral heritage as having been built up to a large extent in an age far earlier than the Hebrews, and having descended to us rather as the composite product of a group of great civilisations and therefore as *the highest and noblest expression of the life of ancient man as a whole, the sublimest message of our Father Man.*

CHAPTER XVII

THE SOURCES OF OUR MORAL HERITAGE

In the preceding chapters we have briefly examined the most important original sources revealing to us the rise and the development of moral convictions in Northeastern Africa from the middle of the Fourth Millennium B.C. until the absorption of Egypt into the Asiatic-Mediterranean empires in the Sixth Century B.C. The ethical development disclosed by these original documents therefore occupied a period of some three thousand years. During this long period Western Asia was likewise bringing forth a group of great civilisations of fundamental importance in the future development of the human race. The oldest of these civilisations was that of Babylonia, the beginnings of which can now be followed some centuries into the Fourth Millennium B.C. The civilisation of the Babylonians achieved some superb developments in art during the Third Millennium B.C., and its vigorous heraldic use of animal figures in balanced antithetic compositions alive with power and action has influenced the decorative art of all subsequent history. This art was profoundly affected by the archaic myths of Western Asia, especially those of Babylonia, which early found powerful literary expression, and disclosed astonishing vitality, so that they were current far beyond the borders of Babylonia and furnished much of the content of early decorative art in Western Asia. The Babylonian Deluge Myth thus found its way westward to the Mediterranean and, circulating in Syria and Palestine, eventually found its way into Hebrew literature, whence it has descended to us in the Old Testament. Allusions to these myths are found throughout the literature of the Hebrews, especially in their religious songs, which we call the Psalms.

With the exception of its interest in art, however, the older Babylonian civilisation remained surprisingly materialistic. It was not until the rise of the Chaldean power (Neo-Babylonia) in the Sixth Century B.C. and the subsequent supremacy of the Persians after Cyrus, that the Babylonians disclosed outstanding intellectual interests and their noble astronomers laid the foundations upon which the astronomical science of the Greeks was later built up. As a people, the Babylonians were essentially a commercial folk, chiefly interested in business and its regulation by law. An able British Assyriologist has said of the Babylonians: "No other people was so perpetually devoted to the acquisition of shekels, so completely absorbed in the pursuit of prosperity in this life."[1] Their caravans and those of Assyria pushed westward into Asia Minor, Syria, and Palestine far back in the Third Millennium B.C. Before 2000 B.C. cuneiform business documents were common in eastern Asia Minor, and Palestine was quite commonly using Babylonian cuneiform writing by the Fifteenth Century B.C. Along with Babylonian business came the commercial usages and laws followed by the Babylonian merchants. Some of the same laws that have come down to us in the Code of Hammurapi became current also in Palestine before Hebrew days, and through the Old Testa-

[1] *Early History of Assyria,* p. 338, by Sidney Smith, Keeper of the Department of Egyptian and Assyrian Antiquities in the British Museum (Vol. I, New York, 1928).

ment have found their way into Western civilisation, where Hebrew law and the laws of the Babylonian Hammurapi meet together again on the study table of the modern orientalist. It was doubtless in practical contacts like those of business that Palestinian life also received such institutions as the Babylonian Sabbath. Whether he likes it or not, the Western man of business living in the Near Orient at the present day must needs conform to the current calendar of sacred days when no business is done, and it will not have been otherwise with the Palestinian merchants when transacting business with those of Babylonia.

It was therefore in external usages and ritual observances rather than in the essential content of religion that Palestine most easily adopted Babylonian beliefs and ideas. Like the Egyptians, the earliest Babylonians had beheld their gods in the forces of nature, and their earliest divinities were nature gods. In a remarkable hymn which must have been employed in the worship of Sin, the Moon-god, in his temple at Ur, we find the priestly author clearly disclosing the background of nature in which he involuntarily beheld the Moon-god functioning, but at the same time shifting him over into the affairs of men, attributing to him not only the creation of all material things but also the establishment of human institutions like the state, including the government and the state religion and especially the moral life of men: "Thy word bringeth forth truth and righteousness, so that men speak the truth." This noble hymn, with its majestic picture of the Moon-god's sway, including his introduction and maintenance of moral life, demonstrates the existence of reflective minds among the priests who officially carried on the duties of the state religion in ancient Babylonia. The priest who wrote this hymn has, to be sure, devoted but a very small amount of space to the moral aspect of the Moon-god's dominion. He is more interested in the unlimited power of the god over the material resources of the land, and the bulk of the hymn is devoted to this side of the picture. Out of forty-eight lines comprising the entire hymn, the priestly author has devoted to "truth and righteousness" possibly two lines, and with certainty only *one*. With some omissions the hymn is as follows:

"Merciful, gracious father, who holdeth[2] the life of the whole land in his hand;
Lord, thy divinity is like the distant heaven, a broad sea full of fruitfulness,
Who createth the land, foundeth the temples, nameth their names;
Father, who begetteth gods and men, causeth dwellings to be set up, and initiateth offerings;
Who summoneth the kingship, handeth over the sceptre, and fixeth destiny to distant days;
Mighty prince, whose spacious heart no god seeth through,

. . . .

Lord, who fixeth the decision of heaven and earth, whose command no one altereth,
Who holdeth fire and water, who guideth the living creatures, what god was thy peer?
In heaven—who is exalted? Thou alone art exalted!
On earth—who is exalted? Thou alone art exalted!
When thy word resoundeth in heaven, the gods of the upper world throw themselves down on their faces;
When thy word resoundeth on earth, the gods of the lower world kiss the ground.
When thy word riseth aloft like the wind, it maketh to flourish meadow and springs;

[2] The inconsistency in the person of the verbs is in the original.

When thy word sinketh down to earth, the green herbage is brought forth.
Thy word maketh fat stall and herd, spreadeth out the living creatures;
Thy word bringeth forth truth and righteousness, so that men speak the truth,
Thy word is the distant sky, the covered earth, which no one seeth through,
Thy word, who comprehendeth it? Who is equal to it?

. . . .

Look upon thy house! Look upon thy city! Look upon Ur!"[3]

Here is religious aspiration on a high plane, which must inevitably have exerted a wide influence in Western Asia. In a period long before the rise of Hebrew religion, it reminds us of the Hebrew Psalms. Our specific task however is not concerned with religion as a whole, but especially with moral ideas and beliefs. What was the moral content of Babylonian life? What moral reflections have the Babylonians left us? The fact that their sculpture shows no discernible evidence of portraiture is significant of their lack of interest in the interpretation of human character or the portrayal of human traits. They were not given to reflection on the divergences between types of character as displayed in the contrast between the lives of good and evil men. Striking evidence of this attitude of mind is the fact that there was no judgment in the hereafter, for good and bad alike were after death consigned to the same *Sheol,* the same shadowy subterranean abode. Nevertheless the Babylonians had developed the belief that Shamash, the Sun-god, who as in Egypt was the god of justice, disapproved of unsocial

[3] After Hugo Gressman, *Altorientalische Texte zum Alten Testament,* pp. 241–242 (2d ed. enl., Berlin, 1926).

conduct. In a hymn to Shamash this belief is unequivocally expressed:

"O Shamash, out of thy net no evil-doer escapes,
Out of thy snare no sinner flees.
As for him who breaks an oath, thou punishest him quickly,
And he who does not respect sacred things cannot escape thee.
Thy broad net is spread out for the evil-doer,
Who lifted up his eyes to the wife of his companion . . .
If thy weapon is raised against him, there is no saviour;
If he stands in the court, not even his father can help.
To the word of the judge not even his brothers make rejoinder;
With a brazen trap he is unfailingly covered.
As for him who plans evil, thou destroyest his horn,
And as for him who takes the part of the evil-doer, he loses the ground under his feet.
The unjust judge thou makest behold shackles,
As for him who takes a bribe and bends the right,
Him dost thou burden with punishment.
He who does not take a bribe, who espouses the cause of the weak,
Is well pleasing to Shamash: he will live long.
The careful judge, who renders a just judgment,
Prepares himself a palace, a princely residence is his dwelling . . .
Like water of the eternal well-springs there is everlasting seed
To him who deals piously and well, and who knows not deceit . . .
But he who is basely minded is recorded with the writing stylus;
And as for them who do evil, their seed hath no permanence."[4]

Here indeed are reward for the worthy and retribution for the guilty, with recognition of the social character of the offences; but such recognition does not characterise the broad current of Babylonian life or the habitual conceptions of evil as they are found throughout Babylonian

[4] After A. Ungnad, *Die Religion der Babylonier und Assyrer*, pp. 187–188 (Jena, 1921).

literature. The penitential psalms of the Babylonians are commonly quoted as expressions of their poignant consciousness of sin; but it is obvious that they contain no evidence of having offended against human society. Westermarck has shrewdly observed, "In none of the penitential psalms known to us is there any indication that the notion of sin comprised offences against fellow men." In the feeling of the Babylonians, offences were merely ceremonial transgressions against the god and there might indeed be no ground at all for the god's anger. The penitential psalms clearly indicate that the evil consequences, which the offender so passionately pleads he may escape, are due not to disapproval of evil conduct by the god, but, as Westermarck has noted, "to the curses of the injured party."[5] This conclusion is in entire harmony with the general observation that the ethical convictions of the Babylonians, in which we cannot as yet discern any clear development, were not a fundamentally important element in the lives, either of the people or of their rulers. This fact is very strikingly demonstrated by the famous law code of Hammurapi, in which the penalties and verdicts are graded according to the social station of the litigant or the offender, the man of high station receiving substantially more favourable consideration than the man of low birth. We recall that Egyptian sages and noblemen continually reiterate their disregard of social distinctions, saying, "I did not exalt the great above the humble," the terms designating a man of rank as contrasted with an ordinary citizen, literally, a "little one." Social position or high rank gave no Egyptian any advantage in the eyes of the law. We remember that the Pharaoh instructed the grand vizier that his duty was "not to

[5] *Op. cit.*, Vol. II, pp. 702–703.

show respect of persons to princes and councillors," and this principle was thus embedded in the very constitution of the Egyptian state. The sense of social justice, which lies at the very foundation of moral development, was very imperfect or lacking altogether among the Babylonians, and their civilisation therefore did not contribute essentially to the moral history of Western Asia.

Another possible source of such influences in the early history of Western Asia, which we should notice even in such a rapid summary as this, is to be found in the high moral sense of the Hittites, fragments of whose laws are now available. The most remarkable example is the recognition of the moral character of international obligations by one of the Hittite kings in the Thirteenth Century B.C. The Hittite sovereign admits an unprovoked attack upon the Egyptian Empire under Ramses II and, recognising the moral wrong of which he has been guilty, attributes a pestilence with which his people were suffering to the anger of his god, who has sent the pestilence as punishment for the offence thus committed. A development of the sense of justice and moderation is observable in a milder revision of the Hittite code by King Khattushil, which he contrasts with the severity of the older code before his time. Nearly 200 paragraphs of this code, comprising a large part of it, have survived on clay tablets. It is noticeable that the Hittites also graded their legally established penalties according to the political status of the offender, the penalty being milder if he is a local native than if he is a subject of a neighbouring state. There is still a vast amount of excavation and of study of the Hittite monuments to be achieved before we shall have in hand a full knowledge of the character of Hittite civilisation. Meanwhile the indications are that the Hittites probably had some influence on the moral development of Western Asia. It is important to notice, however, that Hittite civilisation was of little weight until far down in the Second Millennium B.C., at a period relatively late in the history of oriental civilisation.

During their captivity in the east, at a late stage in their religious development, the Hebrews came into intimate contact with Persian civilisation and learned something of the religion of Zoroaster. Zoroastrianism was a dualism which called on every man to stand on one side or the other; to fill his soul with the Good and the Light or to dwell in the Evil and the Darkness. These forces were all personified. Whatever course a man pursued, he must expect a judgment hereafter. The prominence of the judgment, unknown before Zoroaster in Western Asia, creates a strong presumption that Zoroaster drew much from Egyptian religion.

Six weeks after I had written the preceding statement and after it was already in type, I was standing for the first time among the scanty wreckage of the palace of Cyrus the Great, not half an hour's walk from his tomb at Pasargadæ. Of this now well nigh vanished building only a pilaster or two of heavy stone masonry still remain standing, with the laconic cuneiform inscriptian in Old Persian: "I Cyrus [made it]." One of these stone piers, a door-post, still displays a relief sculpture representing a tall human figure, a semi-divine being with two pairs of wings beautifully spread, one of the ancestors of our Biblican angels. I recognised it as a relief which I had before seen published,[6] but on inspecting the weath-

[6] See Friedrich Sarre, *Die Kunst des alten Persien* (Berlin, 1922); and Friedrich Sarre and Ernst Herzfeld, *Iranische Felsreliefs,* Tafel XXVIII, and pp. 155–165 (Berlin, 1910).

ered sculpture more closely something suddenly became evident, which had never attracted my attention before: *the head of the winged being was surmounted by the crown of Osiris, the Egyptian god of the judgment hereafter!* Such symbolism is always significant in the ancient art of the East. This winged monitor had been standing for nearly 2500 years in the doorway of the palace of Cyrus, and every visitor that entered there beheld him wearing the crown judgment after death. It can, therefore, hardly be doubted that, like so much in Persian architecture and art, the Zoroastrian judgment hereafter was drawn from Egypt.

Since I left Persia, Professor Ernst Herzfeld[7] in reporting on his work among the old Persian monuments writes me that he has been copying a long and unpublished inscription on the front of the tomb of Darius the Great, and that it contains a statement of ethics and ideal human conduct. For example Darius says, "Right I have loved, and Wrong I have not loved. My will was that no injustice should be done to any widow or orphan, and that injustice should be done to orphans and widows was not my will. I strictly punished the liar, (but) him who laboured I well rewarded." We must await full publication of this extraordinary new message from Darius the Great, but the quotations which Herzfeld has sent sound surprisingly like an echo of the social teachings of the Egyptian wise men. There is plenty of evidence that the post-Exilic religious development of the Hebrews was affected by the teachings of Zoroaster, and that among

[7] Professor Herzfeld is Field Director of the Persian Expedition of the Oriental Institute, now engaged in the excavation of the palaces of Persepolis, the neighbouring tombs of the Persian emperors at Naksh-i-Rustum, and other sites around Persepolis.

the international influences to which the development of Hebrew morals was exposed, we must include also the teachings of the great Medo-Persian prophet.

Before the rise of the Hebrew monarchy late in the Eleventh Century B.C. there had developed a whole series of civilised states along the eastern end of the Mediterranean between the Hittite region on the north and the borders of Egypt on the south. For the history of civilisation perhaps the most important of these peoples were the Phœnicians. Important elements of Egyptian and Babylonian civilisation formed a substantial factor in the culture and life of the prosperous harbour cities, the commercial centres of the Phœnician coast. Thence these foreign threads were easily woven into the fabric of Hebrew life. Of Phœnician moral development, however, we know practically nothing. In the territory of Palestine, later occupied by the Hebrews, the Canaanites, the predecessors of the Hebrews, had passed through a civilised development which was over a thousand years old when the Hebrew invasion of Palestine took place. Of this refined and highly developed pre-Hebrew civilisation of Palestine, the historical inscriptions of Egypt and Babylonia, together with archæological excavation, have taught us much. As we have already seen, Babylonian culture had an important and lasting influence on Canaanite Palestine, and it was chiefly through the Canaanites that the influences of Babylonian art, literature, and religion were received by the Hebrews. The region had furthermore long been dominated by Egyptian civilisation. The Egyptians had begun to hold the Phœnician coast over two thousand years before the Hebrews entered Palestine. Egyptian armies had marched across Palestine before 2500 B.C. Having conquered Western Asia to the Euphrates in the

Sixteenth Century B.C., the Pharaohs held Palestine as a subject country for over four centuries, and indeed were the rulers of Palestine for two centuries after the Hebrews settled there. Canaanite civilisation had therefore reached an advanced stage under centuries of Egyptian occupation and was tinctured through and through with Egyptian elements when the Hebrews invaded the country. The Hebrews consequently, on entering Palestine, were in immediate contact with a highly advanced composite civilisation of the Canaanites, built up largely out of Babylonian and Egyptian elements. This Canaanite civilisation had already passed through a long social experience during which there developed also many cultural elements due to the Canaanites themselves. Indeed it was without doubt the very language which the Hebrew invaders found in Palestine, the Canaanitish speech, current there at that time, which the Hebrews adopted and which has descended to us as the Hebrew of the Old Testament. Unhappily we know little of the moral history of these people before the Israelitish invasion.

Summing up the situation of Palestine in its various aspects, therefore, we see that *geographically* it lay on a narrow natural bridge between the Mediterranean Sea on the one hand and the Arabian Desert on the other—an intercontinental bridge which had formed the highway connecting Africa and Asia from prehistoric times. *Politically* Palestine was in antiquity, as it still is today, an international football. *Culturally,* as we have just been observing, it was within the commercial territory so long dominated by Babylonian business, while at the same time it lay directly under the eaves of the great structure of Egyptian civilisation. A people settling in Palestine therefore found itself not only in the midst of an already old and largely Egyptianised civilisation of the region itself, but also looking out upon much older civilisations on either hand in Asia and Africa. Out of this far-reaching international *milieu* of the ancient Near East which enveloped Palestine, came forth the moral ideas which eventually furnished the dominant ethical conceptions of the Western world. They came through the medium of the surviving fragments of Hebrew literature, the moral content of which, as we have seen, was far from being an exclusive contribution of the Hebrews.

It is an extraordinary fact that this great moral legacy should have descended to Western civilisation from a politically insignificant people living at the southeast corner of the Mediterranean. They gained national organisation only a decade or two before 1000 B.C. and endured as a unified nation only about a century at most. After the break-up of this tiny nation, its two surviving fragments struggled on; one of them for a matter of two centuries longer, and the other, after an additional century and a quarter of precarious semi-independent existence among the great powers of the ancient oriental world, likewise suffered complete annihilation not long after 600 B.C. Beginning thus less than three decades before 1000 B.C., the independent national life of the ancient Hebrews, or a part of them, lasted about four and a quarter centuries, and was ended early in the Sixth Century B.C. This period of Hebrew national life thus fell almost entirely within the first half of the last thousand years B.C. At that time the cultural development of both Egypt and Babylonia had fallen into stagnation and had become a tradition of ancient history.

Within the limited compass of this book it is of course quite impossible to offer even a sketch of the religious and moral history of the ancient Hebrews. Our task however does require us to disclose the more important foreign factors in their ethical development. In order to do this, some of the outstanding facts in Hebrew history must be recalled if we are to recognise the foreign elements in Hebrew ethical development.

The Hebrews appear in the arena of history for the first time in the Tell el-Amarna Letters, the earliest of which are to be dated not long after 1400 B.C., that is, from a time far older than any surviving Hebrew literature. These cuneiform letters disclose to us bodies of the Hebrew nomads drifting into Palestine, then under Egyptian sovereignty, and entering mercenary military service there. We know nothing more of them for nearly two hundred years, until an Egyptian monument set up at Thebes (Luxor) by Merneptah, son of Ramses II, a decade or two before 1200 B.C. preserves to us a hymn of victory in which we find the boast:

"Israel is wasted, his seed is not."

This was in the period of the Judges, when Hebrew national life was still very undeveloped and there was little or no centralisation or national organisation. The Hebrew people were still very largely the product of their long centuries of pastoral life as nomadic herdsmen on the desert fringes before they entered Palestine. They still carried with them the rude and barbarous habits of the desert tribesmen and even the half-savage practices of a primitive stage of life, like the slaying of first-born children as a sacrifice to the tribal god. These local gods might be such a sinister demon of a hill-top or a brook as that sombre goblin of the night, with whom Jacob wrestled at the Brook Jabbok and whom he forced to flee in fear before the breaking dawn. In the desert south of Judea such a local spirit was called an "ēl," which is not a proper name but the old Semitic word for a local "god." It has descended to us in the very name of Isra-ēl, the name given to Jacob by the being with whom he had wrestled, and in a group of such names as Micha-ēl, which means "who is like ēl." Farther north in Canaan, the local gods of the Canaanites were called "baals" or lords.

It is evident that some of the Hebrew nomads, after having taken refuge in Egypt in time of famine, were subjected to slavery, from which a Hebrew of statesman-like gifts and notable powers of leadership, who placed himself at their head, delivered them and thus became the first great Hebrew leader whose name has come down to us. It is important to notice that his name, Moses, was Egyptian. It is simply the Egyptian word "mose" meaning "child," and is an abridgement of a fuller form of such names as "Amen-mose" meaning "Amon-a-child" or "Ptah-mose," meaning "Ptah-a-child," these forms themselves being likewise abbreviations for the complete form "Amon-(has-given)-a-child" or "Ptah-(has-given)-a-child." The abbreviation "child" early became a convenient rapid form for the cumbrous full name, and the name Mose, "child," is not uncommon on the Egyptian monuments. The father of Moses without doubt prefixed to his son's name that of an Egyptian god like Amon or Ptah, and this divine name was gradually lost in current usage, till the boy was called "Mose."[8] The leadership of Moses, the courage and skill with which he delivered his people from foreign bondage, the deliverance itself, accompanied by some natural catastrophe which destroyed

[8] The final *s* is an addition drawn from the Greek translation of the Old Testament. It is not in the Hebrew which has "mosheh."

a body of pursuing Egyptian troops—all these found an imperishable place in Hebrew tradition and gave the Hebrews an initial heritage of glory which was the earliest influence welding them together as a nation.

At some stage in these early incidents Moses had tarried in the wilderness south of Palestine among a desert tribe known as Midianites, and especially with one of their sacred ministrants named Jethro, from whom he learned of their local god, "Yahveh," or "Jahveh."[9]

This region from Sinai northward, especially along the tremendous chasm of the Dead Sea and the Jordan Valley, abounds in geological evidences of relatively recent volcanic action. A Hebrew tradition of the destruction of Sodom and Gomorrah, two cities in this area, by "fire and brimstone" from the skies (Gen. 19:23–28), is undoubtedly a vague reminiscence of a volcanic eruption not yet forgotten by the local tribes in early Hebrew times. As described in the Old Testament, the escape of the Hebrews from Egypt was accompanied by wonders quite evidently volcanic in character. The peculiar manifestation of Yahveh as "a pillar of fire" or "a pillar of cloud," and his appearance on Mount Sinai *by day* with "thunders and lightnings and a thick cloud" are obviously volcanic phenomena. It has long been recognised therefore that Yahveh was a local volcano god, who had his localised seat in Mount Sinai. Through the influence of Moses the Hebrews cast out their ancient ēls and adopted Yahveh as their sole god. For this extraordinary deed there must have been some stronger motive than the in-

[9] The growing sacredness of this name led the Jews to pronounce a Hebrew word for "Lord" in its place. This practice finally resulted in the loss of the ancient pronunciation of Yahveh, and its four consonants YHVH, pronounced with the vowels of the Hebrew word "Lord," thus became Jehovah (Yehovah), a form of the name which had no ancient existence at all.

fluence of their great leader. It is evident that the deliverance from Egyptian task-masters was accompanied by some terrible manifestation of Yahveh's power. There is much basis for the view that as the Israelites pressed on in flight an eruption of Sinai, a volcanic mountain, began, and we might conjecture that it was the accompanying earthquake and a resulting tidal wave which caused the engulfment of a body of pursuing Egyptian troops. However this may be, the belief that, as the Hebrews entered his territory near Mount Sinai, Yahveh delivered them by some tremendous manifestation of his power and favour, gained a permanent place in Hebrew tradition. Long afterwards when his national sanctuary had been fixed at Jerusalem, his Israelitish worshippers pictured Yahveh as coming from Sinai in power and splendour to take up his abode on Mount Zion.

The colorless local ēls of the earlier Hebrews, gods, who had no proper names, no identities, and no historical background, continued as feeble competitors of Yahveh after the Israelites had settled in Palestine. More powerful rivals were the Canaanite baals. Notwithstanding their adoption of Yahveh as their national god, there were many Hebrews who still believed in other gods, such as the baals, and often reverted to them. The very name Yahveh, being a proper name like Apollo or Mercury, implied the existence of other gods with similar personal names; and in the first commandment that Yahveh laid upon the Israelites he himself recognised the existence of the other gods when he said, "Thou shalt have no other gods before me." The process by which the Israelites made the transition from the service of many gods to belief in a sole God of the universe was a slow and gradual one, occupying many centuries.

Similarly their conception of the character of their god passed through many stages from the days when they delighted in the power of their nature god to crush and slaughter the Canaanites, until they gained the vision of a merciful and righteous Father. It is especially in the writings of the Hebrew prophets that we are still able to observe some of the steps in the development by which the Israelites outgrew their nature god. Although he continued to bear the name of the old volcano god, Yahveh, the Hebrew people gradually came to behold him as a force in human society.

The Egyptian background out of which Moses had developed into a great national leader must in itself have contributed to his vision of Yahveh's place in the life of his people. Born in Egypt and bearing an Egyptian name, Moses enjoined his countrymen to adopt an enormously ancient Egyptian custom, the rite of circumcision, which in his day had been practiced among the Nile-dwellers for at least three thousand years and more.[10] Hebrew tradition always attributed the origin of this rite to Moses, and the fact that he adopted as a universal distinguishing mark of the Israelite a sacred Egyptian practice, with which he had obviously been acquainted in Egypt from childhood days, is unequivocal contemporaneous evidence that he was consciously drawing upon his knowledge of Egyptian religion. He was no slavish imitator of Egyptian practices, however, as is shown by the fact that having received his god Yahveh from the Midianites, a desert people too primitive and unskilled in the arts to make

[10] The bodies of Egyptians exhumed from the earliest prehistoric cemeteries, back of 4000 B.C., have disclosed the evidence of circumcision, whenever the body is sufficiently well preserved to make observation possible. The actual performance of the operation by the Egyptian surgeon is depicted in an Egyptian tomb relief of the Twenty-seventh or Twenty-eighth Century B.C. in the cemetery of Memphis.

images of their god, he left Yahveh unpictured and imageless, just as the Midianites had done. He retained, however, some reminiscences of Egyptian religious images. He himself carried a magically potent staff, doubtless a serpent staff, in which dwelt the power of Yahveh, and for the healing of the people he set up a shining brazen image of a serpent, obviously one of the many serpent divinities of Egypt. This image of an Egyptian divinity remained with the Hebrews long after they had settled in Palestine. They continued to burn incense to it for five centuries after Moses' time, and it was not removed from the temple in Jerusalem until the reign of Hezekiah, late in the Eighth Century B.C. (II Kings 18:4).

Down into the Christian Era the Hebrews preserved a tradition that Moses was learned in "all the wisdom of the Egyptians" (Acts 7:22), and we can hardly question the correctness of this tradition. It is only in recent years that we have been able to understand the surviving sources of Egyptian life sufficiently well to realise that the "wisdom of the Egyptians" was primarily social contemplation. Moses must therefore have been familiar with the writings of the Egyptian social prophets, the oldest of which, as we have seen, had been in circulation for fifteen hundred years when Moses began the teaching of his people. It is obvious that a man brought up with such literature around him would feel the need of a religion of ethical content for his people. How much moral and ethical teaching Moses may have left with them, it is now very difficult to determine. The reader may decide for himself whether a leader who had set up a brazen serpent for worship by his people, an image which was preserved and worshipped for centuries in the national sanctuary, could also have laid upon each Hebrew householder the command, "Thou shalt not make unto thee a graven image, nor (the likeness of) any form that is in heaven above, or that is in the earth beneath, or that is in the water under the earth." Each commandment in the Decalogue is addressed to a householder, in the second person singular, "thou." It is obvious that when the Decalogue was written the Hebrews had already made the transition from a pastoral life on the desert grasslands to a settled agricultural life in towns, where social influences were shaping religious belief and enriching its content. Landownership, a thing unknown to the nomads, and to some extent also commercial life in towns were creating a small class of rich townsmen, while the majority were left still poor. Class rivalries, with their inevitable antipathies and resulting instructive social experience, began to arise.

Social contrasts were much more noticeable after the establishment of the Hebrew monarchy. The attractions of wealth and commercial life were felt even by the new Hebrew kings. The wealthy trading kings of Phœnicia naturally influenced the outlook of the Israelitish rulers. Solomon made a commercial partnership with Hiram, king of Tyre, and himself launched out as a horsetrader, importing fine breeds from Egypt, where he doubtless enjoyed special advantages through his father-in-law the Pharaoh, and thence exporting the animals northward, he sold them in the horse-markets of the Hittite country. He had his stables at a number of points throughout the country, and this situation becomes very real when we stand among the remains of the actual stables of Solomon uncovered in the ruins of his powerful provincial fortress city of Megiddo (Armageddon) on the Carmel Ridge.

In a situation of sharply contrasted social classes, there developed a social arena such as we have seen arising on the Nile almost two thousand years earlier. It was conditions like these which had awakened a new sense of enduring values in Egypt. In the same way men of humane spirit and social vision among the Hebrews began to feel the voice of conscience as a social force, and the Age of Character, in response to such impulses, was beginning in Israel, as it had done so long before in Egypt. The old rites and the religious usages of ritual and sacrifice began to decline in value as contrasted with worthy character. We recall the remarkable words of the unknown Heracleopolitan king to his son Merikere, a thousand years before the day of Moses, "More acceptable is the virtue of the upright man than the ox of him that doeth iniquity" (p. 156). The trenchant discrimination of the old Pharaoh's moral insight had evidently not been confined to Egypt; the roll that contained his instruction to his son must have found its way to Palestine, for identically the same idea, in very similar words, appeared early in the ethical development of the Hebrews: "Behold, to obey is better than sacrifice, and to hearken than the fat of rams" (I Sam. 15:22). This emphasis on "hearkening" sounds like an echo from the Maxims of Ptahhotep, who instructed his son, over fifteen hundred years before Samuel's time, on the value of "hearkening" (see p. 130). The superiority of character over ritual observances was set forth by the Hebrew wise men in the Book of Proverbs in words which are again an echo of the Heracleopolitan sage: "To do righteousness and justice is more acceptable to Yahveh than sacrifice" (Prov. 21:3). That the Hebrew wise man was following Egyptian thought at this point is interestingly disclosed by the immediately preceding verse

(Prov. 21:2), "But Yahveh weigheth the hearts." In the ancient East there was only one faith in which we find the god *weighing* the human heart, and that was Egyptian religion with its Osirian judgment.

We have seen how unmistakably such discrimination between the value of character and merely external observances had been the product of social experience in Egypt. In Israel the same social experience was going on at a greatly accelerated pace, because of the literary and the ethical heritage upon which the Hebrews had entered. They found such fundamental truths in the writings and the experience of their great African neighbor, but they were fast making this experience also their own. It must be a people's *own* discernment of the enduring values of human character, however, which must lie at the base of any securely established moral development. It is of course only the realm of high ethical values which furnishes the motives and yields the situations for a literature of real power. It is therefore no accident that the first three centuries of Hebrew life after the foundation of the monarchy produced the most finished literary artistry which up to that time the ancient world had anywhere attained. The most convincing illustration of the new-found Hebrew skill in dramatic, picturesque, and humanly appealing narrative is the story of Joseph, and the culmination of this beautiful tale is the moral steadfastness of the exiled youth, a stranger in a foreign land, who hazards his life without hesitation in the preservation of his own personal purity of character, not for the maintenance of prudish or ascetic ideals, but out of respect for the honour of a master who trusts him. It is an extraordinary fact that this crowning incident of the story is drawn from an Egyptian folk tale, which must have gained currency in

Canaanite Palestine, where the gifted writer of the Joseph story learned of it.

The story is now commonly known as the Tale of the Two Brothers. The gods who appear as the two brothers, the chief characters in the tale, are pictured in the naïve imagination of the folk tale as two peasants, whose names, Anubis and Bata, disclose them as divinities who had a place in the religion of Egypt at an enormously remote date. Anubis, the elder brother, is married; Bata, the younger, lives with the married pair almost as their son, when the idyllic round of picturesque rustic life is forever ended by a shameful act of the wife. She beholds the youth one day carrying five sacks of grain at once upon his stalwart shoulder, and she is smitten with love for him. Then as she makes her advances, "the youth was like the Upper Egyptian panther for rage at the evil words which she had spoken to him and she feared greatly. He spake to her and said, 'Lo, thou art with me like a mother and thy husband is with me like a father, for he being older than I hath brought me up. What is then this shameful thing that thou hast said to me? Say it not again to me and I will tell it to no man, nor will I let it come forth from my mouth to any one.' And he took up his burden and went forth to the field." Deceived by his wife into believing a perverted version of the affair foisted upon him by the false woman, Anubis lay in wait for his younger brother to slay him. He stationed himself behind the stable door with his weapon in his hand, and as the youth approached driving his herd before him, the two foremost cows, so often led to the finest pasturage by their young herdsman, now in gratitude warned him of the danger, and the youth turned about and fled.

This moral ordeal of the youth in the Story of the Two

Brothers is the finest example of steadfast integrity of soul, not only in the literature of Egypt, but in the entire literature of the ancient Orient down to that time. It is highly significant that it should have been *this* incident in the whole range of Egyptian literature which so attracted the interest of the Hebrew author that he was led to employ it as a supreme demonstration of the stainless character of his hero. When Mohammed heard this tale some fourteen hundred years later, he promptly wove it into the Koran. The story has frequently reappeared in varied guise throughout the history of literature for some three thousand years since it first arose on the Nile, and it has likewise had a place of some importance in the history of Western painting. The ethical significance of its adoption in Hebrew literature is of fundamental importance, for its mere presence is convincing evidence that in the Eighth Century B.C. the Israelites had already entered the Age of Character.

In an age of such moral vision the old Midianite nature god of the desert, who had led the Israelites into Palestine and had found savage pleasure in the slaughter of the Canaanites, was gradually transformed in the Hebrew conception of him, till he became a God of righteousness, who likewise demanded righteousness in the character of his worshippers. While this transformation, growing out of their own social experience, was in no small degree due to the Hebrews themselves, nevertheless the religious thinking of these dwellers in Palestine was in this instance, as in so many other similar experiences, drawing substantially from the heritage of the past as they found it in the Canaanitish communities with which they had gradually coalesced. That heritage was filled with Egyptian ideas of the character of the Sun-god as a righteous ruler of men. We find a Hebrew prophet assuring his people, "Unto you that fear my name shall the sun of righteousness arise with healing in its wings."[11] We recall that personified "Righteousness," the goddess Maat, was believed by the Egyptians to be a daughter of the Sun-god. Identified by the possession of wings, "the sun of righteousness" of the Hebrews can be nothing else than a reference to the winged Egyptian Sun-god (see Fig. 3), for none of the old Hebrew conceptions of Yahveh had ever pictured him with wings. Recent excavations at Samaria have revealed the fact that these Egyptian conceptions of the righteous Sun-god were common in Palestinian life. In the ruins of the palace of the Israelitish kings at Samaria the excavators discovered some carved ivory relief plaques once forming the decorative incrustation that adorned the furniture of the Hebrew sovereigns. Among these carvings appears a piece bearing the figure of the goddess "Righteousness" (Maat) borne aloft by a solar genius of Heliopolis as he offers the figure, probably to the Sun-god. The entire design is Egyptian in content, but the workmanship shows clearly that the carving was done by Palestinian craftsmen (see Fig. 18, *B*). Hebrew workmen were therefore familiar with such Egyptian designs, and Hebrews of high station beheld these symbols of the Egyptian Sun-god's righteousness every day adorning the very chairs in which they sat.

The winged Sun-god of the Nile was not only known to the Hebrews as a God of righteousness, but also as the beneficent protector of his worshippers. Four times the Hebrew Psalmists refer to the protection found "under (or in) the shadow of thy wings." As we have before ob-

[11] Mal. 4:2.

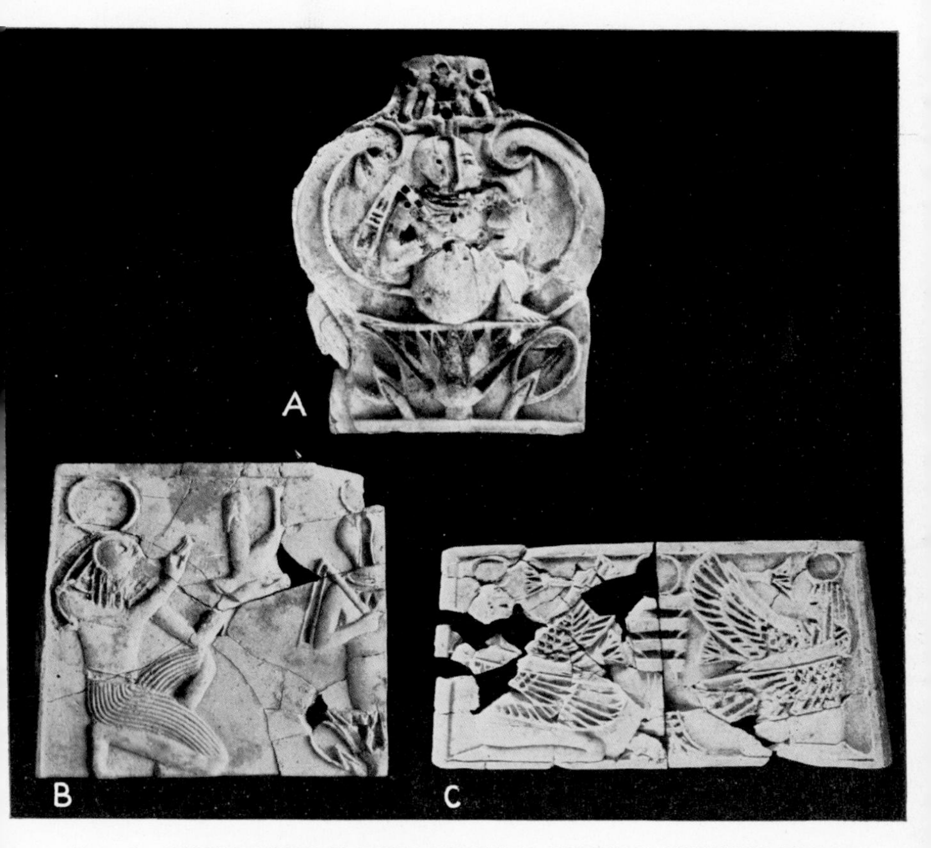

Fig. 18. CARVED IVORY PLAQUES DEPICTING EGYPTIAN DIVINITIES FROM THE PALACE OF THE HEBREW KINGS AT SAMARIA

Part of the decorative incrustation on furniture from the palace of the northern Hebrew kings (about 850 to 750 B.C.), illustrating the royal luxury denounced by the Hebrew prophets. *A.* The child Horus rising from a lotus blossom. *B.* Egyptian falcon-headed Solar divinity with sun-disk on head, offering seated image of the goddess Maat ("Righteousness")—one form of "the sun of righteousness." *C.* Winged goddesses (Isis and Nephthys) protecting the symbol of Osiris. Excavated at Samaria by the Harvard Expedition. (*By courtesy of Professor Kirsopp Lake.*)

served, Yahveh was not pictured by the Hebrews as possessing wings; on the other hand, we have impressive sculptured portraits of the Pharaohs with the Sun-god as a falcon hovering with wings outstretched in protection over the sovereign (see Figs. 9 and 19).

The Egyptian Sun-god conceived as a righteous sovereign was therefore among the influences which contributed to transform Yahveh into a righteous ruler of men. In this development the rise of the Hebrew kingship was a valuable influence. The Israelites gradually gained a vision of an ideal king and this vision contributed powerfully to the conception of Yahveh as a righteous sovereign. We have already seen that a thousand years before the rise of the Hebrew monarchy the social prophets of Egypt raised the cry for social justice and looked for an ideal age of human happiness under the beneficent rule of a righteous king. They denounced the corruption and oppression under which the poor and the humble suffered at the hands of the rich and powerful, and repeatedly their denunciations were delivered in the presence of the king himself. The writings of such men as Ipuwer and Neferrohu (see pp. 194–203) were current as we have seen by 2000 B.C., and there is convincing reason for the conclusion that they found early circulation in Western Asia especially among the Phœnicians, who as close neighbours of the Hebrews are shown by the Old Testament to have influenced them powerfully.

A fall of rock from the face of the sea-cliffs at ancient Byblos on the Phœnician coast north of Beyrut ten years ago disclosed the rock-hewn burial chamber of a Phœnician king of the same age as the Egyptian social prophets whom we have been discussing. This discovery together with the excavation of the royal Byblite cemetery which followed has revealed to us a series of tombs in which the Phœnician kings of Byblos were interred. These tombs are essentially Egyptian in their character, construction, and content, for they contained massive stone sarcophagi of Egyptian type, in which the royal bodies were laid, and they were equipped with vessels and jewelry of great splendour, all either made in Egypt and bearing the names of Twelfth Dynasty Egyptian Pharaohs, or executed in Phœnicia in the Egyptian manner. These burials demonstrate beyond doubt the dominance of Egyptian mortuary and religious customs in Phœnicia at this time. With such religious practices drawn from the land of the Nile, it can hardly be doubted that the rolls of the Egyptian social prophets were likewise known in Phœnicia. A great series of tombs excavated on the eastern slopes of the hill of Armageddon (Megiddo) have been found to contain large numbers of Egyptian scarabs and other sacred symbols of the same age as that of the Egyptian social prophets. It is probable therefore that the Messianic social doctrines of Egypt were known in Western Asia as early as 2000 B.C., and as a result the Canaanites would have been acquainted with them long before the Hebrew invasion of Palestine. In the Twelfth Century B.C. in the Hebrew age of the Judges, Zakarbaal, the Phœnician king of Byblos, admitted to an Egyptian envoy at his court, whom he had otherwise treated with great disrespect, that civilisation had come to Phœnicia from Egypt. He said: "Amon equips all lands; he equips them, having first equipped the land of Egypt, whence thou comest. For craftsmanship came forth from it to reach my place of abode; and teaching came forth from it to reach my place of abode."[12] It is obvious that these words disclose the rec-

[12] See the author's *Ancient Records,* Vol. IV, pp. 282–283.

FIG. 19. "UNDER THE SHADOW OF THY WINGS"

In a temple relief at Medinet Habu (Luxor) we see the Sun-god as a falcon hovering with wings protectingly outspread over the head of the last great king of the Egyptian Empire, Ramses III, as he gives audience to his grand vizier and other officials. We have seen the same Solar falcon hovering above the head of King Khafre over sixteen centuries earlier (Fig. 9). As a figure of divine protection "the shadow of thy wings" occurs four times in the Hebrew Psalms (17:8; 36:7; 57:1; and 63:7). (*Oriental Institute photograph.*)

ognition that Egypt was a source of superior civilisation in that age.

In this connection it is important to point out that the Egyptian envoy witnessed an outbreak of prophetic ecstasy on the part of a Phœnician youth just such as characterised the earlier form of prophecy among the Hebrews, as for example in the case of Saul, and the origin of the proverb "Is Saul also among the prophets?" The teachings of the Egyptian social prophets would then have been already part of the Phœnician or Canaanitish religious tradition for centuries when the "social question" aroused men of sensitive moral feeling among the Hebrews, like Amos and Hosea in the Eighth Century B.C. Just as in Egypt the Hebrew prophets' message was at first little more than denunciation of social injustice.[13] Just as in Egypt the stage and the dramatic setting for these denunciations is often the royal court or they are even addressed to the king himself. Just as in Egypt the vision of the Hebrew prophet passed from denunciation to a picture of a new age when the advent of a just king should usher in the reign of righteousness. We recall Noferrohu's picture of that reign: "Righteousness shall return to its place, unrighteousness shall be cast out." At this point we find the Hebrew prophet rising to majestic conceptions of the world-wide moral mission of his people, quite surpassing the picture of the golden future drawn by the Egyptian Messianic teachers. It should be borne in mind however that the entire conception of a Messianic age grew out of the social reflections of the Egyptian thinkers when as yet such pictures of ideal human possibilities had nowhere dawned upon the soul of

[13] The similarity between the message of the Hebrew prophets and that of the Egyptian sages was noticed by Eduard Meyer in his *Die Israeliten und ihre Nachbarstämme*, pp. 451 ff. (Halle, 1906).

man. In a world where might had always made right and power was the supreme word, the Egyptian social dreamers looked beyond actual conditions and dared to believe in an age of ideal justice. When the Hebrew prophet caught the splendour of this vision and rose to a higher level he was standing on the Egyptian's shoulders. It is important that the modern world should realise that the Messianic vision had a history of more than a thousand years before the Hebrew nation was born. This supreme form of social idealism is our inheritance from the *human* past, not exclusively from any *one* people.

In the realm of *conduct* also the Hebrew prophets likewise drew upon the literature of proverbs and fables, which before 1000 B.C. had already gained international currency. In trying to demonstrate that Assyria was but an instrument in the hand of Yahveh, the prophet Isaiah draws a picture of rebellious implements which is clearly of foreign origin, when he says: "Shall the axe boast itself against him that heweth therewith? Shall the saw magnify itself against him that wieldeth it? As if a rod should wield them that lift it up, or as if a staff should lift up him that is not wood" (Isaiah 10:15). The source of this kind of fable was at first supposed to be India, but Maspero long ago found the earliest known fable of this type on an Egyptian writing tablet in the Turin Museum.

The Hebrew prophets were greatly impressed by the contrast between the upright man and the wicked as pictured in the writings of the Egyptian wise men. Amenemope's remarkable picture of the two trees has been adopted by Jeremiah:

AMENEMOPE	JEREMIAH
"The hot-head serving in the temple,	Cursed is the man that trusteth in man,

AMENEMOPE

He is like a tree growing in the forest.
In a moment he loseth his branches,
And findeth his end in the ⌜timber-dock⌝.
He is floated far away from his place,
And the fire is his grave.

The truly prudent man, who putteth himself aside,
Is like a tree growing in a garden,
He flourisheth and multiplieth his fruit,
He abideth in the presence of his lord,
His fruit is sweet, his shade is pleasant,
And he findeth his end in the garden.
(Amenemope, VI, 1–12)

JEREMIAH

And maketh his flesh his arm,
And whose heart departeth from Yahveh.
For he shall be like the heath in the desert
And shall not see when good cometh,
But shall inhabit the parched places in the wilderness,
A salt land and not inhabited.

Blessed is the man that trusteth in Yahveh
And whose trust Yahveh is.
For he shall be as a tree planted by the waters
That spreadeth out its roots by the river,
And shall not fear when heat cometh,
But its leaf shall be green;
And shall not be careful in the year of drought,
Neither shall cease from yielding fruit. (Jer. 17:5–8)

In contemplating Amenemope's pleasing picture of the two trees, one is inevitably reminded of the first Psalm:

Blessed is the man that walketh not in the counsel of the wicked,
Nor standeth in the way of sinners,
Nor sitteth in the seat of the scornful,
But his delight is in the law of Yahveh,
And on his law doth he meditate day and night.
And he shall be like a tree planted by the streams of water,
That bringeth forth its fruit in its season,
Whose leaf also doth not wither,

And whatsoever he doeth shall prosper.
The wicked are not so,
But are like the chaff which the wind driveth away.
Therefore the wicked shall not stand in the judgment.

It is important to notice that "the judgment" appearing here is *the only mention of it in the entire Book of Psalms.* This is a significant hint, for a judgment hereafter, as we have already seen, was the contribution of Egyptian civilisation. The emphasis on the streams of water in the Hebrew picture is also significant, for the southern half of Palestine was semi-desert, and scarcity of water was a chronic hardship as it is to this day. On the other hand, in Egyptian writing the hieroglyph for "garden" is the picture of a garden pool; the mere mention of a garden therefore means water, which is regarded as a matter of course, and hence is not specifically mentioned in Amenemope's description. The parallel with the Hebrew form is therefore closer than it seems. Of interest is the Psalmist's alteration, abandoning the tree and employing "chaff" as the figure for the wicked, while Jeremiah preferred the parched "heath in the desert," of which there were plentiful examples in his native Judea.

The age and place of the social and religious reformers whom we call the Hebrew prophets in the history of their developing moral and religious life is now clearly understood and well established by the work of modern scholars. On the other hand the same cannot be said of the *religious songs* of the Hebrews, for there is wide difference of opinion among Hebrew scholars and historians regarding the age of the Psalms. There has been an immoderate tendency to regard them as of very late origin, and even to place them all after the Hebrew exile. Religious hymns, however, were common at a very early date both in Babylonia and in Egypt, and there would consequently seem to be no reason why the Palestinians, whether Canaanites or Hebrews, should not have adopted this form of literature long before the Hebrew exile, just as we have seen the prophets of the Hebrews appropriating the social visions of Egypt. We cannot doubt that the prophet Jeremiah was acquainted with Amenemope's picture of the two trees, and it must equally well have been known to the author of the first Psalm. We have already noticed that the Hebrew psalmists drew a picture of divine protection from the sheltering wings of the Egyptian Sun-god. Similarly it is obvious that they were acquainted with the great sun-hymn of Ikhnaton. Here again it is likely that the Egyptian original had gained currency in Palestine or Phœnicia long before the rise of Hebrew psalmody. Ikhnaton produced his hymn before the middle of the Fourteenth Century B.C. and his vindictive enemies would obviously not have allowed it to circulate in Egypt for six or seven centuries until long after 1000 B.C., when the Hebrews became interested in it. We must suppose that it passed into Asia in Ikhnaton's time and that it there escaped destruction at the hands of his enemies. After it had been translated into some Semitic dialect of Western Asia, possibly Phœnician, Aramaic, or Hebrew, it suffered a good deal of modification. An examination of the parallel passages from Psalm 104 which have been included with the translation of the hymn (see pp. 282–284), discloses the surprising extent to which not only the content of Ikhnaton's hymn, but also the succession of its ideas and its external arrangement, have been preserved in the Asiatic version. These correspondences can by no possibility be the result of accident, and they demonstrate the presence of a large part of an Egyptian devotional song in an edited and modified form in the Hebrew Psalter.

Nearly a generation has passed since the present writer first called attention to the extraordinary similarity between Psalm 104 and the Sun-hymn of Ikhnaton.[14] At that time it was not possible to do more than to demonstrate the similarity; it was safer to draw no conclusions based upon the fact. The researches and discoveries which have ensued however have essentially altered our situation. We now have an Egyptian original from which whole passages of the Hebrew Old Testament were translated and edited. Such a penetrating and devout student of Hebrew literature as the lamented Hugo Gressmann has therefore without hesitation recognised the Egyptian source of Psalm 104, which reached Palestine as he believed through Phœnicia. Gressmann goes even farther in identifying foreign influences in the Hebrew Psalms. He says: "The oldest mythological *motif* in the [Hebrew] hymns was that of the creation of the world, and it (together with the creation myth) probably originated in Babylonia. The *motif* of the divine care of the world was a later idea, which made its way into Palestinian Psalmody under the influence of Egypt."

The hymn of Ikhnaton thus reveals to us the source of the Hebrew Psalmist's recognition of the gracious goodness of God in the maintenance of his creatures, even the most insignificant. The Hebrew attitude toward nature as a realm disclosing the benevolent solicitude of the creator thus had its source in this and similar songs of Egypt. The realisation of this goodness or kindness of God, expressed in the hymn of Ikhnaton and especially later in

[14] See the author's *History of Egypt,* pp. 371–374 (1st ed., New York, 1905).

the age of personal piety in Egypt, may likewise have had an important influence on the rise of personal religion among the Hebrews. It would be interesting to know also, what place the hymn of Ikhnaton may have had among the influences which gradually led the Hebrews to monotheism. Some place among such influences is highly probable. As sovereign of a nation exercising world dominion, Ikhnaton had gained international vision which we have seen clearly reflected in his great hymn. A poem of such universal outlook, breathing such unqualified monotheism, circulating in Western Asia centuries before the prophetic literature of the Israelites arose, is likely to have had some influence on the internationalism which later was forced upon the Hebrew prophets by the critical position of their people as they seemed to be more and more the plaything of the great powers, till Yahveh, their once local desert god, emerged upon their vision as supreme over all nations, directing the movements of all the kings of the earth and able to control their hostile purposes for the good of Israel and eventually of all the world. Such a point of view leads to recognition of a moral order of the world. We recall that Ikhnaton's supreme word as he endeavoured to introduce Solar monotheism in the Fourteenth Century B.C., was "righteousness." His movement had been the logical development of the old Solar doctrine, which recognized the supremacy of Maat "righteousness" as the *national* moral order. Ikhnaton's hymn expands this national sovereignty of "righteousness" into an *international* moral order of the world under a sole god. It is not easy to demonstrate the migration of ideas. Recent research however has placed us in a position to demonstrate the fundamental fact that the Hebrews read the moral and religious literature of other nations and adopted the ideas they found there sometimes in the very phraseology of the foreign original.

There is nothing in the whole range of the literature of the Hebrews which has more profoundly impressed Western civilisation than their proverbial admonitions to right conduct, which we call the Book of Proverbs. Its lofty vision of character and the penetrating moral wisdom of this book have entered the very substance of our modern conceptions of worthy living, and, in the picturesque rendering of the King James version, its shrewd apothegms are daily current among us. The current phrase "the proverbs of Solomon" has led the average reader to regard the book as the work of wise King Solomon. It begins indeed with an attribution to Solomon at the head of Chapter 1 and this attribution is repeated at the beginning of Chapter 10, as if it were the title of another collection of Solomon's proverbs. A third collection bearing the name of Solomon begins with Chapter 25, while the last two chapters of the book are attributed to two otherwise unknown authors, one of whom was a woman. On the evidence of the Old Testament itself, therefore, the Book of Proverbs is obviously a compilation. Besides these five once separate collections of maxims in the Book of Proverbs, there is still another, making six in all. In the midst of Chapter 24, even the English translation discloses a title: "These also are [Words] of the Wise," introducing a brief section which is perhaps an appendix of unknown authorship. Buried in the heart of Chapter 22, without any editorial indication by the translators, even of the Revised Version, we find what is obviously the beginning, if not the title, of another section (22:17), called "The Words of the Wise," just as we found it in Chapter 24. Who were "the Wise,"—for the Hebrew word (*ḥaḳa-*

mîm) is in the plural—the social teachers, who wrote this section of about a chapter and a half? Until very recently no one has been able to answer this question, but the publication of a papyrus, which had long reposed in the British Museum, has revealed the author as none other than our old friend Amenemope! All Old Testament scholars of any weight or standing now recognise the fact that this whole section of about a chapter and a half of the Book of Proverbs[15] is largely drawn *verbatim* from the Wisdom of Amenemope; that is, the Hebrew version is practically a literal translation from the Egyptian. It is likewise obvious that in numerous other places in the Old Testament not only in the Book of Proverbs, but also in the Hebrew law, in Job, and as we have already noticed in Samuel and Jeremiah, Amenemope's wisdom is the source of ideas, figures, moral standards, and especially of a certain warm and humane spirit of kindness.

We have already touched upon the fact that there are foreign elements in the Book of Proverbs, which the ancient editors have not hesitated to indicate in the titles. The wise man Agur, whose maxims form Chapter 30, and King Lemuel, who owed his proverbs forming Chapter 31 to his mother, were obviously not Hebrews. The international atmosphere in which Solomon's proverbs grew up is clearly disclosed by the first Book of Kings (4:30–31): "And Solomon's wisdom excelled the wisdom of all the children of the east (the Bedouin), and all the wisdom of Egypt. For he was wiser than all men; than Ethan the Ezrahite, and Heman, and Calcol, and Darda, the sons of Mahol, and his fame was in all the nations round about." Their non-Hebrew names show that all of these wise men were foreigners, from the Hebrew point of

[15] Chapters 22:17, to 23:11.

view. It has long been known that the famous judgment of Solomon was of East Indian origin. Nevertheless research has never before disclosed an ancient oriental composition in a non-Palestinian tongue, from which an entire section of the Old Testament was unquestionably translated.

This discovery is of such far-reaching significance, that, at the risk of wearying the reader, some examples of the evidence must be presented here. The "Words of the Wise" in the Hebrew Book of Proverbs, and in the Wisdom of Amenemope, begin as follows:

AMENEMOPE	PROVERBS
Incline thine ears to hear my sayings,	Incline thine ear, and hear the Words of the Wise,
And apply thine heart to their comprehension.	And apply thine heart unto my knowledge.
For it is a profitable thing to put them in thy heart,	For it is a pleasant thing if thou keep them within thee,
But woe to him who transgresses them.	If they be established together upon thy lips.
(Amenemope III, 9–12)	(Prov. 22: 17–18)

The purpose of such instruction is then defined by the Proverbs, and is also indicated by Amenemope, as essentially practical efficiency in official business:

AMENEMOPE	PROVERBS
In order to return a report to the one that sent him. (Amenemope I, 6)	That thou mayest carry back words of truth to them that send thee. (Prov. 22:21)

The phrase "words of truth" is corrupt in the Hebrew; what is intended is of course an equivalent to the Egyptian "report." Both in Proverbs and Amenemope, however, the moral purpose of the instruction is evident throughout. A few examples are very instructive:

AMENEMOPE	PROVERBS
Remove not the landmark on the boundary of the fields,	Remove not the ancient landmark;
. . . . . .	And enter not into the fields of the fatherless. (Prov. 23:10)
Be not greedy for a cubit of land,	
And trespass not on the boundary of the widow. (Amenemope VII, 12–15)	

It is interesting to note that before the discovery of the Wisdom of Amenemope, the Old Testament critics had suggested that the word "ancient" which in Hebrew resembles the word "widow" was doubtless a manuscript error for "widow," and they therefore made the passage read,

> "Remove not the landmark of the widow,
> And enter not into the fields of the fatherless."

The discovery of the Egyptian source makes this emendation certain.

Perhaps the most striking of the many parallels that might be cited are the warnings regarding riches:

AMENEMOPE	PROVERBS
Weary not thyself to seek for more,	Weary not thyself to be rich
When thy need is (already) secure.	. . . .
If riches be brought to thee by robbery,	
They will not abide the night with thee.	

AMENEMOPE	PROVERBS
When the morning cometh they are no longer in thy house.	Wilt thou set thine eyes upon that which is not?
. . . .	
They have made themselves wings like geese,	For riches certainly make themselves wings,
And they have flown to heaven.	Like an eagle that flieth toward heaven.
(Amenemope IX, 14–X, 5	(Prov. 23:4–5)

The line which we have omitted in the Proverbs version is again corrupt in the Hebrew, and it is probable that it can be restored by study of the Egyptian, but such critical problems cannot be undertaken in a book of this character.

Before 2000 B.C. the Egyptian social sages had held up riches for comparison with character, and had pronounced decidedly in favor of character (see p. 137). The futility of material possessions, especially in the next world, had been fully recognised, and the social thinkers dwell upon many different aspects of the folly of dependence upon riches. In dealing with this subject as frequently as the Proverbs of the Hebrews do, they are obviously under the influence of the Egyptian sages. The following parallel may serve as a further illustration:

AMENEMOPE	PROVERBS
Better is poverty in the hand of God,	Better is little with the fear of Yahveh,
Than riches in the storehouse.	Than great treasure and trouble therewith.
Better are loaves when the heart is joyous,	Better is a portion of herbs, where love is,
Than riches in unhappiness.	Than a stalled ox and hatred therewith.
(Amenemope IX, 5–8)	(Prov. 15:16–17)

Another parallel on the same subject is the following:

AMENEMOPE	PROVERBS
Better is praise as one whom men love,	Better is a dry morsel and quietness therewith,
Than riches in the storehouse. (Amenemope XVI, 11–12)	Than an house full of feasting with strife. (Prov. 17:1)

The subsequent history of the Hebrews would not lead us to suspect that they have been indifferent to financial power or business success; nor did the editor of the Old Testament Book of Proverbs ignore Egyptian wisdom along this line, as we shall see. The reader may have noticed that these admonitions in the Book of Proverbs regarding wealth and luxury are not drawn from the Words of the Wise (Prov. 22:17–24:22). This fact is important and fuller study of the Proverbs will undoubtedly disclose how dependent upon Amenemope were the Hebrew editor's ideas throughout the Book of Proverbs. Another example outside the limits of the Words of the Wise is found below, in the warning against vindictiveness and revenge (Prov. 20:22).

Amenemope is much concerned to warn youth against hotheadedness, or association with men of this type. The Hebrew editor likewise warns:

AMENEMOPE	PROVERBS
Fraternise not with the hot-tempered man,	Make no friendship with a man of heat,
And press not upon him for conversation. (Amenemope XI, 13–14)	And with a wrathful man thou shalt not go. (Prov. 22:24)

The common word for the reckless man of hot temper in Amenemope's wisdom is simply the "hot one," and it is interesting to observe that the original Hebrew of this passage literally rendered means the "man of heat," a phrase which is not found elsewhere in the Old Testament, and is evidently an effort to carry over the Egyptian term. Reckless anger and revenge are condemned both by the Proverbs and Amenemope:

AMENEMOPE	PROVERBS
Say not, "I have found a protector,	Say not thou, "I will recompense evil."
Now I can attack the hated man."	Wait for Yahveh, and he will save thee.
. . . .	(Prov. 20:22)
Set thyself in the arms of God,	
Until thy silence overthroweth them (his enemies).	
(Amenemope XXII, 1–8)	

In the same way Amenemope advises strongly against quarrelling with the "hot-mouthed," for "God will know how to answer him" (V, 10–17), which is again parallel with the Proverbs: "Wait on Yahveh, and he shall save thee."

Much more suited to Egyptian life than to that of the Hebrews are Amenemope's admonitions regarding behaviour in the presence of lordly superiors, for in Egypt appropriate deportment on the part of a young official was absolutely indispensable to a successful career. Just as elegant court manners in Paris under the later Louis' spread to less cultivated capitals of Europe, so refined deportment and palace formalities of official intercourse freshly introduced among a people of rude desert background under the youthful Hebrew monarchy were strongly influenced by the long-established courtesies of the Pharaoh's court, whose officials had ruled Palestine for centuries. The Hebrew editor of Proverbs, therefore, did not hesitate to commend Egyptian official courtesy to the Israelites of his day:

AMENEMOPE	PROVERBS
Eat not bread in the presence of a great man,	When thou sittest to eat with a ruler
Nor offer thy mouth in his presence.	Consider diligently what is before thee;
If thou sate thyself with unpermissible food,	For thou wilt put a knife to thy throat
It is but pleasure of thy spittle.	If thou be a man given to appetite.
Look (only) upon the dish that is before thee,	Be not desirous of his dainties;
And let it furnish thy need.	Seeing they are deceitful food.
(Amenemope XXIII, 13–18)	(Prov. 23:1–3)

The translators of the Revised Version were uncertain whether to render: "what is before thee" or "him who is before thee." Amenemope's "dish that is before thee" settles the question. The Hebrew editor has altered the order of ideas, and has shifted his "deceitful food," which corresponds to the Egyptian "unpermissible food" (literally "wrong food") to the last line. This admonition of Amenemope is very old, for it was drawn from the wisdom of Ptahhotep and was therefore some two thousand years old in Amenemope's time. In Ptahhotep's words the advice is much more intelligible: "If thou art a man of those who sit (at meat) by the seat of a man greater than thou, take when he gives to thee what he puts before thee; look not at what is before him; look (only) at what is before thee, and bombard him not (literally, "shoot him not") with many glances (do not stare at him). . . . Turn thy face downward until he addresses thee, and speak only when he has addressed thee."[16] Here then is a He-

[16] There is much other evidence of the dependence of Amenemope on Ptahhotep, showing that Amenemope is employing the already ancient wisdom liter-

brew sage laying upon youthful Israelites admonitions of courtesy which had guided young Egyptian officials at the court of the Pharaohs in the days when the pyramids were rising two thousand years earlier. This passage is therefore probably the oldest material in the Old Testament. We have here a striking example of how Hebrew life in Palestine developed under the influence of millennia of social experience which had already become ancient history when the Israelitish nation arose.

There is perhaps no saying in the Book of Proverbs oftener quoted in our modern age of dominant business interests than the commendation of the man who knows his job:

> Seest thou a man skillful in his business?
> He shall stand before kings.

The Septuagint, the ancient Greek translation of the Old Testament, does not have the verb, "Seest thou," but begins with "A man, etc." Grimme has shown that the introductory verb belongs to the preceding verse of the Hebrew text.[17] Having made this correction we find that the following parallelism results:

AMENEMOPE	PROVERBS
A scribe skillful in his office, He shall find himself worthy of being a courtier. (Amenemope XXVII, 16–17)	A man skillful in his business, He shall stand before kings. (Prov. 22:29)

We might continue indefinitely with such parallels, but

ature of the Egyptians for building up his book of thirty chapters. The fact is important because of the effort on the part of some Biblical scholars to place Amenemope at a late date, and thus regard him as a borrower from the Hebrew Proverbs!

[17] "Weiteres zu Amen-em-ope und Proverbien," in ***Orientalistische Literaturzeitung***, Vol. 28 (1925), col. 59.

doubtless the examples cited are sufficient to demonstrate the fact that the Hebrew Book of Proverbs has embedded in it a substantial section of an earlier Egyptian book of wisdom. This borrowing was done, as was quite natural in such an age, without acknowledgment. It is not a little interesting, however, to find in the Book of Proverbs an unmistakable reference to Amenemope's book, although the reference is naturally not by title, nor in an age so remote, by mention of the Egyptian wise man's name. In the introduction to the Words of the Wise, we find the following curious inquiry, the translation of which has much puzzled the editors of the Revised Version:

> Have I not written unto thee excellent things,
> Of counsels and knowledge? (Prov. 22:20)

The Revision Committee has inserted a marginal remark regarding "excellent things," calling attention to the fact that "The word is doubtful." The early Hebrew editors themselves had some doubts about it also, for they inserted another spelling of the word in the margin of the Hebrew manuscript, and as thus spelled by the ancient Hebrew editors, the word means *"thirty."* If we accept this word, the query would then read:

> Have I not written unto thee thirty,
> Of counsels and knowledge?

At first sight this old reading seems to furnish only nonsense; but when we observe, as Erman did, that Amenemope divided his book into thirty chapters and numbered them, all becomes clear. In Palestine the Egyptian roll must have been called something like the "Thirty Chapters of Wisdom," from which it would seem that an abbreviated form, of merely "Thirty," eventually arose.

Without any change in the actual Hebrew text the proper rendering, as suggested by Grimme, furnishes us the following parallel:

AMENEMOPE	PROVERBS
Consider for thyself these thirty chapters,	Have I not written to thee "Thirty,"
That they are satisfaction and instruction.	Wherein are counsels and knowledge?
(Amenemope XXVII, 7–8)	(Prov. 22:20)

This extraordinary mention of the current title of a foreign work from which an Old Testament writer was liberally borrowing makes it certain that he had in his hands a Hebrew translation of Amenemope's book, which was complete, that is, contained all thirty chapters of the Egyptian original, otherwise the title "Thirty" would have had no meaning. To retain its meaning the Hebrew compiler of the Proverbs, though he did not retain all of the available thirty chapters, nevertheless employed exactly thirty proverbs in his abridged edition (Prov. 22:17–24:22).

As he has contemplated these passages from the old Hebrew book of wisdom side by side with the Egyptian source from which they were drawn, the reader will doubtless have made for himself an observation of outstanding significance. Besides the portions really *translated,* it is obvious that the Hebrew editor of Proverbs has not slavishly and mechanically lifted the Egyptian wise sayings from the text of the Palestinian translation. There is little likelihood that we shall ever see that translation. Perhaps the Palestinian translator himself produced the freely edited renderings we have found in the Book of Proverbs, so that the editor of Proverbs was indeed merely quoting the translation. However that may be, the significant fact is that the form of Amenemope's wisdom as it reappears in the Book of Proverbs shows clearly that the Hebrew translator or editor appropriated the *ideas* chiefly and developed them with penetrating insight into life and superb literary skill, often *in language largely his own*. Some obvious illustrations make this fact quite clear. Riches take "wings" in both Egypt and Palestine, but in Egypt they are the wings of geese, while in Palestine, where there were no marshes swarming with wild geese, the translator substitutes the eagle. In Egypt a successful man of business affairs was regularly a "scribe," but in Palestine, where this was not the case, the translator makes him merely a "man" whose further description as one "skillful in his business" quite clearly identifies him. In Egypt over a thousand years before the appearance of the Book of Proverbs man's outstanding debt to the Sun-god was the gift of water, and its universality is made an argument for the equality of all men. But in Palestine, where there was little water and drought was common, Yahveh's act of creation, to which every man owed his being, was made the reason for the equality of all, notwithstanding the distinction between wealth and poverty:

COFFIN TEXTS (see p. 221)	THE BOOK OF PROVERBS (22:2)
I have made the great waters that the pauper like the lord might have use of them.	The rich and the poor meet together; Yahveh is the maker of them all.

We have already touched upon the fact that there is in Amenemope's wisdom a spirit of resignation to the will of God, which strikes a deeply religious note of unmistakable influence both on the wise men and the prophets of Palestine. In Amenemope's beautiful admonition: "Set thyself in the arms of God," we can hardly fail to recognise the source, of which we have an echo in the words of the so-called Blessing of Moses,

> "The eternal God is a dwelling place,
> And underneath are the everlasting arms."

Amenemope's ideal is the man who thus depends on God and silently endures wrong, confident of divine vindication. Is it an accident that the later Hebrew tradition of the character of Moses says of him: "Now the man Moses was very meek above all the men that were upon the face of the earth" (Num. 12:3), whereas in the earlier tradition he is represented as a very vigorous, self-reliant, and aggressive man of action, brooking no wrong towards himself or his people? Professor Sellin has called attention to the fact that the older Hebrew ideal of character depicted a man of action, strength, and wisdom, endowed with wealth and numerous children; but that after the middle of the Eighth Century B.C. there appeared a strikingly opposed conception of the meek, lowly, gentle and silent man, detached from material possessions. This ideal culminated in the picture of the suffering servant: "He will not cry nor lift up his voice, nor cause it to be heard in the street" (Isaiah 42:2), and especially in Isaiah's lofty conception: "He was oppressed, yet when he was afflicted he opened not his mouth; as a lamb that is led to the slaughter, and as a sheep that before its shearers is dumb, so he opened not his mouth" (Isaiah 53:7). Amenemope continually finds his ideal in the "silent" man who leaves his cause with God. Knowing as we now do that his book was read in Jerusalem, and that it was being excerpted and quoted by the Hebrew sages and prophets, we may fairly raise the question, whether the conception of the silent sufferer in Israel is not to be traced back to the social thinkers of Egypt. In any case it is now clear that social idealism, built up on lofty conceptions of character, the earliest known and in that age the *only* transcendentalism, arose in Egypt before 2000 B.C. and the actual books containing it were being read in Jerusalem by the men who produced those writings which we now call the Old Testament.

How could it indeed have been otherwise? Just as the literatures of modern Europe have grown up saturated with our ancient inheritance from Greece and Rome, so it was in Palestine inevitable that the Hebrews should be profoundly influenced in their thinking and their writing by the literature of the great nation which had held Palestine as its cultural and political province longer than Rome held Gaul. In receiving a great and inspiring moral and religious heritage from the Hebrews, therefore, we may regard it as a demonstrated fact that we have inherited a two-fold legacy, which is made up in the *first* place of some thousands of years of human experience in the Ancient Near East, chiefly Egypt, *before the Hebrew nation arose,* and was then in the *second* place marvellously deepened and enriched out of their own social experience by the prophets and sages of Israel themselves.

The interpenetration of culture influences between Palestine and its neighbours on all sides has long been obvious on the basis of the Hebrew writings alone. They reveal the constant passage of foreign merchant caravans; when the Hebrews need smiths they call them in from the Philistine towns; Solomon's architects designed his temple at Jerusalem on the ground plan of an Egyptian temple and the skilled craftsmen for building it were sent to Solomon from his friend King Hiram of Tyre; King Ahab of Israel married a Phœnician princess and protected her introduction of foreign divinities; and so we might go on indefinitely. To these obvious indications in the Old Testament itself we must now add those of modern archæological discovery. Excavation in Palestine has revealed a long list of foreign wares marketed there, numerous foreign decorative designs which came in with such things, and countless other evidences of foreign influence. The furniture in Ahab's palace at Samaria was adorned with ivory carvings depicting foreign gods, especially those of Egypt (see Fig. 18). A volume might be written on the foreign culture elements which pervaded Palestine before the Hebrews settled there and continued to be even more influential after the rise of the Hebrew monarchy. It might long ago have been equally obvious that Hebrew literature, as an expression of Hebrew life, must, like that life itself, inevitably be saturated with the culture forces from without, in law, in mythology, in religion as a whole, and not least in moral convictions. We have seen that in law and mythology the Hebrews drew much from Babylonian civilisation; but in morals, in religion, and in social thinking in general with which we are chiefly concerned in this book, the Hebrews built up their life on Egyptian foundations. After they settled in Palestine the Israelites were dwelling in a land which was Egyptian territory and had been so for centuries. It remained Egyptian for centuries after the Hebrew occupation began, and even so late as the reign of Solomon, the Egyptian Pharaoh presented to the Hebrew king the city of Gezer, a strong city of Palestine which was almost under the eaves of Jerusalem.

The fundamental conclusions that form the basis of moral convictions, and continue to do so in civilised life at the present day, had already been reached in Egyptian life long before the Hebrews began their social experience in Palestine, and those Egyptian moral convictions had been available in written form in Palestine for centuries when the Hebrews settled there. The enrichment which these teachings received, as the outgrowth of Hebrew life and thought, are of priceless value to humanity; but in recognising this fact we should not fail to realise that the moral sentiments of civilised society originated in a period far earlier than the long accepted "age of revelation," and have descended to us of the present day from an epoch when the writings of the Hebrews did not yet exist. The sources of our inheritance of moral tradition are therefore far from having been confined to Palestine, but must be regarded as including also Egyptian civilisation. The channel by which this inheritance has reached the Western world has chiefly been the surviving Hebrew literature preserved in the Old Testament. The disappearance of the ancient oriental civilisations, on the basis of which that of the Hebrews was built up, the resulting loss by the Western world of all understanding of the writing and languages of these vanished civilisations so that they lapsed into silence two thousand years ago, left Hebrew literature shining like a lonely beacon light surrounded by the deepest darkness. The recent scientific recovery of some knowledge of the lost oriental civilisations is therefore illuminating the darkness, and surrounding Israel with a light that is some thousands of years older. Had the Western world never lost all knowledge of the origins and development of civilisation, it would never have occurred to any one to place Hebrew history anywhere else than as the culmination of a long preceding development of morals and religion. Certainly no theological doctrine of one people exclusively enjoying a divine revelation could ever have arisen—a doctrine which has blinded us for centuries to our noble inheritance of universal human aspiration, not limited to the history or the experience of any one people.

The greatest constructive contribution which the recovery of the lost ancient oriental civilisations is making therefore, is the restoration to us of an inheritance as broad as the horizon—a heritage left us by the life of man as a whole. Herein lies the greatest of all revelations that we can now demonstrate as a process of history, and as a result of social experience, man's dawning comprehension of the difference between right and wrong conduct, and the supreme value of that growing comprehension as *an unfinished historical process.* It is the recovery of the lost civilisations that has enabled us to demonstrate that we have barely emerged from pre-moral darkness, that the dawn of conscience is just behind us, and that we still stand in the sun-rise of the age of character.

I believe it was Louis Agassiz who, after studying the resistless action of the Swiss glaciers and watching the massive boulders and fragments of rock brought down in the grip of the ice, to be dropped at the bidding of the summer sun in a wandering rampart of tumbled rocks skirting the mouth of the valley, at length realised that this glacial action had been going on for ages, and the imposing truth burst upon him that the geological processes of past æons which have made the earth, are still going on at the present day, that they have never ceased, that they will never cease. After this brief survey of the development of morals, it is perhaps a fair analogy to conclude that the same is true of the ethical evolution of man.

EPILOGUE

"That which all things educe, which freedom, cultivation, intercourse, revolutions, go to form and deliver, is CHARACTER; that is the end of nature, to reach unto this coronation of her king."
—(Emerson, Essay on "Politics.")

"I love history because it shows me the birth and progress of justice; and I find it all the more beautiful in that I see in it the ultimate development of nature."—(Letters of H. Taine.)

I

NATURE AND HUMAN FRIENDLINESS

It is narrated of the biologist Haeckel that some one once put to him the following provocative question:

"If in some way you could address a question to the Universe and be assured of a truthful answer, what question would you ask?"

Haeckel remained for some moments absorbed in thought, and then he said, "The question I would most like to see answered is this: Is the Universe friendly?"

Here is indeed a profound and suggestive question. The ethical evolution traced in the preceding pages places us in a position to discuss this question of Professor Haeckel in the light of new facts, some of them very recently ascertained and therefore probably unknown to him, but nevertheless indispensable to the discussion. It has long been recognised that the business of the historian is to present his conclusions, to indicate as far as is practicable the basic documents out of which his conclusions grow, and having done this, not to moralise but to regard his task as ended. If the reader has exercised the necessary patience, he has been able to survey the most important documentary evidence revealing the origins and early history of our inherited morals marshalled in the preceding chapters. Besides such discussion as this evidence required, I am not, as a historian, entitled to say anything more. Nevertheless the far-reaching significance of the evidence itself and the conclusions flowing from them tempt me to some additional observations quite outside of my competence. Within the frame-work of an epilogue, if there is such a thing, one may perhaps be permitted to say whatever one pleases.

Returning now to Professor Haeckel's question, it is with some feeling of presumption that I say I would have liked to ask *him* a question: "Where did you get that word 'friendly?'" For Professor Haeckel seems to have accepted the word *friendly* as a matter of course, just as the natural scientist accepts *matter* as a given factor, for which he is not called upon to account. But the word "friendly" is *not* a matter of course. Its very appearance in Professor Haeckel's question really answers the question itself, and he should have been called upon to account for the word. If Professor Haeckel had not long since passed on, it would have been interesting to hear his answer. His response would perhaps have been something like this: "Why, it is a word common to all the modern languages of civilisation." But it has long been recognised that language is far more than merely a vehicle for the expression of thought. It is a vehicle so built up out of man's experience that it is, historically speaking, to some extent a *record* of his experience in all its manifold aspects, social, industrial, scientific, mechanical, artistic, moral, religious, governmental or what not. Turning for example to an important item of our mechanical experience, we find that the words: "garage,"[1] "chauffeur," "chassis," "tonneau," and the like, form a little group which began to be common in English speech about a generation ago. The appearance and the foreign source of this little group of words, probably for thousands of years, will continue to demonstrate two historical facts in our experience: *first,* the introduction of the automobile late in the Nineteenth Century and *second,* its origin and earliest general use as a practical device in France.

An interesting example in earlier human life is the word "byblos," which appeared in Europe perhaps as early as 1000 B.C. and entered Greek speech as the word for "papyrus paper." The earliest emergence of this word in Greek probably several centuries before 500 B.C. is indication of the first introduction of paper into Europe; and its non-Greek, foreign name (from which came our word "Bible") is an unmistakable evidence that the immediate source of the earliest paper in Europe was the Phœnician city of Byblos on the North Syrian coast.

Buried thus in the constituents of language we find the evidence for the introduction of two very tangible human devices: the automobile introduced among us in our own time, and papyrus paper first imported into Europe over twenty-five hundred years ago. Now what is true of these two words for new mechanical devices is of course equally true of the less tangible qualities of advancing human life, as it rose from savagery or barbarism to the attainment of those inner values, which would give rise to such words as "friend," "friendly," "friendliness." If so, then when Professor Haeckel asked his question: "Is the uni-

[1] I believe the French origin of this derivative from *"gare"* or *"garer"* is now questioned.

verse friendly?" did he not overlook the significance of the very existence of the word "friendly"? In our examination of the records of ancient Egypt we have found disclosed in its speech and its history the emergence and early development of those human qualities suggested by the word "friendly."

It is, to be sure, true that if he were sharing in this discussion, Professor Haeckel might make an effective rejoinder which would seem to be along this line: "How does your demonstrated historic emergence of the word 'friendly' answer my original question? Granted that physical man has issued from the background of the developing universe, and granted that human experience has developed friendliness, you are talking of *human experience;* whereas I asked my question about the *universe.* What has human experience to do with the universe?"

Although the idea is older than Locke, it seems to have been his premises which drove the philosophers to the conclusion that man is a part of nature. That was a conclusion of the philosophers based of course on *philosophical* premises. Today the researches of palæontology and of prehistoric archæology are able to follow the physical man as he rises out of the geological ages and issues from the natural world. Physically at least he has therefore been more and more clearly disclosed as a part of nature. The earliest surviving written documents of his past furthermore reveal to us his rise into an age of ethical consciousness. This fact seems to have been curiously overlooked. We are no longer dependent on the philosophers, as in Goethe's time, for a mere *supposition* that man is an outgrowth of nature. The documents of the Ancient Near East demonstrate the fact *historically.*

The story of human beginnings as recently disclosed by

research in the Ancient Near East is showing quite clearly that human experience, *not* philosophically speaking, but *historically* speaking, is the latest stage of the history of the universe. Human experience is therefore the outcome of the history of the universe, as far as it is discernible to us.

In the story of human advance which we have been following, we picked up the threads of developing human life at the point where man became the first known implement-making creature at least several hundred thousand, perhaps even a million, years ago. At that stage he is regarded today as the common property of the palæontologists and geologists on the one hand, and of the archæologists on the other. In studying this remote age, we humanists thus jostle elbows with the natural scientists—an experience helpful to both. As found at the dawn of the Stone Age, man is still regarded as a subject for the investigations of the natural scientist, nor does science suggest a point at which man ceased to be a part of the developing universe. Although it involves us in some repetition let us again cast a swift glance backward over his career since then, and see if we can find a point where man ceased to be a part of an evolving universe.

However rapidly, we have in this book been able to follow the oldest known ancestors of civilisation in their hunting life across the wide stretches of the Sahara plateau at a remote period when its now desert uplands were still green and verdure-covered. The palæontologist tells you that this primitive hunter roaming the prehistoric forests of the Sahara was a creature which issued from the developing life of the universe—that he was still an inseparable part of the universe. Across all North Africa we watch the far-reaching mantle of green slowly fading through a hundred thousand years or more; we see the parklands and forests of the Sahara gradually disappearing, while the falling waters of a Sahara lake alongside the Nile Valley, like the sinking sand in an hourglass, measure for us the long ages during which the shrinking rainfall of North Africa gradually transformed the whole vast Sahara into a waterless waste of rock and sand. When the savage hunters, thus forced to forsake the desert plateau, had dropped into the Nile Valley, did they cease to be a part of the developing universe?

When thereupon they penned up the wild creatures in great stockades to become domesticated cattle, sheep, goats, and asses; when they not only ate the seed of the wild grasses, but began to plant and cultivate them as barley and wheat, and thus finally renouncing their wandering life as hunters and settling in little villages as shepherds and husbandmen, did they cease to be a part of the developing universe?

When those prehistoric villages of shepherds and plowmen, scattered for seven or eight hundred miles along the Nile, were transformed by many thousands of years of social evolution into the earliest known great state of several million souls, possessing metal and writing, controlled by a highly organised government and erecting the greatest buildings ever produced in the ancient world, a demonstration of their tremendous conquest of material forces, did they then somehow cease to be a part of the developing universe?

When at the dawn of so-called "history" some centuries before 3000 B.C., the ferment of social forces began and the stress of the remotest known age of social friction, going on for a thousand years, issued at last before 2000 B.C. in the earliest crusade for social justice and in efforts to usher in a new age of brotherly kindness, the reign of "friendliness," must we sever these earliest social idealists from the preceding stages of the developing universe?

Herein lies the fundamental value of the results of the disclosures that have come to us from the geological strata and the ancient cities and cemeteries of the Orient. These discoveries reveal to us a new and imposing panorama of stage after stage of advancing human development. At its beginning man visibly emerges from the geological ages and after several hundred thousand years, he rises from purely material conquest to visions of brotherly kindness. Yonder the emergence of physical man in the bestial savagery of the geological ages and here a humane world employing the word "friendly," about which Professor Haeckel addressed his penetrating question to the universe! While between these two stages lies the connecting development, demonstrable as yet only in the progress of early life along the Nile. We have seen it like a great social laboratory with its human life reaching back into those remote secular processes which have formed the present surface of the globe, and we have thus found the Nile Valley to be a unique arena where the struggle of the advancing life of man may be surveyed, from the appearance of physical man, through all the succeeding conquests of his rising career, until we see him catching the vision of human brotherhood and friendliness.

II

THE GREAT TRANSFORMATION AND THE SLOWNESS OF HUMAN DEVELOPMENT

Professor Haeckel's objection then (if we may, perhaps unjustly, assume that he would have made it), that human experience is not a stage of the development of the universe, receives for the first time an *historical* refutation in early Egypt. We have been rapidly examining a few milestones marking the long road by which man has passed from his conquest of the material world to the amazing discovery of inner values, the victory over self and the vision of social responsibility. These social documents have placed us in a position to realise that we have been following a process which not only belongs to the history of the universe, but is furthermore the most tremendous transformation in that history in so far as it is known to us.

That transformation is really the subject of this book, and with it the supreme fact that the great transformation, as we shall call it, is still incomplete and is therefore still going on. We have been endeavouring to disclose its genesis and follow its early history. It introduced not only into human life, but for the first time also into the universe as known to man, new conceptions and new words as symbols for them—conceptions which designate forces transcending the processes of matter and shifting us into a world of human motives and possibilities individual and racial, of which mankind is only now becoming dimly conscious. It is especially the *beginning* of the great transformation which is marked by significant new words. Professor Haeckel's word "friendly" was but one in a group of such words appearing for the first time and therefore like finger-posts directing man into a new road, and becoming for us historical monuments proclaiming the advent of the Age of Character. We have already referred to the fact that an Egyptian surgical treatise, written early in the Third Millennium B.C., contains the earliest mention of the word "brain." At that time there was of course no word already current designating the brain which the author of the treatise could employ. He took an ordinary word meaning a soft or semi-fluid, pasty mass like marrow, and to avoid misunderstanding added the genitive, "of the skull." His new term, the "mass of the skull" or "marrow of the skull," then functioned as the designation of the brain, in the earliest known discussion of it. This surgical anatomist of nearly five thousand years ago already knew that the brain was the seat of consciousness and of control of the limbs. His scientific knowledge, however, was too recent to displace the older belief that the heart was the seat of intelligence. When, therefore, these early men became conscious of a function of human intelligence, which discriminated between right and wrong conduct, they involuntarily applied to it the old word "heart," meaning the moral discernment exercised by the heart. Thus the new conception, man's ability to make moral distinctions, that is to say, his conscience, was finally also designated by the word "heart." Under that name the new-born conception "conscience" not only began its history as a social force, but continued it, as we have seen, for thousands of years to the present day under the same name. It may be of interest to the clergy and other moral teachers of today to know that the once new meaning of the old word "heart" which it gained some five thousand years ago has made it a monument of the great transformation which we are considering.

It was this new *function* of human intelligence which made possible the discernment of character, and it is not a little interesting to note the point when the word "character" itself first occurs in human speech. It began to appear in the Pyramid Age, and early became the subject of reflective comment. In the wisdom of Ptahhotep the wise old vizier reminds his son, "Precious to a man is the virtue of his son, and good character is a thing remembered" (p. 137). This earliest occurrence of the word thus belongs in the Twenty-seventh Century B.C. Then some five centuries later in the Instruction Addressed to Merikere, the Pharaoh refers to "God, who knoweth character" (p. 157). The word itself is very interesting. Its original meaning is "to shape, to form, to build," and it was early employed especially to designate the work of the potter in shaping clay vessels on his wheel. Its derived meaning, "character," is strikingly parallel to our own "character," a Greek word meaning the impression of an engraved seal on the yielding clay or wax, or of a die on the metal in striking a coin. We have seen the new capacities which these new words proclaimed, operating as social forces, and bringing about a new order, which the moral sages of Egypt also discerned and for which they had a term, "Maat," meaning "right, righteousness, justice, truth," and the moral order in which these things were the controlling forces. It is these terms, together with "conscience" and "character," all emerging historically in the written records of Egypt between 3000 and 2000 B.C., which are for us monuments of the transformation of life on our planet.

In this epoch-making transformation, occurring for the first time on our globe, and so far as we know, for the first time in the universe, the Egyptians were the discoverers of character. It is fundamentally important that the modern world should realise how recent is that discovery. Civilisation is built up on character, and the foundations are therefore still so new that we need feel no discouragement if the building has not yet exhibited the stability we may yet hope to see it achieve. Mr. Mencken's withering jibes are without doubt often deserved, and the very obvious need of repairs in the structure furnishes ample opportunity for amusing commentary in the pages of *Punch* and *Life*, or the plays of Bernard Shaw who finds attitudinising far too easy and profitable to be displaced by any effort to take the human adventure seriously. More disinterested and substantially grounded convictions that the building is damaged quite beyond restoration are not wanting. Oswald Spengler proclaims the final downfall of Western civilisation. It would not be difficult to demonstrate that his dismal Jeremiads are based on surprising ignorance of the facts of human development. Spengler makes extensive use of Egyptian civilisation. Had he been adequately acquainted with it, he would have found in it no support for his pessimistic conclusions. The marvel is that a creature rising out of animal savagery should have advanced to *begin* the great transformation at all, and it should give us little concern that in carrying on its further development man has at times faltered, or even decidedly lost ground for a time.

All serious-minded people are sorely perplexed and some of us are wholly disillusioned at the spectacle of modern man so largely dominated by the destructive power which science and his enormously increased weapon-making ability have placed in his hands. Men of science are paying much attention to the fact that man's power, both creative and destructive, has been developing for such an enormous period of time, especially since it has just been disclosed that the Pekin Man of probably a million years ago was not only able to build a fire, the earliest known example of fire kindled by man, but that he also *wrought stone weapons.* He thus emerges as the earliest known human creature able to fashion weapons. But neither the men of science nor the historians are evaluating man's present situation in full recognition of the fact that the emergence of conscience as a social force is an event of yesterday, as truly a datable event as the gradual introduction of metal, and that the resulting Age of Character is therefore little more than about four thousand years old. The career of man, like other processes of nature, is a slow development, and the great transformation may be as slow in completion as the process of man's physical evolution. In the several hundred thousand years that lie between the recently discovered Pekin Man and the Neanderthal Man the human brain increased about 50 per cent in size. In the relatively long period since the Neanderthal Man our brain has not increased in size at all. The rate of man's development is therefore appallingly slow. The high noon of that ethical day, which is now only dawning, is still far away, and there is great need of patience, the patience of him who has learned to wait, if need be, in expectant silence. Perhaps there is no better example of the slowness of the development of the human soul than the following parallel between the thoughts of an Egyptian Wise Man of three thousand years ago and a modern reflective novelist:

AN ANCIENT EGYPTIAN WISE MAN OF ABOUT 1000 B.C.

"O Amon, thou sweet Well for him that thirsteth in the desert; it is closed to him who speaketh, but it is open to him who is silent. When he who is silent cometh, lo, he findeth the Well." (See above, p. 318.)

CHARLES MORGAN IN *The Fountain,* A.D. 1932.

"Yet he was not unquiet; rather did he seem to have entered the innermost court of quietness itself, where, like a stream from the ground, the fountain of the spirit was rising." (p. 107.)

Such reflections on the meditative spirit were of course characteristic of the ancient East, but a similar parallel may be drawn from the life of action and adventure:

THE EGYPTIAN SINDBAD, ABOUT 2000 B.C.	VIRGIL
"Happy he who tells of his misfortunes after they are past."	"Et haec olim meminisse juvabit."

And after life is over, whether meditative or adventurous and filled with action, the reflections of Spenser in praise of death are like an echo of our ancient Egyptian Job, whom we called the Misanthrope (p. 168):

THE EGYPTIAN JOB	SPENSER, "THE FAERIE QUEENE"
"Death is before me today, Like the recovery of a sick man, Like going forth into a garden after sickness. . . . . Death is before me today, Like the course of the freshet, Like the return of a man from the war-galley to his house."	"He there does now enjoy eternal rest, ... Is not short pain well borne that brings long ease, And lays the soul to sleep in quiet grave? Sleep after toil, port after stormy seas, Ease after war, death after life, does greatly please." —(Speech of Despair).

And such relatively recent echoes are not lacking, even in an English churchyard:

TOMBSTONE OF AN EGYPTIAN NOBLE ABOUT 2100 B.C.	TOMBSTONE OF AN ENGLISHMAN IN BURFORD CHURCHYARD, OXFORDSHIRE, 18TH CENTURY
A man's virtue is his monument, (But) forgotten is the man of evil repute.	Praises on stone are titles vainly lent, A man's good name is his best monument.

Myriads of examples might be marshalled here to show how, millennium after millennium, the generations thus go on, each accumulating its own experience, and to no small extent repeating and re-expressing the meditative experience of the ages that have gone before.

III

THE GREAT TRANSFORMATION—AN EXPRESSION OF HUMAN EXPERIENCE

However slowly experience may accumulate, it is profoundly important that we should recognise the historical fact that the great transformation which we have been discussing was the product and the result of human experience, that the moving force of human development since then has been human experience, and that it is *man's own experience* which has been and continues to be his greatest teacher. In enacting the Eighteenth Amendment the people of the United States tried an experiment, and social experience demonstrated that the attempt to control social habits was a failure. Social experience is an inexorable teacher. No thoughtful student of the Hebrew literature which we call the Old Testament can fail to feel its power, or to recognise the fundamentally important part which it has played in the advance of Western civilisation. Yet we must also recognise the fact that the Old Testament, as a fragment of ancient Hebrew literature, is likewise a record of human experience. We have been linking up the higher life of our own modern Western world with its ultimate sources in the life of man in the Ancient Orient, over two thousand years before Hebrew history began. In doing so we have found not only the origins of moral feeling, but also whole chapters of social history—the life of a great nation as it unfolded for some three thousand years, developing the earliest profound moral vision, and as a result of that experience, bringing forth ripe moral convictions expressed in a considerable literature. Not only so, but we have seen this development going on and producing this literature many centuries before the beginning of what the old-time theologians called the "age of revelation," and we have demonstrated as a historical fact that this literature not only survived into the so-called "age of revelation," but that it also had a profound effect upon the moral and religious development of the Hebrews, from whom we received our greatest moral heritage.

The sources of our inheritance of moral teaching extend far beyond the borders of Palestine, and include the whole Ancient Near East, especially Egypt, where the earliest transcendental vision of social idealism arose. We have never before been able to discern the larger source of this moral and idealistic heritage, because the channel by which it has reached the Western world has been Hebrew literature. Nor have we before been aware of the composite, international origin of this literature. The now unwelcome idea of a discriminatory revelation, which excluded all other peoples and was confined to only *one,* grew up at a time when Western civilisation was completely unacquainted with the rise of man or the history of civilisation preceding the Hebrews. We repeat, therefore, that no such conception of an exclusive revelation to one people could ever have arisen, if the languages of the Ancient Orient had not been lost and their records no longer intelligible to any one, so that the moral and religious literature of the great civilisations some thousands of years older than the Hebrews disappeared.

Perhaps the most valuable contribution of archæological excavation is its revelation of the social and moral development achieved by the ancient oriental societies long before Hebrew literature arose. For this revelation of modern science is one of the most profound and far-reaching importance. It has disclosed to us the fact that, as far as our chief *moral* legacy is concerned, we are the heirs of the *early life of man as a whole,* especially as it developed around the eastern end of the Mediterranean. Obviously we are not here considering the invaluable accretions which that legacy received as the result of the moral reflection of ancient and modern Europe.

In my feeling this new and historically sound conception of Hebrew literature rather enhances than detracts from its value, disclosing as it does a new vision of the wider human sources of influence which have been so deeply wrought into the very substance of Western civilisation. We hear much of a "new humanism." Its soul will be found in the modern study of the soil in which the earliest moral germs took root and brought forth fruit. Oriental research has revealed to us the fact that the soil which brought forth the finest flower of social idealism was human life. In thus recognising that man's vision of ideal human character is far older than the "age of revelation" we have gained a new and a broader basis for our faith in man.

IV

THE NEW PAST AS A NEW MORAL INFLUENCE

Lord Acton has well said that "next to the discovery of the New World, the recovery of the ancient world is the second landmark that divides us from the Middle Ages and marks the transition to modern life." In this distinguished historian's judgment, therefore, the two great forces which led men out of the Middle Ages into modern life were a vision which looked both *forward* and *backward,* and which not only caught the limitless possibilities of the *future* in the New World after 1492, but also drew the profoundest inspiration from the newly recovered *past,* as they learned to know it in the surviving writings and other important works of its greatest men. What was the "ancient world," the past, to which Lord Acton referred? It had not revealed to the earliest modern men the slightest intimation of the great transformation. The only past known to the men who were emerging from the Middle Ages was, as we all know, the Biblical story followed by the history of Greece and Rome. Now the process of recovering the ancient world which began at the dawn of the Renaissance did not cease with the Renaissance, but, as we have seen, has gone on through all the centuries since then, and with quickening strides, especially during the last two generations. We listen now not only to the voices of Isaiah and David, of Socrates and Cicero, as did the men of the Renaissance, but also to the voices of the great oriental sovereigns in the proud stories of their conquest of the Mediterranean, to the prophets of Egypt proclaiming the golden age of social justice, to the voice of Cheops (Khufu) telling in terms of colossal masonry architecture the triumphs of the first great organised state, to the voice of the earliest smelter of metals singing in the tinkle of his primitive anvil the song of man's coming conquest of the earth, to the voice of remote and long-forgotten generations of men heard now only in the message of ever more carefully wrought stone implements, to the voice of geological ages muttering in the savage gutturals of incipient human speech which we seem to hear resounding through prehistoric forests reechoing to the first articulate utterances of those now hardly discernible creatures, about to become men. Back through the æons into historic and prehistoric deeps like these we now look, and listen to the echoes that come to us out of the vista of the ages. It was with such a vision before him that Tennyson looked down into the cradle of his firstborn and said, "Out of the deeps, my child"; and such a vision of the New Past, just beginning to dawn upon the minds of modern men, has values as yet all unproved. He who really discerns this vision has begun to read the glorious Odyssey of human kind, disclosing to us man issuing from the darkness of the eternities and with uplifted face pushing out upon the sunlit ocean of time to make conquest of treasure unspeakable, of worlds surpassing all his dreams—the supreme adventure of the ages.

I have sometimes wondered whether any vision that could conceivably dawn upon the human soul as a moving impulse to self-expression in art or literature might be compared with the realisation of human possibilities as disclosed in the transformation of human life which we have been endeavouring to follow in this book. There can be no doubt that Emerson saw by sheer intuition what we have set forth as a historically demonstrable process. Otherwise however, the human soul has never given it expression except possibly in music. When I listen to the terrifying power of the opening theme in Beethoven's Fifth Symphony and then follow the transition to the serene triumph of the last movement it has seemed to me that, like Emerson, Beethoven must have realised by the noble intuitions of his exalted soul the deep and fundamental fact which underlies human hope, the supreme possibilities of character rising out of the deeps of an unfathomable universe.

As we look back upon its past, the human adventure has no value or significance except as we see it rising impressively towards the great transformation and the discovery of the highest human values in the Age of Character. It is the incompleteness of the great transformation which should make the vision of man's long pilgrimage a moral influence, not by assimilation of the actual content of any ancient faith, but by some vision of the rising trail of which such faiths are only the guide posts disclosing to us the course of the trail. For it is easy to misunderstand the value of ancient oriental experience in religion and morals. One of the commonest and most regrettable spectacles of modern life, especially in America and England, is that of enraptured femininity contemplating the lofty truths fondly believed to be enshrined in some ancient oriental faith, and forgetting all that ages of social experience have contributed in developing, elevating, and enriching all the surviving religions of ancient origin. To ignore these later centuries of ennobling development and, turning backward, to adopt without change the germinal stages of some ancient faith is as reasonable as it would be for the thirsty individual seeking refreshment on a hot day to go and lie down under an acorn and regale himself on a watermelon seed!

My friend James Harvey Robinson has warned us against subjection to the past in his profoundly suggestive book, *The Mind in the Making;* but I believe he is speaking of thoughtless *subservience* to the past. The course of sound progress is a wisely balanced mean between the lessons of experience and new vision. What I am endeavouring to do in these final reflections of this book is to remind the reader of the fact that an unprejudiced study of human experience, especially if it is newly revealed, is often the stimulus and the inspiration to new vision. Consider some of the outstanding facts revealed by the examination of the early moral history of mankind, which we have just been making. To repeat: we have found in the first place that moral development on our planet is an unfinished process, and in this fact lies our greatest reason for hopefulness. As a result we find in the second place, that man is morally still a mere child playing in a nursery full of the most dangerous toys, which he has not yet learned to handle and with which he continually inflicts serious injury, not only on himself but on the whole structure in which he lives. Recent economic history would indicate that man's infantile limitations are not confined to morals. Finally, having recognized the nature of moral progress as shown by early human history to have been a product and an outgrowth of social experience, modern man is for the first time in a position to put forth his hand and, consciously co-operating with the inherent factors in his situation, to influence and expedite the process of moral advancement.

Professor Thomas H. Morgan[2] has made it quite clear that physical evolution is a process the nature and the laws of which must be studied by actual experimentation. If social development is a thing which we are entitled to call "evolution," the application of experimentation is obviously beset with difficulties. Such a social laboratory as Egypt, however, throws valuable light on the processes of higher human evolution, and suggests the possibility of a

[2] See Thomas Hunt Morgan, *The Scientific Basis of Evolution* (New York, 1932).

world in which government and leadership, avoiding the pitfall of sumptuary legislation, might consciously endeavour to develop conditions favourable to enlightened moral progress and to influences more effective than those now operative.

We are the first generation of men and women who are able to look back, and surveying the vast length of the entire human career, to follow the course of the great transformation as far as it has now advanced. Ours are the first minds so placed as to realise that the emergence of conscience and the rise of a sense of social responsibility after 3000 B.C., which began the great transformation, were events of yesterday. Those events marked our Father Man's approach to the frontiers of a New Country. Today we his children have hardly crossed those frontiers to begin the exploration of the New Country beyond. We stand in hesitation upon its outer margins, the beauty and sublimity of its distant prospects are hidden from us by the mists of human frailty, or blackened by the stifling smoke of greed, selfishness and World War. Blinded and dismayed we have stumbled and faltered with the foothills of the New Country all before us, while beyond them, if we would but lift our eyes, are glorious glimpses of the Delectable Mountains. Towards their still unscaled heights points the long and rising trail behind us, revealing to us, as it has risen from savagery to *character,* an unconquerable buoyancy of the human soul that has somehow issued from the deeps and risen so high.

In using the words "unconquerable buoyancy of the human soul," I am not employing a meaningless rhetorical phrase. I first used those words years ago in a convocation address, after returning from a journey among the buried cities of the Ancient Orient, when I felt as never before the meaning of the great fact that in the life that once pulsed along the streets of those now long vanished cities, man had for the first time risen from the conquest of material resources to visions of social idealism so vital that they have continued to be a power among us who are building Western civilisation in the light of the great truths which still shine out of the East. That phrase "unconquerable buoyancy of the human soul" suggests far more than is expressed in the mere words, but let me assure the reader that those words represent a reality, an irrefutable fact in human life, whether past or present, a fact with which such men as Oswald Spengler and all the other pessimists do not deal, for they seem totally unconscious of it. It is a thing as demonstrably present in the spirit of man, as the circulation of the blood in his physical body. What other force has been the driving power in that amazing transformation from savagery to character, the beginnings of which we have been following? What carried the early man from purely material conquest to a recognition of the inner vision and its irresistible attraction? A philosopher like Bergson proclaims something which he calls the *élan vital;* but I am not dealing with philosophical conceptions, for I am not a philosopher. I am discussing the history of man and something which, especially in its earlier stages, is quite unmistakably disclosed as a force visibly present and operative for several hundred thousand years, and which I believe is still at work. No one can define it, or tell what it is, but like the force of gravitation, we can observe what it does. I am using the present tense advisedly: we have only to look around us in this depression which has culminated in 1933 to realise that the historical buoyancy of the human soul is still with us.

From that dim and distant day when a human creature struck out the first flint implement, through all the ages until now, when man belts the globe with the radio or plans to annihilate whole cities with poison gas-bombs from the sky, the course of human life has prevailingly been a career of material achievement. For several hundred thousands years this Age of Material Conquest has gone on and still goes on. But yesterday, as it were, through the dust of an engrossing conflict our Father Man began to catch but faintly the veiled glory of the moral vision, and to hear a new voice within, responding to a thousand promptings, old and new. It was interfused of love of home, of wife and children, of love of friends, and love of neighbours, of love of the poor and lonely and oppressed, of love of country and veneration of the Sovereign; and all these which were new, mingling with a vastly older reverence, the love of cloud and hilltop, of forest and stream, of earth and sea and sky, and not least of the earth's green mantle which every year burgeoned with life and nourishment for the children of men.

Thus the old nature gods were shifted into a new world of social forces and thus they were fused into one with a god of human needs and human aspiration, a Universal Father in whom men began to see all the highest values that their own social experience had revealed to them.

A past like that has accumulated a priceless body of man's experience which the rising line of human advance has validated as possessing still valuable elements of strength which it is fatal to neglect as factors in our own modern life. In his admirable book, *A Preface to Morals,* Walter Lippmann[3] has discussed with great penetration the crumbling foundations of moral authority. In such a

[3] New York, 1929.

situation I believe there is moral power in contemplation of the ancestry of the finest things in human living. The most precious possessions of the human soul, the indomitable purpose to preserve the consciousness of rectitude, and to press on towards new conquests in character—these things are not only rooted deep in human experience, but they came into the life of man as new values out of a range of his experience, the power of which as a surviving influence in human society has by no means been exhausted. The surviving documents demonstrate historically that the thing which was long called "the moral consciousness of mankind" has grown up with each generation out of the discipline and the emotions of family life, supplemented by reflection and the teaching of experienced elders. The supreme values which lie within the human soul have therefore, as a matter of historical fact, entered the world for the first time through the operation of those gentle and ennobling influences which touch us continually in our family life. Whether in the beginning they were anywhere else out yonder in this vast universe, we shall never know; but they were not anywhere here upon our globe until the life of father, mother, and children created them. It was the sunshine and the atmosphere of the earliest human homes that created ideals of conduct and revealed the beauty of self-forgetfulness.

Bertrand Russell, in his latest book[4] espousing the cause of communism, tells us that the most important change which communism would introduce is the abolition of the family and, throwing human experience entirely overboard, he advocates this change. Notwithstanding the revolt of the new generation, human experience cannot be

[4] *Education and the Social Order* (London, 1932).

annihilated, nor can the traits it has produced in us be obliterated or ignored. The young people of today have indeed revolted against authority, whether it be that of the church or the mandate of Scripture. To invoke authority is always to invite opposition, especially in the minds of youth. But the human past shines upon us like a great light, and there is no need to invoke authority. If any young readers take up this book, I beg them merely to contemplate the facts of human experience now revealed to us in fuller measure than ever before. There are other sources of reverence besides the declarations of Scripture or the pronouncements of the church. Men like William Morris and Walt Whitman have loved and reverenced the life of man on earth, and have found inspiration and guidance in the contemplation of its relationships. There is one supreme human relationship, that which has created the home and made the family fireside the source out of which man's highest qualities have grown up to transform the world. As historical fact, it is to family life that we owe the greatest debt which the mind of man can conceive. The echoes of our own past from immemorial ages bid us unmistakably to venerate, to cherish, and to preserve a relationship to which the life of man owes this supreme debt.

V

POWER AND CHARACTER

As a result of the great transformation the life of man on earth has become a struggle between the *new* ideals of self-forgetfulness that arose but yesterday, and the deep-seated passion for power, which is as old as the human race itself. Man's ancient love of power is enormously older than the Age of Character and it has thus far been so dangerously victorious over new-born conscience and character that we are faced with the grave question of the survival of civilisation. Sir Alfred Ewing in his presidential address before the British Association for the Advancement of Science thus summarised man's present situation: "The command of nature has been put into his hand before he knows how to command himself."[5]

That the vision of the New Past may influence the conduct of the *individual* I am profoundly convinced. Whether *nations* or *mankind as a whole,* realising this vision, will find in it a really potent influence towards quenching international hatreds, or better still for building up international feelings of brotherhood and generous regard, may seriously be doubted. Mr. H. G. Wells has been very optimistic in his expressions on this question, and I wish I could share his optimism; but having spent many years in almost daily contemplation of the monuments of human power, I have gained impressions which I do not find it easy to dispel.

We have been watching the development of early characteristics of the human soul, and in doing so we have been observing especially the emergence of the higher values. But we might have called upon a vast host of ancient monuments which would have revealed the other side of the picture, and especially the most dangerous opposing force, man's growing eagerness for power as national organisation advanced, until the machinery of human government became the organised expression of the thirst for power—the appetite for the exercise of force.

In wandering for years through the ancient lands of the Near East I have been impressed with this outstand-

[5] *New York Times,* September 25, 1932, editorial page.

ing fact: the insistent monuments now surviving in all those distant lands have been primarily expressions of man's *power*. It is as if his struggle with the forces of nature, a struggle which has now been going on for perhaps a million years, had imbued him with a defiant consciousness that he could win only by fighting his way through as he met the opposing forces of the natural world which challenged him on every hand. It was with this same attitude of relentless force that he met his own human fellows when the long struggle for supremacy eventually arose among the earliest nations. Today you may enter one of the lonely valleys of Sinai and find there, suddenly confronting you, the tall figure of an Egyptian Pharaoh carved in relief upon the face of the rock wall. There he has been standing since the Thirty-fourth Century before Christ, the oldest historical monument in the world. With uplifted weapon he is about to crush the skull of an Asiatic captive whom he has thrust down upon his knees before him. A monument of brutal force, it was a declaration of possession by right of conquest, serving imperious notice on the Asiatics that the king of Egypt had crossed from Africa into Asia and had taken possession of the surrounding copper and turquoise mines. Here, then, at the beginning of historical monuments and written records, the conquest of natural resources emerges as a fundamental motive of national action, and the monument which reveals it strikes the note of force which has dominated human history ever since.

Just after the armistice in Europe, while the fighting was still sporadically continuing in Western Asia, I marched up the Euphrates through the hostile Arab tribes in the endeavour to reach Western civilisation again. Our Oriental Institute expedition was the first western party for many months to attempt the crossing of the bandit-infested desert from Baghdad to the Mediterranean. On the seventh day from Baghdad we entered a vast fortress on the Middle Euphrates, called by the modern natives Salihiyeh. Its ancient name was at that time still unidentified, and as we entered its colossal walls and passed around a corner, suddenly there rose before us a high wall covered with an imposing painting in many colors depicting in life-size a group of eleven people reverently absorbed in worship. We stood gazing in amazement at these wonderful figures looking gravely down upon us, as suddenly disclosed as if they had been conjured up by magic from the silent wastes of the desert which stretched out far below us. They had been uncovered a few days before by the British East Indian troops as they "dug themselves in" against the surrounding hordes of hostile Arab tribesmen. Eagerly the next day, with the aid of the same East Indian troops, we uncovered several other walls, on one of which, as the encumbering rubbish was slowly removed, we gradually saw revealed to us a group of Roman soldiers with the commander, their tribune standing at their head. His name, Julius Terentius, was written on the wall in front of his figure and he was leading in official worship his garrison of Roman legionaries which once occupied this desolate desert stronghold, far outside of the finally established eastern frontier of the Roman Empire on the Euphrates. In a Greek inscription on the painting I found also the ancient name of the lost city. It was called Doura and here we had found the easternmost representation of Roman soldiers ever discovered.[6]

[6] See the author's *Oriental Forerunners of Byzantine Painting* (University of Chicago Press, 1924). The site is now undergoing systematic excavation by

It was an impressive moment as I realised that there in the heart of the Syrian desert, nearly three hundred miles east of the Mediterranean, I was looking upon the easternmost forces of a vast military machine which stretched westward the length of Western Asia and of all Europe besides, to the shores of the Atlantic and the British Isles, over three thousand miles away. My mind moved far across the desert to the great figure of Pharaoh on the rock wall in the lonely valley in Sinai where monuments of such power had begun. Then as nation followed nation, and empire displaced empire for nearly four thousand years, power had found its culmination in the Roman colossus which stretched from the Atlantic to the Euphrates. Thrilling is a badly overworked word, but there were thrills enough in this glimpse at the magnificent pageant of Roman supremacy, as one contemplated here on the wall the scarlet banner of a Roman legion borne by the *signifer* at the head of these troops who were maintaining the majesty of Roman military power in the desert wastes on the banks of the distant Euphrates so long ago. It was, as I have said, nearly four thousand years from these Romans on the Euphrates back to the lonely monument of the Pharaoh among the copper mines of Sinai. At the end of those four millennia *power* was outwardly still the supreme force in the developing life of man.

A few weeks later I was sitting with Sir Herbert Samuels, the first British Governor of Palestine, in the beautiful gardens of the British Residency on the Mount of Olives. Behind us toward the setting sun, lay Jerusalem, the Holy City, while before us was the tremendous rift

a Franco-American expedition sent out by the French *Académie des Inscriptions,* and Yale University.

of the Jordan Valley and the Dead Sea, with the blue and purple mountains of Moab behind them. The depression of the mighty chasm before us had recently been vividly illustrated by a tale which Lord Allenby had told me of his campaign in Palestine. He sent a dispatch to the War Office one day, which read:

"This morning our bombing planes, flying six hundred feet below the sea, bombed the Turkish positions in the Jordan Valley."

Seven hundred feet below those planes were the mouth of the Jordan and the surface of the Dead Sea. That is to say the surface of the Dead Sea is one thousand three hundred feet below sea level, and its bottom is one thousand three hundred feet further down, below the surface of its salt waters. With its bottom, therefore, two thousand six hundred feet below sea level, it is the lowest chasm in the surface of our globe, and looming over it are the mountains about Jerusalem rising as high above the sea as the bottom of the Dead Sea is below it. The difference is more than five thousand feet, indeed almost exactly a mile. Viewed from the summit of the Mount of Olives, the scene is an appalling picture of the terrible forces which wrought it, as if some giant hand, thrusting in its titanic fingers, had rent the very earth in twain, and left a chasm a mile deep. As Sir Herbert and I sat contemplating this scene, it seemed to us that it was perhaps the most terrifying demonstration of natural force which human eyes could behold. There were no men when that chasm was torn open, and when man appeared he was met by forces like that wherever he turned. By the operation of such forces terrestrial history went on, and we find an echo of some of its terrors in the story of Sodom and Gomorrah. It was in such terrible manifestations as these that the early men of this region saw their gods. It was in the personification of the volcanic forces upon which we were looking down, that the Hebrews discerned the earliest god of Israel and it was long before they imbued his nature of terrifying power with traits of *human* friendliness. Then we looked just a few miles north and there nestling on the slopes of the gaunt Judean hills, looking down upon the awful chasm, we saw the little village which had been the birthplace and the home of the Hebrew prophet Jeremiah. He had looked down all his life on this same tremendous panorama of the merciless power of natural processes, and yet he had been aware of a world of inner forces which he believed imperishable when he represented his God as saying: "I will put my law in their inward parts, and in their heart will I write it." (Jer. 31:33.)

It was a scene which made very real the fact that somehow the amazing shift from a world of purely natural forces to one of imperishable human values had really taken place out yonder in the Ancient Near East. Then as we sat overlooking Jeremiah's little village we turned our eyes southwestward across the barren hills of Judea, behind which lay the Nile Valley, the home of the earliest men who had felt the power of ideals of conduct—ideals which began the great transformation—and we recalled how, two thousand years before Jeremiah was born, the Egyptian social sages had been the first men to discern the worth of character and the inner values of the human heart; and how their writings had passed over into Palestine and borne rich fruit in the life of the Hebrews. Thus, stimulated by social vision which had arisen on the Nile, the Hebrew prophets became a beacon light for all the world. Gradually we began to discern in its larger outlines the age-long sweep of the whole human drama, as it had begun to unfold among those ancient lands of the Near East.

That was a great memory as again on another day I looked out from the summit of the mound of Armageddon northward across the storied plain which bears its name, to the highlands of Galilee. There among the hills of Nazareth the child Jesus must often have looked down upon this battlefield of the ages. The cloud shadows were creeping slowly across those misty hills of Nazareth only eight miles away. Peeping out of the *débris* at my feet, where our excavations were clearing it away, were the battlements of Armageddon, which dominated this historic plain. This fortress city, a monument of human power, must have been visible from those hills of Nazareth. For ages of the reign of force they had looked down upon scenes of conquest and bloodshed on the plain below—ages whose highest gods were divinities of violence and carnage, the delight of such fierce prophets as Elijah; and after ideals of human conduct from the Nile had slowly eclipsed such bloody gods, there dawned among those hills of Nazareth a God of brotherly kindness—the vision of a Jewish carpenter's son, whose tiny Galilean village lies just behind the brow of the northern hills so clearly visible from the battlements of Armageddon. As Jeremiah, looking forth from his little village, beheld the titanic forces of *nature* and still held fast to his faith in the inner values, so the youthful prophet of Nazareth, having grown up with the traditional scene of the brutal forces of *human* power daily before his eyes, nevertheless clung to his vision of the new kingdom within. *In Palestine* this is indeed the supreme transformation, from Elijah to Jesus, from Carmel and Armageddon to Nazareth.

But this culmination *in Palestine* was a later process, a fruition made possible by that far earlier transformation, —what we have called the "great transformation"—which lifted man from the exclusive struggle with nature alone and shifted him into a new arena, the struggle with *himself* for the conquest of his own soul and those new values which transcend the material world and make up the substance of a new reality which we call character. We have seen that the forces which wrought this earlier transformation were born in Egypt and passed thence to Palestine and the later world. It was no merely accidental coincidence that Hebrew history should have traced Hebrew national origins back to Egypt, a tradition of which there is an echo in the Christian belief, "Out of Egypt have I called my son."

Today in the lands of the Ancient East we too look out upon the works of nature and the works of man, and in a New Crusade of scientific endeavour, we are striving to recover the story of both. But already we have discerned enough to realise that they are *one:* that the processes of nature and the unfolding life of man are but chapters of the same great story; that looking down into that appalling chasm of the Dead Sea which so terribly confronts us with Professor Haeckel's question, we may find an answer which natural science cannot give us—an answer which comes to us only as we contemplate human experience in the Ancient East and realise that the culmination of a developing universe is *character.*

It has been the purpose of this book to furnish an historical demonstration that the process of human advance which brought forth character is still unfinished—is still going on. The possibilities of its future are *unlimited,* and it is our responsibility to bring the vast significance of this new fact to bear as a practical influence upon our own conduct. In doing so we gain the full realisation that we are no longer carrying forward merely traditional truths and inherited teachings with which we may have little sympathy, but just as the light of character once dawned in a darkness which had never known such light before, so there is no reason to doubt the growth of that light to illumine realms of being that still lie all unrealised in the unfathomed ages toward which our limited vision of to-day looks out but does not see.

INDEX